Biometric Recognition: Latest Advances and Prospects

Biometric Recognition: Latest Advances and Prospects

Guest Editors

Yunlong Wang
Zhaofeng He
Caiyong Wang
Jianze Wei
Min Ren

MDPI

Basel • Beijing • Wuhan • Barcelona • Belgrade • Novi Sad • Cluj • Manchester

Guest Editors
Yunlong Wang
Institute of Automation
Chinese Academy of Sciences
Beijing
China

Zhaofeng He
School of Artificial Intelligence
Beijing University of Posts
and Telecommunications
Beijing
China

Caiyong Wang
School of Intelligence Science
and Technology
Beijing University of Civil
Engineering and Architecture
Beijing
China

Jianze Wei
Institute of Microelectronics
Chinese Academy of Sciences
Beijing
China

Min Ren
School of Artificial Intelligence
Beijing University of Posts
and Telecommunications
Beijing
China

Editorial Office
MDPI AG
Grosspeteranlage 5
4052 Basel, Switzerland

This is a reprint of the Special Issue, published open access by the journal *Electronics* (ISSN 2079-9292), freely accessible at: https://www.mdpi.com/journal/electronics/special_issues/RIVJJ1NSVM.

For citation purposes, cite each article independently as indicated on the article page online and as indicated below:

Lastname, A.A.; Lastname, B.B. Article Title. *Journal Name* **Year**, *Volume Number*, Page Range.

ISBN 978-3-7258-5931-3 (Hbk)
ISBN 978-3-7258-5932-0 (PDF)
https://doi.org/10.3390/books978-3-7258-5932-0

Contents

About the Editors

Yunlong Wang

Yunlong Wang is currently an Associate Professor at the New Laboratory of Pattern Recognition (NLPR), State Key Laboratory of Multimodal Artificial Intelligence Systems (MAIS), Institute of Automation, Chinese Academy of Sciences (CASIA), China. He received his B.E. and his Ph.D. at the Department of Automation, University of Science and Technology of China, majoring in pattern recognition and intelligent systems. His research focuses on pattern recognition, machine learning, light field photography and biometrics. He has published over 60 papers in top-tier academic journals (*TPAMI, IJCV, TIP, TIFS*, etc.) and conferences (ICML, ICCV, ECCV, AAAI, etc.). He also owns over 20 issued patents, including 2 US patents and 4 PCT patents. He received the Best Paper Runner-up at IJCB 2020 and the Best Student Paper Award at IJCB in 2023.

Zhaofeng He

Zhaofeng He is currently a Professor at the School of Artificial Intelligence, Beijing University of Posts and Telecommunications, Beijing, China. He received his B.S. in electronic engineering and information science from the University of Science and Technology of China (USTC), Hefei, China, in 2005, and his Ph.D. in computer applied technology from the National Laboratory of Pattern Recognition, Institute of Automation, Chinese Academy of Sciences (CASIA), Beijing, China. His research interests include computer vision, biometrics, intelligent game decision-making, and AI + IC. He has published over 100 papers in top-tier academic journals (*TPAMI, TIFS*, etc.) and conferences (ICCV, CVPR, etc.). He also owns over 90 issued patents.

Caiyong Wang

Caiyong Wang is currently an Associate Professor at the School of Intelligence Science and Technology, Beijing University of Civil Engineering and Architecture, China. He received his Ph.D. in pattern recognition and intelligent systems from the Institute of Automation, Chinese Academy of Sciences (CASIA), China, in 2020. Prior to his PhD, he worked as an Algorithm Engineer at LUSTER LightTech Group and Cheetah Mobile. He received his B.E. in applied mathematics from Xinjiang University, China, in 2013, and his M.S. in computational mathematics from Xiamen University, China, in 2016. His research interests include biometrics, computer vision, and pattern recognition. He has received the Honorable Mention Paper Award at ICB 2019 and the Best Student Paper Award at IJCB 2023.

Jianze Wei

Jianze Wei is currently an Associate Professor at the Communication and Information Engineering Center, Institute of Microelectronics, Chinese Academy of Sciences, China. He received his Ph.D. from the University of Chinese Academy of Sciences, majoring in computer application technology. His research focuses on image retrieval, transfer learning, and biometrics. He has published over 10 papers in top-tier academic journals (*TIP, TIFS*, etc.) and conferences. He also owns 6 issued patents.

Min Ren

Min Ren is currently an Associate Professor at the School of Artificial Intelligence, Beijing University of Posts and Telecommunications, Beijing, China. He received his B.S. in mechanical engineering and automation from the National University of Defense Technology, Changsha, China, in

2013, and his Ph.D. in pattern recognition and intelligent systems from the Institute of Automation, Chinese Academy of Sciences (CASIA), Beijing, China. His research interests include pattern recognition, biometrics, and adversarial learning. He has published over 10 papers in top-tier academic journals (*TPAMI*, *IJCV*, *TIFS*, etc.) and conferences (ICCV, CVPR, AAAI, etc.).

electronics

Editorial

Editorial: Biometric Recognition—Latest Advances and Prospects

Yunlong Wang [1,*], Zhaofeng He [2], Caiyong Wang [3], Jianze Wei [4] and Min Ren [2]

1 New Laboratory of Pattern Recognition, Institute of Automation, Chinese Academy of Sciences, Beijing 100190, China
2 School of Artificial Intelligence, Beijing University of Posts and Telecommunications, Beijing 100876, China
3 School of Intelligence Science and Technology, Beijing University of Civil Engineering and Architecture, Beijing 102616, China
4 Institute of Microelectronics, Chinese Academy of Sciences, Beijing 100029, China
* Correspondence: yunlong.wang@cripac.ia.ac.cn

We are pleased to present this Special Issue of *Electronics*, dedicated to exploring cutting-edge advancements in Biometric Recognition. As digital identity becomes integral to the "Internet of Everything," this collection showcases interdisciplinary innovations spanning sensor design, algorithmic robustness, multi-modal fusion, and real-world applications. Below, we summarize the key contributions and extend our gratitude to all participants involved.

1. Research Highlights

1.1. Face Recognition and Animation

- Contribution 1 introduces a prior structure-assisted network for identity-preserving face animation, leveraging segmentation and landmarks to enhance realism under motion transfer.
- Contribution 2 addresses asymmetric matching across heterogeneous models (e.g., ResNet vs. Transformer) using learnable anchors that are critical for edge-device deployment.

1.2. Ocular Biometrics

- Contribution 3 adapts the Segment Anything Model with a novel "IrisAdapter" for high-precision segmentation, overcoming domain gaps between natural and iris images.
- Contribution 4 achieves efficient multi-modal ocular segmentation (periocular/sclera/iris/pupil) in noisy environments via shape priors and cross-attention.
- Contribution 5 produces a pioneering VR periocular dataset with periocular images acquired in VR environments, identities and abundant emotion annotations, enabling implicit authentication and affective computing studies.

1.3. Noise-Robust Authentication

- Contribution 6 mitigate flicker noise and IR reflections in periocular images captured by head-mounted display devices, achieving 6.39% EER via reflection removal and SE blocks.
- Contribution 7 enhance voice-based two-factor authentication (2FA) with a GMM-based web solution, optimizing thresholds for varying acoustic conditions.

1.4. Emerging Modalities and Applications

- Contribution 8 design an open-environment multi-spectral palm vein system with supervised feature learning (<1% EER).

https://doi.org/10.3390/electronics14153108

- Contribution 9 produce ultra-wideband (UWB) based real-time leg movement recognition (95% accuracy), enabling seamless human–robot interactions.
- Contribution 10 combine the CNN and Transformer (CrowdCCT) for weakly supervised crowd counting, excelling in hybrid feature fusion.

1.5. Security and Ethical Considerations

- Contribution 11 critically review ML vulnerabilities in biometrics (e.g., data poisoning, deepfakes), urging defenses against adversarial threats.

2. Future Outlook

The work herein signals three key trajectories for biometrics:

- **Cross-spectral integration** (e.g., visible/infrared/multi-spectral fusion) will drive seamless authentication in non-cooperative environments.
- **Lightweight, explainable AI** must evolve to balance accuracy with ethical imperatives, addressing bias, privacy, and adversarial threats.
- **Metaverse-ready biometrics** will require novel sensors and generative models for immersive identity verification.
- **Ethical guardianship** must embed privacy-by-design principles and rigorous ethical frameworks in future advances to prevent the misuse of sensitive biological data.

We expect more collaborations to build trustworthy, inclusive, and ethically grounded biometric systems for an interconnected world.

Acknowledgments: We thank all contributing authors for their rigorous research advancing developments in biometrics community. We extend our thanks to peer reviewers whose expertise ensured the scientific quality and novelty of published works and Special Issue guest editors for their service in shaping this interdisciplinary discourse.

Conflicts of Interest: The authors declare no conflict of interest.

List of Contributions

1. Zhao, G.; Xu, J.; Wang, X.; Yan, F.; Qiu, S. PSAIP: Prior Structure-Assisted Identity-Preserving Network for Face Animation. *Electronics* **2025**, *14*, 784. https://doi.org/10.3390/electronics14040784.
2. Kim, J.; Ng, T.-S.; Teoh, A.B.J. Learnable Anchor Embedding for Asymmetric Face Recognition. *Electronics* **2025**, *14*, 455. https://doi.org/10.3390/electronics14030455.
3. Jiang, J.; Zhang, Q.; Wang, C. SAM-Iris: A SAM-Based Iris Segmentation Algorithm. *Electronics* **2025**, *14*, 246. https://doi.org/10.3390/electronics14020246.
4. Zhang, Y.; Wang, C.; Li, H.; Sun, X.; Tian, Q.; Zhao, G. OcularSeg: Accurate and Efficient Multi-Modal Ocular Segmentation in Non-Constrained Scenarios. *Electronics* **2024**, *13*, 1967. https://doi.org/10.3390/electronics13101967.
5. Seok, C.; Park, Y.; Baek, J.; Lim, H.; Roh, J.-H.; Kim, Y.; Kim, S.; Lee, E.C. AffectiVR: A Database for Periocular Identification and Valence and Arousal Evaluation in Virtual Reality. *Electronics* **2024**, *13*, 4112. https://doi.org/10.3390/electronics13204112.
6. Baek, J.; Park, Y.; Seok, C.; Lee, E.C. Noise-Robust Biometric Authentication Using Infrared Periocular Images Captured from a Head-Mounted Display. *Electronics* **2025**, *14*, 240. https://doi.org/10.3390/electronics14020240.
7. Kamiński, K.A.; Dobrowolski, A.P.; Piotrowski, Z.; Ścibiorek, P. Enhancing Web Application Security: Advanced Biometric Voice Verification for Two-Factor Authentication. *Electronics* **2023**, *12*, 3791. https://doi.org/10.3390/electronics12183791.
8. Wu, W.; Li, Y.; Zhang, Y.; Li, C. Identity Recognition System Based on Multi-Spectral Palm Vein Image. *Electronics* **2023**, *12*, 3503. https://doi.org/10.3390/electronics12163503.
9. Noh, M.; Ahn, H.; Lee, S.C. Real-Time Human Movement Recognition Using Ultra-Wideband Sensors. *Electronics* **2024**, *13*, 1300. https://doi.org/10.3390/electronics13071300.

10. Cai, Y.; Zhang, D. A Weakly Supervised Crowd Counting Method via Combining CNN and Transformer. *Electronics* **2024**, *13*, 5053. https://doi.org/10.3390/electronics13245053.
11. Ghilom, M.; Latifi, S. The Role of Machine Learning in Advanced Biometric Systems. *Electronics* **2024**, *13*, 2667. https://doi.org/10.3390/electronics13132667.

electronics

MDPI

Article

PSAIP: Prior Structure-Assisted Identity-Preserving Network for Face Animation

Guangzhe Zhao, Jun Xu, Xueping Wang *, Feihu Yan and Shuang Qiu

School of Intelligence Science and Technology, Beijing University of Civil Engineering and Architecture, Beijing 100044, China; zhaoguangzhe@bucea.edu.cn (G.Z.); 2108550022060@stu.bucea.edu.cn (J.X.); yanfeihu@bucea.edu.cn (F.Y.); 1108140023038@stu.bucea.edu.cn (S.Q.)

* Correspondence: wangxueping@bucea.edu.cn

Abstract: Face animation aims to render the source image according to the motion of the driving images while preserving the identity information of the source image. Despite significant advancements with the introduction of additional information, the literature lacks a thorough exploration of identity preservation. This paper proposes a Prior Structure-Assisted Identity-Preserving (PSAIP) network for face animation. Specifically, we introduce the additional priors of portrait segmentation images and face landmarks, which provide rich face geometric information while masking background interference to generate more realistic face images. Furthermore, we design an identity-enhancing generator network to adaptively fuses the identity feature information extracted from the source portrait and motion representations. Also, we utilize an identity-aware feature loss based on segmentation to avoid background distractions and monitor the identity preservation ability of the model. Extensive experiments on the VoxCeleb dataset and HDTF dataset show that our method is superior in identity preservation and realistic visual effects.

Keywords: face animation; prior structure; identity preserving; feature fusion; generative adversarial networks

1. Introduction

Face animation refers to inputting a face video as well as a static face image; the former is called the driver video and the latter is called the source image, and then capturing the relative changes in the pose as well as the expression of the character from the driver video, so as to drive the character in the source image to make the same expression and movement. It is worth noting that preserving the identity information of the source image is a crucial goal in this task. This task plays a crucial role in multimedia applications such as film production [1], human–computer interaction [2], digital human animation [3,4], and virtual reality [5].

Generating high-quality face animation videos usually requires fulfilling two crucial conditions: (1) pose preservation, i.e., the pose and expression of the character in the generated video should strictly be consistent with that of the driver character, and (2) identity preservation, i.e., the character in the generated video should retain the same identity as the source character. Although previous studies [6–13] have attained increased video fidelity and higher pose preservation capabilities, identity preservation is still a challenging problem, especially when the identity of the source portrait and the driver portrait differs greatly. Certainly, due to the inherent diversity in facial geometries among individuals, the alterations in expressions are not uniform or consistent across all faces. In addition, the human visual system is susceptible to small deviations in facial geometry.

With the rapid development of Generative Adversarial Networks (GANs) [14], many deep learning-based methods [6,7,15–17] have shown promising results in face animation. Siarohin et al. [6] animate input faces by learning dense motion fields conditioned on unsupervised motion-specific keypoints, but the generated video faces undergo geometrical deformations. Zhao et al. [7] can better model the facial movements through the thin-plate spline transformation. Meanwhile, the background of the image interferes with the detection of the keypoints, resulting in the semantic misalignment of the keypoints. In contrast, Agarwal et al. [8] provide before and after background information through portrait masks, but lack more accurate motion flow, making the video unrealistic. Zhang et al. [9] predict the motion field through predefined face landmarks, which can better maintain the geometry of the face, but cannot model the face details well due to the lack of texture information of the face. Therefore, the prior knowledge, i.e., face geometry and textures, should be considered together for better identity preservation.

Furthermore, existing generative networks [6,7,10,18] warp the source image through different processing methods, but most of them ignore the importance of identity information in the warping process. For example, Siarohin et al. [6] directly use the flow field to warp the source image, Wang et al. [10] improve the fidelity of the result by adaptively fusing the occlusion mask, and Zhao et al. [7] perform multi-resolution occlusion masks to make the features more fully fused. However, all these methods inevitably lose subtle identity-aware features, resulting in the identity loss problem. Therefore, more identity features should be taken into account in the generator model.

To solve the above issues, in this paper, we design a prior structure-assisted identity-preserving network for face animation, which better preserves portrait identity in three ways. First, we use an additional prior to provide rich face structure information for the network structure. Specifically, we employ the mediapipe [19] model to generate portrait segmentation images and 468 head landmarks. The segmentation image can effectively separate the foreground and background information of the image and reduce the interference of background on keypoints detection. The landmark can provide richer face geometric information. Second, we design an identity-enhancing generator network to enhance the perceived identity by fusing the identity features of the source portrait. Specifically, we adaptively fuse the identity feature information extracted from the source portrait as well as the motion representations learned from the source and driver frames through the Identity Adaptive Denormalization (IADE) layer to better synthesize identity-preserving face animation effects. Finally, we introduce a segmented image-based identity-aware feature loss for the model. To ensure that the identity information of the portrait can be better preserved while preventing the interference of background information, we compute the dissimilarity between the source segmented portrait and the generated segmented portrait as a loss to supervise the identity preservation capability of the model. Both the qualitative and quantitative results demonstrate the superior performance of our method when equipped with these three components (see Figure 1 for an illustration of our face animation results).

The main contributions are summarized as follows:

- We propose an additional face structure prior to provide richer face geometric information to the model and improve the reasonableness of the generated results.
- We design an identity-enhancing generator network to enhance the identity-awareness by fusing the identity features of the source portraits. This significantly reduces the identity loss during the generation process.
- We introduce a segmented image-based identity-aware feature loss to improve the identity preservation of the model.

Figure 1. Example results generated by our PSAIP. The left two columns are self-reconstruction and the right two columns are cross-reconstruction. The model can animate the source image to generate a realistic portrait image according to the driving image.

2. Related Works

2.1. Face Animation

Researchers have taken many different approaches to face animation. Early studies [20,21] mainly used computer graphics techniques that required human intervention to animate faces. Most recently, deep learning-based methods have been gradually developed, and related studies can be categorized into two parts: dense motion learning-based methods and face prior assisted-based methods.

Dense Motion Learning-Based Methods. Dense motion learning-based methods refer to the modeling of relative motion flows in different regions of the image by unsupervised means or conditioned on unsupervised keypoints, and the dense motion flows are superimposed to generate a warp field. For example, Wiles et al. [15] directly estimated the relative motion fields by unsupervised means using deep neural networks. Siarohin et al. [16] employed U-Net [22] to predict multiple pairs of keypoints unsupervised to estimate transformations of the animation. The follow-up work FOMM [6] utilized affine transformations to estimate motion near multiple keypoints, generating more accurate motion fields and thus significantly improving the quality of motion transfer. Wang et al. [23] introduced 3D spatial keypoints to estimate dense motion fields and enhance the representation in 3D space to model more flexible and accurate motion. Siarohin et al. [17] replaced unsupervised keypoints with planar regions on 2D that can be rotated and scaled by PCA [24], and propose to model foreground and background motion separately. Zhao et al. [7] proposed the thin-plate spline (TPS) [25] transformation to replace the affine transformation for estimating the optic flow for the relative motion of the keypoints. As a non-linear transformation, TPS allows for a more flexible estimation of the optical flow and can be better used for large-scale motion. TPSMM [7] produced state-of-the-art results in dense motion learning-based methods. These methods described above can model flexible and accurate motion flows, but have the obvious disadvantage of lacking a face prior and ignoring the rich information about face geometry.

Face Prior Assisted-Based Methods. Due to the specificity of faces, using predefined face prior for face animation is also an effective way. Some previous approaches [9,26–29] chose to use some prior knowledge of faces (e.g., face landmarks, 3DMM [30]) as conditions to train the warping field in a self-supervised manner. Zakharov et al. [19] constructed a neural rendering system using the SPADE layer [31], and generated a low-frequency component and a high-frequency component, then fused the two components to obtain the final result. Zhao et al. [27] presented an efficient model by combining local motion and global motion, and this model can be better implemented to animate face images through sparse landmarks. However, these landmarks are not dense enough to produce accurate warping flows. Zhang et al. [9] generated more accurate motion fields by predicting motion fields from dense face landmarks. Ren et al. [28] proposed a model for controlling face motion using the parameters of the 3D Morphable Model (3DMM) [30], which generated face images with accurate motion and realism based on free control. Wang et al. [10] modeled faces using a 3DMM to generate more realistic faces. Although these methods preserve the geometry of the face well, the warping fields of these methods do not use accurate flowing ground truth, are less expressive and flexible, and can only simulate coarse geometric deformations.

In this paper, we introduce a face prior in dense motion learning-based method for face animation. This not only facilitates the provision of richer face structure information, but also generates accurate warped flow fields. We improve the identity preservation capability of the model while ensuring the reasonableness of the generated results.

2.2. *Generative Adversarial Network*

Recently, Generative Adversarial Networks (GANs) [14] were trained to synthesize realistic images, which generally consist of a generator and a discriminator. Due to its powerful generative capabilities, GANs have achieved significant success in face animation.

There have been a number of studies [32,33] using the basic framework of GANs for synthesizing realistic faces. Some subsequent algorithms have achieved better generalization by proposing effective morphing modules [6,15–17,34]. There are also works that use an advanced version of GAN for face animation. For example, Tewari et al. [35] extracted the 3DMM parameters of the face and conditioned these parameters to manipulate the pre-trained StyleGAN [36] as a way to animate the face. However, it is not suitable for animating real-world images as it only maps latent variables. Our work builds on the basic GAN framework to complete the face animation through a deformation module, while proposing an effective identity preservation module for better generation.

2.3. *Identity Feature Fusion*

Identity feature fusion is an extremely effective operation in most tasks of face editing, including face swapping [37–39], face synthesis [40,41], and face animation [42,43]. Extensive experiments have demonstrated that performing identity feature fusion can help models better preserve the identity information of characters, which is extremely important for face animation.

In the field of face exchange, FaceShifter [39] extracted the identity of the source portrait and the attributes of the target portrait, and integrated the identity and attribute features for face synthesis through Adaptive Attentional Denormalization (AAD) layers. In the field of audio-driven face animation, Zhong et al. [43] injected extracted audio features into the model through AdaIN [44] as a way to guide speaker generation and ensure lip-synchronization. In the field of video-driven face animation, Zhan et al. [42] employed 3DMM-derived multiple guidance to improve face animation by using the 3DMM-drawn images through SPADE [31] to guide face animation and improve the identity preservation of the model. Many methods [6,16,25,28,45,46] utilized the predicted motion field to directly warp the source image, which inevitably results in identity loss during the generation process. Our method extracts the identity features of the source character and injects them into the encoder, allowing the identity features to be more fully fused for better identity preservation.

3. Methods

3.1. Overview

We design an elaborate framework for face animation, named PSAIP, as shown in Figure 2. PSAIP takes the source image $S \in \mathbb{R}^{H \times W \times 3}$ and the driving image $D \in \mathbb{R}^{H \times W \times 3}$ as inputs. We expect to generate a realistic face image $O \in \mathbb{R}^{H \times W \times 3}$ where the motion information is learned from the driver image while maintaining the identity information of the source image. The proposed method consists of three main components: structural priors to the motion estimator, an identity-enhancing generator network, and an identity-aware feature loss. The structural priors to the motion estimator take S and D as inputs, and generates optical flow of the source and driving images conditioned on the prior knowledge of face structure (see Section 3.2). Moreover, the identity-enhancing generator network performs a warping operation on the encoded S utilizing the optical flow and multi-scale occlusion masks generated by [25], and then adaptively fuses the identity features extracted from S_m at each layer of the decoder to better preserve the source identity (see Section 3.3). For further personalized facial modeling, we introduce identity-aware feature loss for identity-preserving face animation (see Section 3.4).

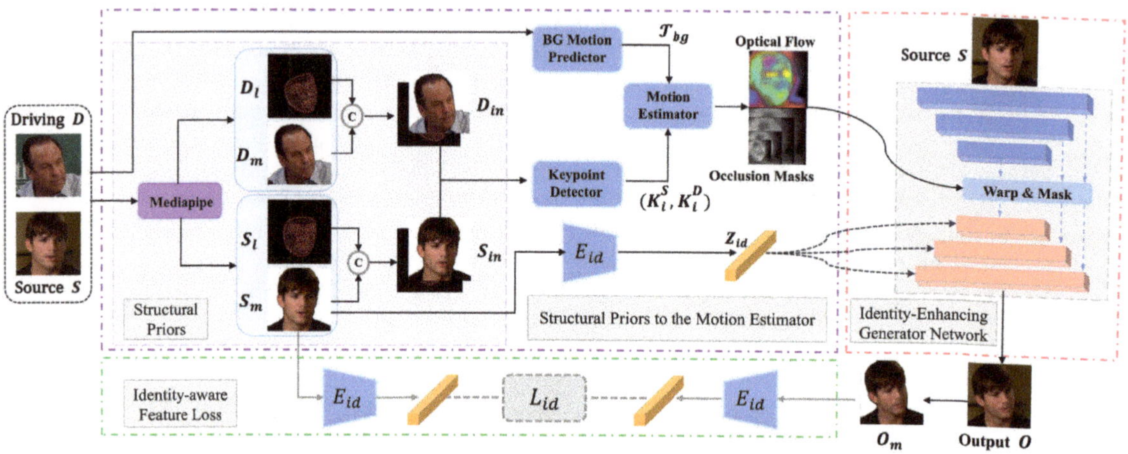

Figure 2. Overview of PSAIP framework. Our approach takes the source and driver images as inputs and uses their portrait segmentation images and facial landmarks as auxiliary priors. We introduce S_{in} and D_{in} to extract keypoints and perform background motion estimation for S and D. We then predict the overall motion optical flow and multiscale masking layers through a motion estimation network. We use E_{id} to extract the identity feature extracts implied by S and fusion them into the generator. Finally, we compute the identity loss between O_m and S_m to ensure the stability of the identity information.

3.2. Structural Priors to the Motion Estimator

Face geometry knowledge and face textures are helpful to guide the model to obtain better identity information in the process of generation. The introduction of these structural prior knowledge is benefit for the keypoint detector with more knowledge about the structure of the portrait and to improve the accuracy of keypoint detection. Among them, the face landmark map provides 468 important landmarks of the face, which provides more geometric information of the face for the keypoint detector and makes the model more focused on the keypoint detection of the face part. Meanwhile, the portrait segmentation image separates the background and foreground information so that the keypoints can only be detected from the foreground, focusing on the face part, without neglecting other important human elements such as hair and neck. In order to learn the motion flow effectively, the keypoint detector is employed to learn the transformation of the foreground, whereas the Background (BG) Motion Estimator is utilized to learn the transformation of the background.

Specifically, we randomly select two frames with different dimensions of $H \times W \times 3$ in the same video, which are used as S and D in the input, respectively. Before performing keypoint detection, mediapipe [19] is employed to preprocess S and D separately to generate the segmented images of the portrait (S_m, D_m) with dimensions of $H \times W \times 3$ and the face landmark maps (S_l, D_l) with dimensions of $H \times W \times 1$. Subsequently, the generated portrait masks ($T_m, T \in (S, D)$) and face landmark maps ($T_l, T \in (S, D)$) are concatenated in a channel fashion to obtain S_{in} and D_{in} with dimensions of $H \times W \times 4$, i.e., $S_{in} = Concat(S_m, S_l)$, $D_{in} = Concat(D_m, D_l)$. Finally, S_{in} and D_{in} are input to the keypoint detector. In this case, the keypoint detector is selected from TPSMM [7] in our framework, and it detects the keypoints $K_i \in \mathbb{R}^{50 \times 2}$ in the image in an unsupervised manner via ResNet18 [47], which is defined as follows:

$$K_i^T = K_p(T_{in}), T \in (S, D), \tag{1}$$

where K_p is the keypoints detector.

In addition, we use S and D as inputs to the BG estimator to perform motion estimation T_{bg} on the background of the image alone, as the background information is also non-negligible in face animation. We use the two generated sets of keypoints K_i^S and K_i^D for predicting the warping optical flow, and we use the motion estimation module from TPSMM to compute the TPS transform between the keypoints, and then fusion T_{bg} to obtain the warping optical flow $M_{s \to d}$ as well as the multiscale occlusion map, i.e.,

$$T_t = TPS(K_i^S, K_i^D), \tag{2}$$

$$M_{s \to d} = EM(T_{kp}, T_{bg}), T \in (S, D), \tag{3}$$

where T_t denotes the TPS transformation between the keypoints (K_i^S, K_i^D); TPS denotes the thin-plate spline transformation function; $M_{s \to d}$ denotes the warped optical flow we obtain; and EM stands for the motion estimation module.

3.3. Identity-Enhancing Generator Network

The direct application of the predicted flow field to warp the source image tends to introduce artifacts and compromise subtle perceptual characteristics. Consequently, a generative network enriched with identity information becomes essential to generate more realistic results, ensuring accuracy in both pose and expression. In this work, we propose an identity-enhancing generator network by using identity features as additional inputs to better preserve the identity of the source character without changing the pose and the expression upfront (see Figure 3a). Initially, we encode the source image. Subsequently, we employ the estimated optical flow to warp the feature map, simultaneously reconstructing the absent regions of the feature map using occlusion masks. Ultimately, in the decoding process, we adaptively integrate identity features into the final output.

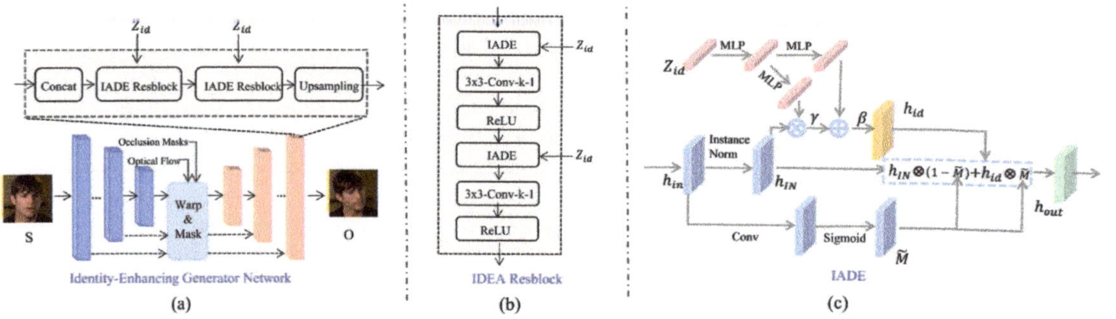

Figure 3. Overview of the Identity-Enhancing Generator Network. (**a**) Detailed structure of the generator, (**b**) detailed structure of the IADE Resblock, and (**c**) detailed structure of the IADE layer.

Identity Adaptive Denormalization (IADE). In order to adaptively adjust the identity feature embedding into the decoder, we propose the Identity Adaptive Denormalization (IADE), which is the main component of IADE Resblock, as shown in Figure 3b,c. During the decoder process, the identity feature Z_{id} of the source image is injected into each IADE Resblock, as shown in Figure 3b. We believe that Z_{id} should be fused adaptively, so we elaborate an IADE layer that uses denormalization for feature fusion. As shown in Figure 3c.

Specifically, the Z_{id} is initially projected onto MLP layers, and subsequently convolved to generate the modulation parameters γ and β. InstanceNorm normalizes the input of IADE layer h_{in} to h_{IN}. Subsequently, the produced h_{IN} is multiplied with the parameter γ and added to the parameter β for normalized activation, and the output is named as the identity-aware feature h_{id}, which is defined as follows:

$$h_{id} = h_{IN} \otimes \gamma + \beta, \quad (4)$$

where $\otimes$ denotes the Hadamard product. Then, the fusion mask $\widetilde{M}$ is generated by Conv and Sigmoid operations:

$$\widetilde{M} = \sigma(Conv(h_{in})). \quad (5)$$

The value of $\widetilde{M}$ is between 0 and 1. Finally, we combine h_{id} and h_{IN} using the mask $\widetilde{M}$ as a weighting parameter to obtain the final output h_{out} of the IADE layer, which is defined as follows:

$$h_{out} = h_{IN} \otimes (1 - \widetilde{M}) + h_{id} \otimes \widetilde{M}. \quad (6)$$

3.4. Identity-Aware Feature Loss

Identity preservation is necessary to generate high-quality face animations. Previous methods provide only image-level supervision and do not constrain the identity feature loss of images. Therefore, we introduce a segmented image-based identity-aware feature loss to supervise the identity preservation capability. To ensure that the identity information of the portrait can be better preserved while preventing the background information from interfering with the loss, we calculate the dissimilarity between the source segmented portrait S_m and the generated segmented portrait O_m as the loss:

$$L_{id} = 1 - cos(E_{id}(S_m), E_{id}(O_m)), \quad (7)$$

where S_m is the portrait segmentation map of the source image, O_m is the portrait segmentation map of the generated image O, and E_{id} is the identity feature extractor. The identity feature extractor is employed to extract identity features from S_m and O_m, respectively, and the dissimilarity is calculated between the two identity features. The identity-aware feature loss constrains the identity similarity between S_m and O_m, i.e., it represents the identity similarity between the source image S and the generated image O. This effectively enhances the capability to maintain the identity of the framework.

3.5. Training Losses

Following [6,7], we use L_r to supervise reconstruction effects at different resolutions. The loss can be expressed as follows:

$$L_r = \sum_i (V_i(D) - V_i(O)), \tag{8}$$

where V_i is the ith layer of the pre-trained VGG-19 network [48].

We utilize the equivariance loss L_e to impose constraints on the keypoint detector:

$$L_e = |K_p(T_r(S_{in})) - T_r(K_p(S_{in}))|, \tag{9}$$

where T_r is the random TPS transformation, and K_p is the keypoints detector.

What is more, we employ the warping loss to additionally constrain the warped coded images within the generator network:

$$L_w = \sum_i |\widetilde{W}(U_i(S) - U_i(D))|, \tag{10}$$

where U_i represents the ith layer in the encoder and $\widetilde{W}$ is the warping operation based on the predicted optical flow $M_{s \to d}$.

The comprehensive loss function is a fusion of the above loss functions:

$$L_s = L_{id} + L_r + L_e + L_w. \tag{11}$$

4. Experiments

4.1. Datasets & Metrics

Datasets: We evaluate our model on the VoxCeleb dataset [49], which contains 22,496 face videos extracted from YouTube. We adopt the same pre-processing strategy as that of [6] to crop faces from the original videos. During pre-processing, each video is cropped and resized to 256 × 256 for training and testing. In total, we obtain 18,025 videos for training and 473 videos for testing. The length of the videos ranges from 64 to 1024 frames.

To further validate the robustness and effectiveness of our model, we also tested the model on the HDTF dataset [50] for validation. This dataset consists of 410 videos from 300 different identities. We reduced the cropped faces to 256 × 256 resolution, and we will obtain all videos as a new test set to evaluate our model again.

Metrics: We calculate the Manhattan Distance (**L1**) to represent the reconstruction capability of the model. For the visual quality and realism of the generated images, we use Fréchet Inception Distance (**FID**) [51,52] for evaluation. The quality of our image generation is evaluated using Structural Similarity Index Measure (**SSIM**) [53] and Peak Signal to Noise Ratio (**PSNR**). Based on previous work [6], we use the Average Euclidean Identity Distance (**AEID**) to measure the degree of preservation of the identity information. We use the widely used face recognition model Open-face [54] to extract the identity features of two faces from the generated video and ground-truth video, and then compute the average Euclidean distance between them. The smaller the AEID distance, the better the identity information is preserved.

4.2. Implementation Details

During training and testing, instead of generating multiple frames as a video, we process them frame by frame. We randomly extract two frames in the same video to be the source image S and driver image D. Before we train the whole model end-to-end, the source and driver frames are pre-processed separately, and we extract the portrait segmentation image and 468 facial landmarks using mediapipe [19] as a geometric prior for the face. We refer to the pre-trained face recognition model ArcFace [55] as our identity feature extractor, because ArcFace has better stability and robustness while meeting our computational needs. In addition, we adjust the weight of the identity loss lid to four different settings with values of 0.2, 0.5, 1, and 2, and finally determine that a weight of 1 yields more reasonable reconstruction results.

We deploy a Tesla V100 GPUs to train the model on the VoxCeleb dataset [49] for about 10 days. We set 100 epochs with a batch size of 16, and repeat the dataset video list 75 times for each epoch. The model is trained by the Adam Optimizer with the initial learning rate being set to 2×10^{-4}.

4.3. Comparisons with Other Methods

To thoroughly assess the efficacy of our PSAIP in the face animation task, we utilize the VoxCeleb dataset and HDTF dataset for a multifaceted comparison with several advanced face animation methods, including X2Face [15], FOMM [6], PIRender [28], and TPSMM [7]. For a fair comparison, we use officially published code for training. For the four models above and the proposed PSAIP, we perform face animation on the test set of 473 videos using two inference strategies (self-reconstruction and cross-reconstruction). We compare the reconstruction results quantitatively and qualitatively. Figure 4 shows our qualitative results with other methods, where the first two rows are self-reconstruction and the last three rows are cross-reconstruction. Tables 1 and 2 show the quantitative results of our PSAIP with other methods.

Self-Reconstruction: Self-reconstruction involves undertaking the face animation task using a scenario where the source image and the driving video feature the same individual. The initial frame of the video is designated as the source image, while the subsequent frames are treated as the driving ones. Under these conditions, our expectation is for the generated video to closely mirror the original video. Therefore, we calculate L1, FID, SSIM, PSNR, and AEID to quantitatively evaluate the generated video in various aspects.

The first two rows of Figure 4 show the effects of the five models under the self-reconstruction strategy. We can observe that X2Face produces obvious warping effects, and FOMM basically maintains the pose of the driving character, but there are artifacts and the face is unreasonable. PIRenderer is of poor quality and not realistic enough. TPSMM maintains the pose and identity of the character well, but due to the lack of a certain facial prior, it is not reasonable in the generation of facial details (such as the eyes of the man in the first row). In contrast, our framework can generate more accurate facial geometric details such as eyes and mouths.

For a more objective comparison, we present in Table 1 the quantitative results evaluated in the Voxceleb dataset, where PSAIP outperforms the other methods under the self-reconfiguration strategy for most of the metrics, and only achieves competitive results for SSIM and FID. To further validate the effectiveness of our model, we conducted test experiments again on the HTDF dataset, and the quantitative results of our test experiments are demonstrated in Table 2. PSAIP clearly achieves optimal results. It is worth noting that our method performs particularly well in terms of AEID values on both datasets. As a result, our model can generate more realistic and reasonable faces with better character preservation.

Figure 4. Qualitative results for self-reconstruction (top two rows) and cross-reconstruction (bottom three rows) on the VoxCeleb dataset.

Cross-Reconstruction: Cross-reconstruction differs from self-reconstruction in that the subjects featured in the source image and the driving video do not share the same identity. Cross-reconstruction is a much more meaningful setup because most real-world applications require the source image and the driver video to be different people. For cross-reconstruction, we first randomly sort the videos in the test set. The first frame of a video is set as the source image, the next video in the sequence is as the driver video, and when the first frame of the last video in the sequence is used as the source image, we use the first video in the sequence as the driver video. With our setup, each video in the test set can be used as both the source and driver video, and the overall frame count of the 473 videos remains the same in the final generated result.

For a qualitative comparison of the cross-reconstruction, we can observe from the last three rows of Figure 4 that ours distinctly exhibits superior visual outcomes. The most obvious of these is that previous methods suffer from a leakage of appearance data from the driving portrait and they produce faces that bear a resemblance to the identity depicted in the driving image. In contrast, our model enhances the facial geometric information, especially details such as eyes and teeth, while more effectively retaining the identity features of the source character. Tables 1 and 2 also include quantitative results for the various methods in the cross-identity setting. In this case, as there is no ground truth to use as a comparison, we only count AEID and FID for the reconstruction results. The AEID-c and FID-c values presented in Table serve as evidence that PSAIP produces videos that are not only more realistic and sensible, but also more effectively preserve the characteristics of the source image.

Table 1. Quantitative results for VoxCeleb self-reconfiguration and cross-reconfiguration. -c indicates cross-reconstruction. The symbol '↓' indicates a preference for smaller values, while '↑' denotes a preference for larger values. The optimal results are emphasized in bold.

Method	L1 ↓	FID ↓	SSIM ↑	PSNR ↑	AEID ↓	FID-c ↓	AEID-c ↓
X2Face [15]	0.0833	39.8220	0.5288	28.4935	0.5156	67.8122	0.7278
FOMM [6]	0.0422	12.2464	0.6901	29.1699	0.1590	17.7347	0.5611
PIRender [28]	0.0592	15.9981	0.6600	29.9740	0.2322	16.8866	0.5971
TPSMM [7]	0.0404	**10.6923**	**0.7881**	30.8830	0.1470	16.5776	0.5597
Ours	**0.0396**	10.7576	0.7873	**30.9882**	**0.1248**	**16.3589**	**0.5407**

Table 2. Quantitative results for HTDF self-reconfiguration and cross-reconfiguration. -c indicates cross-reconstruction. The symbol '↓' indicates a preference for smaller values, while '↑' denotes a preference for larger values. The optimal results are emphasized in bold.

Method	L1 ↓	FID ↓	SSIM ↑	PSNR ↑	AEID ↓	FID-c ↓	AEID-c ↓
X2Face [15]	0.0742	30.2147	0.6347	27.6324	0.6245	63.2147	0.8324
FOMM [6]	0.0373	11.5148	0.7980	28.0126	0.2674	18.3420	0.6421
PIRender [28]	0.0576	12.6485	0.7254	27.9362	0.3072	18.4476	0.7097
TPSMM [7]	0.0298	10.3982	0.8101	28.4267	0.2142	17.7432	0.6207
Ours	**0.0284**	**10.2123**	**0.8135**	**28.4762**	**0.1989**	**17.5497**	**0.6100**

4.4. Ablation Study

To demonstrate the effectiveness and necessity of each of our contributions, we separately set several variants of our model and conduct experiments. **Baseline** indicates the test results of the baseline model; **Baseline + prior** indicates that we add the face priors to the Motion Estimator on the baseline model; **Baseline + prior +** Z_{id} indicates that we design the identity-enhancing generator network based on **Baseline + prior**; and **Ours** indicates the final model after we introduce the face priors to the Motion Estimator, the identity-enhancing generator network, and the identity feature loss.

Figure 5 and Table 3 show the qualitative and quantitative results of our ablation experiments. When the face prior is introduced, more reasonable geometric details of the face can be generated (see Figure 5-Baseline + prior), and the AEID metrics are significantly optimized. When the identity-preserving generator network is updated, more realistic images can be generated (see Figure 5-Baseline + prior + Z_{id}), there is a significant decrease in the L1 reconstruction loss, PSNR and AEID have a more significant improvement. Finally, after introducing the loss of identity features based on segmented images, the face details are adjusted again (see Figure 5-Ours), and the optimal AEID value also shows that this work excels in preserving the identity.

From the above quantitative and qualitative results, each of our works is effective and necessary. What is more, our model can generate more accurate facial geometric details, better preserve the identity information of the characters, and effectively improve the credibility of the generated results.

Table 3. Quantitative ablation study for self-reconstruction. The symbol '↓' indicates a preference for smaller values, while '↑' denotes a preference for larger values. The optimal results are emphasized in bold.

Method	L1 ↓	PSNR ↑	AEID ↓
Baseline	0.0404	30.8830	0.1470
Baseline + prior	0.0404	30.8873	0.1285
Baseline + prior + Z_{id}	0.0398	**31.0086**	0.1269
Ours	**0.0396**	30.9882	**0.1248**

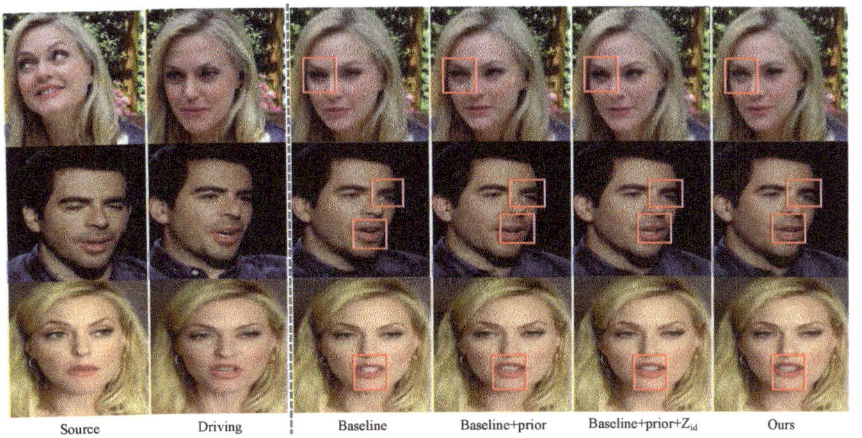

Figure 5. Qualitative ablation study for self-reconstruction. We show the impact of different modules in detail.

4.5. Limitations

Although our method synthesizes photo-realistic results with better identity preservation, there are still some limitations. Figure 6 depicts two typical failures. The right half of the face of the lady in the first row was not reconstructed as accurately as we expected due to the occlusion of the hand in the source image. The man in the second row was reconstructed with a lip and chin section, but the generated image lacks realism. We posit that significant occlusions hinder our model from obtaining sufficient feature information, posing challenges in accurately reconstructing the occluded portions. Improving the occlusion-awareness and auto-repair capabilities might be used for further improvement.

Figure 6. Some fail cases. When the source image is occluded, our model cannot be perfectly reconstructed.

5. Conclusions

In this paper, we propose a Prior Structure-Assisted Identity-Preserving network for face animation, which uses portrait segmentation images and face landmarks to provide rich face structure prior to the model. These prior information effectively improve the structure of reconstructed faces and increase the rationality of the generation. In addition, we design an identity-enhancing generator network to enhance the identity feature information of the source portrait to reduce the identity loss caused by the generation process. Finally, the identity-aware feature loss is introduced to supervise the identity preservation capability of the model. The superiority of our approach is verified through extensive experiments, which demonstrate that PSAIP can preserve more complete and authentic identity features in the source portrait, surpassing state-of-the-art methods across most metrics.

Author Contributions: J.X. provided and implemented the main idea of the research and wrote part of the paper. G.Z., X.W. and F.Y. provided some suggestions and revised the paper. S.Q. also wrote some parts of the paper. All authors have read and agreed to the published version of the manuscript.

Funding: This research was funded by the National Natural Science Foundation of China under grant number 62402026, and grant number 62176018; in part by the R&D Program of Beijing Municipal Education Commission under Grant KM202410016010.

Data Availability Statement: The original contributions presented in this study are included in the article. Our source code is publicly available via: https://github.com/xxxujun/PSAIP (accessed on 2 January 2025). Further inquiries can be directed to the corresponding author.

Acknowledgments: Thanks to my supervisors for their help.

Conflicts of Interest: The authors declare no conflicts of interest.

References

1. Kim, H.; Elgharib, M.; Zollhöfer, M.; Seidel, H.P.; Beeler, T.; Richardt, C.; Theobalt, C. Neural style-preserving visual dubbing. *ACM Trans. Graph.* **2019**, *38*, 1–13. [CrossRef]
2. Adalgeirsson, S.O.; Breazeal, C. MeBot: A robotic platform for socially embodied telepresence. In Proceedings of the ACM/IEEE International Conference on Human-Robot Interaction (HRI), Osaka, Japan, 2–5 March 2010; pp. 15–22.
3. Edwards, P.; Landreth, C.; Fiume, E.; Singh, K. Jali: An animator-centric viseme model for expressive lip synchronization. *ACM Trans. Graph.* **2016**, *35*, 1–11. [CrossRef]
4. Zhou, Y.; Xu, Z.; Landreth, C.; Kalogerakis, E.; Maji, S.; Singh, K. Visemenet: Audio-driven animator-centric speech animation. *ACM Trans. Graph.* **2018**, *37*, 1–10. [CrossRef]
5. Fang, Y.; Tang, J.; Shen, W.; Shen, W.; Gu, X.; Song, L.; Zhai, G. Dual Attention Guided Gaze Target Detection in the Wild. In Proceedings of the IEEE/CVF Conference on Computer Vision and Pattern Recognition (CVPR), Nashville, TN, USA, 19–25 June 2021; pp. 11390–11399.
6. Siarohin, A.; Lathuilière, S.; Tulyakov, S.; Ricci, E.; Sebe, N. First order motion model for image animation. In Proceedings of the Neural Information Processing Systems (NeurIPS), Vancouver, BC, Canada, 8–14 December 2019; Volume 32, pp. 7137–7147.
7. Zhao, J.; Zhang, H. Thin-plate spline motion model for image animation. In Proceedings of the IEEE/CVF Conference on Computer Vision and Pattern Recognition (CVPR), Vancouver, BC, Canada, 18–22 June 2022; pp. 3657–3666.
8. Agarwal, M.; Mukhopadhyay, R.; Namboodiri, V.; Jawahar, C.V. Audio-Visual Face Reenactment. In Proceedings of the IEEE/CVF Winter Conference on Applications of Computer Vision (WACV), Waikoloa, HI, USA, 2–7 January 2023; pp. 5167–5176. [CrossRef]
9. Zhang, B.; Qi, C.; Zhang, P.; Zhang, B.; Wu, H.; Chen, D.; Chen, Q.; Wang, Y.; Wen, F. MetaPortrait: Identity-Preserving Talking Head Generation With Fast Personalized Adaptation. In Proceedings of the IEEE/CVF Conference on Computer Vision and Pattern Recognition (CVPR), Vancouver, BC, Canada, 18–22 June 2023; pp. 22096–22105.
10. Wang, Q.; Zhang, L.; Li, B. SAFA: Structure Aware Face Animation. In Proceedings of the 2021 International Conference on 3D Vision (3DV), Virtual, 1–3 December 2021; pp. 679–688. [CrossRef]
11. Aneja, S.; Thies, J.; Dai, A.; Nießner, M. FaceTalk: Audio-driven motion diffusion for neural parametric head models. In Proceedings of the IEEE/CVF Conference on Computer Vision and Pattern Recognition, Seattle, WA, USA, 16–22 June 2024; pp. 21263–21273.

12. Wang, X.; Ruan, T.; Xu, J.; Guo, X.; Li, J.; Yan, F.; Zhao, G.; Wang, C. Expression-aware neural radiance fields for high-fidelity talking portrait synthesis. *Image Vis. Comput.* **2024**, *147*, 105075. [CrossRef]
13. Peng, Z.; Hu, W.; Shi, Y.; Zhu, X.; Zhang, X.; Zhao, H.; He, J.; Liu, H.; Fan, Z. SyncTalk: The devil is in the synchronization for talking head synthesis. In Proceedings of the IEEE/CVF Conference on Computer Vision and Pattern Recognition, Seattle, WA, USA, 16–22 June 2024; pp. 666–676.
14. Goodfellow, I.; Pouget-Abadie, J.; Mirza, M.; Xu, B.; Warde-Farley, D.; Ozair, S.; Courville, A.; Bengio, Y. Generative Adversarial Nets. In Proceedings of the Neural Information Processing Systems (NeurIPS), Montreal, QC, Canada, 8–13 December 2014; Volume 27, pp. 2672–2680.
15. Wiles, O.; Koepke, A.; Zisserman, A. X2face: A network for controlling face generation using images, audio, and pose codes. In Proceedings of the European Conference on Computer Vision (ECCV), Munich, Germany, 8–14 September 2018; pp. 670–686.
16. Siarohin, A.; Lathuilière, S.; Tulyakov, S.; Ricci, E.; Sebe, N. Animating Arbitrary Objects via Deep Motion Transfer. In Proceedings of the IEEE/CVF Conference on Computer Vision and Pattern Recognition (CVPR), Long Beach, CA, USA, 15–20 June 2019; pp. 2372–2381. [CrossRef]
17. Siarohin, A.; Woodford, O.J.; Ren, J.; Chai, M.; Tulyakov, S. Motion representations for articulated animation. In Proceedings of the IEEE/CVF Conference on Computer Vision and Pattern Recognition (CVPR), Nashville, TN, USA, 19–25 June 2021; pp. 13653–13662.
18. Wang, H.; Liu, F.; Zhou, Q.; Yi, R.; Tan, X.; Ma, L. Continuous Piecewise-Affine Based Motion Model for Image Animation. In Proceedings of the AAAI Conference on Artificial Intelligence, Vancouver, BC, Canada, 20–27 February 2024; Volume 38, pp. 5427–5435.
19. Lugaresi, C.; Tang, J.; Nash, H.; McClanahan, C.; Uboweja, E.; Hays, M.; Zhang, F.; Chang, C.L.; Yong, M.G.; Lee, J.; et al. MediaPipe: A Framework for Building Perception Pipelines. *arXiv* **2019**, arXiv:1906.08172.
20. Blanz, V.; Basso, C.; Poggio, T.; Vetter, T. Reanimating Faces in Images and Video. *Comput. Graph. Forum* **2003**, *22*, 641–650. [CrossRef]
21. Leyvand, T.; Cohen-Or, D.; Dror, G.; Lischinski, D. Data-driven Enhancement Of Facial Attractiveness. *ACM Trans. Graph.* **2008**, *27*, 241–249. [CrossRef]
22. Ronneberger, O.; Fischer, P.; Brox, T. U-net: Convolutional networks for biomedical image segmentation. *Med. Image Comput. Comput.-Assist. Interv.* **2015**, *18*, 234–241.
23. Wang, T.C.; Mallya, A.; Liu, M.Y. One-shot free-view neural talking-head synthesis for video conferencing. In Proceedings of the IEEE/CVF Conference on Computer Vision and Pattern Recognition (CVPR), Nashville, TN, USA, 19–25 June 2021; pp. 10039–10049.
24. Wall, M.E.; Rechtsteiner, A.; Rocha, L.M. Singular value decomposition and principal component analysis. *Pract. Approach Microarray Data Anal.* **2003**, *3*, 91–109.
25. Bookstein, F.L. Principal warps: Thin-plate splines and the decomposition of deformations. *IEEE Trans. Pattern Anal. Mach. Intell.* **1989**, *11*, 567–585. [CrossRef]
26. Zakharov, E.; Ivakhnenko, A.; Shysheya, A.; Lempitsky, V. Fast bi-layer neural synthesis of one-shot realistic head avatars. In Proceedings of the European Conference on Computer Vision (ECCV), Glasgow, UK, 23–28 August 2020; pp. 524–540.
27. Zhao, R.; Wu, T.; Guo, G. Sparse to dense motion transfer for face image animation. In Proceedings of the IEEE/CVF International Conference on Computer Vision (ICCV), Montreal, BC, Canada, 11–17 October 2021; pp. 1991–2000.
28. Ren, Y.; Li, G.; Chen, Y.; Li, T.H.; Liu, S. Pirenderer: Controllable portrait image generation via semantic neural rendering. In Proceedings of the IEEE/CVF International Conference on Computer Vision (ICCV), Montreal, QC, Canada, 11–17 October 2021; pp. 13759–13768.
29. Chen, H.; Zendehdel, N.; Leu, M.C.; Yin, Z. Real-time human-computer interaction using eye gazes. *Manuf. Lett.* **2023**, *35*, 883–894. [CrossRef]
30. Blanz, V.; Vetter, T. A Morphable Model for the Synthesis of 3D Faces. *Semin. Graph. Pap. Push. Boundaries* **2023**, *2*, 157–164.
31. Park, T.; Liu, M.Y.; Wang, T.C.; Zhu, J.Y. Semantic image synthesis with spatially-adaptive normalization. In Proceedings of the IEEE/CVF Conference on Computer Vision and Pattern Recognition (CVPR), Long Beach, CA, USA, 15–20 June 2019; pp. 2337–2346.
32. Thies, J.; Zollhöfer, M.; Nießner, M.; Valgaerts, L.; Stamminger, M.; Theobalt, C. Real-time expression transfer for facial reenactment. *ACM Trans. Graph.* **2015**, *34*, 183. [CrossRef]
33. Kim, H.; Garrido, P.; Tewari, A.; Xu, W.; Thies, J.; Niessner, M.; Pérez, P.; Richardt, C.; Zollhöfer, M.; Theobalt, C. Deep video portraits. *ACM Trans. Graph.* **2018**, *37*, 1–14. [CrossRef]
34. Zakharov, E.; Shysheya, A.; Burkov, E.; Lempitsky, V. Few-Shot Adversarial Learning of Realistic Neural Talking Head Models. In Proceedings of the IEEE/CVF International Conference on Computer Vision (ICCV), Seoul, Republic of Korea, 27 October–2 November 2019; pp. 9458–9467. [CrossRef]

35. Tewari, A.; Elgharib, M.; Bharaj, G.; Bernard, F.; Seidel, H.P.; Pérez, P.; Zollhofer, M.; Theobalt, C. Stylerig: Rigging stylegan for 3d control over portrait images. In Proceedings of the IEEE/CVF Conference on Computer Vision and Pattern Recognition (CVPR), Seattle, WA, USA, 14–19 June 2020; pp. 6142–6151.
36. Karras, T.; Laine, S.; Aila, T. A style-based generator architecture for generative adversarial networks. In Proceedings of the IEEE/CVF Conference on Computer Vision and Pattern Recognition (CVPR), Long Beach, CA, USA, 15–20 June 2019; pp. 4401–4410.
37. Natsume, R.; Yatagawa, T.; Morishima, S. Fsnet: An identity-aware generative model for image-based face swapping. In Proceedings of the Asian Conference on Computer Vision (ACCV), Perth, Australia, 2–6 December 2018; pp. 117–132.
38. Bao, J.; Chen, D.; Wen, F.; Li, H.; Hua, G. Towards Open-Set Identity Preserving Face Synthesis. In Proceedings of the IEEE/CVF Conference on Computer Vision and Pattern Recognition (CVPR), Salt Lake City, UT, USA, 18–22 June 2018; pp. 6713–6722.
39. Li, L.; Bao, J.; Yang, H.; Chen, D.; Wen, F. Advancing high fidelity identity swapping for forgery detection. In Proceedings of the IEEE/CVF Conference on Computer Vision and Pattern Recognition (CVPR), Seattle, WA, USA, 14–19 June 2020; pp. 5074–5083.
40. An S.; Chen, J.; Zhu, Z.; Zhou, F.; Yang, Y.; Ma, Y.; Liu, X.; Zhu, H. ARCosmetics: A real-time augmented reality cosmetics try-on system. *Front. Comput. Sci.* **2023**, *17*, 174706. [CrossRef]
41. Sun, S.; Zhao, B.; Mateen, M.; Chen, X.; Wen, J. Mask guided diverse face image synthesis. *Front. Comput. Sci.* **2022**, *16*, 163311. [CrossRef]
42. Zhang, H.; Ren, Y.; Chen, Y.; Li, G.; Li, T.H. Exploiting Multiple Guidance from 3DMM for Face Reenactment. In Proceedings of the AAAI-23 Workshop on Creative AI Across Modalities (CreativeAI), Washington, DC, USA, 7–14 February 2023; pp. 729–737.
43. Zhong, W.; Fang, C.; Cai, Y.; Wei, P.; Zhao, G.; Lin, L.; Li, G. Identity-Preserving Talking Face Generation with Landmark and Appearance Priors. In Proceedings of the IEEE/CVF Conference on Computer Vision and Pattern Recognition (CVPR), Vancouver, BC, Canada, 17–24 June 2023; pp. 9729–9738.
44. Huang, X.; Belongie, S. Arbitrary style transfer in real-time with adaptive instance normalization. In Proceedings of the IEEE/CVF International Conference on Computer Vision (ICCV), Venice, Italy, 22–29 October 2017; pp. 1501–1510.
45. Qiu, X.; Zhu, R.J.; Chou, Y.; Wang, Z.; Deng, L.J.; Li, G. Gated attention coding for training high-performance and efficient spiking neural networks. In Proceedings of the AAAI Conference on Artificial Intelligence, Vancouver, BC, Canada, 20–27 February 2024; Volume 38, pp. 601–610.
46. Ma, Y.; Liu, H.; Wang, H.; Pan, H.; He, Y.; Yuan, J.; Zeng, A.; Cai, C.; Shum, H.Y.; Liu, W.; et al. Follow-your-emoji: Fine-controllable and expressive freestyle portrait animation. In Proceedings of the SIGGRAPH Asia 2024 Conference Papers, Tokyo, Japan, 3–6 December 2024; pp. 1–12.
47. He, K.; Zhang, X.; Ren, S.; Sun, J. Deep residual learning for image recognition. In Proceedings of the IEEE/CVF Conference on Computer Vision and Pattern Recognition (CVPR), Las Vegas, Nevada, USA, 27–30 June 2016; pp. 770–778.
48. Johnson, J.; Alahi, A.; Fei-Fei, L. Perceptual losses for real-time style transfer and super-resolution. In Proceedings of the IEEE/CVF Conference on European Conference on Computer Vision (ECCV), Amsterdam, The Netherlands, 11–14 October 2016; pp. 694–711.
49. Nagrani, A.; Chung, J.S.; Zisserman, A. VoxCeleb: A Large-Scale Speaker Identification Dataset. In Proceedings of the Interspeech 2017, Stockholm, Sweden, 20–24 August 2017; pp. 2616–2620. [CrossRef]
50. Zhang, Z.; Li, L.; Ding, Y.; Fan, C. Flow-guided one-shot talking face generation with a high-resolution audio-visual dataset. In Proceedings of the IEEE/CVF Conference on Computer Vision and Pattern Recognition, Nashville, TN, USA, 19–25 June 2021; pp. 3661–3670.
51. Heusel, M.; Ramsauer, H.; Unterthiner, T.; Nessler, B.; Hochreiter, S. GANs Trained by a Two Time-Scale Update Rule Converge to a Local Nash Equilibrium. In Proceedings of the Neural Information Processing Systems (NeurIPS), Long Beach, CA, USA, 4–9 December 2017; pp. 6629–6640.
52. Szegedy, C.; Vanhoucke, V.; Ioffe, S.; Shlens, J.; Wojna, Z. Rethinking the inception architecture for computer vision. In Proceedings of the IEEE/CVF Conference on Computer Vision and Pattern Recognition (CVPR), Las Vegas, Nevada, USA, 27–30 June 2016; pp. 2818–2826.
53. Wang, Z.; Bovik, A.C.; Sheikh, H.R.; Simoncelli, E.P. Image quality assessment: From error visibility to structural similarity. *IEEE Trans. Image Process.* **2004**, *13*, 600–612. [CrossRef] [PubMed]
54. Amos, B.; Ludwiczuk, B.; Satyanarayanan, M. Openface: A general-purpose face recognition library with mobile applications. *CMU Sch. Comput. Sci.* **2016**, *6*, 20.
55. Deng, J.; Guo, J.; Xue, N.; Zafeiriou, S. Arcface: Additive angular margin loss for deep face recognition. In Proceedings of the IEEE/CVF Conference on Computer Vision and Pattern Recognition (CVPR), Long Beach, CA, USA, 15–20 June 2019; pp. 4690–4699.

electronics

MDPI

Article

Learnable Anchor Embedding for Asymmetric Face Recognition

Jungyun Kim, Tiong-Sik Ng and Andrew Beng Jin Teoh *

School of Electrical and Electronic Engineering, Yonsei University, Seoul 03722, Republic of Korea; jungyun@yonsei.ac.kr (J.K.); ngtiongsik@yonsei.ac.kr (T.-S.N.)
* Correspondence: bjteoh@yonsei.ac.kr

Abstract: Face verification and identification traditionally follow a symmetric matching approach, where the same model (e.g., ResNet-50 vs. ResNet-50) generates embeddings for both gallery and query images, ensuring compatibility. However, real-world scenarios often demand asymmetric matching, especially when query devices have limited computational resources or employ heterogeneous models (e.g., ResNet-50 vs. SwinTransformer). This asymmetry can degrade face recognition performance due to incompatibility between embeddings from different models. To tackle this asymmetric face recognition problem, we introduce the Learnable Anchor Embedding (LAE) model, which features two key innovations: the Shared Learnable Anchor and a Light Cross-Attention Mechanism. The Shared Learnable Anchor is a dynamic attractor, aligning heterogeneous gallery and query embeddings within a unified embedding space. The Light Cross-Attention Mechanism complements this alignment process by reweighting embeddings relative to the anchor, efficiently refining their alignment within the unified space. Extensive evaluations of several facial benchmark datasets demonstrate LAE's superior performance, particularly in asymmetric settings. Its robustness and scalability make it an effective solution for real-world applications such as edge-device authentication, cross-platform verification, and environments with resource constraints.

Keywords: asymmetric face recognition; face identification; face verification; shared learnable anchor; light cross-attention

1. Introduction

Deep-learning-based face recognition technology has experienced remarkable advancements in recent years and is increasingly employed in various real-world applications. This technology plays a critical role across domains such as missing person searches [1], attendance verification systems [2], and financial security [3], contributing significantly to the recognition of individuals. Particularly in scenarios such as contactless authentication, access control, and real-time monitoring via surveillance cameras, face recognition proves to be highly useful, enhancing both security and convenience.

Deep-learning-based face recognition systems typically rely on a single model to generate embeddings for both gallery and query images, a method commonly referred to as *symmetric face recognition* [4–8]. This approach is highly effective in controlled environments where the same model is consistently employed across all devices. However, relying on a single model is not always feasible in real-world scenarios. Instead, multiple devices often utilize different models to meet computational and memory constraints. For instance, resource-limited edge devices (e.g., smartphones) may adopt lightweight models to minimize computational overhead and memory usage. In contrast, high-performance servers or cloud infrastructures can employ larger and more complex models to maximize the accuracy of face embedding extraction. Such heterogeneous cross-device authentication scenarios commonly arise in financial systems, access control, and IoT ecosystems. Ensuring seamless interoperability in these settings is critical for user convenience and security. Consequently, when designing face recognition systems, it is imperative to account for various model and device environments to provide accurate and consistent embedding compatibility across different models. This variation introduces challenges, as embeddings generated by one model may not align perfectly with those from another, leading to performance degradation and inconsistencies. The illustration of differences between symmetric and asymmetric face recognition is shown in Figure 1.

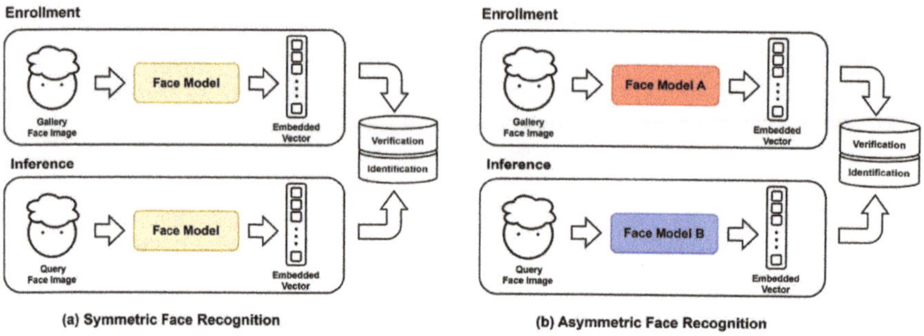

Figure 1. Symmetric and asymmetric face recognition. (**a**) Symmetric face recognition in which both face models are identical for the gallery and query; (**b**) asymmetric face recognition in which models A and B may differ in architecture, training techniques, or optimization strategies.

In practice, deploying heterogeneous models within a face recognition system is often necessary due to differences in hardware capabilities, optimization needs, or specific contextual requirements at the enrollment and query ends, which is known as *asymmetric face recognition* (AFR) [9–11]. For example, a lightweight model might be used on resource-constrained hardware at the query end, while a more sophisticated model operates on a server for enrollment. These practical considerations underscore the importance of ensuring interoperability between different face recognition models, allowing for consistent and reliable performance regardless of device or model variations. Addressing these challenges is crucial for enhancing face recognition systems' robustness, scalability, and adaptability in diverse real-world environments.

A key challenge in AFR lies in the compatibility of facial embeddings generated by different deep-face models (e.g., VGGNets, ResNets with different depths, MobileFaceNet, faceViT, etc.), which can significantly degrade matching performance. When two distinct models produce embeddings for the same face, misalignment or incompatibility between embeddings can result in low match scores, leading to recognition failures even for legitimate users. This issue becomes critical in multi-device ecosystems or systems employing diverse models to meet hardware constraints or specific requirements. For example, a user might authenticate using a smartphone running one model and later access the same system via a tablet using a different model. Without addressing this compatibility issue, the system's ability to provide seamless and reliable authentication across devices is compromised.

Addressing the AFR challenge requires embedding harmonization across models to ensure compatibility without compromising accuracy or computational feasibility. This is not merely a technical hurdle but a critical enabler for modern face recognition systems' robustness, usability, and scalability in diverse applications.

Recent research has made significant strides in addressing the problems of ASR. Wang et al. [9] introduced the Residual Bottleneck Transform (RBT) and integrated it into pretrained gallery and query models, projecting facial embeddings into a unified embedding space. While effective at aligning embedding spaces across models, this method suffers from instability in the unified space, resulting in prolonged training times that limit its practicality in real-time or large-scale applications.

In a complementary effort, Shoshan et al. [10] proposed a method that aligns the gallery embedding space with the query embedding space rather than creating a unified space. This approach achieves greater training stability and improved recognition performance by adjusting gallery embeddings relative to query embeddings. Additionally, they implemented an ensemble strategy using multiple gallery models to enhance the performance further. However, as the number of models increases, so do computational costs, creating a trade-off between recognition accuracy and system efficiency.

We propose the Learnable Anchor Embedding (LAE) model to address the challenges of asymmetric face recognition (AFR) by aligning embeddings within a unified space using Shared Learnable Anchors (SLAs). These anchors serve as dynamic reference points during training, guiding embeddings from heterogeneous models toward alignment and significantly enhancing recognition accuracy.

The Light Cross-Attention Mechanism complements the SLA by directly computing attention scores between facial embeddings and anchors through a dot product. This streamlined approach reduces computational overhead while preserving the ability to capture meaningful relationships between embeddings.

Unlike prior methods such as RBT [9], which suffer from bottlenecks and information loss during dimensional transformations, the LAE framework integrates an SLA and the Light Cross-Attention Mechanism to harmonize embeddings efficiently. The SLA learns critical shared features across models, while the attention mechanism emphasizes and refines these features, ensuring robust compatibility and outstanding performance even in resource-constrained environments.

The main contributions of this paper are as follows:

- We propose the Learnable Anchor Embedding (LAE) model for AFR problems. The LAE model employs shared learnable anchors during training to align embeddings from heterogeneous models within a unified embedding space, significantly improving alignment and enhancing recognition accuracy across heterogeneous models.
- We propose the Light Cross-Attention Mechanism to complement shared learnable anchors by directly computing attention scores between facial embeddings and shared learnable anchors using a dot product, reducing computational complexity and parameter overhead while ensuring efficient and effective embedding transformations for improved AFR performance.
- We demonstrate the effectiveness of the proposed LAE model for AFR across various heterogeneous facial models by evaluating it in verification and identification tasks. Our results highlight the ability of the LAE model to enable the seamless operation of diverse face recognition technologies. This significant improvement in cross-platform compatibility showcases the robustness and versatility of the proposed method, enhancing its practical applicability in real-world scenarios.

2. Related Work

2.1. Asymmetric Face Recognition

Asymmetric Face Recognition (AFR), also called cross-model face recognition, tackles the challenge of ensuring compatibility between embeddings generated by different deep-learning-based face recognition models. This emerging field has garnered some attention. Existing solutions to AFR can be broadly categorized into two types: generative-based approaches and transform-based approaches.

2.1.1. Generative-Based Approaches

Chen et al. [12] introduce the R3 Adversarial Network (R3AN) to address cross-model face recognition challenges. The R3AN framework consists of three main components: reconstruction, representation, and regression, which transform feature distributions between different models. By incorporating adversarial learning, particularly in the reconstruction path, the authors demonstrate improved performance in comparing features from various sources. The study highlights the significance of the AFR problem and presents R3AN as an efficient solution for feature transformation across different face recognition systems. The authors emphasize the framework's efficiency in updating features without storing face images, making it suitable for scenarios requiring frequent model updates.

However, R3AN's reconstruction path may generate blurry, low-detail images that compromise visual quality, while the complex three-path architecture increases the implementation difficulty. The system raises privacy concerns by demonstrating the potential to decode face features into approximate original images, which could be ethically problematic.

2.1.2. Transform-Based Approaches

Wang et al. [9] tackled the challenge of AFR with an integrated representation learning framework tailored for face recognition and person re-identification. This paper proposes a unified representation learning framework by introducing a lightweight Residual Bottleneck Transformation (RBT) module and a new training scheme based on knowledge distillation to optimize embedding spaces. The framework aims to enable correct recognition and retrieval of identities without re-encoding user images, which is crucial for privacy concerns. The method works by aligning feature classes across models and restricting mapped features to have more compact intra-class distributions, resulting in improved compatibility and more discriminative features.

Shoshan et al. [10] introduced an embedding transformation model that aligns the gallery model embeddings with the query model's embedding space, eliminating the need for knowledge distillation. This approach leverages multiple independently trained gallery models built with varying architectures or datasets alongside a single lightweight query model to enhance retrieval accuracy. Additionally, they proposed a method for assessing the uncertainty of gallery images, enabling the filtering of problematic samples to improve the overall system accuracy. This technique allows the query system to effectively interpret embeddings from diverse sources, bolstering the precision and reliability of face recognition systems in complex and heterogeneous environments.

2.2. Backward-Compatible Training

Backward-Compatible Training (BCT) [13,14] is a notion that is closely aligned with AFR. BCT enables new models to generate features directly comparable with existing models, facilitating the adoption of new technologies while preserving compatibility with legacy data. This approach eliminates the need to recompute existing embeddings, streamlining the integration of updated algorithms.

Shen et al. [13] proposed a BCT framework for visual feature learning, ensuring that new embeddings remain comparable to their predecessors, regardless of changes in model architecture, feature dimensions, or loss functions. This framework eliminates the need to reprocess entire datasets during model upgrades. Central to their approach is the concept of "influence loss", which leverages the classifier from the existing model to enhance the robustness and adaptability of BCT.

Building on these advancements, Liang et al. [14] introduced MixBCT, an improved method for addressing the limitations of traditional BCT in image retrieval systems.

MixBCT combines old and new features during training, enabling new models to better align with the distribution of legacy features. By requiring only a single loss function, this approach simplifies the training process and reduces the retraining overhead. MixBCT enhances model compatibility, enabling rapid deployment of new models while maintaining performance consistency with existing systems.

3. Proposed Method

3.1. Overview

Figure 2 illustrates the proposed Learnable Anchor Embedding (LAE) model for addressing asymmetric face recognition problems (ASR). The model ensures compatibility between heterogeneous face recognition models and comprises two phases: training and inference.

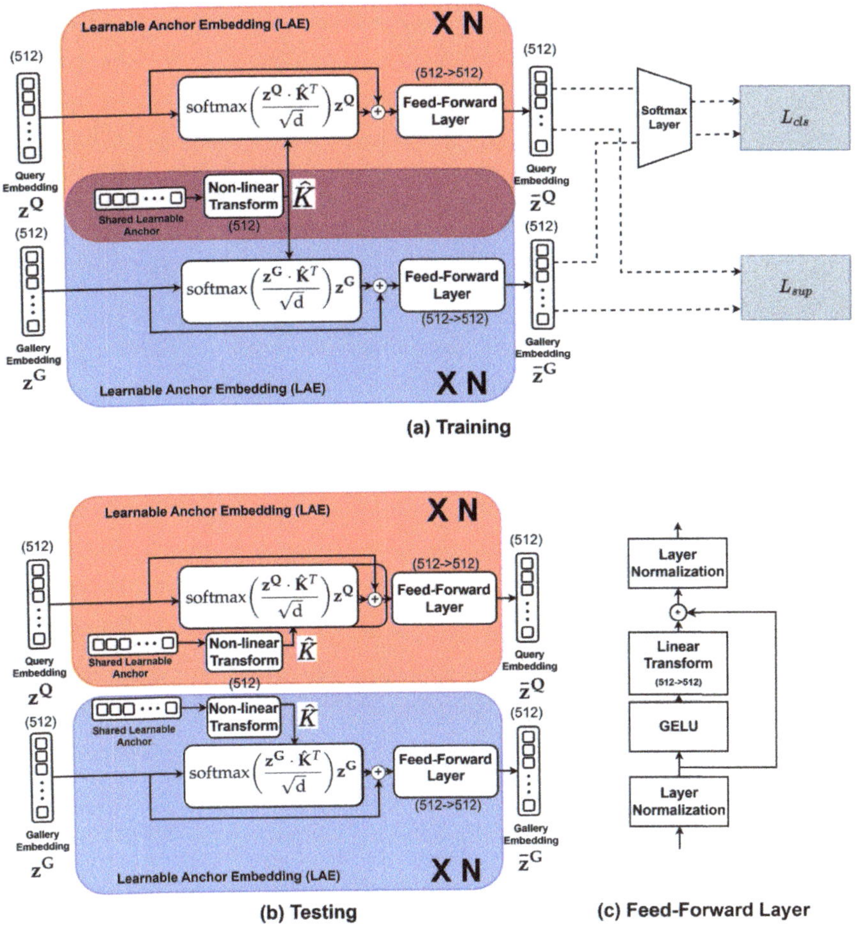

Figure 2. The proposed LAE model: (**a**) The SLA is shared during the training stage. (**b**) The SLA is used separately for the query and gallery during inference. (**c**) Feedforward layer. L_{cls} represents the classification loss, and L_{sup} denotes the supervised contrastive loss. Parentheses indicate dimensions, and the arrow (->) symbolizes transformation.

During the training phase, embeddings $\mathbf{z}^Q$ and $\mathbf{z}^G$ are extracted from the query and gallery face models, which may differ in architecture, feature dimensions, or training methodologies. A Shared Learnable Anchor (SLA), denoted as $\hat{\mathbf{K}}$, acts as a mediator to unify these embeddings. The gallery and query embeddings are refined through their respective light cross-attention blocks and feedforward layers, which capture intricate relationships between embeddings while preserving computational efficiency.

To optimize the transformation, the LAE model is trained using Supervised Contrastive Loss (SupConLoss) [15] and Classification Loss, which ensures that identity-specific discriminative features are retained during the transformation process. This optimization enables the SLA to guide the face embeddings into a unified embedding space that is robust, discriminative, and agnostic to the underlying model differences.

The trained SLA is independently applied to both LAE models during the inference phase, as shown in Figure 2b. It projects the query and gallery embeddings into the unified embedding space, ensuring alignment regardless of the inherent heterogeneity between the models. The transformed embeddings are then utilized for matching.

3.2. Learnable Anchor Embedding Model

The LAE model consists of three key components: a Shared Learnable Anchor (SLA), two independent lightweight cross-attention modules, and their corresponding feedforward networks, each dedicated to processing gallery and query embeddings. This dual-path architecture is designed to optimize feature representations uniquely tailored to the distinct properties of gallery and query embedding, as depicted in Figure 2a.

A softmax layer (classifier) is appended to both LAE models during the training phase to facilitate optimization. However, this softmax layer is removed during inference. The LAE modules operate independently in the inference setup to process gallery and query embeddings, as illustrated in Figure 2b.

Notably, LAE models are modular and can be cascaded sequentially to refine alignment progressively. The details of each component are explored in the subsections below.

3.2.1. Shared Learnable Anchor and Light Cross-Attention Mechanism

The SLA is the foundation for aligning heterogeneous embeddings from gallery and query models within a unified embedding space. Represented as a learnable embedding, $\hat{\mathbf{K}}$, the SLA is dynamically optimized during training through ReLU-activated nonlinear transformations. This adaptability enables the SLA to act as a flexible attractor, pulling the disparate embeddings from both models closer to a shared representation. The SLA ensures compatibility across models with differing architectures, feature dimensions, and training distributions by aligning the embeddings.

To further enhance this alignment, the Light Cross-Attention Mechanism comes into play, building upon the SLA's functionality. Traditional self-attention mechanisms in Transformer [7] rely on separate linear transformations of query, key, and value matrices, leading to significant computational overhead. In contrast, using a dot product, the proposed light cross-attention mechanism simplifies this process by directly computing the attention scores between the facial embeddings and the SLA, bypassing the need for additional linear transformations. This streamlined approach drastically reduces the number of parameters and computational costs while retaining the ability to capture the relationships between the embeddings and the SLA effectively.

The interplay of the SLA and the light cross-attention mechanism is central to the proposed framework. The SLA acts as the anchor, attracting and aligning the embeddings. At the same time, the light cross-attention mechanism reweights the facial embeddings relative to the SLA, refining their positions in the unified embedding space. Together, they form a cohesive system where the SLA provides the target alignment, and the cross-attention mechanism ensures efficient and accurate embedding transformation, driving improved compatibility and performance in asymmetric face recognition tasks.

After computing the attention score, $\mathbf{z} \cdot \hat{\mathbf{K}}^T$, it is divided by the dimension of the SLA to prevent the dot product value from becoming excessively large and stabilize training. Subsequently, the softmax function is applied to convert the attention score into a probability distribution, normalizing the importance of each value to a range of [0, 1]. The resulting importance weights are multiplied by the facial embedding $\mathbf{z}$, generating a re-weighted facial embedding $\hat{\mathbf{z}}$, which is expressed as follows:

$$\hat{\mathbf{z}} = \text{softmax}\left(\frac{\mathbf{z} \cdot \hat{\mathbf{K}}^T}{\sqrt{\text{d}}}\right)\mathbf{z} \quad (1)$$

The RBT [9] relies on a bottleneck process to refine data, which often results in significant information loss, and it depends solely on the loss function to align embeddings within a unified vector space. In contrast, the Shared Learnable Anchor (SLA) and Light Cross-Attention Mechanism collaboratively extract and emphasize shared features across models during the embedding process. The SLA identifies critical features, while the Light Cross-Attention Mechanism assigns weights to these features, enhancing their representation and ensuring efficient interaction between embeddings. This synergy not only preserves information but also amplifies the most significant features, effectively addressing the limitations of previous methods.

3.2.2. Feedforward Layer

As shown in Figure 2c, the feedforward layer (FFL) takes the transformed facial embedding $\hat{\mathbf{z}}$, which has passed through the light cross-attention mechanism, as its input. A linear transformation is initially applied to $\hat{\mathbf{z}}$, incorporating weight matrices and bias terms. Subsequently, the GELU [16] activation function is employed to introduce nonlinearity, enhancing the model's representative capacity.

The output of GELU is then passed through a dropout layer [17], where some neurons are randomly deactivated, helping to prevent overfitting. Following this, a second linear transformation is applied, and the resulting output undergoes dropout before being combined with $\hat{\mathbf{z}}$. Finally, Layer Normalization stabilizes the output and improves the training efficiency.

Algorithm 1 provides a detailed step-by-step procedure for transforming facial embeddings, $\mathbf{z}$, into a unified embedding space. The input $\mathbf{z}$ is derived from a pre-trained face model. During training, the algorithm dynamically generates the Shared Learnable Anchor (SLA) with 512 learnable parameters. In contrast, the testing phase employs pre-trained SLA weights. The SLA, together with $\mathbf{z}$, is processed through the light cross-attention mechanism, producing $\hat{\mathbf{z}}$, where the common feature vectors are adaptively reweighted based on the SLA. Finally, $\hat{\mathbf{z}}$ is passed through a feedforward layer, transforming it into a unified and refined feature vector ready for downstream tasks.

Algorithm 1 Learnable Anchor Embedding (LAE) Model

Input: Facial embedding, $\mathbf{z}^*$, where $* \in \{Q, G\}$
Output: Transformed facial embedding ($\bar{\mathbf{z}}^*$), where $* \in \{Q, G\}$

Step 1: Shared Learnable Anchor (SLA)
if Training **then**
    Generate a 512 random parameters $\bar{\mathbf{k}}$.
    The SLA $\hat{\mathbf{K}} \leftarrow RELU(LinearTransform(\bar{\mathbf{k}}))$.

    $\mathbf{z}^Q$ and $\mathbf{z}^G$ share the same SLA $\hat{\mathbf{K}}$.
else
    Freeze the SLA $\hat{\mathbf{K}}$.
    $\mathbf{z}^Q$ and $\mathbf{z}^G$ utilize the trained SLA $\hat{\mathbf{K}}$.
end if

Step 2: Light Cross-Attention
$\hat{\mathbf{z}}^* \leftarrow \text{softmax}\left(\frac{\mathbf{z}^* \cdot \hat{\mathbf{K}}^T}{\sqrt{\text{d}}}\right)\mathbf{z}^*$

Step 3: Feedforward Layer
$Norm \leftarrow \text{LayerNorm}(\hat{\mathbf{z}}^*)$
$Transformed \leftarrow \text{LinearTransform}(\text{GELU}(Norm))$
$\bar{\mathbf{z}}^* \leftarrow \text{LayerNorm}(Transformed + Norm)$
return $\bar{\mathbf{z}}^*$

3.3. Loss Functions

3.3.1. Classification Loss

In this paper, we utilize ArcFace loss [18] as our classification loss function, as it is designed to boost the discriminative power of facial embeddings. ArcFace achieves this by incorporating an angular margin penalty into the softmax loss, effectively redefining traditional softmax logits in angular terms. By adding a margin to the angle between an embedding and its corresponding class weight, ArcFace ensures tighter clustering of embeddings within the same class while increasing the separation between different classes. This dual enhancement of intra-class compactness and inter-class distinction leads to highly separable and robust embeddings.

ArcFace loss computation is based on the cosine similarity between $\bar{\mathbf{z}}_i$ and $\mathbf{w}_j$, and it is defined as

$$\cos\theta_{i,j} = \frac{\mathbf{w}_j^T \bar{\mathbf{z}}_i}{||\mathbf{w}_j|| \, ||\bar{\mathbf{z}}_i||} \tag{2}$$

Here, i indexes the samples, and j indexes the identity label C. $\bar{\mathbf{z}}_i$ represents the LAE-transformed facial embedding of the i-th sample in a batch with N samples. $\mathbf{w}_j$ denotes the weight embedding associated with the j-th class in the network's last fully connected layer, serving as the classifier for each class. During the training phase, a classifier is incorporated into the final fully connected layer of the LAE model to compute the ArcFace loss. However, this classifier is removed during inference to streamline the model's operation.

Based on Equation (4), ArcFace loss is expressed as

$$L_{ArcFace} = -\frac{1}{N}\sum_{i=1}^{N} \log \frac{e^{s\cdot\cos(\theta_{i,y_i}+m)}}{e^{s\cdot\cos(\theta_{i,y_i}+m)} + \sum_{j=1, j\neq y_i}^{C} e^{s\cdot\cos\theta_{i,j}}} \tag{3}$$

where m is the margin and s is the scaling factor, with values of $m = 0.5$ and $s = 32$ being used in the experiments.

The classification loss L_{cls} is defined as the sum of the ArcFace losses corresponding to the query and gallery LAE models, and it is denoted by L^Q_{ArcFace} and L^G_{ArcFace}, respectively:

$$L_{cls} = L^{Q}_{ArcFace} + L^{G}_{ArcFace} \tag{4}$$

3.3.2. Supervised Contrastive Loss

ArcFace loss enhances inter-class separability by introducing an angular margin, ensuring that embeddings of different classes are well separated in the embedding space. However, real-world data often present challenges such as noisy labels, hard-to-classify samples, and imbalanced distributions. To address these limitations, we integrate Supervised Contrastive Loss (SupConLoss) [15], which complements ArcFace by refining intra-class compactness and improving local pairwise relationships.

SupConLoss achieves this by leveraging relationships between positive pairs (embeddings from the same identity) and negative pairs (embeddings from different identities). For each LAE-transformed embedding $\bar{\mathbf{z}}_i$, it evaluates its similarity to all other transformed embeddings $\bar{\mathbf{z}}_j$, pulling positive pairs closer while pushing negative pairs further apart. This detailed pairwise optimization is particularly effective in handling hard-to-classify samples, such as those near decision boundaries or imbalanced data distributions.

The combination of ArcFace and SupConLoss offers several key benefits. ArcFace establishes strong global separability by optimizing the angular margins between classes, while SupConLoss refines local relationships, ensuring tighter clustering within classes and better separation between difficult pairs. This synergy makes the model robust to challenging data conditions and capable of handling noisy or imbalanced datasets more effectively.

Together, these two loss functions deliver a balanced optimization strategy that enhances inter-class separability and intra-class compactness. They significantly boost the model's discriminative power by complementing each other, resulting in superior performance across large-scale and fine-grained datasets, particularly in challenging scenarios.

The loss function is formulated as follows:

$$L_{sup} = \frac{1}{N}\sum_{i=1}^{N}\frac{1}{|P(i)|}\sum_{p\in P(i)} -\log\frac{\exp(\bar{\mathbf{z}}_i \cdot \bar{\mathbf{z}}_p/\tau)}{\sum_{a\in A(i)}\exp(\bar{\mathbf{z}}_i \cdot \bar{\mathbf{z}}_a/\tau)} \tag{5}$$

where $P(i)$ denotes the set of all positive samples $\bar{\mathbf{z}}_p$ that belong to the same class as sample i, and $A(i)$ represents the set of all anchor samples $\bar{\mathbf{z}}_a$ excluding sample i. In our exposition, each sample in the batch is used as an anchor one time. The term τ is a temperature hyperparameter used to scale the similarity scores. It is set to 0.07 in the experiments.

3.3.3. Total Loss

The total loss used to optimize the LAE model is defined as follows:

$$L_{total} = L_{cls} + L_{sup} \tag{6}$$

4. Experiments

4.1. Setup

4.1.1. Training Dataset

We used MS1M-Retina [19] as the training dataset for the LAE model. MS1M-Retina is a comprehensive facial image collection that is well suited for training face recognition models, as it includes a wide range of facial expressions, lighting conditions, and angle variations, which enhance the model's performance. As it is a large-scale facial image dataset, it helps the model effectively learn various facial transformations. For comprehensive details about the MS1M-Retina dataset, please refer to the Appendix A.1.

4.1.2. Testing Dataset

For testing, we utilized datasets for two main purposes: performance comparison with state-of-the-art (SOTA) methods [9,10] and evaluation of the model's generalization ability.

The testing datasets used include IJB-B [20], IJB-C [21], LFW [22], CALFW [23], CPLFW [24], and RFW [25]. IJB-B is a large-scale dataset containing images and videos capturing facial variations under different conditions, allowing us to evaluate the model's robustness in various environments. IJB-C is an extension of IJB-B, encompassing more diverse identities and conditions, thereby providing a more challenging evaluation scenario. LFW is a widely used benchmark for face verification featuring unconstrained facial images. CALFW is a variation of LFW designed to test age variation's impact on face recognition. CPLFW is another variation of LFW created to evaluate face recognition performance under pose variations, thus assessing the model's robustness to pose changes. RFW is used to evaluate the model's performance across different racial groups, helping to highlight potential biases and measure recognition accuracy without racial bias. For more details about the testing datasets, please refer to the Appendices A.2–A.7.

4.1.3. Experimental Setup

The hardware platform used for the experiments included an NVIDIA RTX 4080 Super graphics card, an Intel(R) Core(TM) i7-14700KF processor, and a total of 64 GB of DDR4 RAM (four 16 GB). The software environment consisted of CUDA version 12.6 and NVIDIA driver version 560.35.03, with PyTorch 2.5.1 installed.

The facial recognition models utilized in this study include MobileFaceNet (MBF) [4], ResNet50 (Res50) [5], ResNet152 (Res152) [5], Swin Transformer Tiny (SwinTransformerT) [6], and Swin Transformer Small (SwinTransformerS) [6]. MBF, SwinTransformerT, and SwinTransformerS are lightweight models designed for efficiency, while ResNet50 and ResNet152 are larger, more complex models with greater computational demands.

To ensure fairness, these face models utilized the standard configurations and the pre-trained weights provided by Face X Zoo [26]. The Swin Transformer used images of size 224×224, whereas the other face models [4,5] used images of size 112×112.

The LAE and SOTA models were trained for 15 epochs, starting with an initial learning rate of 0.1, which decreased at 5 and 10 through learning rate scheduling. The batch size was consistently set to 512 across all models.

4.2. Performance Criteria

We used well-established face recognition metrics to assess the proposed model's performance. For verification tasks, the Receiver Operating Characteristic (ROC) curve was employed to measure the True Positive Rate (TPR) at a False Positive Rate (FPR) of 10^{-3}. This metric effectively captures the model's ability to verify identities while minimizing false positive occurrences.

The Cumulative Match Characteristic (CMC) curve was used for identification tasks, with the top-1 identification accuracy being reported at a False Alarm Rate (FAR) of 10^{0}.

The evaluation extended across large-scale datasets, such as IJB-B and IJB-C, and smaller benchmarks, including LFW, CALFW, CPLFW, and RFW. These smaller datasets were analyzed using verification accuracy (ACC), a straightforward yet reliable metric for binary classification. This diverse set of metrics enabled a comprehensive evaluation of the model's robustness across various scenarios, including cross-pose, cross-age, and racial diversity.

4.3. Performance Comparison

Table 1 comprehensively compares the state-of-the-art (SOTA) models, focusing on their verification and identification performance. This evaluation includes symmetric configurations, such as MBF vs. MBF and Res50 vs. Res50, and asymmetric configurations, such as MBF vs. Res50. All experiments were conducted under consistent conditions, with careful parameter tuning to ensure a fair and unbiased assessment.

Table 1. A comparison of the verification and identification performance for symmetric and asymmetric configurations and SOTA models.

Approaches	Configurations	Params	FLOPs	IJB-C		IJB-B		LFW	CALFW	CPLFW	RFW
				Ver. (%)	Id. (%)	Ver. (%)	Id. (%)	ACC (%)	ACC (%)	ACC (%)	ACC (%)
-	(MBF, MBF)	-	-	91.2	90.2	89.6	89.2	99.5	93.7	82.7	90.5
-	(Res50, Res50)	-	-	96.3	95.3	95.3	94.4	99.7	95.3	88.2	95.6
-	(MBF, Res50)	-	-	0.0	0.0	0.8	0.0	50.7	51.3	49.3	50.5
Wang et al. [9]	(MBF, Res50)	1.08 M	1.08 M	88.2	87.7	86.4	87.1	98.7	93.1	84.4	86.8
Shoshan et al. [10]	(MBF, Res50)	1.08 M	1.08 M	92.5	90.2	87.4	87.9	99.2	94.0	85.3	91.4
Ours	(MBF, Res50)	1.06 M	1.05 M	93.8	92.3	92.3	91.3	99.6	94.5	86.2	92.3

The results reveal that symmetric configurations, particularly MBF vs. MBF and Res50 vs. Res50, achieved high accuracy across the verification and identification tasks. However, the asymmetric configuration (MBF vs. Res50) showed significantly poorer performance, especially on the IJB-B and IJB-C datasets. This stark contrast emphasizes the challenges of addressing AFR problems and reveals the limitations of existing models in such scenarios.

In the proposed approach, we emphasize storage requirements and computational complexity as critical metrics for evaluating model efficiency and real-world applicability. Specifically, Params (number of parameters) and FLOPs (floating-point operations per second) serve as principal indicators, allowing us to measure the model size and computational load explicitly. By doing so, we ensure that our model maintains a lightweight footprint suitable for resource-constrained environments while preserving high performance.

From this perspective, we conducted a systematic comparison of our proposed method against the SOTA techniques introduced by Wang [9] and Shoshan et al. [10]. Despite operating with only 1.06 M parameters and 1.05 M FLOPs, our model significantly improves the computational efficiency and achieves superior performance on large-scale datasets compared with the competing methods. For instance, on the IJB-C dataset, it achieved 93.8% verification and 92.3% identification rates, outperforming all existing approaches. Likewise, on the IJB-B dataset, it demonstrated excellence by achieving 92.3% verification and 91.3% identification rates. These results underscore the strength of our approach in maintaining high accuracy despite its lightweight design.

Beyond these large datasets, our method also excelled on other benchmark datasets. It achieved an outstanding accuracy of 99.6% on LFW, setting a new benchmark for this widely used test set. On more challenging datasets such as CALFW and CPLFW, our method recorded accuracies of 94.5% and 86.2%, respectively, outperforming all competitors. Moreover, it achieved an accuracy of 92.3% on the RFW dataset, showcasing its robustness and generalization capabilities across diverse recognition tasks.

These experimental results highlight the strength of our approach. Its ability to balance computational efficiency with exceptional accuracy demonstrates its potential as a robust and versatile face recognition solution under challenging asymmetric configurations.

5. Ablation Experiments

5.1. MLP vs. LAE Models

In this ablation study, we compare the performance of a baseline model utilizing an MLP as a nonlinear transformation module with our proposed LAE model. Both approaches employ the same loss functions, combining ArcFace and SupConLoss to ensure a fair comparison.

The query facial embeddings are generated using a pre-trained MobileFaceNet, while the gallery embeddings are derived from a pre-trained ResNet50. For the baseline, the MLP module takes a 512-dimensional facial embedding as input, processes it through a single nonlinear transformation layer, followed by a linear transformation layer, and outputs a 512-dimensional embedding. Notably, both the MLP and LAE models are designed to be stackable, allowing for flexibility in the module configuration.

Table 2 highlights the impact of stacking MLP and LAE modules on the performance metrics. For the MLP module, increasing the number of stacked layers leads to linear growth in parameters and FLOPs, accompanied by modest improvements in verification (Ver) and identification (Id) accuracies. For instance, when the number of MLP modules increases from one to four, the verification accuracy improves from 88.1% to 89.3%, while the identification accuracy rises from 85.3% to 87.1%.

Table 2. Verification and identification accuracy with the number of stacked LAE and MLP modules. The numbers in parentheses represent the numbers of stacked modules.

The Number of Modules	Params	FLOPs	IJB-C	
			Ver. (%)	Id. (%)
MLP (1)	1.05 M	1.05 M	88.1	85.3
MLP (2)	2.10 M	2.11 M	88.6	85.8
MLP (3)	3.15 M	3.16 M	89.0	86.7
MLP (4)	4.20 M	4.21 M	89.3	87.1
LAE (1)	0.53 M	0.54 M	93.6	92.0
LAE (2)	1.06 M	1.07 M	93.8	92.3
LAE (3)	1.59 M	1.62 M	93.7	92.1
LAE (4)	2.12 M	2.17 M	93.6	91.9

In contrast, the LAE module demonstrates its peak performance with one or two modules, beyond which the performance stabilizes or slightly declines. Specifically, verification accuracy improves marginally from 93.6% with one module to 93.8% with two but begins to drop when additional modules are introduced. This suggests that the LAE module achieves optimal performance with a limited number of layers, while excessive stacking may risk overfitting and diminishing returns.

5.2. Light Cross-Attention Ablation

This subsection explores three variants of the lightweight cross-attention mechanism: no transform, linear transform, and nonlinear transform. As illustrated in Figure 2, the lightweight cross-attention mechanism consists of two key components: cross-attention and a transformation layer. We investigate configurations without transformation and cases employing linear and nonlinear transformations to analyze their versatility. This systematic comparison sheds light on the role of transformation layers in enhancing cross-attention effectiveness.

Table 3 summarizes the impact of different transformation strategies on verification (Ver) and identification (Id) performance. The no-transform and linear transform configurations achieved identical verification accuracy of 93.6%, while the nonlinear transform slightly improved, reaching 93.8%. This indicates that the introduction of nonlinearity enhances verification performance, albeit modestly.

Table 3. Ablation study on the light cross-attention mechanism.

Transformation Type	No Transform	Linear Transform	Non-Linear Transform
Ver. (%)	93.6	93.6	93.8
Id. (%)	89.1	89.0	89.3

The nonlinear transform again outperformed the other configurations in terms of identification accuracy, achieving 89.3% compared with 89.1% for no transform and 89.0% for the linear transform. Notably, the linear transform resulted in a small dip in performance compared with the no-transform configuration.

These findings highlight the added representational power that the nonlinear transformation provides, which leads to consistent verification and identification performance improvements over simpler alternatives.

5.3. Loss Function Ablation

This subsection studies the impact of Arcface loss and SupConloss in the proposed model. Table 4 highlights ArcFace Loss's and SupConLoss's effects on verification and identification performance. The '✓' indicates that a loss is applied, while '-' denotes its absence.In the first row, only ArcFace Loss is used, resulting in a verification accuracy of 96.1% and an identification accuracy of 70.6%. In the second row, when only SupConLoss is applied, the verification accuracy rises significantly to 98.2%, and the identification accuracy improves to 88.4%. Finally, combining ArcFace Loss and SupConLoss yields the best results, with the verification accuracy reaching 98.5% and the identification accuracy increasing to 92.3%.

Table 4. Ablation study on loss functions.

Classification Loss	SupConLoss	IJB-C	
		Ver. (%)	Id. (%)
✓	-	96.1	70.6
-	✓	98.2	88.4
✓	✓	98.5	92.3

These findings underline the significant contribution of SupConLoss to boosting verification and identification performance. SupConLoss achieves much better results than using only the classification loss. Furthermore, the ArcFace Loss and SupConLoss combination demonstrates a synergistic effect, delivering the highest overall performance in both metrics.

5.4. Ablation on Asymmetric Models Matched with IJB-C

In this subsection, we describe an additional ablation study conducted for various asymmetric models that were matched with IJB-C. As presented in Table 5, the comparative analysis reveals that combinations involving SwinTransformer models (Tiny and Small) consistently deliver superior accuracy. For example, pairing ResNet50 as the query model with SwinTransformerS as the gallery model achieves a verification accuracy of 98.8% and an identification accuracy of 93.4%, outperforming most other combinations involving MobileFaceNet or ResNet models. Notably, configurations that exclusively use SwinTransformer models, such as SwinTransformerT paired with SwinTransformerS, achieve the best overall performance, with a verification accuracy of 98.9% and an identification accuracy of

95.8%. These findings emphasize the enhanced performance of Transformer-based models when used in tandem.

MobileFaceNet combinations with SwinTransformer also demonstrated strong performance, outperforming those involving ResNet. For instance, pairing MobileFaceNet with SwinTransformerS achieved a verification accuracy of 98.7% and an identification accuracy of 93.3%. This setup resolved the AFR problem and confirmed the compatibility between CNN- and Transformer-based models. These results underscore the critical role of pre-trained model selection in determining the effectiveness of individual components and overall system performance.

Table 5. Ablation study on the matching of various asymmetric models.

Query Model	Gallery Model	IJB-C	
		Ver. (%)	Id. (%)
MobileFaceNet	ResNet50	98.5	92.3
MobileFaceNet	ResNet152	98.5	92.5
ResNet50	ResNet152	98.5	92.5
MobileFaceNet	SwinTransformerT	98.6	92.9
MobileFaceNet	SwinTransformerS	98.7	93.3
ResNet50	SwinTransformerT	98.7	93.1
ResNet50	SwinTransformerS	98.8	93.4
SwinTransformerT	SwinTransformerS	98.9	95.8

6. Conclusions

This paper introduces Learnable Anchor Embedding (LAE), a novel model designed to tackle the challenges of Asymmetric Face Recognition. The LAE model employs a Shared Learnable Anchor (SLA) to align face embeddings from heterogeneous models into a unified embedding space, greatly improving compatibility across asymmetric face recognition systems. The model incorporates a Light Cross-Attention Mechanism to enhance the efficiency further, enabling effective embedding transformation while keeping the computational complexity and parameter overhead to a minimum. The proposed LAE model exhibits exceptional alignment capabilities and achieves high face recognition accuracy across diverse asymmetric configurations involving heterogeneous models. The experimental results on verification and identification tasks demonstrate its effectiveness in ensuring robust cross-platform compatibility. Future research will focus on developing a more generalized training approach. This will enable the LAE framework to retain its performance when paired with alternative pre-trained models, further broadening its applicability.

Author Contributions: Conceptualization, J.K.; methodology, J.K.; software, J.K.; validation, T.-S.N.; formal analysis, J.K.; investigation, J.K.; resources, J.K. and A.B.J.T.; data curation, J.K. and T.-S.N.; writing—original draft preparation, J.K.; writing—review and editing, J.K., T.-S.N. and A.B.J.T.; visualization, J.K.; supervision, A.B.J.T.; project administration, A.B.J.T.; funding acquisition, A.B.J.T. All authors have read and agreed to the published version of the manuscript.

Funding: This work was supported by the National Research Foundation of Korea (NRF) with a grant funded by the Korean government (MSIP) (NO. NRF-2022R1A2C1010710).

Institutional Review Board Statement: Not applicable.

Informed Consent Statement: Not applicable.

Data Availability Statement: This literature involves publicly available datasets, MS1M-Retina (https://drive.google.com/file/d/1JgmzL9OLTqDAZE86pBgETtSQL4USKTFy/view, 18 January 2025) [19], IJBB (https://github.com/deepinsight/insightface/tree/master/recognition/_evaluation_/ijb, 18 January

2025) [20], IJBC (https://github.com/deepinsight/insightface/tree/master/recognition/_evaluation_/ijb, 18 January 2025) [21], LFW (http://vis-www.cs.umass.edu/lfw, 18 January 2025) [22], CALFW (http://whdeng.cn/CALFW/index.html?reload=true, 18 January 2025) [23], CPLFW (http://www.whdeng.cn/CPLFW/index.html?reload=true, 18 January 2025) [24], and RFW (http://whdeng.cn/RFW/testing.html, 18 January 2025) [25].

Conflicts of Interest: The authors declare no conflicts of interest.

Appendix A. Dataset Details

Appendix A.1. MS1M-Retina

MS1M-Retina is derived from the MS-Celeb-1M dataset [19], where face images have been preprocessed using the Retina-Face detector [27]. All images are cropped and aligned to a resolution of 112 × 112 pixels, resulting in a total of 5.1 million images corresponding to 93k distinct identities. Figure A1 shows sample data from the dataset.

(a) (b) (c) (d) (e)

Figure A1. Samples of the MS1m-Retina dataset.

Appendix A.2. IJBB

The IJBB dataset comprises 1845 subjects, including 21,798 images, 55,026 video frames, and 12,115 templates. The dataset retains its original resolution, with faces provided in an uncropped and unaligned state, requiring additional preprocessing before being used for facial recognition tasks. It incorporates various variations such as pose, illumination, expression, resolution, and occlusion, and it is specifically designed to evaluate the performance of facial recognition algorithms in unconstrained environments. Supporting both verification and identification protocols, the dataset is widely used for research purposes. Due to the inclusion of sensitive information, its access and usage require approval from NIST, and licensing restrictions prohibit the direct display or sharing of images.

Appendix A.3. IJBC

The IJBC dataset comprises 130,000 images and over 300,000 face annotations designed for robust facial recognition and detection tasks. The dataset captures significant pose, illumination, expression, resolution, and occlusion variations, ensuring a comprehensive evaluation of algorithmic performance in real-world conditions. With high-quality annotations such as bounding boxes and landmarks, IJBC supports both verification and identification protocols. It is widely utilized in research, particularly for evaluating algorithm generalization in unconstrained scenarios. Access to the dataset requires approval due to sensitive content, and licensing restricts the public display of the data.

Appendix A.4. LFW

The LFW dataset contains 13,233 images of faces collected from the web. This dataset consists of 5749 identities with 1680 people with two or more images. In the standard LFW evaluation protocol, the verification accuracies are reported on 6000 face pairs.

Appendix A.5. CALFW

The CALFW dataset comprises 13,233 images of 5749 identities, and it is specifically designed to address the challenges of cross-age facial recognition in unconstrained environments. The dataset introduces deliberate intra-class variations by including 3000 positive pairs with significant age gaps and 3000 negative pairs with matched gender and race, minimizing inter-class attribute differences. All images have high-quality annotations, including landmarks for face alignment, and they are available in aligned and unaligned formats.

CALFW maintains the same size and protocol as the LFW dataset to enable direct performance comparisons while emphasizing real-world challenges such as age variations. It supports a verification protocol with "same/different" pairs, ensuring consistency with standard face verification benchmarks. The dataset is openly available, but appropriate citation is required for academic use.

Appendix A.6. CPLFW

The CPLFW dataset comprises 13,233 images of 5749 identities, specifically designed to address the challenges of cross-pose facial recognition in unconstrained environments. To introduce deliberate pose variations within intra-class variance, the dataset includes 3000 positive pairs with significant pose differences and 3000 negative pairs with matched gender and race, minimizing inter-class attribute differences. All images have high-quality annotations, including landmarks for face alignment, and they are available in aligned and unaligned formats.

CPLFW maintains the same size and protocol as the LFW dataset to enable direct performance comparisons while emphasizing real-world challenges such as pose variations. It supports a verification protocol with "same/different" pairs, ensuring consistency with standard face verification benchmarks. Pose differences between positive pairs in CPLFW are significantly larger than in LFW, making CPLFW a more challenging dataset for evaluating algorithms under cross-pose conditions.

Access to the CPLFW dataset is openly available, but appropriate citation is required for academic use.

Appendix A.7. RFW

The Racial Faces in-the-Wild (RFW) dataset is a testing benchmark designed to study racial bias in face recognition. It consists of four subsets: Caucasian, Asian, Indian, and African, each containing approximately 3000 identities and 6000 image pairs for face verification. This structure enables fair evaluation and comparison of algorithm performance across racial groups.

References

1. Zheng, L.; Yang, Y.; Hauptmann, A.G. Person re-identification: Past, present and future. *arXiv* **2016**, arXiv:1610.02984.
2. Sawhney, S.; Kacker, K.; Jain, S.; Singh, S.N.; Garg, R. Real-time smart attendance system using face recognition techniques. In Proceedings of the 2019 9th International Conference on Cloud Computing, Data Science & Engineering (Confluence), Noida, India, 10–11 January 2019; IEEE: New York, NY, USA, 2019; pp. 522–525.
3. Boragule, A.; Yow, K.C.; Jeon, M. On-device Face Authentication System for ATMs and Privacy Preservation. In Proceedings of the 2023 IEEE International Conference on Consumer Electronics (ICCE), Las Vegas, NV, USA, 6–8 January 2023; IEEE: New York, NY, USA, 2023; pp. 1–4.
4. Chen, S.; Liu, Y.; Gao, X.; Han, Z. Mobilefacenets: Efficient cnns for accurate real-time face verification on mobile devices. In Proceedings of the Biometric Recognition: 13th Chinese Conference, CCBR 2018, Urumqi, China, 11–12 August 2018; Proceedings 13; Springer: Berlin/Heidelberg, Germany, 2018, pp. 428–438.
5. He, K.; Zhang, X.; Ren, S.; Sun, J. Identity mappings in deep residual networks. In Proceedings of the Computer Vision—ECCV 2016: 14th European Conference, Amsterdam, The Netherlands, 11–14 October 2016; Proceedings, Part IV 14; Springer: Berlin/Heidelberg, Germany, 2016; pp. 630–645.

6. Liu, Z.; Lin, Y.; Cao, Y.; Hu, H.; Wei, Y.; Zhang, Z.; Lin, S.; Guo, B. Swin transformer: Hierarchical vision transformer using shifted windows. In Proceedings of the IEEE/CVF International Conference on Computer Vision, Montreal, BC, Canada, 11–17 October 2021; pp. 10012–10022.
7. Vaswani, A.; Shazeer, N.; Parmar, N.; Uszkoreit, J.; Jones, L.; Gomez, A.N.; Kaiser, L.; Polosukhin, I. Attention Is All You Need *arXiv* **2017**, arXiv:1706.03762.
8. Phan, H.; Le, C.X.; Le, V.; He, Y.; Nguyen, A. Fast and Interpretable Face Identification for Out-Of-Distribution Data Using Vision Transformers. In Proceedings of the IEEE/CVF Winter Conference on Applications of Computer Vision, Waikoloa, HI, USA, 3–8 January 2024; pp. 6301–6311.
9. Wang, C.Y.; Chang, Y.L.; Yang, S.T.; Chen, D.; Lai, S.H. Unified representation learning for cross model compatibility. *arXiv* **2020**, arXiv:2008.04821.
10. Shoshan, A.; Linial, O.; Bhonker, N.; Hirsch, E.; Zamir, L.; Kviatkovsky, I.; Medioni, G. Asymmetric image retrieval with cross model compatible ensembles. In Proceedings of the IEEE/CVF Winter Conference on Applications of Computer Vision, Waikoloa, HI, USA, 3–8 January 2024; pp. 1–11.
11. Zhao, W.; Zhu, X.; He, Z.; Zhang, X.Y.; Lei, Z. Cross-Architecture Distillation for Face Recognition. In Proceedings of the 31st ACM International Conference on Multimedia, Ottawa, ON, Canada, 29 October–3 November 2023; pp. 8076–8085.
12. Chen, K.; Wu, Y.; Qin, H.; Liang, D.; Liu, X.; Yan, J. R3 adversarial network for cross model face recognition. In Proceedings of the IEEE/CVF Conference on Computer Vision and Pattern Recognition, Long Beach, CA, USA, 15–20 June 2019; pp. 9868–9876.
13. Shen, Y.; Xiong, Y.; Xia, W.; Soatto, S. Towards backward-compatible representation learning. In Proceedings of the IEEE/CVF Conference on Computer Vision and Pattern Recognition, Seattle, WA, USA, 13–19 June 2020; pp. 6368–6377.
14. Liang, Y.; Zhang, Y.; Zhang, S.; Wang, Y.; Xiao, S.; Xiao, R.; Wang, X. MixBCT: Towards Self-Adapting Backward-Compatible Training. *arXiv* **2023**, arXiv:2308.06948.
15. Khosla, P.; Teterwak, P.; Wang, C.; Sarna, A.; Tian, Y.; Isola, P.; Maschinot, A.; Liu, C.; Krishnan, D. Supervised contrastive learning. *Adv. Neural Inf. Process. Syst.* **2020**, *33*, 18661–18673.
16. Hendrycks, D.; Gimpel, K. Gaussian error linear units (gelus). *arXiv* **2016**, arXiv:1606.08415.
17. Srivastava, N.; Hinton, G.; Krizhevsky, A.; Sutskever, I.; Salakhutdinov, R. Dropout: A simple way to prevent neural networks from overfitting. *J. Mach. Learn. Res.* **2014**, *15*, 1929–1958.
18. Deng, J.; Guo, J.; Xue, N.; Zafeiriou, S. Arcface: Additive angular margin loss for deep face recognition. In Proceedings of the IEEE/CVF Conference on Computer Vision and Pattern Recognition, Long Beach, CA, USA, 15–20 June 2019; pp. 4690–4699.
19. Guo, Y.; Zhang, L.; Hu, Y.; He, X.; Gao, J. Ms-celeb-1m: A dataset and benchmark for large-scale face recognition. In Proceedings of the Computer Vision—ECCV 2016: 14th European Conference, Amsterdam, The Netherlands, 11–14 October 2016; Proceedings, Part III 14; Springer: Berlin/Heidelberg, Germany, 2016; pp. 87–102.
20. Whitelam, C.; Taborsky, E.; Blanton, A.; Maze, B.; Adams, J.; Miller, T.; Kalka, N.; Jain, A.K.; Duncan, J.A.; Allen, K.; et al. IARPA Janus Benchmark-B Face Dataset. In Proceedings of the 2017 IEEE Conference on Computer Vision and Pattern Recognition Workshops (CVPRW), Honolulu, HI, USA, 21–26 July 2017; pp. 592–600. [CrossRef]
21. Maze, B.; Adams, J.; Duncan, J.A.; Kalka, N.; Miller, T.; Otto, C.; Jain, A.K.; Niggel, W.T.; Anderson, J.; Cheney, J.; et al. Iarpa janus benchmark-c: Face dataset and protocol. In Proceedings of the 2018 International Conference on Biometrics (ICB), Gold Coast, Australia, 20–23 February 2018; IEEE: New York, NY, USA, 2018; pp. 158–165.
22. Huang, G.B.; Mattar, M.; Berg, T.; Learned-Miller, E. Labeled faces in the wild: A database forstudying face recognition in unconstrained environments. In Proceedings of the Workshop on Faces in 'Real-Life' Images: Detection, Alignment, and Recognition, Marseille, France, 12–18 October 2008.
23. Zheng, T.; Deng, W.; Hu, J. Cross-age LWF: A database for studying cross-age face recognition in unconstrained environments. *arXiv* **2017**, arXiv:1708.08197.
24. Zheng, T.; Deng, W. Cross-pose lfw: A database for studying cross-pose face recognition in unconstrained environments. *Beijing Univ. Posts Telecommun. Tech. Rep* **2018**, *5*, 5.
25. Wang, M.; Deng, W.; Hu, J.; Tao, X.; Huang, Y. Racial faces in the wild: Reducing racial bias by information maximization adaptation network. In Proceedings of the IEEE/CVF International Conference on Computer Vision, Seoul, Republic of Korea, 27 October–2 November 2019; pp. 692–702.
26. Wang, J.; Liu, Y.; Hu, Y.; Shi, H.; Mei, T. Facex-zoo: A pytorch toolbox for face recognition. In Proceedings of the 29th ACM International Conference on Multimedia, Virtual, 20–24 October 2021; pp. 3779–3782.
27. Deng, J.; Guo, J.; Zhou, Y.; Yu, J.; Kotsia, I.; Zafeiriou, S. Retinaface: Single-stage dense face localisation in the wild. *arXiv* **2019**, arXiv:1905.00641.

electronics

MDPI

Article

SAM-Iris: A SAM-Based Iris Segmentation Algorithm

Jian Jiang [1], Qi Zhang [1,*] and Caiyong Wang [2]

1 School of Information and Cyber Security, People's Public Security University of China, Beijing 100038, China; 2022211480@stu.ppsuc.edu.cn
2 School of Intelligence Science and Technology, Beijing University of Civil Engineering and Architecture, Beijing 100044, China; wangcaiyong@bucea.edu.cn
* Correspondence: qi.zhang@ppsuc.edu.cn

Abstract: The Segment Anything Model (SAM) has made breakthroughs in the domain of image segmentation, attaining high-quality segmentation results using input prompts like points and bounding boxes. However, utilizing a pretrained SAM model for iris segmentation has not achieved the desired results. This is mainly due to the substantial disparity between natural images and iris images. To address this issue, we have developed SAM-Iris. First, we designed an innovative plug-and-play adapter called IrisAdapter. This adapter allows us to effectively learn features from iris images without the need to comprehensively update the model parameters while avoiding the problem of knowledge forgetting. Subsequently, to overcome the shortcomings of the pretrained Vision Transformer (ViT) encoder in capturing local detail information, we introduced a Convolutional Neural Network (CNN) branch that works in parallel with it. This design enables the model to capture fine local features of iris images. Furthermore, we adopted a Cross-Branch Attention mechanism module, which not only promotes information exchange between the ViT and CNN branches but also enables the ViT branch to integrate and utilize local information more effectively. Subsequently, we adapted SAM for iris image segmentation by incorporating a broader set of input instructions, which included bounding boxes, points, and masks. In the CASIA.v4-distance dataset, the E1, F1, mIoU, and Acc of our model are 0.34, 95.15%, 90.88%, and 96.49%; in the UBIRIS.v2 dataset, the E1, F1, mIoU, and Acc are 0.79, 94.08%, 88.94%, and 94.97%; in the MICHE dataset, E1, F1, mIoU, and Acc were 0.67, 93.62%, 88.66%, and 95.03%. In summary, this study has improved the accuracy of iris segmentation through a series of innovative methods and strategies, opening up new horizons and directions for large-model-based iris-segmentation algorithms.

Keywords: iris segmentation; pretrained large models; segment anything model; large model fine-tuning

1. Introduction

Iris-recognition technology necessitates a thorough analysis of eye images, which includes not only identifying the iris texture with individual characteristics but also dealing with non-iris components such as eyelids, eyelashes, and reflections. Accurate iris segmentation is critical for further image processing and feature extraction [1]. Inaccurate segmentation can result in image-pixel misalignment, which reduces the accuracy of iris recognition. As a result, researchers are constantly looking for more efficient algorithms to accurately segment the iris area from complex eye images, eliminate other interfering factors, and improve the overall performance of the iris-recognition system. The principle of iris segmentation is illustrated in Figure 1.

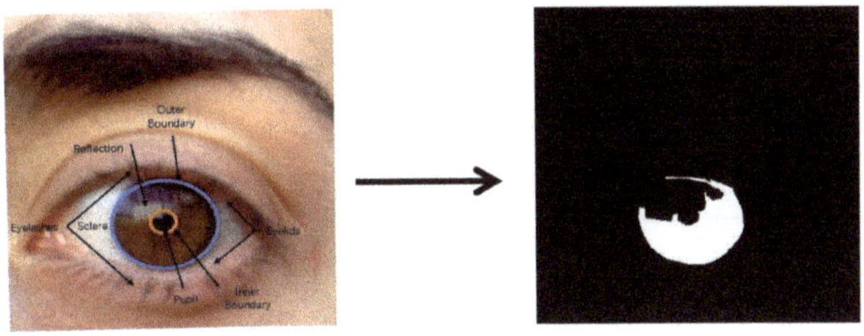

Figure 1. Iris segmentation. The figure on the left represents the components of the human eye, where the part between the orange inner circle and the blue outer circle is the part to be segmented, and the figure on the right represents the segmentation mask, where the white part is the part to be segmented correctly.

Conventional iris-segmentation techniques, such as edge detection and Hough transform methods, are put to the test in terms of performance and stability when confronted with undesirable conditions such as eye occlusion, image blurring, insufficient resolution, or reflections. As a result, improving the accuracy and reliability of iris segmentation under these non-ideal conditions has emerged as a major focus of current research. The use of deep learning algorithms, including advanced image segmentation architectures such as FCN [2], U-Net [3], Transformer [4], provide a more accurate and stable solution for iris segmentation due to their powerful feature learning and boundary recognition abilities.

The applicability of U-Net to iris-segmentation tasks was first studied in depth and the computational efficiency of the algorithm was explored in detail by Lozej et al. [5]. Wu et al. [6] proposed a model Dense U-Net combining U-Net and DenseNet to improve iris-segmentation accuracy under non-ideal conditions. Zhang et al. [7] further developed the field by proposing the FD-U-Net algorithm, which utilizes dilation convolution instead of the traditional convolution operation, thus making significant progress in extracting global features, especially in processing the details of iris images. It shows excellent performance in handling the details of iris images, which enables the algorithm to maintain its outstanding performance in heterogeneous iris-segmentation tasks as well. Wang et al. proposed IrisParseNet [8], an efficient multitasking iris-segmentation method based on U-Net. The method models the iris mask and its parameterized inner and outer boundary information through a unified multitask network framework, which not only enhances the robustness and generalization ability of the algorithm but also provides a solid technical foundation for iris segmentation under non-ideal conditions. The Transformer architecture, with its unique self-attention mechanism, has revolutionized the domain of natural language processing with its ability to efficiently capture long-distance dependencies. With its gradual application in the field of image segmentation, this innovative technique is beginning to show its potential in visual tasks. Sun et al. [9] took an exploratory step in the field of iris segmentation by proposing HTU-Net, a hybrid architecture that incorporates Transformer. The architecture employs a convolutional layer in the encoding stage to capture the intensity of local features while utilizing the Transformer to capture correlation information at a distance. In the decoding stage, by introducing a gating mechanism, HTU-Net is able to capture rich multi-scale contextual information. In addition, Sun et al. designed the pyramid center perception module to further enhance the ability to capture global features of the iris, while Gu et al. [10] further advanced the field by deeply integrating the Swin Transformer [11] with the U-Net architecture, which dramatically improves the iris region by accurately modeling contextual information interactions between image pixels separation accuracy from background noisy pixels. Meng et al. [12] proposed a bilateral segmentation backbone network that combines the advantages of

Swin Transformer and CNN for more efficient feature extraction. They also introduced the Multi-scale Information Feature Extraction Module, a module capable of extracting finer-grained multi-scale spatial information, as well as the Channel Attention Mechanism Module to enhance the discriminability of iris regions.

The Segment Anything Model (SAM), a groundbreaking development by Meta, has revolutionized the realm of image segmentation. It boasts superior capabilities for segmenting intricate scenes and a multitude of objects. In addition, the SAM model is designed to have GPT-like Prompt-based working capability compared to models such as U-Net, FRED-Net [13], OR-Skip-Net [14], etc., which means that it can use simple textual commands or clicking prompts to edit the image during image segmentation tasks which is not common in traditional models such as U-Net. However, when applying it to specific tasks, such as iris segmentation, we face a unique set of challenges. These challenges require us to fine-tune the model to fit more specialized and specific application scenarios. Therefore, we make a series of improvements to SAM to obtain better iris-segmentation results. The contributions of this paper are summarized in the following aspects:

1. The Segment Anything Model (SAM) was applied to the field of iris segmentation in this paper, confirming the great potential and efficacy of large pretrained models in handling this intricate visual task. This also opens up new avenues for future research on iris-segmentation algorithms based on large models.
2. Adapter technique has been proven to be an efficient strategy for fine-tuning large models to fit specific tasks. In this paper, we present an innovative plug-and-play adapter, the IrisAdapter, which is specifically designed to capture iris domain-specific information. The introduction of this adapter allows us to perform effective feature learning on iris images without comprehensively updating the entire model parameters while ensuring that the original knowledge of the model is preserved to avoid the problem of knowledge forgetting. More importantly, the application of IrisAdapter significantly reduces the computational and economic costs associated with large-scale model training.
3. In order to cope with the inadequacy of the pretrained ViT encoder in extracting localized detail information of iris images, this paper introduces a CNN branch that works in parallel with ViT. This design enables the model to capture the fine local features of iris images through the CNN branch. Furthermore, we employ a Cross-Branch Attention mechanism module, the introduction of which not only facilitates the information exchange between the ViT and CNN branches but also enables the ViT branch to integrate and utilize the local information of iris images more effectively. Through this fusion strategy, our model significantly enhances the ability to recognize iris details while maintaining the sensitivity of ViT to global contextual information, thus improving the overall segmentation performance.

2. Related Work

2.1. Segment Anything Model

Over the past few years, there has been a surge of inspiration drawn from large-scale language models like ChatGPT and GPT, and many researchers have devoted themselves to developing models with similar capabilities. These models not only have strong generalization capabilities, but also can be quickly adapted and scaled to the target task domain with a very small number of samples or even in the case of zero samples. Meta's FAIR Lab has recently released the Segment Anything Model (SAM) [15], a model at the forefront of image segmentation technology that promises to revolutionize the field of computer vision. The architecture and pipeline of SAM is shown in Figure 2. The pipeline of SAM is as follows: receive input image and prompt information, extract features by image encoder, process prompts by Prompt Encoder, generate segmentation mask by mask decoder, process disambiguation by data engine, and finally output accurate segmentation result. Intensively trained on millions of images and over a billion masks, SAM is capable of accurate image segmentation based on a wide range of prompts such as foreground/background points, bounding boxes, masks, text, and more. Impressively, SAM is able to provide effective segmentation results even when the prompt information is not sufficiently clear. SAM's core strength lies in its rich knowledge accumulated through training on large-scale data, which has allowed it to learn and master the basic concepts of objects. Based on this deep understanding, SAM is able to segment any object, even when faced with never-before-seen objects, without additional training or fine-tuning, demonstrating excellent zero-sample generalization capabilities. This capability not only reflects SAM's advancement in the domain of image segmentation but also heralds the great potential of large pretrained models in solving complex visual problems.

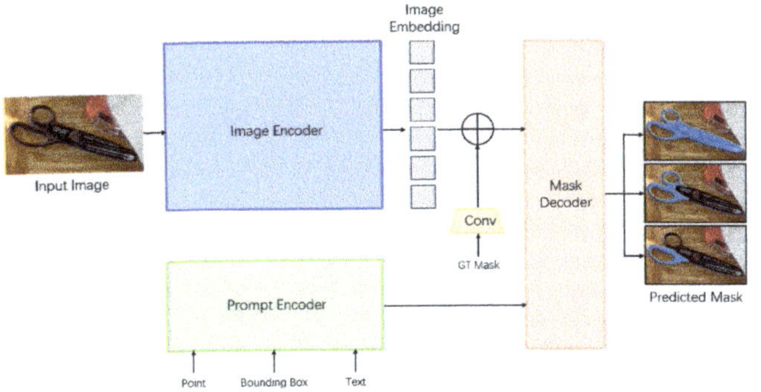

Figure 2. SAM architecture.

2.2. *Task-Specific SAM Fine-Tuning*

SAM offers a superior framework for interactive segmentation, making itself a benchmark for image segmentation that relies on prompts. However, due to the domain differences between natural images and iris images, the performance of SAM shows a significant degradation when applied to iris images. The reason for this can be attributed to the method of data acquisition: iris images are captured using specific protocols and specialized sensors and are presented in different modes (near-infrared, visible light). These images are, therefore, based on a set of physical properties and energy sources that are very different from natural images. Therefore, the research in this paper fine-tunes SAM for a specific iris-segmentation dataset.

There are many studies on fine-tuning SAM in specific tasks. Chen et al. proposed SAM adapters [16], which employ domain-specific information or visual cues to segment networks through the use of simple but effective adapters. Ma et al. [17] collected 11 medical image datasets with different modalities and fine-tuned the SAM mask decoder on more than 1 million masks while preserving the original bounding box prompts. Deng et al. [18] proposed a multi-bounding box-triggered uncertainty estimation method for SAM, which has achieved a significant improvement in retinal image segmentation. Wu et al. proposed MSA [19], which utilizes an adapter technique to integrate medical-specific knowledge into SAM. Zhang et al. [20] proposed SAMed to integrate low-rank [21] into SAM. These preceding studies show that fine-tuning strategies or adapters can improve the performance of SAM on specific tasks. In order to combine the advantages of both the base model and the domain-specific model, Farmanifard et al. [22] developed a pixel-level iris-segmentation model, IrisSAM, and the primary innovation of this research lies in the integration of different loss functions when fine-tuning SAM on eye images. Li et al. [23] propose nnSAM, which represents an integration of the SAM model with nnUNet, enhancing the precision and robustness of medical image segmentation.

2.3. Interactive Segmentation

Interactive segmentation is the splitting of the foreground and background that the user needs to be segmented by providing certain interactive information by the user, including clicks, bounding boxes, closed curves, non-closed curves, and other interactive methods. It is characterized by obtaining information from the guidance of user interaction. The algorithm then iteratively improves the segmentation based on user feedback. Interactive segmentation is useful in many applications that require precise extraction of objects, such as medical image segmentation [24].

3. Methodology

3.1. Overview

Inheriting the decoder and prompt encoder of the original SAM, SAM-Iris improves the image encoder to better adapt to the iris-segmentation task. The architecture and pipeline of SAM-Iris is shown in Figure 3. First, we adjust the input resolution of the image encoder by reducing it from 1024 × 1024 to 256 × 256, and this improvement significantly enhances the computational efficiency of the model. Then, to compensate for the lack of local feature extraction in the original ViT encoder, we introduce a CNN branch dedicated to capturing fine local information in the image, thus enhancing the model's iris details. Then, by introducing the CBA (Cross-Branch Attention) module, we realize the effective information exchange between the CNN branch and the ViT branch, and this cross-branch synergy enables the model to comprehensively utilize the advantages of the two branches to generate richer and more accurate feature representations. Finally, the outputs of the CNN branch and the ViT branch are merged to form an image embedding through which the encoder and decoder predict the iris mask. Furthermore, SAM requires post-processing to generate high-quality segmentation masks after the segmentation task, which includes up-sampling, which up-samples the dimensions of the model output to the dimensions of the original image, and binarization, which converts the up-sampled mask prediction results to binary masks through binarization.

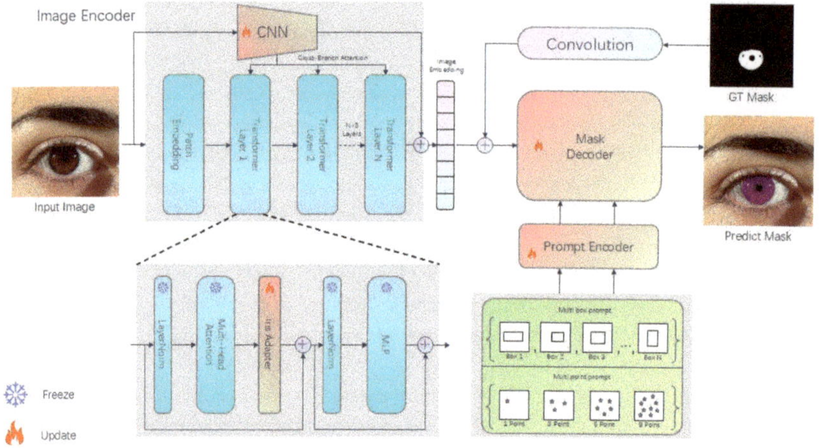

Figure 3. The architecture and pipeline of SAM-Iris, where "Freeze" means not updating the parameters and "Update" means updating the parameters.

3.2. Adapter

As computer hardware performance improves and the number of pretrained large model parameters increases, full fine-tuning while training downstream tasks becomes expensive and time-consuming. Based on this, the emergence of an Adapter alleviates the above problem. Adapter inserts parameters for downstream tasks into each layer of the pretrained model freezes the body of the model during fine-tuning, and trains only the task-specific parameters, thus reducing the computational power overhead during training. In the SAM model, the image encoder, as the component with the largest number of parameters, is the most important part of the SAM model. As such, we keep the original encoder parameters frozen during the fine-tuning process while equipping each Transformer module with an adapter. The implementation strategy is as follows: first, the resolution of the input feature map is efficiently reduced to $C \times 1 \times 1$ using global average pooling to achieve a compact representation of the features. Subsequently, these compressed channel embeddings are further compressed by a linear layer, followed by another linear layer, to reduce the compressed embeddings to the original dimension. This compression and reduction process not only preserves the key information but also enhances the representation of the features. Finally, the reduced channel embeddings are multiplied element-by-element with the original feature maps, and the results obtained will be used as inputs to the next layer to provide a richer and finer feature representation for the model. To further enhance the performance of the model, we introduce skip connections after each adapter, a design that not only preserves more low-level features but also promotes the effective fusion of features at different levels, thus enhancing the model's ability to capture details. With this innovative adapter technique, we are able to significantly improve the performance and adaptability of the model in iris-segmentation tasks while maintaining computational efficiency. The structure of IrisAdapter is shown in Figure 4.

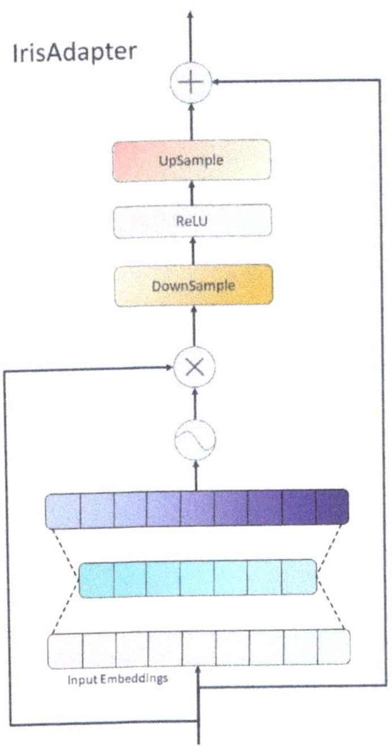

Figure 4. The structure of IrisAdapter.

3.3. Prompt Encoder

The SAM model's prompt encoder is highly capable, offering support for four modes of prompts: point, bounding box, mask, and textual prompts. Given the lack of pretrained models for matching iris images to text, this study focuses on fine-tuning the other three prompt modes. Compared to previous approaches that use only a single prompt for fine-tuning, the research work in this paper provides an innovative extension to retain the three prompt modes of point, bounding box, and mask. Specifically, the model proposed in this paper employs an integrated strategy that utilizes both sparse prompts (points and bounding boxes) and dense prompts (masks). For the treatment of point prompts, we employ position-encoded vector embedding combined with two learnable vector embeddings, which represent the positions of the foreground and background, respectively, and enrich the expressive power of the point prompt by their sum. For bounding box prompts, we use the position encoding of the points where the upper left and lower right corners are located, as well as the learnable embedding vectors representing these two corners, to accurately capture the features of the bounding box. For the application of dense prompt, in this paper, We employ the low-resolution feature maps produced following the model's initial iteration as a mask prompt. Utilizing two convolutional embeddings, we reduced the input mask's dimensions by a factor of four, concurrently modifying the number of output channels to one quarter and one sixth of the initial input channels, respectively. Ultimately, by using a 1×1 convolutional kernel, the channel dimensions are mapped to 256 to ensure that the feature maps are sufficiently expressive while remaining informative. This combined use of sparse and dense prompts not only improves the model's capacity for capturing iris image features but also enhances the model's adaptability and flexibility to different prompt modes, providing powerful technical support for accurate segmentation and analysis of iris images. The structure of Prompt Encoder is shown in Figure 5.

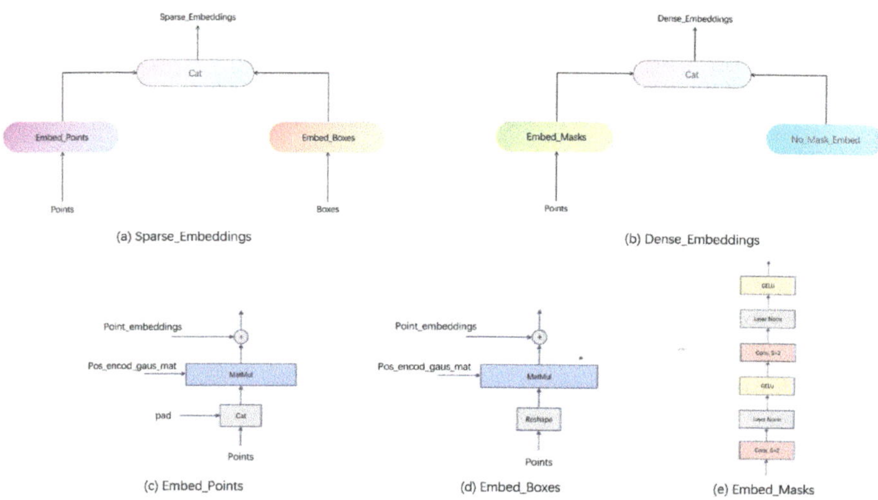

Figure 5. The structure of Prompt Encoder.

3.4. Mask Decoder

In this study, we used the original mask decoder of the SAM model, preserved its structure, and did not make any changes. During the training process, we focused on continuously optimizing and updating the parameters of the mask decoder. This decoder is composed of a pair of Transformer layers: a dynamic mask prediction header responsible for generating the initial prediction of the mask and an intersection-to-union (IoU) score regression header that focuses on improving the match between the predicted mask and the real mask. This design is not only lightweight and efficient but also very powerful in terms of functionality. In the model's default mode of operation, it is able to generate three independent mask predictions for each prompt simultaneously. By comparing these predictions, the model selects the mask with the highest IoU score as the optimal solution, which guides the parameter updates. This approach ensures that the model is able to continuously improve itself during the training process, gradually increasing the accuracy and reliability of the mask predictions.

3.5. CNN Branch

The CNN branch is made up of a succession of convolution-pooling blocks that are linked consecutively. To be precise, the input data initially traverses a single convolutional block, which is then succeeded by a trio of sequential convolutional-pooling blocks. In this process, the spatial dimensions of the feature maps output from the CNN branch are matched to the feature maps of the ViT branch. In the following section of the CNN branch, these convolutional layers are sequentially iterated four times. Each convolutional layer is equipped with a 3 × 3 convolutional kernel for the convolution operation, and each convolutional-pooling hierarchy contains a maximum pooling layer with a step size and a pooling kernel of 2 following the convolutional layer. The structure of a single convolutional block is shown in Figure 6.

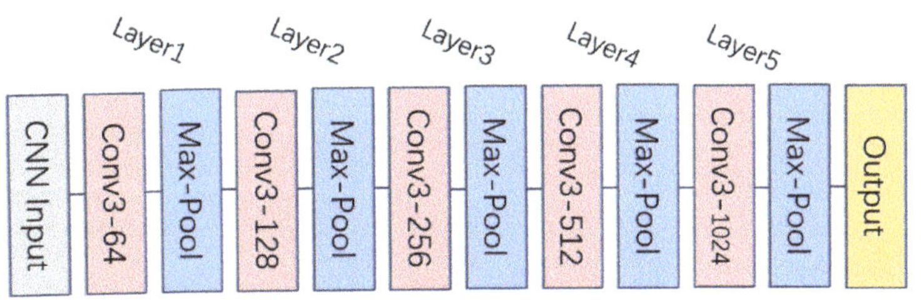

Figure 6. The structure of a single convolutional block.

3.6. Cross-Branch Attention

The Cross-Branch Attention (CBA) module facilitates an information exchange pathway between the CNN and ViT branches, enhancing the model's ability to incorporate missing local information. The structure of Cross-Branch Attention module is shown in Figure 7. For the feature map F_V from the ViT branch and the feature map F_C from the CNN branch, the representation formula is as follows.

$$CBA(\mathcal{F}_V, \mathcal{F}_C) = \left(\sigma\left(\frac{\mathcal{F}_V M_q (\mathcal{F}_C M_k)^T}{\sqrt{d_m}}\right) + R\right)(M_v) \quad (1)$$

where σ denotes the SoftMax function. $M_q \in \mathbb{R}^{d \times d_m}$, $M_k \in \mathbb{R}^{d \times d_m}$, $M_v \in \mathbb{R}^{d \times d_m}$ denotes Q, K, and V in the attention mechanism, denotes the relative position encoding, and $R \in \mathbb{R}^{hw \times hw}$ denotes the dimensionality of the CBA module, d_m denotes the dimensionality of the CBA module.

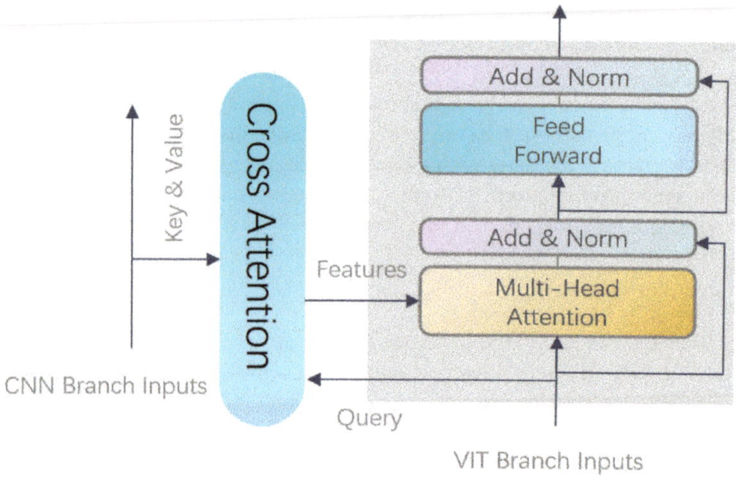

Figure 7. The structure of Cross-Branch Attention module.

3.7. Loss Function

In the iris-segmentation task, the number of non-iris pixels is much larger compared to the number of iris pixels, and this class imbalance problem can seriously interfere with the segmentation performance. To address the problem, we employ a combined loss function that includes Dice Loss, Focal Loss, and IoU Loss to supervise the model's training process.

Dice Loss, originating from a seminal paper [25], was specifically designed to address the strong imbalance that exists between positive and negative samples in segmentation tasks. This loss function, with its unique advantages, optimizes the model's performance when dealing with unbalanced datasets and improves the model's accuracy in recognizing a small number of categories. Dice Loss, by assessing the resemblance between the model's predictions and the actual labels, prompts the model to focus more on positive samples that constitute a minor part of the dataset. This approach effectively equalizes the influence of various categories and ensures the model's capacity for generalization and robustness, as detailed further below:

$$L_{dice} = 1 - \frac{2|Predicted \cap Target|}{|Predicted| + |Target|} \tag{2}$$

where *Predicted* represents the mask predicted by the model and *Target* represents the true mask.

IoU Loss (Intersection over Union loss) [26] is a loss function that measures the degree of overlap between predicted and true results and evaluates the performance of a model by calculating the ratio of intersection and concatenation between the predicted and true masks. The core principle of this loss function is that it provides intuitive feedback on the model's performance by quantifying how well the predicted mask matches the true mask. IoU Loss is particularly suited to segmentation tasks that require high accuracy, as defined below:

$$L_{IoU} = -\frac{|Predicted \cap Target|}{|Predicted \cup Target|} \tag{3}$$

Focal Loss [27] was introduced to address a common challenge in iris-segmentation tasks—the significant imbalance between positive and negative samples. This loss function is an innovative extension of the traditional cross-entropy loss function, which effectively adjusts the sensitivity of the loss function to different samples by introducing a dynamic scaling factor γ. The core idea of Focal Loss is to reduce the weight of its contribution to the loss function during training for samples that are easily correctly categorized by the model, i.e., easy-to-distinguish samples, and to increase the weight for samples that are difficult to be accurately recognized by the model, i.e., hard-to-distinguish samples, increase their weights, thus prompting the model to focus on these challenging samples more quickly. In this way, Focal Loss optimizes the model's learning process, enabling the model to learn and distinguish those elusive details in the iris-segmentation task more efficiently, and significantly improves the model's ability to recognize a small number of classes of samples. Its formula is as follows:

$$L_{Focal} = (1 - p_t)^{\gamma} \cdot \log p_t \tag{4}$$

$$\begin{cases} p_t = p, y = 1 \\ p_t = 1 - p, otherwise \end{cases} \tag{5}$$

where p_t denotes the probability that the model is predicted to be a foreground, and γ is a dynamic scaling factor to adjust the balance between positive and negative categories. The value of p ranges from 0 to 1 and is the probability that the model predicts a mask.

Finally, the joint loss function is formulated as, where w and s are tunable hyperparameters:

$$L_{total} = w * L_{Focal} + L_{dice} + s * L_{IoU} \tag{6}$$

3.8. Fitune Strategy

In this paper, we draw on the essence of the SAM model as well as other interactive segmentation methods and train the model in depth by simulating the process of interactive segmentation. Specifically, for each batch of data, we employ a training strategy of 9 iterations. In the crucial first iteration, we initiate the segmentation process by randomly selecting a foreground point or bounding box as a sparse prompt with the same probability. The foreground points are carefully sampled from the real mask, while the bounding box is a maximal enclosing rectangular box computed based on the real mask, with points at its four corners allowed to have an offset of up to 5 pixels in order to increase the robustness of the model. In the first iteration, we adopted a comprehensive update strategy, updating the parameters of the adapter, prompt encoder, and mask decoder simultaneously. This comprehensive update provides a solid starting point for the model to capture key features of the image more accurately in subsequent iterations. Starting from the second iteration, we adopt a more flexible sparse prompt strategy by randomly selecting 1, 3, 5, or 9 points as prompt, which not only increases the diversity of the training but also motivates the model to learn to segment efficiently with different numbers of prompt. At the same time, the model uses the low-resolution feature maps generated in the previous iteration as dense prompts for the current iteration, and this strategy enables the model to gradually refine its understanding of the mask in successive iterations. In the last iteration, as well as randomly selected intermediate iterations, we only provide a dense prompt, which aims to guide the model to focus on extracting information from the existing feature prompt to further improve the accuracy and reliability of its predictions.

4. Experiments and Analysis of Results

4.1. Introduction to the Dataset

In this paper, we assess the performance of our proposed model across three iris-segmentation datasets: CASIA.v4-distance, UBIRIS.v2, and MICHE. These three datasets cover a variety of challenging factors such as different spectra (visible and near-infrared), devices, and distances, and their dataset-related information is shown in Table 1.

Table 1. Experimental dataset. Where NIR denotes near-infrared light and VIS denotes visible light.

Dataset	Train	Test	Resolution	Device	Spectral
CASIA.v4-distance	300	100	640 × 400	CASIA long-range iris camera	NIR
UBIRIS.v2	500	445	400 × 300	Canon EOS 5D	VIS
MICHE	680	191	400 × 400	iPhone 5 Samsung Galaxy S4 Samsung Galaxy Table2	VIS

CASIA.v4-distance [28]: This dataset was captured using a CASIA long-range iris camera in near-infrared light. We use the same protocol as [29] for experiments, which contained 400 iris images at 640 × 480 resolution. The first 300 images from the first 30 subjects were used for training, and the last 100 images from the last 10 subjects were used for testing.

UBIRIS.v2 [30]: This dataset was captured under visible light conditions using a Canon EOS 5D camera. A subset of 1000 UBIRIS.v2 images at 400 × 300 resolution was used in the NICE.I [31] competition. We use the same protocol [31] as NICE.I competition for experiments, which selected 945 of these images to be manually labeled, of which 500 images were used for training and 445 images for testing.

MICHE [32]: This dataset was created in order to evaluate and develop algorithms for visible light iris images captured on the mobile device. It includes visible light iris images captured by three mobile devices (iPhone 5, Samsung Galaxy S4, Samsung Galaxy Table2) under unconstrained conditions. We use the same protocol as [8] for experiments, which selected 871 visible light images from MICHE, which contains 680 training images and 191 images for testing.

4.2. Metric

FP (False Positive) denotes the number of pixels that predicted the non-iris region as the iris region, and TN (True Negative) denotes the number of correctly predicted pixels in the non-iris region, FN (False Negative) denotes the number of pixels for which the iris region is predicted as a non-iris region, and TP (True Positive) denotes the number of pixels for which the iris region is correctly predicted.

4.2.1. mIoU

The mIoU represents the average intersection ratio for the type of pixel points in the iris image. A larger value of mIoU represents a better segmentation result where k represents the number of classes. The formula for mIoU is as follows.

$$mIoU = \frac{1}{k+1}\sum_{i=0}^{k}\frac{TP}{FN+FP+TP} \tag{7}$$

4.2.2. F1

The F1 Score is calculated from Precision and Recall. A larger value of F1 Score means better segmentation results. The formula for F1 Score is as follows.

$$F1 = \frac{2 \times Precision \times Recall}{Precision + Recall} \tag{8}$$

$$Precision = \frac{TP}{TP+FP} \tag{9}$$

$$Recall = \frac{TP}{TP+FN} \tag{10}$$

4.2.3. E1

E1 denotes the ratio of inconsistent pixels to the total pixels obtained by computing the dissimilarity of the predicted segmented image to each pixel in the ground truth. The smaller the value of E1, the better the segmentation result is, and the calculation formula is as follows.

$$E1 = \frac{\sum_{k=1}^{N} \sum_{i,j \in (m,n)} G(i,j) \oplus O(i,j)}{N \times m \times n} \tag{11}$$

where N denotes the number of iris images, m as well as n denotes the width and height of the iris images, $G(i,j)$ and $O(i,j)$ denote the predicted segmentation results and the pixels of the labeled images, respectively, and $\oplus$ denotes the logical heterodyne operation.

4.2.4. Accuracy

Accuracy represents the ratio of the number of correctly predicted pixel points to the total number of pixels in the iris image. A larger value of Acc represents a better segmentation result and is calculated as follows.

$$Acc = \frac{TP + TN}{TP + FN + FP + TN} \times 100\% \tag{12}$$

4.3. Experimental Setup

This paper introduces an algorithm that is fully developed using the PyTorch framework and is trained on a single Nvidia RTX 4090 GPU. Considering the limitations of computational resources, and especially given the concentration of parameters in the encoder part of the SAM model, we chose to use ViT-B (Base) as the encoder for fine-tuning the model. Given the relatively limited dataset available for training, we set the batch size to 2 and employed an Adam optimizer with a learning rate of 0.0001 and a weight decay of 0.01 throughout the training process. To ensure that the model could fully learn and generalize on the limited data, the training process was conducted over 15 epochs. Prior to the commencement of the training process, the resolution of the images was uniformly adjusted to normalize them to 256 × 256 pixels. In the case of images with a width or height less than 256 × 256 pixels, a strategy of zero edge padding was employed to ensure the integrity and proportion of the image were maintained. In all other instances, a bilinear interpolation technique was utilized to resize the image, therefore guaranteeing that the quality and details were correctly handled during the zoom-in process.

4.4. Analysis of Experimental Results

4.4.1. Comparison Experiment

As shown in Table 2, our model demonstrates exceptional performance on a multitude of iris-segmentation datasets, including CASIA.v4-distance, UBIRIS.v2, MICHE-I. In the comparative experiments, a variety of algorithms were selected for analysis, including the traditional algorithm RTV-L 1 [33]. This was complemented by the inclusion of several advanced algorithms, including CNN-based U-Net [3], Deeplab V3+ [34], MFCNs [29], CNNHT [35], and IrisParseNet [8], as well as Transformer-based Swin Transformer [11] and TransUNet [36]. An analysis of the results indicates that the model introduced in this study surpasses CNN-based models across all four performance metrics. This result unequivocally demonstrates the superiority of the self-attention mechanism in Transformer in capturing long-distance dependent information in images, which markedly enhances the segmentation performance. Moreover, the Transformer-based algorithms Swin Transformer and TransUNet demonstrate superior performance compared to their CNN-based counterparts, further substantiating the efficacy of the self-attention mechanism. The encoder and decoder of the SAM-Iris model are both comprised of a Transformer layer, wherein the encoder incorporates the pretrained large-scale model ViT-B and the IrisAdapter module, a novel addition that endows the model with enhanced iris image feature extraction capabilities. Notably, the incorporation of bounding boxes and point prompts enhances the model's precision in defining the iris's annular area, which in turn effectively steers the segmentation algorithm towards higher accuracy. In comparison with the current state-of-the-art Transformer algorithms, Swin Transformer and TransUNet, SAM-Iris has been demonstrated to possess superior iris-segmentation capabilities.

Table 2. Comparison of experimental results. Where an upward arrow indicates that a larger value is better, and a downward arrow indicates that a smaller value is better.

Methods	CASIA.v4-Distance				UBIRIS.v2				MICHE-I			
	E1↓	F1↑	mIoU↑	Acc↑	E1↓	F1↑	mIoU↑	Acc↑	E1↓	F1↑	mIoU↑	Acc↑
RTV-L 1 [33]	0.68	87.55	78.25	81.04	1.21	85.97	77.63	88.83	2.42	79.24	71.47	88.97
U-Net [3]	0.42	93.96	88.84	91.28	0.91	91.59	84.67	92.50	0.76	92.63	86.67	93.36
Deeplab V3+ [34]	0.53	92.43	86.83	-	0.88	91.16	85.90	-	0.77	91.93	85.79	-
MFCNs [29]	0.59	93.09	-	-	0.90	91.04	-	-	0.74	92.01	-	-
CNNHT [35]	0.56	92.27	86.58	89.01	0.97	90.34	82.98	91.14	0.80	91.41	85.27	91.66
IrisParseNet [8]	0.41	94.25	89.52	93.29	0.84	91.78	84.88	92.31	0.66	93.05	87.27	92.53
SwinTransformer [11]	0.40	94.52	89.68	93.91	0.99	91.46	83.96	91.52	0.91	91.34	84.67	92.39
SwinUNet [37]	0.37	94.67	90.03	94.22	0.92	92.37	84.64	92.72	0.71	91.34	86.93	93.79
TransUNet [36]	0.39	94.51	89.72	93.27	0.91	91.55	84.57	91.67	0.73	92.71	86.75	93.10
MedSAM [17]	0.47	92.94	86.81	92.67	0.93	90.58	83.27	90.75	0.81	92.02	84.95	93.04
IrisSAM [22]	0.45	93.79	87.82	93.58	0.93	91.12	84.05	92.43	0.80	92.06	84.25	92.15
Ours	**0.34**	**95.15**	**90.88**	**96.49**	**0.79**	**94.08**	**88.94**	**94.97**	**0.67**	**93.62**	**88.66**	**95.03**

Visual comparisons of the iris-segmentation results from SAM-Iris are depicted in Figures 8 and 9. In the subplots of these result comparisons, blue-colored areas represent true positives (correct predictions), while red areas represent false positives (incorrect predictions in non-iris regions), and green represents true negative pixels (incorrect predictions in iris regions). Observing the results, it can be found that the method proposed in this paper not only accurately segments the outer and inner contours of the iris region but also enables the image encoder to learn iris features more efficiently, therefore effectively avoiding incorrect segmentation of the pupil region. In addition, the method also shows higher accuracy when dealing with eyelash occlusion and highlight regions, successfully excluding factors that are not related to the iris region. This improvement is mainly attributed to the enhancement of the CNN branch, which significantly improves the information extraction ability of the image encoder in localized regions, thus improving the prediction quality of the iris mask. With this comprehensive strategy, SAM-Iris not only achieves a significant improvement in overall segmentation accuracy but also demonstrates its excellent performance in detail processing.

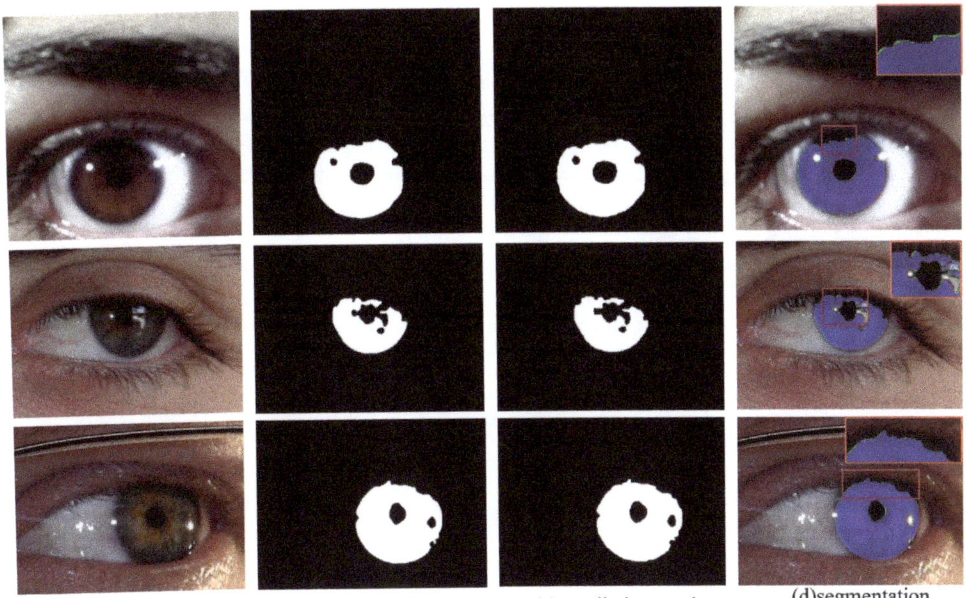

Figure 8. Visualization of visible light iris-segmentation results. Blue-colored areas represent true positives, red areas represent false positives, and green represents true negative pixels.

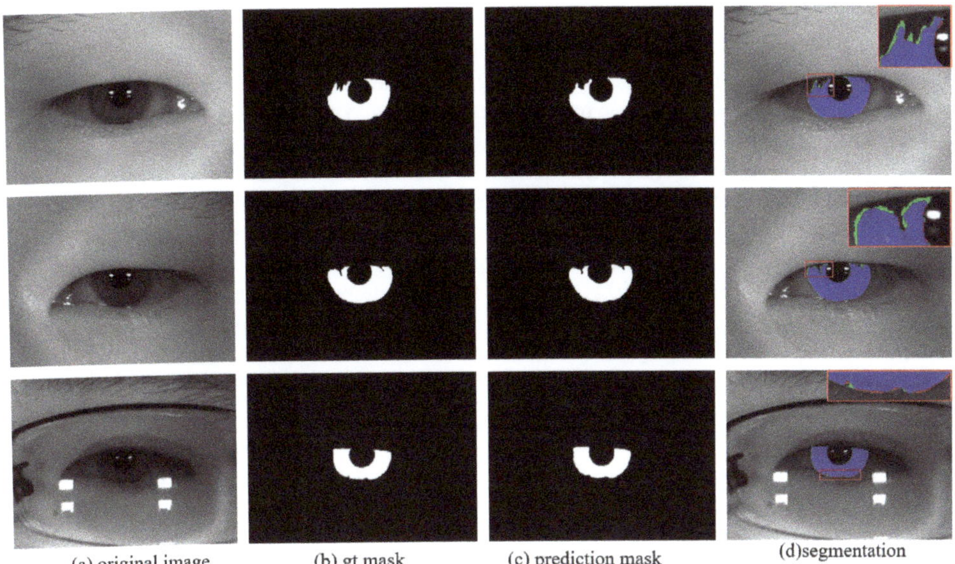

Figure 9. Visualization of NIR iris image segmentation results. Blue-colored areas represent true positives, red areas represent false positives, and green represents true negative pixels.

4.4.2. Ablation Experiment

As detailed in Table 3, this section presents a comprehensive set of ablation studies designed to assess the individual impact of each component on enhancing performance. For consistency, the iris images in all four sets of experiments were resized to 256 × 256 pixels.

The first set of experiments used the original SAM model without fine-tuning. The results show that the model performs poorly in segmenting iris regions and lacks the ability to generalize to specific iris-segmentation tasks. This finding emphasizes the need for targeted fine-tuning of the SAM model. The next three sets of experiments further validated that the fine-tuned SAM model can be effectively adapted to the target domain. In the second and third sets of experiments, the results showed that the IrisAdapter adapter was able to significantly improve the image encoder's ability to extract iris features, thus confirming the effectiveness of the adapter technique in optimizing the SAM model. In addition, the second and fourth sets of experiments demonstrated the importance of local information in improving the quality of iris segmentation, and the experimental results proved that the CNN branch successfully introduced key local features for the ViT branch, further enhancing the model's capacity to capture iris details.

Table 3. Results of the ablation study. Where an upward arrow indicates that a larger value is better, and a downward arrow indicates that a smaller value is better.

Methods	CASIA.v4-Distance				UBIRIS.v2				MICHE-I			
	E1↓	**F1↑**	**mIoU↑**	**Acc↑**	**E1↓**	**F1↑**	**mIoU↑**	**Acc↑**	**E1↓**	**F1↑**	**mIoU↑**	**Acc↑**
NoFitune-SAM	3.78	37.33	24.97	64.41	6.47	32.17	21.42	77.03	5.19	43.84	31.05	67.26
SAM+IrisAdapter	0.44	91.43	88.07	96.15	0.91	93.19	87.41	94.22	0.82	91.47	84.66	92.45
SAM+CNNBranch	3.77	56.86	40.48	52.26	4.97	57.41	41.89	66.68	4.31	48.96	33.77	57.02
Ours	**0.34**	**95.15**	**90.88**	**96.49**	**0.79**	**94.08**	**88.94**	**94.97**	**0.67**	**93.62**	**88.66**	**95.03**

4.4.3. Prompt Experiment

The SAM model is pretrained by an interactive promptable segmentation method, where a series of prompts (points, boxes, masks, etc.) are simulated for each training image, and the loss is defined as the deviation between the model's predicted mask and the true mask. This interactive capability allows SAM to obtain reasonable segmentation results in a single interaction, which is usually not the case with traditional models. The data in Table 4 reflect in detail the performance of the iris-segmentation task when using a bounding box (Bbox) and different numbers of point prompt (1 point, 3 points, 5 points, 9 points) on different datasets. It is noticeable that as the number of point prompts increases incrementally, the model's performance metric remains largely constant. This suggests that using an appropriate number of point prompts is advantageous for enhancing the precision of iris segmentation. However, when the number of point prompt exceeds a certain threshold, the performance improvement is not significant, indicating that more point prompts are not better, but there is an optimal number of prompts. In addition, point prompt demonstrates an advantage in improving iris-segmentation performance compared to the bounding box prompt. Point prompts are able to localize key regions of the iris more accurately, which allows the model to understand and segment the iris contour in greater detail. This performance improvement further confirms the superiority of point prompts over bounding box prompts in iris-segmentation tasks. Taken together, these findings provide important guidance: when designing SAM-based iris-segmentation algorithms, an appropriate amount of point prompts should be considered to optimize performance and also highlight the effectiveness of point prompts in accurately capturing iris features.

Table 4. Prompt comparison experiment results.

Prompt Mode	CASIA.v4-Distance				UBIRIS.v2				MICHE-I			
	E1↓	F1↑	mIoU ↑	Acc↑	E1↓	F1↑	mIoU↑	Acc↑	E1↓	F1↑	mIoU↑	Acc↑
Bbox	0.36	94.89	90.45	96.11	0.72	93.24	87.83	94.02	0.68	93.35	88.27	94.95
1 Point	**0.34**	**95.15**	**90.88**	**96.49**	**0.79**	**94.08**	**88.94**	**94.97**	**0.67**	**93.62**	**88.66**	**95.03**
3 Points	0.37	94.68	90.22	96.03	0.73	93.20	87.79	93.92	0.68	93.33	88.27	94.87
5 Points	0.37	94.66	90.21	96.01	0.73	93.20	87.79	93.92	0.68	93.31	88.25	94.84
9 Points	0.37	94.67	90.22	96.01	0.73	93.19	87.77	93.91	0.68	93.33	88.27	94.87

4.4.4. Interactive Segmentation Visualization

Figure 10 provides a visualization of the segmentation effect of the NIR iris image, with different prompts to see the differences in the segmentation results. Starting from the original image in Figure 10a, we can see the original unsegmented iris image, which provides a reference for the subsequent visualization. In Figure 10b–f, it can be seen that the model is able to segment the iris region accurately and interactively under different prompt modes that are considered to be set.

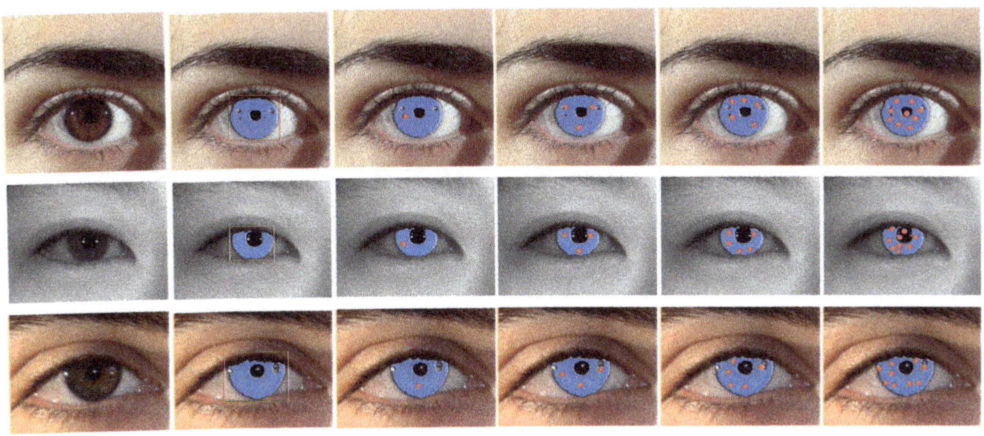

(a) original image (b) bounding box (c) 1 point (d) 3 points (e) 5 points (f) 9 points

Figure 10. Interactive segmentation results.

5. Conclusions

In this paper, we have successfully applied the Segment Anything Model (SAM) to the iris-segmentation domain through a series of innovative research efforts, confirming the great potential and effectiveness of large pretrained models in handling this complex visual task. We propose the IrisAdapter adapter as a plug-and-play tool that effectively captures iris domain-specific information while avoiding a full update of the entire model parameters, reducing the computational and economic cost of the training process. In addition, by introducing a CNN branch working in parallel with ViT and a Cross-Branch Attention mechanism module, our model makes significant progress in extracting local detail information of the iris image, enhances the ability to recognize iris details, and improves the overall segmentation performance. Future work can further explore and optimize the adapter technique for a wider range of application scenarios and requirements. Meanwhile, we will also focus on how to further improve the SAM model's ability to extract local features as well as pre-training large model fine-tuning techniques to achieve higher accuracy iris segmentation.

Author Contributions: Conceptualization, J.J. and Q.Z.; methodology, J.J; software, J.J.; validation, J.J.; formal analysis, J.J. and Q.Z.; investigation, Q.Z. and C.W.; resources, Q.Z. and C.W.; data curation, J.J.; writing—original draft preparation, J.J.; writing—review and editing, Q.Z., C.W.; visualization, J.J.; supervision, Q.Z.; project administration, Q.Z.; funding acquisition, Q.Z., C.W. All authors have read and agreed to the published version of the manuscript.

Funding: This research was funded by the National Natural Science Foundation of China (61906199, 62106015) and the Beijing Natural Science Foundation (4242018).

Data Availability Statement: The dataset presented in this study is available. All data used in the study can be obtained from publicly available databases and emails from the author's mailbox.

Conflicts of Interest: The authors declare no conflict of interest.

References

1. Nguyen, K.; Proença, H.; Alonso-Fernandez, F. Deep Learning for Iris Recognition: A Survey. *ACM Comput. Surv.* **2024**, *56*, 1–35 . [CrossRef]
2. Long, J.; Shelhamer, E.; Darrell, T. Fully convolutional networks for semantic segmentation. In Proceedings of the 2015 IEEE Conference on Computer Vision and Pattern Recognition (CVPR), Boston, MA, USA, 7–12 June 2015; pp. 3431–3440.
3. Ronneberger, O.; Fischer, P.; Brox, T. U-Net: Convolutional Networks for Biomedical Image Segmentation. In *Medical Image Computing and Computer-Assisted Intervention—MICCAI 2015*; Springer International Publishing: New York, NY, USA, 2015; pp. 234–241.
4. Dosovitskiy, A.; Beyer, L.; Kolesnikov, A.; Weissenborn, D.; Zhai, X.; Unterthiner, T.; Dehghani, M.; Minderer, M.; Heigold, G.; Gelly, S.; et al. An Image is Worth 16 × 16 Words: Transformers for Image Recognition at Scale. In Proceedings of the International Conference on Learning Representations, Virtual Event, Austria, 3–7 May 2021. Available online: https://openreview.net/forum?id=YicbFdNTTy (accessed on 22 October 2020).
5. Lozej, J.; Meden, B.; Struc, V.; Peer, P. End-to-End Iris Segmentation Using U-Net. In Proceedings of the 2018 IEEE International Work Conference on Bioinspired Intelligence (IWOBI), San Carlos, Costa Rica, 18–20 July 2018; pp. 1–6.
6. Wu, X.; Zhao, L. Study on Iris Segmentation Algorithm Based on Dense U-Net. *IEEE Access* **2019**, *7*, 123959–123968. [CrossRef]
7. Zhang, W.; Lu, X.; Gu, Y.; Liu, Y.; Meng, X.; Li, J. A Robust Iris Segmentation Scheme Based on Improved U-Net. *IEEE Access* **2019**, *7*, 85082–85089. [CrossRef]
8. Wang, C.; Muhammad, J.; Wang, Y.; He, Z.; Sun, Z. Towards Complete and Accurate Iris Segmentation Using Deep Multi-Task Attention Network for Non-Cooperative Iris Recognition. *IEEE Trans. Inf. Forensics Secur.* **2020**, *15*, 2944–2959. [CrossRef]
9. Sun, Y.; Lu, Y.; Liu, Y.; Zhu, X. Towards More Accurate and Complete Iris Segmentation Using Hybrid Transformer U-Net. In Proceedings of the 2022 IEEE International Joint Conference on Biometrics (IJCB), Abu Dhabi, United Arab Emirates, 10–13 October 2022; pp. 1–10.
10. Gu, Z.; Wang, C.; Tian, Q.; Zhang, Q. A Symmetrical Encoder-Decoder Network with Transformer for Noise-Robust Iris Segmentation. *J. Comput. Aided Des. Comput. Graph.* **2022**, *34*, 1887–1898. [CrossRef]
11. Liu, Z.; Lin, Y.; Cao, Y.; Hu, H.; Wei, Y.; Zhang, Z.; Lin, S.; Guo, B. Swin Transformer: Hierarchical Vision Transformer using Shifted Windows. In Proceedings of the 2021 IEEE/CVF International Conference on Computer Vision (ICCV), Montreal, QC, Canada, 10–17 October 2021; pp. 9992–10002.
12. Meng, Y.; Bao, T. Towards More Accurate and Complete Heterogeneous Iris Segmentation Using a Hybrid Deep Learning Approach. *J. Imaging* **2022**, *8*, 246. [CrossRef] [PubMed]
13. Arsalan, M.; Kim, D.; Lee, M.; Owais, M.; Park, K. FRED-Net: Fully residual encoder–decoder network for accurate iris segmentation. *Expert Syst. Appl.* **2019**, *122*, 217–241. [CrossRef]
14. Arsalan, M.; Kim, D.; Owais, M.; Park, K. OR-Skip-Net: Outer residual skip network for skin segmentation in non-ideal situations. *Expert Syst. Appl.* **2020**, *141*, 112922. [CrossRef]
15. Kirillov, A.; Mintun, E.; Ravi, N.; Mao, H.; Rolland, C.; Gustafson, L.; Xiao, T.; Whitehead, S.; Berg, A.; Lo, W.; et al. Segment Anything. *arXiv* **2023**. [CrossRef]
16. Chen, T.; Zhu, L.; Deng, C.; Cao, R.; Wang, Y.; Zhang, S.; Li, Z.; Sun, L.; Zang, Y.; Mao, P. SAM-Adapter: Adapting Segment Anything in Underperformed Scenes. In Proceedings of the IEEE/CVF International Conference on Computer Vision (ICCV) Workshops, Paris, France, 2–3 October 2023; pp. 3367–3375.
17. Ma, J.; Wang, B. Segment Anything in Medical Images. *arXiv* **2023**, arXiv:2304.12306. [CrossRef] [PubMed]
18. Deng, G.; Zou, K.; Ren, K.; Wang, M.; Yuan, X.; Ying, S.; Fu, H. SAM-U: Multi-box Prompts Triggered Uncertainty Estimation for Reliable SAM in Medical Image. In *Medical Image Computing and Computer Assisted Intervention—MICCAI 2023 Workshops*; Springer: Cham, Switzerland, 2023; pp. 368–377.

19. Wu, J.; Ji, W.; Liu, Y.; Fu, H.; Xu, M.; Xu, Y.; Jin, Y. Medical SAM Adapter: Adapting Segment Anything Model for Medical Image Segmentation. *arXiv* **2023**. [CrossRef]
20. Zhang, K.; Liu, D. Customized Segment Anything Model for Medical Image Segmentation. *arXiv* **2023**. [CrossRef]
21. Hu, E.; Shen, Y.; Wallis, P.; Allen-Zhu, Z.; Li, Y.; Wang, S.; Wang, L.; Chen, W. LoRA: Low-Rank Adaptation of Large Language Models. *arXiv* **2021**. [CrossRef]
22. Farmanifard, P.; Ross, A. Iris-SAM: Iris Segmentation Using a Foundation Model. 2024. Available online: https://api.semanticscholar.org/CorpusID:267616903 (accessed on 9 February 2024).
23. Li, Y.; Jing, B.; Li, Z.; Wang, J.; Zhang, Y. nnSAM: Plug-and-play Segment Anything Model Improves nnUNet Performance. *arXiv* **2024**. [CrossRef]
24. Wang, G.; Zuluaga, M.; Li, W.; Pratt, R.; Patel, P.; Aertsen, M.; Doel, T.; David, A.; Deprest, J.; Ourselin, S.; et al. DeepIGeoS: A Deep Interactive Geodesic Framework for Medical Image Segmentation. *IEEE Trans. Pattern Anal. Mach. Intell.* **2019**, *41*, 1559–1572. [CrossRef] [PubMed]
25. Milletari, F.; Navab, N.; Ahmadi, S. V-Net: Fully Convolutional Neural Networks for Volumetric Medical Image Segmentation. In Proceedings of the 2016 Fourth International Conference on 3D Vision (3DV), Stanford, CA, USA, 25–28 October 2016; pp. 565–571.
26. Yu, J.; Jiang, Y.; Wang, Z.; Cao, Z.; Huang, T. UnitBox: An Advanced Object Detection Network. In Proceedings of the 24th ACM International Conference on Multimedia, Amsterdam, The Netherlands, 15–19 October 2016; pp. 516–520. [CrossRef]
27. Lin, T.; Goyal, P.; Girshick, R.; He, K.; Dollár, P. Focal Loss for Dense Object Detection. In Proceedings of the 2017 IEEE International Conference on Computer Vision (ICCV), Venice, Italy, 22–29 October 2017; pp. 2999–3007.
28. BIT B. I. Test. Casia-v4 Database. 2020. Available online: http://www.idealtest.org/dbDetailForUser.do?id=4 (accessed on 12 July 2021).
29. Liu, N.; Li, H.; Zhang, M.; Liu, J.; Sun, Z.; Tan, T. Accurate iris segmentation in non-cooperative environments using fully convolutional networks. In Proceedings of the 2016 International Conference on Biometrics (ICB), Halmstad, Sweden, 13–16 June 2016; pp. 1–8.
30. Proenca, H.; Filipe, S.; Santos, R.; Oliveira, J.; Alexandre, L. The UBIRIS.v2: A Database of Visible Wavelength Iris Images Captured On-the-Move and At-a-Distance. *IEEE Trans. Pattern Anal. Mach. Intell.* **2010**, *32*, 1529–1535. [CrossRef] [PubMed]
31. Proenca, H.; Alexandre, L. The NICE.I: Noisy Iris Challenge Evaluation—Part I. In Proceedings of the 2007 First IEEE International Conference on Biometrics: Theory, Applications, and Systems, Crystal City, VA, USA, 27–29 September 2007; pp. 1–4.
32. De Marsico, M.; Nappi, M.; Riccio, D.; Wechsler, H. Mobile Iris Challenge Evaluation (MICHE)-I, biometric iris dataset and protocols. *Pattern Recognit. Lett.* **2015**, *57*, 17–23. [CrossRef]
33. Zhao, Z.; Kumar, A. An Accurate Iris Segmentation Framework Under Relaxed Imaging Constraints Using Total Variation Model. In Proceedings of the 2015 IEEE International Conference on Computer Vision (ICCV), Santiago, Chile, 7–13 December 2015; pp. 3828–3836.
34. Chen, L.; Zhu, Y.; Papandreou, G.; Schroff, F.; Adam, H. Encoder-Decoder with Atrous Separable Convolution for Semantic Image Segmentation. *arXiv* **2018**. [CrossRef]
35. Hofbauer, H.; Jalilian, E.; Uhl, A. Exploiting superior CNN-based iris segmentation for better recognition accuracy. *Pattern Recognit. Lett.* **2019**, *120*, 17–23. [CrossRef]
36. Chen, J.; Lu, Y.; Yu, Q.; Luo, X.; Adeli, E.; Wang, Y.; Lu, L.; Yuille, A.; Zhou, Y. TransUNet: Transformers Make Strong Encoders for Medical Image Segmentation. *arXiv* **2021**. [CrossRef]
37. Cao, H.; Wang, Y.; Chen, J.; Jiang, D.; Zhang, X.; Tian, Q.; Wang, M. Swin-Unet: Unet-like Pure Transformer for Medical Image Segmentation. In Proceedings of the ECCV Workshops, Montreal, BC, Canada, 11–17 October 2021. Available online: https://api.semanticscholar.org/CorpusID:234469981 (accessed on 12 May 2021).

electronics

MDPI

Article

OcularSeg: Accurate and Efficient Multi-Modal Ocular Segmentation in Non-Constrained Scenarios

Yixin Zhang [1,2], Caiyong Wang [1,2,*], Haiqing Li [1,2], Xianyun Sun [1,2], Qichuan Tian [1,2] and Guangzhe Zhao [1,2]

1 School of Electrical and Information Engineering, Beijing University of Civil Engineering and Architecture, Beijing 100044, China; zhangyixin@stu.bucea.edu.cn (Y.Z.); haiqing_li@stu.bucea.edu.cn (H.L.); sunxianyun@stu.bucea.edu.cn (X.S.); tianqichuan@bucea.edu.cn (Q.T.); zhaoguangzhe@bucea.edu.cn (G.Z.)

2 Beijing Key Laboratory of Robot Bionics and Function Research, Beijing 100044, China

* Correspondence: wangcaiyong@bucea.edu.cn

Abstract: Multi-modal ocular biometrics has recently garnered significant attention due to its potential in enhancing the security and reliability of biometric identification systems in non-constrained scenarios. However, accurately and efficiently segmenting multi-modal ocular traits (periocular, sclera, iris, and pupil) remains challenging due to noise interference or environmental changes, such as specular reflection, gaze deviation, blur, occlusions from eyelid/eyelash/glasses, and illumination/spectrum/sensor variations. To address these challenges, we propose OcularSeg, a densely connected encoder–decoder model incorporating eye shape prior. The model utilizes Efficientnetv2 as a lightweight backbone in the encoder for extracting multi-level visual features while minimizing network parameters. Moreover, we introduce the Expectation–Maximization attention (EMA) unit to progressively refine the model's attention and roughly aggregate features from each ocular modality. In the decoder, we design a bottom-up dense subtraction module (DSM) to amplify information disparity between encoder layers, facilitating the acquisition of high-level semantic detailed features at varying scales, thereby enhancing the precision of detailed ocular region prediction. Additionally, boundary- and semantic-guided eye shape priors are integrated as auxiliary supervision during training to optimize the position, shape, and internal topological structure of segmentation results. Due to the scarcity of datasets with multi-modal ocular segmentation annotations, we manually annotated three challenging eye datasets captured in near-infrared and visible light scenarios. Experimental results on newly annotated and existing datasets demonstrate that our model achieves state-of-the-art performance in intra- and cross-dataset scenarios while maintaining efficient execution.

Keywords: ocular segmentation; iris segmentation; sclera segmentation; biometric recognition; shape prior

1. Introduction

As a form of single-modal ocular biometrics, iris recognition has gained widespread recognition as a reliable authentication method due to its unique, stable, accurate, and noninvasive characteristics [1]. It has found extensive applications across various domains, including public safety, border control, mobile payment, and the metaverse. Additionally, in recent years, research has indicated that other ocular modalities (as illustrated in Figure 1), such as sclera and periocular [2,3], can effectively complement the iris recognition, substantially enhancing its suitability, accuracy, and security [4–7]. To exploit multi-modal ocular traits for recognition, the initial step is to perform multi-modal ocular segmentation on the input eye image. As depicted in Figure 2, this study concentrates on the simultaneous segmentation of the periocular (as a background class), sclera, iris, and pupil regions. As a result, the segmented region of interest (ROI) images of the periocular, sclera, and iris are further fed into their corresponding feature extractors to extract multi-modal identity features for fusion recognition. As for the pupil, it can serve various purposes, such as fatigue detection and gaze estimation [8]. Given that multi-modal ocular segmentation occurs during the pre-processing stage, any inaccuracies in segmentation could result in the loss of identity-related modality information or the introduction of distracting textures. Such inaccuracies can substantially impair the accuracy of multi-modal ocular recognition [9,10].

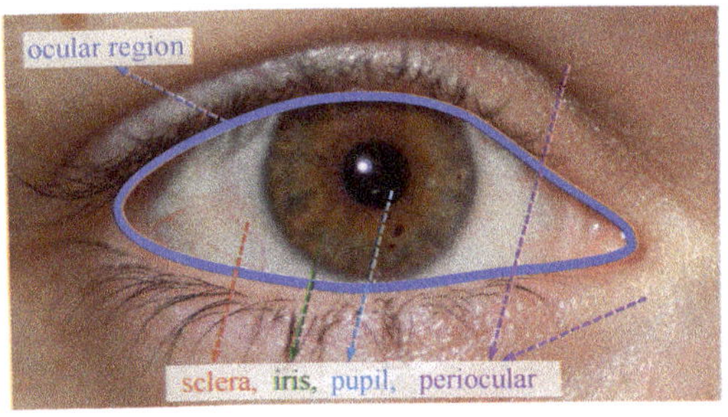

Figure 1. Periocular and ocular components (sclera, iris, and pupil). The eye image is from the SBVPI [11] dataset.

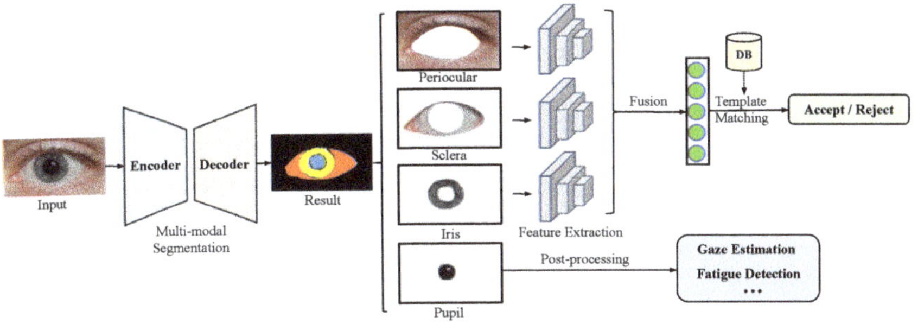

Figure 2. A standard multi-modal ocular recognition pipeline typically incorporates multi-modal segmentation to identify the regions of interest (ROIs) for fusion recognition.

Biometric recognition usually occurs in constrained scenarios. However, with the deepening of its application in our daily lives, it has become a trend to develop ocular biometrics in non-constrained scenarios (e.g., at-a-distance, on-the-move, and visible illumination), which would greatly reduce the constraints for user cooperation and imaging conditions. However, under these conditions, the segmentation process is highly susceptible to various noise factors such as specular reflection, gaze deviation, motion/defocus blur, occlusions from eyelid/eyelash/glasses, as well as environmental changes such as variations in illumination/spectrum/sensor. In addition, as a pre-processing operation, it should also be computationally efficient for practical deployment. Overall, achieving accurate and efficient multi-modal ocular segmentation is inherently challenging.

Some efforts have been made in the literature to enhance the accuracy of multi-modal ocular segmentation. Early approaches, such as EyeNet [12] and MinENet [13], primarily utilized classic CNN architectures like ResNet [14] to assess the feasibility of multi-modal ocular segmentation tasks. Subsequently, several models based on improved encoder–decoder architecture, such as RITnet [15], SCN [16], and Eye-UNet [17], were proposed to elevate segmentation accuracy further. In recent years, to enhance segmentation performance with limited annotated datasets, methods based on semi-supervised learning have been proposed [18]. Hassan et al. introduced a new framework named SIPFormer [19], which integrates transformer architecture for this multi-modal segmentation task. At the same time, it improves segmentation accuracy and introduces many parameters, reducing model efficiency. Additionally, most current methods are trained and evaluated on datasets from a single collection environment with limited samples, such as OpenEDS [20], which may not adequately reflect the performance in real-world ocular recognition scenarios. Therefore, substantial challenges remain in developing efficient, accurate, and generalizable multi-modal ocular segmentation models.

More specifically, several challenges are highlighted in the multi-modal ocular segmentation task: (i) Current models exhibit inadequate adaptability to environmental fluctuations, encompassing factors like illumination, resolution, and contrast, among others, coupled with heightened computational complexity, constraining their applicability in resource-constrained settings like embedded devices. (ii) Most current models utilize an end-to-end pixel-wise semantic segmentation strategy for multi-modal ocular segmentation. However, they often fail to effectively leverage prior knowledge concerning the overall eye shape and the spatial distribution of different modalities. Consequently, this limitation hinders the extraction of contextual features, rendering the models prone to segmentation errors. (iii) The availability of finely annotated multi-modal ocular datasets in real-world open environments is scarce. Furthermore, certain datasets mentioned in the literature, like OpenEDS [20], exhibit limited accessibility or are not specifically collected for ocular biometrics.

This paper proposes a novel multi-modal ocular segmentation approach, named OcularSeg, to address the challenges above. The proposed approach is an encoder–decoder model like U-Net [21]. Specifically, the encoder employs the lightweight Efficientnetv2 [22] as the backbone for extracting multi-level visual features while mitigating computational complexity. Since the initially extracted hierarchical features are relatively coarse and lack discrimination for multi-modal ocular traits, we further introduce the Expectation–Maximization Attention (EMA) [23] module to alleviate this problem. Unlike certain mechanisms that require generating large attention maps, resulting in high computational complexity and consuming significant GPU memory—such as the self-attention mechanism in Transformer [24]—the EMA module is designed based on the Expectation–Maximization [25] algorithm. This allows it to dynamically adjust attention weights within the neural network and integrate spatial information. Such a design enhances the model's perceptual and discriminative abilities in noisy environments, thereby achieving coarse aggregation of ocular features and effectively improving the accuracy of prediction results.

In the decoder, we focus more on the information differences between different levels and consider that the semantic features at the deep level are richer and more likely to capture intricate ocular parts; hence, we propose a bottom-up densely connected subtraction module. It starts from the deepest level and applies subtraction units to the feature maps at all scales larger than the current one. This facilitates the exchange of cross-resolution feature information while accentuating useful distinctions between features, thereby eliminating interference from redundant components. Moreover, we incorporate the prior knowledge of ocular by integrating the boundary-guided prior and semantic-guided prior as supplementary constraints within the model structure and training procedure. This optimization enhances the model's predictive capabilities across various modalities and diminishes mis-segmentation. Lastly, we manually annotate three diverse multi-modal ocular datasets collected under visible and near-infrared light conditions with noise to assess the model's accuracy and generalization in real-world open environments. Experimental findings on self-collected and publicly available datasets show that our model achieves state-of-the-art performance in intra- and cross-dataset scenarios while maintaining low computation costs.

In summary, our main contributions can be summarized as follows:

- We present OcularSeg, a highly efficient and accurate, densely connected encoder–decoder model tailored for multi-modal ocular segmentation. This model integrates a lightweight EfficientNetv2 as its backbone, an EMA module for aggregating features from different modalities, and a bottom-up dense subtraction module to refine prediction results through feature exchange across different levels.
- We incorporate prior knowledge of eye shape, including boundary-guided and semantic-guided priors, to offer additional and refined guidance for the model's predictions

regarding shape, position, and structural relationships between different modalities. This inclusion substantially enhances the accuracy of our method.

- We manually annotate three diverse eye image datasets collected under various environmental conditions, encompassing illumination, resolution, and spectrum differences. These datasets are meticulously categorized for periocular, sclera, iris, and pupil pixels. Combining these datasets with existing ones demonstrates our method's effectiveness, superiority, and efficiency for multi-modal ocular segmentation across intra- and cross-dataset scenarios.

The structure of this paper is as follows: Section 2 reviews related work, while Section 3 elaborates on our multi-modal ocular segmentation framework. The experimental settings, including datasets and evaluation protocols, are detailed in Section 4. In Section 5, we present and analyze the experimental results quantitatively and qualitatively. Finally, Section 6 concludes the paper and discusses future work.

2. Related Work

Few studies have concentrated on multi-modal ocular segmentation, particularly for delineating multiple ocular regions from images using a single segmentation model. Rot et al. [26] pioneered the training of a convolutional encoder–decoder network based on SegNet [27], categorizing pixels into six classes: pupil, iris, sclera, eyelashes, canthus, and periocular (as listed in Table 1). Subsequently, Ref. [28] manually annotated 500 eye images from the NICE. I competition dataset [29], expanding on NICE. I's two-category real iris segmentation mask to encompass 10 semantic categories. Their work achieved comparable segmentation accuracy utilizing FCN networks [30]. In another approach, Ref. [31] designed a miniature multi-scale segmentation network (Eye-MS) founded on multi-scale interconnected convolutional modules. They also developed a lightweight variant named Eye-MMS, containing only 80k parameters, to preserve performance while reducing parameters.

The eye segmentation challenge organized by Facebook research was conducted on the OpenEDS dataset [20]. Kansal et al. proposed Eyenet [32] to address this challenge, employing residual connections, multi-scale supervision, a squeeze-and-excitation module [33], and a convolutional block attention module [34]. MinENet [13] was introduced to streamline model complexity by removing redundancy within the central layer of ENet [35], which utilizes a dilated and asymmetric convolution design. Chaudhary et al. proposed the RITnet architecture [15], amalgamating DenseNet [36] and U-Net [21], integrating pre-processing enhancement operations and boundary-aware loss functions to produce clear regional boundaries.

Table 1. Comparison of the proposed method with other multi-class ocular segmentation methods.

Method	Backbone	Dataset	Spectrum		Modality	Weakness
			NIR	VIS		
Rot et al. [26]	SegNet	MASD [37]	-	✓	S/I/P/E/C/PO	The dataset is relatively small, consisting of 120 samples.
D. et al. [28]	FCN	NICE.I [29]/MobBIO [38]	-	✓	S/I/P/E/C/PO/SR/EB/H/GF	The computational demands and rough annotation.
Eye-MMS [31]	-	OpenEDS [20]	✓	-	S/I/P/PO	The model is simple and the accuracy is poor.
EyeNet [12]	ResNet50	OpenEDS [20]	✓	-	S/I/P/PO	Large number of parameters and additional optimization.
MinENet [13]	ENet	OpenEDS [20]	✓	-	S/I/P/PO	Only the modifications in the model architecture.

Table 1. *Cont.*

Method	Backbone	Dataset	Spectrum		Modality	Weakness
			NIR	VIS		
RITnet [15]	U-Net/DenseNet	OpenEDS [20]	✓	-	S/I/P/PO	It is computationally intensive and includes pre-processing.
iBUG [39]	VGG-16/ResNet101	iBUG (Proprietary) [39]	-	✓	S/I	Utilized for iris-only and sclera-only segmentation, including pre-processing and post-processing operations.
Eyenet [32]	ResNet	OpenEDS [20]	✓	-	S/I/P/PO	Contains extensive post-processing.
EyeSeg [40]	-	OpenEDS [20]	✓	-	S/I/P/PO	Contains redundant processing.
SCN [16]	SegNet	Proprietary [16]	-	✓	S/I	Introduced a large number of parameters.
Ocular-Net [41]	lite-residual	NICE-II [42]/SBVPI [11]	✓	-	S/I	Trains each region individually, working on one region at a time.
SSL [18]	-	OpenEDS [20]	✓	-	S/I/P/PO	Poor for low-quality images.
SIPFormer [19]	Transformer	CASIA [43]	✓	-	S/I/P/PO	Contains a large number of parameters, as well as a large number of pre-processing and post-processing.
Eye-UNet [17]	ResNet	OpenEDS [20]	-	✓	S/I/PO	Inference time is not ideal.
OcularSeg (Ours)	Efficientnetv2	Proprietary	✓	✓	S/I/P/PO	Rigorous training is required.

S = Sclera, I = Iris, P = Pupil, E = Eyelashes, C = Canthus, PO = Periocular (background), SR = Specular reflections, EB = Eyebrows, H = Hair, GF = Glass frames, NIR = Near-infrared, VIS = Visible light.

Subsequently, Ref. [39] introduced a low-resolution ocular segmentation dataset, offering two types of annotations: 30 keypoints and pixel-level annotations. They conducted preliminary eye segmentation investigations using deformable model-based methods and DeepLab with Atrous CNN+CRF, respectively. EyeNet [12] tackled multiple heterogeneous tasks related to gaze estimation and user semantic understanding. In addition, the feature encoding layer utilized ResNet50 as the backbone and integrated feature pyramid (FPN) [44] to capture the information across different scales. Similarly, EyeSeg [40] incorporated two key components: residual connections and dilated convolutional layers. This combination substantially improved performance without considerably increasing computational complexity. Furthermore, Luo et al. [16] introduced a shape-constrained network (SCN), which first uses VAE-GAN [45] to learn shapes, and employed pre-trained networks to regularize the training of SegNet. They curated and annotated a dataset comprising 8882 ocular images from 4461 facial images with varying resolutions, lighting conditions, and head poses. Subsequently, Naqvi et al. proposed Ocular-Net [41], a deep-learning-based lite-residual network. Additionally, Kothari proposed EllSeg [46], a simple three-category full ellipse segmentation framework, to extend the traditional encoder–decoder architecture. The results demonstrated that predicting pupil and iris centers and directions yielded superior performance compared to pixel-level segmentation models.

Hassan et al. [19] introduced SIPFormer, a novel framework comprising encoder, decoder, and transformer modules designed for joint segmentation. Their approach includes a pre-processing stage to enhance eye features while suppressing information from the periocular regions. By leveraging transformer modules, SIPFormer demonstrates improved feature learning capabilities, resulting in high accuracy in segmenting multi-modal features. Similarly, Eye-UNet [17] tackled the segmentation challenge posed by low-quality human eye images captured outdoors. Initially, they curated a dataset of 5000 low-quality eye images with varying lighting conditions, occlusions, and motion blur. Based on U-Net architecture, their proposed network replaces the backbone network with Resnet18 and integrates an attention mechanism and a deep supervision module [47].

The field of ocular segmentation is dynamically evolving, witnessing the emergence of novel architectures and fusion strategies for multi-model data. Early studies predominantly focused on a single spectrum, such as visible light, employing traditional deep-learning techniques. While these methods succeeded under specific conditions, their limitations become apparent with increasing data volume and task complexity. To address these challenges more effectively, we advocate for a deep learning architecture amalgamating traditional and modern prior knowledge methods. By doing so, we aim to accurately capture subtle features and structures in eye images, offering a comprehensive solution for ocular segmentation.

3. Methodology

3.1. Overview

The proposed OcularSeg model is designed to perform joint segmentation of the periocular, sclera, iris, and pupil from ocular scans. A high-level overview of the model is depicted in Figure 3. This architecture begins by extracting features using a lightweight network, yielding five feature embeddings $E_i, i \in \{1,2,3,4,5\}$ through five distinct feature extraction stages. Subsequently, a convolution filter having size (3×3) pixels is applied individually to each feature embedding to reduce the channels to 64 and further minimize parameter redundancy. The resulting features are passed through the EMA module for feature aggregation. Following this, different levels of features are directed to the dense subtraction module, producing the decoder feature map $D_i, i \in \{1,2,3,4,5\}$. Ultimately, each D_i progressively contributes to the decoder and is combined with eye shape prior to generate the final predictions.

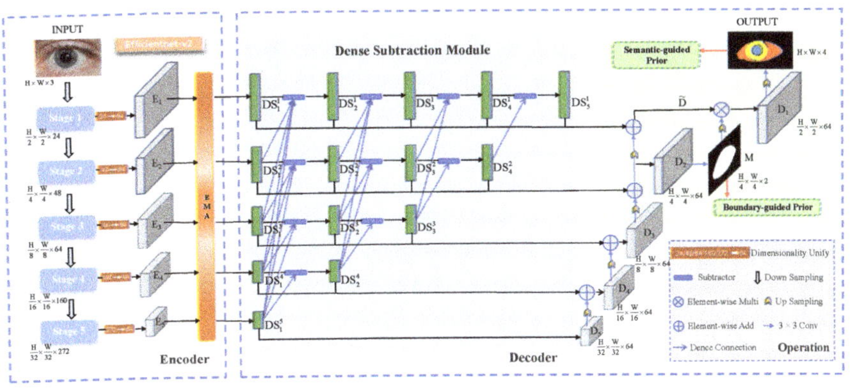

Figure 3. Overview of the proposed OcularSeg model.

3.2. Feature Extraction

We adopt the lightweight Efficientnetv2 [22] as the backbone to extract five levels of features. Then, a convolution filter having size (3×3) pixels is applied to the feature map output by each encoder block, standardizing the number of channels to 64. This facilitates subsequent operations and reduces the number of parameters. The resulting latent features E_i are then fed into the EMA [23] network, as shown in Figure 4. The attention mechanism is rethought from the perspective of the Expectation–Maximization (EM) [25] algorithm. Specifically, the EM algorithm is employed to identify a more compact base set μ and then operate the attention on this set. Through dynamic learning and adjustment of attention weights, we can obtain discriminative feature representations, enabling the model to focus more on key regions and specific semantic categories. Details are described as follows:

Starting with an input feature map E_i of size $(C \times H \times W)$ pixels, where C, H, and W denote the number of channels, height, and width, respectively, it is reshaped into an $N \times C$ matrix by flattening it along the spatial dimensions ($N = H \times W$ for simplicity). Herein, $E_i^j \in \mathbb{R}^C$ represents the C-dimensional feature vector at pixel j. The EMA module comprises three key operations: responsibility estimation (A_E), likelihood maximization (A_M), and data re-estimation (A_R). Given the input $E_i \in \mathbb{R}^{N\times C}$ and initial bases $\mu \in \mathbb{R}^{K\times C}$, A_E estimates latent variables $Z \in \mathbb{R}^{N\times K}$, resembling the Expectation (E) step in the EM algorithm. Subsequently, A_M utilizes this estimation to update the bases μ, resembling the Maximization (M) step in the EM algorithm. The A_E and A_M steps alternate for a fixed number of iterations (here, we empirically set it to 3). Finally, with the converged μ and Z, A_R reconstructs the original E_i as Y.

This algorithm treats the construction base μ as the learnable parameter and the attention map Z as the latent variable. The objective is to find the maximum likelihood estimate of the parameters. It has been demonstrated that the complete data likelihood $\ln p(E_i, Z)$ monotonically increases with the iteration of EM steps. The E step computes the expectation value for each position, leveraging the current attention weights and feature representations to estimate the significance associated with each position. The M step utilizes the estimated E values to adjust the attention weights, thereby directing the model's focus towards features deemed more critical for the current ocular segmentation task. This module is integrated into the feature extraction stage of the segmentation model, called the EMA unit. By alternating the E step and the M step, the EMA module dynamically learns and adjusts the attention weights. Consequently, the updated Z and μ better reconstruct the original ocular data E_i, reducing intra-class feature differences and rendering features more compact.

In summary, the operation of A_E in the t-th iteration is formulated as

$$Z^{(t)} = \text{softmax}\left(\lambda E_i \left(\mu^{(t-1)}\right)^{\top}\right), \; i \in \{1,2,3,4,5\}, \tag{1}$$

where λ is a hyperparameter that controls the distribution of Z.

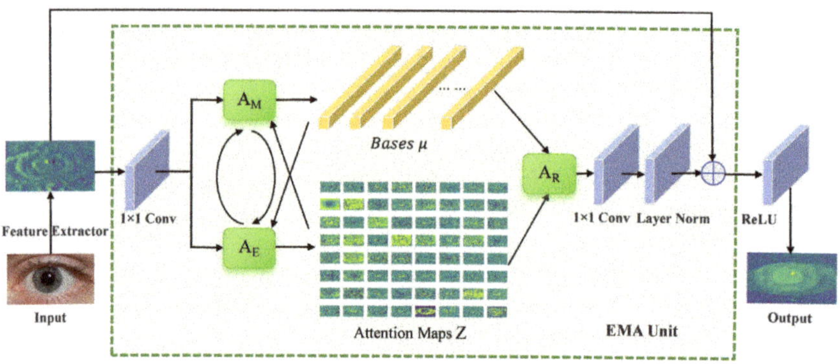

Figure 4. Overall structure of the EMA unit, where A_E and A_M execute alternately.

3.3. Dense Subtraction Module

In the classic U-shaped segmentation architecture, various feature levels undergo gradual fusion within the decoder via element-wise addition or concatenation. Nonetheless, these conventional operations often lead to substantial redundancy, undermining the complementary relationship between features at disparate levels and resulting in inaccurate segmentation. To alleviate this problem, we propose a bottom-up dense subtraction module (DSM), where each subtractor module is designed based on the multi-scale subtraction unit (MSU) from M^2SNet [48]. Concretely, the subtractor employs all-one convolutional filters of size (1 × 1), (3 × 3), and (5 × 5) pixels to compute detail and structure differences based on pixel–pixel and regional patterns, defined as follows:

$$\begin{aligned} Subtractor(DS_h\,,\,DS_l) = Conv(& \\ \mid F(DS_h)_{1\times1} \ominus F(DS_l)_{1\times1} \mid +& \\ \mid F(DS_h)_{3\times3} \ominus F(DS_l)_{3\times3} \mid +& \\ \mid F(DS_h)_{5\times5} \ominus F(DS_l)_{5\times5} \mid),& \end{aligned} \tag{2}$$

where $\ominus$ is the element-wise subtraction operation, and $F(\cdot)_{n\times n}$ represents a convolutional filter of size $(n \times n)$ pixels. The subtractor captures complementary information from DS_h and DS_l, representing high-level and low-level semantic features, respectively, and emphasizes their differences, thereby enriching information for the decoder.

As depicted in Figure 3, to obtain high-level complementary information at multiple feature levels, we horizontally and vertically connect multiple subtractors to compute a series of differential features with varying orders and receptive fields. Subsequently, we aggregate scale-specific features DS_1^i and cross-scale differential features $DS_{n\neq1}^i$ between the corresponding and higher levels. This process can be expressed as follows:

$$DS_i^k = \sum_{j=k+1}^{7-i} \left| Subtractor(DS_{i-1}^j\,,DS_{i-1}^k) \right|, \tag{3}$$

where i and k represent the row and column indices of the feature maps in DSM, respectively. Notably, the channel number of each feature map is kept uniform. This process aids in further restructuring semantic information after feature extraction and aggregation from the original backbone, thereby facilitating efficient segmentation of the eye region.

3.4. Decoder with Eye Shape Priors

Finally, the results generated by the DSM are input into the decoder for feature enhancement and up-sampling. The decoder feature map D_i is obtained as

$$D_i = \sum_{k=1}^{6-i} DS_k^i + UP[Conv(D_{i+1})], \quad i = 2,3,4,5. \tag{4}$$

where $Conv$ denotes the convolution filter of size 3 × 3 pixels and UP represents the up-sampling operation.

Due to the fixed positional relationship between each modality imposed by the ocular region's physiological structure and functional requirements, a specific aggregation of eye features exists. Considering this property, we incorporate the convex hull [49] of the ocular region, design the eye shape within the decoder part to constrain the ocular region, and guide the model to focus more effectively on key regions of the eye image. As illustrated in Figure 5a, we integrate the boundary-guided prior into the high-resolution layer D_1. Initially, a convolution filter having size (3 × 3) pixels is applied to D_2, followed by a softmax operation to generate a binary supervised signal M. Subsequently, M undergoes a slicing operation to acquire a probability-valued feature map, which is then element-wise multiplied with the result of the up-sampling operation on D_2 to obtain D_1. The formulation is as follows:

$$M = softmax[Conv(D_2)], \tag{5}$$

$$\widetilde{D} = \sum_{i=1}^{5} DS_i^1 + UP[Conv(D_2)], \tag{6}$$

$$D_1 = \widetilde{D} \otimes UP(M\,[:,1,:,:]), \tag{7}$$

where $Conv$ denotes the convolution filter of size 3 × 3 pixels, UP represents the up-sampling operation, and the notation $\otimes$ signifies element-wise multiplication.

By augmenting visual features, the boundary-guided eye shape prior can furnish more accurate and reliable information in ocular image analysis. This constraint mechanism is anticipated to elevate performance and accuracy in processing and analyzing eye images, particularly in tasks necessitating refined modeling of visual attention regions.

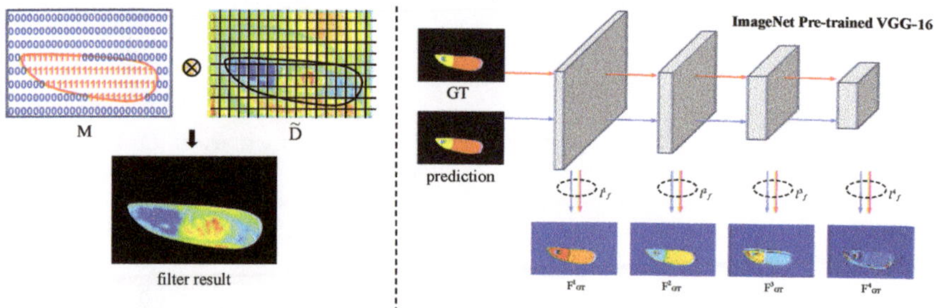

(a) **Boundary-guided Prior** (b) **Semantic-guided Prior**

Figure 5. An illustration of the proposed eye shape priors.

When observing a person's eyes, discernible features encompass the ocular regions and the positional relationships among the periocular, sclera, iris, and pupil areas. The pupil typically manifests as a black circular region positioned centrally within the eye. The iris, between the black pupil and the white sclera, presents as a colored circular region, while the sclera encompasses the iris. The periocular region, comprising the skin around the eyes, may exhibit various textures surrounding the above ocular modalities. These components collectively contribute to the distinct semantic features of each individual's eye. We aim to fine-tune a pre-trained VGG network to correct and enhance feature discrepancies between prediction results and ground truth progressively, from shallow to deep layers. This process, termed semantic-guided prior, captures the semantic relationships between different modalities by supervising the generation of 4-classes prediction results.

It is evident that low-level feature maps harbor abundant information, whereas high-level feature maps encapsulate more location information, as depicted in Figure 5b. We extract multi-scale features from the prediction and ground truth, respectively. Subsequently, the feature difference between them is computed as loss L_f:

$$L_f = l_f^1 + l_f^2 + l_f^3 + l_f^4, \quad (8)$$

where l_f^i is described as

$$l_f^i = \left\| F_P^i - F_G^i \right\|_2, \quad i = 1,2,3,4, \quad (9)$$

where F_P^i and F_G^i represent the feature maps extracted from prediction results and ground-truth labels at layer i from shallow to deep, respectively. Thus, l_f^i is calculated as the Euclidean distance (L2-Loss) between two feature maps at the same level.

3.5. Training Objectives

During the training process, we utilize three loss functions to optimize the entire model: boundary-guided prior loss, semantic-guided prior loss, and regular semantic segmentation loss. Specifically, for the boundary-guided prior loss, we employ a combination of cross-entropy loss [50] and dice loss [51] for joint optimization to learn the ocular masks of the eye regions. Mathematically, it is formulated as L_B:

$$L_B = \alpha \cdot L_{CE}^b + \beta \cdot L_{Dice}^b. \quad (10)$$

The semantic-guided prior loss is expressed as L_f, as described in Section 3.4. For the regular semantic segmentation loss L_S, we employ structure loss, consisting of cross-entropy loss and IoU loss, to learn multi-modal (4-classes) ocular segmentation results. Mathematically, the function of L_S is formulated as

$$L_S = \delta \cdot (L^s_{IoU} + L^s_{CE}). \tag{11}$$

Overall, these loss functions are jointly optimized as follows:

$$L_{total} = L_B + L_S + \gamma \cdot L_f. \tag{12}$$

In the loss functions above, the terms α, β, γ, and δ are tunable hyperparameters. The L_{CE} and L_{Dice} terms are commonly employed in training models for semantic segmentation tasks. While the gradient calculation of L_{CE} is more intuitive, facilitating easier optimization, L_{Dice} effectively addresses pixel category imbalance, making it suitable for our eye images. Additionally, the L_{IoU} loss aids in suppressing false positives by quantifying the intersection-over-union ratio between the prediction masks and the ground-truth masks.

4. Experimental Settings

This section outlines the experimental setup for the ocular segmentation task. We commence by introducing the dataset collected and annotated for this purpose. Subsequently, we describe the performance metrics utilized and discuss recent state-of-the-art baseline methods for comparative evaluation. Finally, we provide detailed insights into implementing the proposed method and any reproduced methods used in the study.

4.1. Datasets

We are dedicated to constructing comprehensive and accurate datasets to address the existing scarcity data, enabling the model to perform effectively across various real-world application scenarios. Our experiments gathered five standard datasets, each potentially containing different ocular modalities and image qualities. For instance, MOBIUS is a dataset of low quality, encompassing annotations for all four required modalities, whereas SBVPI is of high quality but only includes sclera and periocular modalities. The specifics of these datasets are outlined in Table 2; each of them is divided into two subsets, where 80% of the images are randomly selected for training and the remaining 20% for testing. We augmented the annotations based on the original datasets, ensuring the availability of all necessary annotations for experimental training, as depicted in Figure 6.

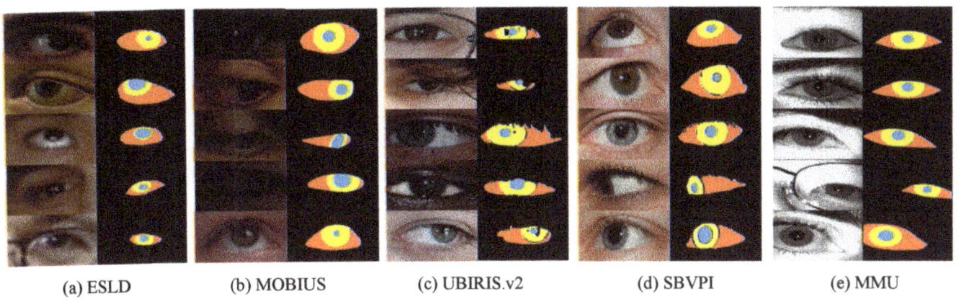

Figure 6. Example images and corresponding ground-truth segmentation masks of five datasets.

Table 2. Summary of the datasets used in our method.

Subset	Spectrum	Quality	Images	Training Set	Testing Set	Input Size	Original	Supplement
ESLD [52]	VIS	low	2353	1882	471	256 × 128	S/I/P/PO	-
MOBIUS [53]	VIS	low	3500	2800	700	288 × 160	S/I/P/PO	-
UBIRIS.v2 [54]	VIS	low	919	735	184	288 × 160	I	S/P/PO
SBVPI [11]	VIS	high	1233	986	247	288 × 160	S/PO	I/P
MMU [55]	NIR	low	993	794	199	288 × 160	-	S/I/P/PO

S = Sclera, I = Iris, P = Pupil, PO = Periocular (background), NIR = Near-infrared, VIS = Visible light.

It is important to note that within these five datasets in Figure 6, (a), (b), and (e) are categorized under coarse labeling, while (c) and (d) fall under elaborate labeling. Coarse labeling provides complete information without noise, simulating real-world scenarios where labeling may lack detail and comprise only basic structural information. By incorporating these coarse annotations, we aim to enhance the model's robustness, enabling it to handle better challenges, such as missing or incomplete annotations that may arise in real-world environments. In contrast, elaborate annotations prioritize offering high-quality and accurate information, potentially including noise, occlusions, or other complexities, to ensure the model receives adequate guidance when learning crucial features. This is particularly crucial for tasks demanding high data accuracy, such as medical image recognition, where capturing subtle structures accurately is paramount. By leveraging both coarse and elaborate annotations in our experiments, we seek to further enhance the model's ability to handle diverse modalities, balance its performance across different annotation levels, and enable it to adapt flexibly to various application scenarios. The relevant information for each dataset is as follows:

ESLD [52] is a multi-type ocular structure dataset comprising ocular images captured by standard cameras under natural lighting conditions and synthetic ocular images. The dataset is obtained through three primary methods: (i) capturing facial images of users during computer usage; (ii) obtaining facial images from public datasets captured with standard cameras under natural lighting conditions; (iii) generating synthetic eye images using the UnityEye software (https://www.cl.cam.ac.uk/research/rainbow/projects/unityeyes/tutorial.html (accessed on 16 May 2024)). These acquisition methods yielded 1386, 804, and 1600 eye images. Subsequently, 40 feature points within the ocular region are annotated on the original images, and ocular images of varying sizes are normalized to dimensions of 256×128 pixels. This dataset serves as valuable support for researchers investigating changes in users' emotional and psychological states through the analysis of ocular images. The ground-truth iris/sclera/pupil/periocular segmentation masks were manually labeled by the dataset owner.

MOBIUS [53] was developed for mobile ocular biometrics in uncontrolled environments. It comprises 16,717 RGB images of 200 eyes from 100 Caucasian subjects, with an image resolution of 3000×1700 pixels. Images in the dataset were captured under various gaze directions (left, right, straight, and up) using three different mobile phones, i.e., Sony Xperia Z5 Compact (made by Sony, in Tokyo, Japan), Apple iPhone 6s (made by Apple Inc., in Cupertino, CA, USA), and Xiaomi Pocophone F1 (made by Xiaomi, in Beijing, China), resulting in considerable variability in image quality. We utilize a subset of this dataset specifically for ocular segmentation research, where annotations for the four modalities were manually created by the dataset owner.

UBIRIS.v2 [54] was originally collected for less-constrained iris recognition. It includes 11,102 RGB images from 261 subjects captured on the move and at a distance with a Canon EOS 5D camera (made by Canon Inc., in Tokyo, Japan). In the experiment, we utilize the subset from the NICE. I competition [29], where each image was manually labeled with iris mask. We also manually annotated the ground-truth masks of sclera, pupil, and periocular regions.

SBVPI [11] is a high-quality ocular dataset tailored for sclera recognition, but it is also suitable for iris and periocular recognition research. It consists of 1858 RGB images of 110 eyes from 55 Caucasian subjects, captured with a DSLR camera in a controlled laboratory setting, with a resolution of 3000×1700 pixels. Similar to MOBIUS, images in SBVPI were captured under four different gaze directions (left, right, straight, and up). We employ a subset of this dataset for our experiments, and manually annotate the iris and pupil masks for each image based on the sclera and periocular segmentation annotations previously provided by the dataset owner. Notably, the image quality in SBVPI is substantially higher than that of all other datasets.

MMU [55] is provided by the Malaysian Multimedia University and captured under near-infrared light conditions. The dataset comprises two subsets, MMU1 and MMU2, categorized based on noise exposure and image quality. MMU1 contains 450 iris images with less noise, while MMU2 contains 995 images captured at a distance, with a 320×238 pixels resolution. These images exhibit various types of noise, such as eyelashes, eyelids, occlusions, specular reflections, uneven lighting, nonlinear deformation, and low contrast. We manually labeled a subset with ground-truth iris/sclera/pupil/periocular segmentation masks for our experiments.

Our experimental design aimed to ensure the model's robust performance across a wide range of data qualities and complexities. This comprehensive evaluation validates the model's efficacy and adaptability in real-world applications, enabling it to be generalizable and handle data with diverse modalities and annotation levels.

4.2. Evaluation Metrics

To measure the performance of multi-modal ocular segmentation, we compute the Precision (P), Recall (R), F_1-score (F_1), Intersection over Union (IoU), and Dice score (Dice) for each modality, respectively, and then take the mean value of all modalities as the whole evaluation metrics. The single-modal performance metrics are defined as follows:

- Precision (P): It measures the proportion of correctly predicted pixels to the total number of predicted pixels, calculated as $\frac{TP}{TP+FP}$.
- Recall (R): It measures the proportion of correctly predicted pixels relative to the total number of ground-truth pixels, formulated as $\frac{TP}{TP+FN}$.
- F_1-score (F_1): Defined as the harmonic mean between precision and recall, given by $2 \cdot \frac{P \cdot R}{P+R}$. It is a balance metric between precision and recall and is considered as the prior metric for comparing different methods.
- Intersection over Union (IoU): Represents the ratio between (i) the size of the intersection of the predicted and ground-truth regions and the size of their union, calculated as (ii) $\frac{TP}{TP+FN+FP}$.
- Dice score (Dice): Another measure of the overlap between predicted results and ground-truth labels, commonly used in segmentation tasks. It is calculated as $\frac{2TP}{2TP+FN+FP}$.

TP represents the number of true positives, indicating correctly predicted pixels; *FP* stands for false positives, representing background pixels incorrectly predicted as pixels; and *FN* denotes false negatives, indicating pixels incorrectly predicted as background pixels. These metrics are bounded in 0 and 1, where a higher value indicates a better segmentation result. In addition, the multi-class receiver operating characteristic (ROC) and precision–recall (PR) curves are generated by varying the decision threshold to yield different binary segmentation masks, thereby evaluating the overall segmentation performance.

4.3. Implementation Details

The proposed model is implemented in PyTorch (Version: 1.8.0) and initialized with the Efficientnetv2 [22] pretrained on ImageNet. Throughout the experiment, we standardized the image resolutions of different datasets to a fixed size using bilinear interpolation, as outlined in Table 2, to facilitate batch processing. We employed the SGD optimizer to optimize our model, with a batch size of 8, momentum of 0.9, and weight decay of 1×10^{-4}. Our learning rate policy followed the polynomial decay, where the learning rate is multiplied by $(1 - \frac{iter}{max\_iter})^{power}$ with the power of 0.9. We set the initial learning rate to 0.1 and the maximum iteration to 30,000. The hyperparameters α, β, γ, and δ were configured to 1, 1, 0.1, and 1, respectively. All experiments were conducted using a single NVIDIA RTX 3090 GPU (made by NVIDIA Corporation, in Santa Clara, CA, USA).

5. Experimental Results

5.1. Comparison with State-of-the-Art

In this section, we assess the performance of multi-modal ocular segmentation on the collected datasets. To ensure a fair comparison, we evaluate not only classical CNN-based semantic segmentation models such as U-Net [21], DeepLabv3+ [56], and transformer-based methods like TransUNet [57] but also recent ocular segmentation methods like EyeSeg [40] and Eye-UNet [17]. As the base model of our proposed OcularSeg, M^{2}SNet [48] is also used for comparison. We retrain these baseline methods on the same training datasets used for our proposed method. As outlined in Section 4.3, we utilized the proposed method to predict segmentation results for four categories, subsequently computing Precision, Recall, F1, IoU, and Dice metrics for different methods. The comparison results are presented in Table 3.

Table 3. Comparison of the proposed OcularSeg method with existing methods on five datasets. The bold values represent the best performances.

Dataset	Method	Precision (%) ↑	Recall (%) ↑	F_1(%) ↑	IoU (%) ↑	Dice(%) ↑
ESLD	U-Net [21]	87.3481	83.8864	85.9616	76.2965	82.8186
	DeepLabv3+ [56]	87.6251	86.5164	87.0468	77.8608	83.6691
	TransUNet [57]	**87.8762**	86.3939	87.1206	77.9557	84.3116
	M^{2}SNet [48]	87.3153	87.6695	87.4766	78.4824	84.6058
	EyeSeg [40]	87.2658	84.0316	85.5464	75.7187	82.0045
	Eye-UNet [17]	87.6377	86.8893	87.2518	78.1396	84.3350
	OcularSeg (ours)	87.4155	**88.2361**	**87.8214**	**78.9869**	**84.9862**
MOBIUS	U-Net [21]	91.5314	91.1735	91.3513	84.6038	90.3752
	DeepLabv3+ [56]	90.7674	92.5963	91.6383	84.9759	90.6610
	TransUNet [57]	**92.2497**	90.7409	91.4758	84.7980	90.3963
	M^{2}SNet [48]	92.1401	91.8056	91.9716	85.5650	90.9405
	EyeSeg [40]	90.6816	88.9764	89.8077	82.1804	88.2383
	Eye-UNet [17]	92.2172	90.3344	91.2222	84.2480	89.6927
	OcularSeg (ours)	92.1548	**92.6767**	**92.4134**	**86.2826**	**91.4060**
UBIRIS.v2	U-Net [21]	92.2269	93.5845	92.8452	87.0086	90.1322
	DeepLabv3+ [56]	92.7268	93.8245	93.2649	87.6711	90.8170
	TransUNet [57]	93.2628	93.7707	93.5077	88.0714	91.2042
	M^{2}SNet [48]	91.8245	**95.0000**	93.3620	87.8614	91.0248
	EyeSeg [40]	91.4751	93.7088	92.5234	86.4000	89.2864
	Eye-UNet [17]	92.9044	93.9907	93.4320	87.9459	90.7327
	OcularSeg (ours)	**94.2200**	93.1717	**93.6832**	**88.3299**	**91.3085**
SBVPI	U-Net [21]	95.4764	96.8177	96.1145	92.5744	95.6842
	DeepLabv3+ [56]	95.2275	97.1899	96.1734	92.6796	95.7601
	TransUNet [57]	95.9070	96.9274	96.4031	93.0974	96.0489
	M^{2}SNet [48]	95.8556	96.7834	96.2979	92.9049	95.8969
	EyeSeg [40]	94.6019	96.2444	95.3999	91.2714	94.7392
	Eye-UNet [17]	**96.4776**	95.7972	96.1274	92.5865	95.7257
	OcularSeg (ours)	95.2585	**97.7663**	**96.4817**	**93.2409**	**96.1035**
MMU	U-Net [21]	95.2909	95.4245	95.3484	91.2482	95.1574
	DeepLabv3+ [56]	95.0387	95.6079	95.2998	91.1421	95.1575
	TransUNet [57]	96.0650	94.7250	95.3441	91.2222	95.1254
	M^{2}SNet [48]	95.3193	94.1703	94.6143	89.9287	94.3720
	EyeSeg [40]	**96.2267**	93.5702	94.8473	90.3489	94.6760
	Eye-UNet [17]	93.4111	95.0539	94.2011	89.3189	94.0891
	OcularSeg (ours)	95.2293	**95.9017**	**95.5616**	**91.6152**	**95.4080**

It can be seen that our proposed method demonstrates the best performance in most metrics across all datasets, particularly low-quality ones. However, it is noteworthy that our method does not consistently achieve optimality in terms of the Precision metric. Our analysis indicates that this phenomenon may arise due to the model's tendency to become more aggressive in predicting positive (target) categories during iteration, thereby increasing false positives. Several specific issues contribute to this behavior, including the following: (i) Imbalanced category distribution: In scenarios where the ocular region occupies a relatively small portion of the image compared to background categories, the model may overpredict the target category to ensure a higher Recall. Consequently, this behavior can increase false positives in the background, resulting in lower Precision. (ii) Model prediction bias: Semantic segmentation models are often biased toward larger objects or more prominent image regions. This bias can cause the model to overpredict target categories, consequently increasing Recall. However, due to this bias, some predictions may lack accuracy, leading to lower Precision. (iii) The trade-off between Recall and Precision: A trade-off exists between Recall and Precision, wherein increasing Recall typically leads to a decrease in Precision and vice versa. This trade-off reflects the model's inherent balance between accurately capturing all relevant instances of the target category (Recall) and minimizing false positives (Precision). To comprehensively evaluate the model's performance, it is essential to consider multiple metrics rather than focusing solely on a single metric. Evaluating the model using a combination of metrics provides a more holistic understanding of its performance across various aspects.

Furthermore, we conducted a detailed analysis of the OcularSeg performance by examining the receiver operating characteristic (ROC) and precision–recall (PR) curves for each category on the MOBIUS dataset, as illustrated in Figure 7. In the ROC curves depicted in Figure 7a, we observed that our proposed method accurately predicts the positive labels in each category after careful training. Comparatively, the precision–recall curves in Figure 7b are more sensitive to the unbalanced categories, making them particularly suitable for our ocular segmentation task and demonstrating the superiority of our algorithm more intuitively. Additionally, the area-under-the-curve (AUC) values, represented as the area in the figure, serve as quantitative indicators of the model's superior predictive performance. Among these, the micro-average (https://sklearn-evaluation.ploomber.io/en/latest/classification/micro_macro.html (accessed on 16 May 2024)) performs excellently in addressing category imbalance and effectively reflects the overall performance, especially when the sample size of some categories substantially outweighs others. Conversely, the macro-average is suitable for scenarios where each category is treated equally and remains unaffected by category imbalance.

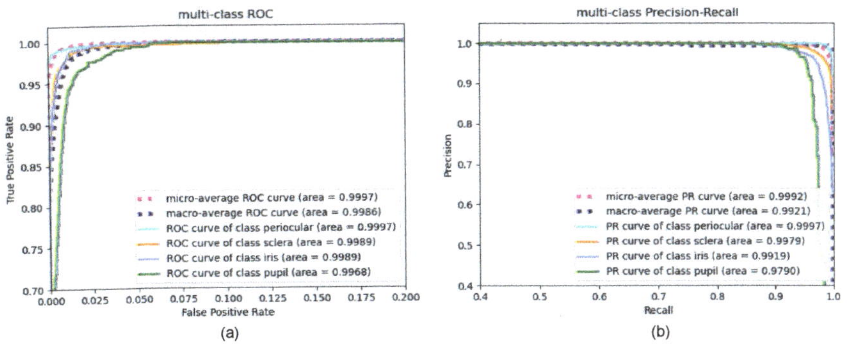

Figure 7. (**a**) Receiver operating characteristic (ROC) and (**b**) precision–recall (PR) curves generated by our proposed method, OcularSeg, for each class on the MOBIUS dataset.

5.2. *Qualitative Evaluation*

Here, a qualitative evaluation is performed to further analyze the proposed model. To this end, we select several representative and challenging eye images from all datasets for experiments, and different segmentation models are used for comparisons. The visualization results are shown in Figure 8. It can be seen that our OcularSeg model outperforms other baseline models in accurately segmenting four ocular modalities across the majority of samples. Nevertheless, we acknowledge that there is still room for improvement in existing methods when dealing with lower-quality datasets such as the ESLD and MOBIUS. This could be attributed to the presence of serious noise interference in the dataset such as blur, occlusions, specular reflection, and uneven illumination, coupled with potential errors in annotations.

In non-constrained scenarios, apart from normally captured eye images, a variety of variables such as changes in head pose, errors in eye movement tracking, or illumination variations often result in the occurrence of almost closed, fully closed, or misaligned eyes in the captured images. These extreme cases are of significant interest to the research community as they reflect the robustness of the model in real-world applications. For this reason, we select several representative samples from the low-quality UBIRIS.v2 [54] dataset for testing. Figure 9 shows their multi-modal ocular segmentation results using the proposed OcularSeg. As can be seen, our model is still able to accurately segment the multi-modal ocular structures in the face of these adverse factors. Therefore, visual results demonstrate that the opening and closing state or position of the eyes does not significantly affect the accuracy of our model in most cases.

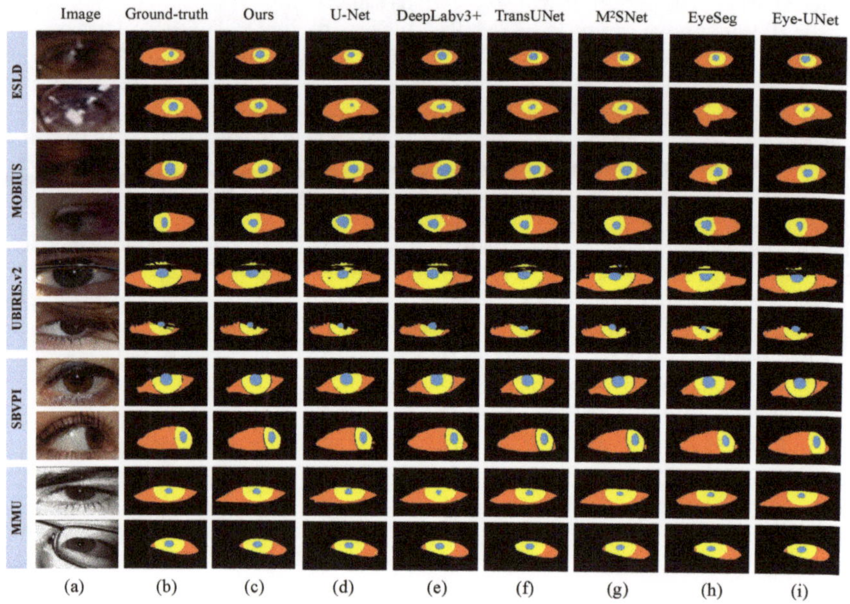

Figure 8. Multi-modal ocular segmentation results of challenging samples on multiple datasets. (**a**) Original images, (**b**) Ground-truth labels, (**c**) OcularSeg (ours), (**d**) U-Net, (**e**) DeepLabv3+, (**f**) TransUNet, (**g**) M^2SNet, (**h**) EyeSeg, (**i**) Eye-UNet.

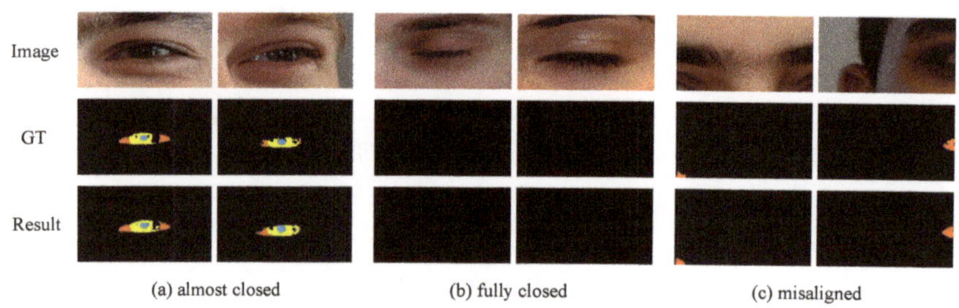

Figure 9. Multi-modal ocular segmentation results of extreme cases using the proposed OcularSeg, including (**a**) almost closed eye images, (**b**) fully closed eye images, and (**c**) misaligned eye images, which are from the UBIRIS.v2 [54] dataset.

5.3. Comparison with Single-Modal Segmentation Techniques

In this section, we compare the performance of the multi-modal OcularSeg model to the performance of the OcularSeg model trained only for a single modal by leveraging the low-quality ESLD and MOBIUS datasets. The single-modal OcularSeg model is trained by removing two eye shape priors and modifying the final number of segmentation categories to two (modality and background). As a result, both OcularSeg variants have approximately the same set of parameters. The experimental results are shown in Tables 4 and 5.

As we can see from the results, the multi-modal OcularSeg model consistently outperforms the single-modal OcularSeg model in terms of F_1, IoU, and Dice metrics across different datasets for segmenting each individual modality. For example, on the ESLD dataset, the multi-modal OcularSeg model achieves the F_1 metric improvements by 0.0303%, 0.8639%, 0.8884%, and 1.2606%, respectively, for the periocular, sclera, iris, and pupil categories. Besides, corresponding improvements on the MOBIUS dataset are 0.0615%, 0.5704%, 0.8595%, and 2.1062%, respectively. Figure 10 also visually shows the improvements of the multi-modal OcularSeg model over the single-modal OcularSeg model in terms of the IoU metric. These results suggest the potential advantages of multi-modal ocular segmentation in enhancing the performance of single-modal ocular segmentation.

Table 4. Comparison of multi-modal and single-modal segmentation results on ESLD with the proposed OcularSeg. The bold values represent the best performances.

Dataset	Category	Precision (%) ↑	Recall (%) ↑	F_1 (%) ↑	IoU (%) ↑	Dice (%) ↑
ESLD	Periocular (single-modal)	98.5216	**99.1404**	98.8300	97.6871	98.8114
	Periocular (multi-modal)	**98.9457**	98.7750	**98.8603**	**97.7462**	**98.8373**
	Sclera (single-modal)	**85.0790**	80.9840	82.9810	70.9124	80.1791
	Sclera (multi-modal)	83.7979	**83.8919**	**83.8449**	**72.1836**	**81.1347**
	Iris (single-modal)	**88.0152**	85.9134	86.9516	76.9154	84.1478
	Iris (multi-modal)	86.7830	**88.9230**	**87.8400**	**78.3167**	**85.1080**
	Pupil (single-modal)	**80.7008**	78.2368	79.4497	65.9059	73.5095
	Pupil (multi-modal)	80.1353	**81.3545**	**80.7403**	**67.7012**	**74.8650**

Table 5. Comparison of multi-modal and single-modal segmentation results on MOBIUS with the proposed OcularSeg. The bold values represent the best performances.

Dataset	Category	Precision (%) ↑	Recall (%) ↑	F_1 (%) ↑	IoU (%) ↑	Dice (%) ↑
MOBIUS	Periocular (single-modal)	98.8133	**99.181**	98.9968	98.0135	98.9827
	Periocular (multi-modal)	**99.0999**	99.0168	**99.0583**	**98.1343**	**99.0455**
	Sclera (single-modal)	**93.9194**	91.9747	92.9369	86.8057	92.3554
	Sclera (multi-modal)	93.5948	**93.4199**	**93.5073**	**87.8063**	**92.9326**
	Iris (single-modal)	91.0376	90.8156	90.9265	83.3625	89.7834
	Iris (multi-modal)	**91.4323**	**92.1424**	**91.7860**	**84.8189**	**90.6959**
	Pupil (single-modal)	**84.5237**	81.9092	83.1959	71.2269	80.7107
	Pupil (multi-modal)	84.4922	**86.1277**	**85.3021**	**74.3711**	**82.9499**

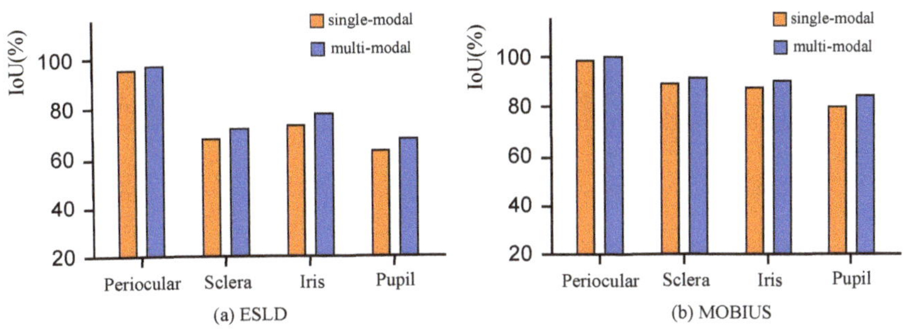

Figure 10. Performance comparison of single-modal and multi-modal segmentation on (**a**) ESLD and (**b**) MOBIUS datasets with the proposed OcularSeg.

For the observed improvements in performance, we analyze that the reason may be as follows: (1) The richer information and stronger complementary provided by multi-modal segmentation enable the model to robustly resist the interference of noise frequently encountered in single-modal scenarios. (2) Multi-modal segmentation alleviates the problem of foreground–background category imbalance during segmentation. These experimental findings further highlight the advantages of our multi-modal ocular segmentation model and offer valuable insights for enhancing single-modal segmentation methods.

5.4. Cross-Domain and Cross-Spectrum Evaluation

Addressing the generalization challenge of multi-modal ocular segmentation, we endeavor to assess performance across domains and spectral ranges using the datasets provided. Leveraging the diversity of label annotations in these datasets, we conduct a cross-domain evaluation using UBIRIS.v2 and SBVPI for visible light scenarios. At the same time, we utilize MOBIUS and MMU datasets for the cross-spectral problem. The experimental results are summarized in Tables 6 and 7.

Table 6. Cross-domain performance comparison on UBIRIS.v2 and SBVPI.

Training	Testing	Precision (%) ↑	Recall (%) ↑	F_1 (%) ↑	IoU (%) ↑	Dice (%) ↑
UBIRIS.v2	SBVPI	93.4298	88.2239	90.5547	83.1643	90.4116
SBVPI	UBIRIS.v2	79.7851	90.7899	83.7912	73.5187	80.2446

Table 7. Cross-spectral performance comparison on MOBIUS and MMU.

Training	Testing	Precision (%) ↑	Recall (%) ↑	F_1 (%) ↑	IoU (%) ↑	Dice (%) ↑
MOBIUS	MMU	93.6960	89.0114	91.0423	84.3484	90.7386
MMU	MOBIUS	84.7607	60.2717	66.2934	54.2809	62.6713

In evaluating visible light cross-domain performance, we assess the model's ability to generalize to a new domain by learning visible light features. This analysis aids in understanding the model's adaptability across diverse visible light datasets and offers valuable insights for real-world applications. As illustrated in Figure 11, the visualization highlights the model's robust generalization performance in the visible light domain. Notably, the model demonstrates effective transfer learning between the UBIRIS.v2 and SBVPI datasets, indicating its proficiency in capturing common visible light features. Consequently, the model achieves satisfactory segmentation across different data sources, bolstering the feasibility of ocular biometrics applications in varied visible light conditions.

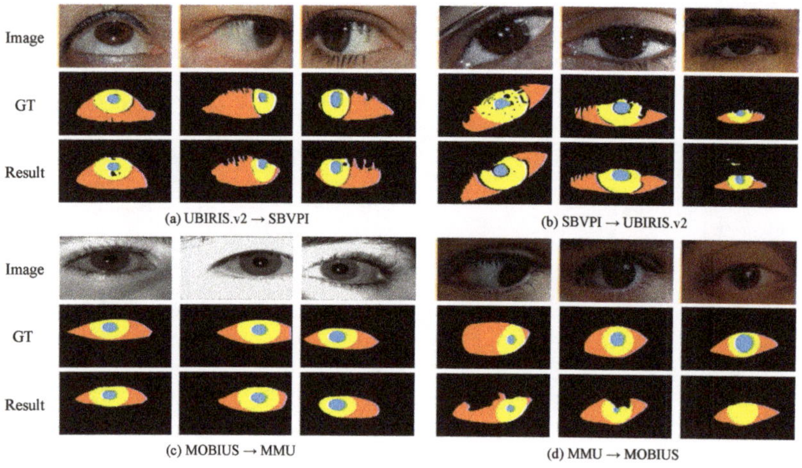

Figure 11. Visualization of cross-domain (**a**,**b**) and cross-spectral (**c**,**d**) segmentation results using the proposed OcularSeg.

The assessment of cross-spectral performance introduces additional complexities compared to cross-domain evaluation. In our experiments using MOBIUS for visible light and MMU for near-infrared light, we observed a disparity in performance. Specifically, the model exhibited better performance when generalized from the visible to the near-infrared spectrum, whereas the reverse, near-infrared to visible light generalization yielded comparatively lower results. This observation underscores the inherent challenges of adapting models to eye images captured across different spectral ranges.

Our experimental findings underscore the persistent challenges encountered in cross-domain and cross-spectral segmentation tasks. While we have made strides in achieving favorable outcomes on specific datasets, extending model performance to diverse conditions remains intricate. These challenges stem from fundamental differences in image features, resolutions, and lighting conditions inherent to each dataset, making accurate generalization across varied environments difficult. Consequently, achieving satisfactory performance on one dataset does not guarantee similar results on others. Moreover, addressing the cross-spectral problem amplifies the complexity of model adaptation to diverse spectral bands. Effectively coping with this challenge necessitates the model's sensitivity and adaptability to comprehend and capture the distinct information in different spectral ranges. Successfully navigating these complexities demands a deeper understanding of the intricate relationships between specific spectral bands and robust adaptation strategies.

5.5. Computational Complexity Analysis

In this section, we analyze the computational complexity of the proposed model during both the training and testing phases. First, we compare the convergence speed and performance of different segmentation models in the training. Therefore, we draw their corresponding IoU curves (Figure 12a) and loss curves (Figure 12b) with respect to the epochs, which are generated on the validation set and training set of the ESLD dataset, respectively. It should be noted that the original training set is partitioned into a final validation set comprising 10% of the data and a final training set consisting of the remaining 90% during the model development.

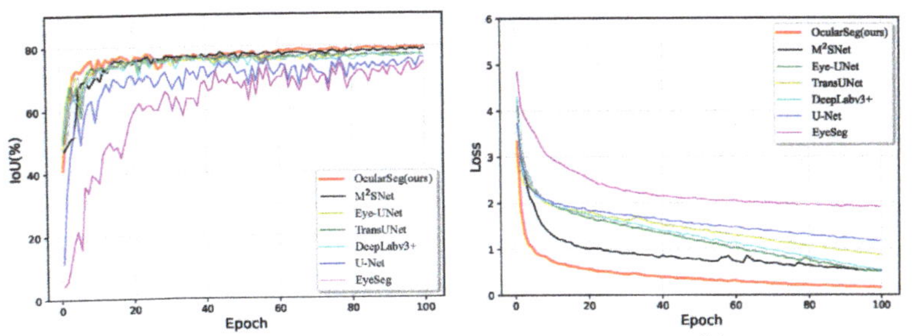

(a) (b)

Figure 12. IoU curves (**a**) and loss curves (**b**) of different segmentation models.

By observing the overall trend of the curves, we have the following findings: (1) For all methods, the IoU metric gradually increases while the loss value decreases over time until they all reach stability. (2) Our OcularSeg model exhibits the fastest convergence speed at the initial stages and maintains the highest performance throughout. Hence, we can conclude that compared to several baselines, our OcularSeg model does not impose a heavier training burden; instead, it demonstrates higher accuracy in most of the training time.

Secondly, we evaluate the computational complexity of different segmentation models in the testing. The model parameter amount, FLOPs, running time, and frames per second (FPS) are calculated in the consistent simulation environment, where the latter three metrics are with respect to the input of 288×160 pixels. From the results in Table 8, we can observe that (1) our OcularSeg model exhibits a more compact computational load regarding model parameters than other majority methods and (2) our OcularSeg model can process 24.08 FPS and requires 6.55 GFLOPs and 41.53 ms to process a single image. Although there are some gaps between our method and the most simplified one regarding inference efficiency, it is crucial to note that while the most simplified method may be computationally more efficient, it sacrifices segmentation accuracy. Overall, thanks to the strategies employed for optimizing the model structure, such as lightweight feature extraction and cross-layer connections in DSM, our OcularSeg model achieves a good balance between performance and efficiency, rendering it feasible for real-time biometric applications.

Table 8. Computational complexity analysis. The bold and underlined values represent the best and second-best performances, respectively.

Metrics	OcularSeg (Ours)	U-Net [21]	DeepLabv3+ [56]	TransUNet [57]	M^2SNet [48]	EyeSeg [40]	Eye-UNet [17]
Params (M) ↓	<u>22.65</u>	39.40	59.34	93.19	27.7	**0.25**	31.04
FLOPs (G) ↓	<u>6.55</u>	61.70	18.76	128.68	6.92	**3.28**	41.92
Runtime (ms) ↓	41.53	**10.70**	34.66	48.57	27.74	<u>11.79</u>	12.95
FPS ↑	24.08	**93.46**	28.85	20.59	36.05	<u>84.82</u>	77.22

5.6. Ablation Study

We refine our research through ablation studies conducted on the challenging ESLD [52] dataset to validate the effectiveness of the core components of our method. The experimental results are detailed in Table 9, where the symbol ✓ denotes the inclusion of the module, whereas ✗ indicates its absence. Among the evaluation metrics, Precision, Recall, and F_1 are notably influenced by data imbalance. Therefore, we prioritize IoU and Dice for their ability to comprehensively and accurately capture the degree of overlap between prediction results and ground truth. Starting with Efficientnetv2 as the baseline, with simple subtraction cells as setting a, we analyze the contribution of each component in detail.

Table 9. Ablation experiments of the four parts in our proposed method. Here, Prior1 represents the boundary-guided prior and Prior2 is the semantic-guided prior. The bold values represent the best performances.

Settings	EMA	DSM	Prior1	Prior2	Precision (%) ↑	Recall (%) ↑	F_1 (%) ↑	IoU (%) ↑	Dice (%) ↑
a	✗	✗	✗	✗	85.9952	85.9889	85.6497	76.7358	82.5455
b	✓	✗	✗	✗	86.4852	87.9172	86.1581	76.9980	83.4262
c	✓	✓	✗	✗	85.8027	87.9969	86.7555	77.3918	84.3962
d	✓	✓	✓	✗	**88.2327**	86.8165	87.5091	78.5481	84.8176
e (ours)	✓	✓	✓	✓	87.4155	**88.2361**	**87.8214**	**78.9869**	**84.9862**

In setting b, we enhance the original baseline model by integrating the EMA algorithm, which aggregates the features of ocular modalities in the spatial domain after feature extraction. Incorporating this module yields gains of 0.26% and 0.88% on the evaluation metrics IoU and Dice, respectively. Moving to set c, we interconnect DSM across layers to accentuate feature disparities between adjacent layers, effectively mitigating the interference of redundant features. This enhancement encourages the model to extract richer semantic information, and the quantitative metrics in the experimental results corroborate the effectiveness of this component, with improvements of 0.39% and 0.97% in IoU and Dice, respectively.

Finally, in settings d and e, the position, shape, and internal topological relationship among modalities are supervised by the boundary-guided prior and the semantic-guided prior. Compared with the previous modules, the eye shape prior proves more effective in performance enhancement, underscoring the efficacy of our proposed eye shape prior constraints. Especially, in d, we introduce the convex hull as an extra boundary supervision. This step is akin to using manually annotated labels, providing more accurate guidance for the ocular boundary by leveraging external forces. Compared to internal annotations of the eye, convex hull is often smoother and relatively accurate. Therefore, by utilizing such prior knowledge for auxiliary supervision, precise boundary information of the target is provided, enabling the model to better understand the spatial location and shape of the ocular during learning. Additionally, this prior weakens noise around the ocular, helping to reduce errors and noise in prediction results, thus enhancing the accuracy and generalization capability of the segmentation model. Overall, this represents a global optimization, whereas improvements in other modules often only optimizes specific feature representations locally, leading to limited performance gains. Quantitative results also demonstrate the effectiveness of the boundary-guided prior in segmentation performance compared to other modules.

6. Conclusions and Future Work

This study investigates the multi-modal ocular segmentation task in non-constrained scenarios, including near-infrared and visible light illumination conditions. To tackle this challenge comprehensively, we have annotated multiple challenging datasets and developed an effective segmentation model (OcularSeg). Our model encompasses lightweight feature extraction, feature aggregation, bottom-up dense connection layers, and guidance from eye shape priors, ultimately achieving state-of-the-art performance. We particularly emphasize performance enhancement compared to single-modal approaches and explore feasibility issues in cross-domain and cross-spectral contexts.

Future research directions will prioritize further optimization of the model to enhance its generalization ability and adaptability, especially for ocular images spanning different domains and spectral ranges. We will introduce more advanced domain adaptation techniques and inter-domain normalization methods, and enhance the model's ability to perceive spectral differences. Despite the progress made, there remains a pressing need to expand the size of available datasets, which currently hampers the training of more sophisticated segmentation models. Additionally, we will focus on algorithm optimization to improve efficiency and actively explore hardware acceleration solutions to ensure real-time inference.

Author Contributions: Conceptualization, Y.Z. and C.W.; methodology, Y.Z.; software, Y.Z.; validation, H.L.; formal analysis, Y.Z. and X.S.; investigation, C.W. and H.L.; resources, C.W.; data curation, Y.Z. and H.L.; writing—original draft preparation, Y.Z.; writing—review and editing, C.W., Q.T. and G.Z.; visualization, Y.Z. and X.S.; supervision, C.W.; project administration, C.W.; funding acquisition, C.W. All authors have read and agreed to the published version of the manuscript.

Funding: This research was funded by the National Natural Science Foundation of China (62106015), the Beijing Natural Science Foundation (4242018), the Young Elite Scientist Sponsorship Program by BAST (BYESS2023130), and the Pyramid Talent Training Project of BUCEA (JDYC20220819).

Data Availability Statement: The UBIRIS.v2 dataset is publicly available at http://iris.di.ubi.pt/ubiris2.html (accessed on 16 May 2024). The SBVPI and MOBIUS datasets are publicly available at https://sclera.fri.uni-lj.si/datasets.html (accessed on 16 May 2024). The ESLD dataset is publicly available at http://www.cjig.cn//html/jig/2022/8/20220802.htm (accessed on 16 May 2024). The MMU dataset is publicly available at https://www.kaggle.com/datasets/naureenmohammad/mmu-iris-dataset (accessed on 16 May 2024). Our code and ocular segmentation annotations for UBIRIS.v2, SBVPI, and MMU are publicly available via https://github.com/koala0623/OcularSeg (accessed on 16 May 2024).

Conflicts of Interest: The authors declare no conflicts of interest.

References

1. Nguyen, K.; Proença, H.; Alonso-Fernandez, F. Deep Learning for Iris Recognition: A Survey. *ACM Comput. Surv.* **2024**, *56*, 1–35. [CrossRef]
2. Evangeline, D.; Parkavi, A.; Bhutaki, R.; Jhawar, S.; Pujitha, M.S. Person Identification using Periocular Region. In Proceedings of the 2024 International Conference on Intelligent and Innovative Technologies in Computing, Electrical and Electronics (IITCEE), Bangalore, India, 24–25 January 2024; pp. 1–6. [CrossRef]
3. Li, H.; Wang, C.; Zhao, G.; He, Z.; Wang, Y.; Sun, Z. Sclera-TransFuse: Fusing Swin Transformer and CNN for Accurate Sclera Segmentation. In Proceedings of the 2023 IEEE International Joint Conference on Biometrics (IJCB), Ljubljana, Slovenia, 25–28 September 2023; pp. 1–8. [CrossRef]

4. Nigam, I.; Vatsa, M.; Singh, R. Ocular biometrics: A survey of modalities and fusion approaches. *Inf. Fusion* **2015**, *26*, 1–35. [CrossRef]
5. Umer, S.; Sardar, A.; Dhara, B.C.; Rout, R.K.; Pandey, H.M. Person identification using fusion of iris and periocular deep features. *Neural Netw.* **2020**, *122*, 407–419. [CrossRef] [PubMed]
6. Gragnaniello, D.; Poggi, G.; Sansone, C.; Verdoliva, L. Using iris and sclera for detection and classification of contact lenses. *Pattern Recognit. Lett.* **2016**, *82*, 251–257. [CrossRef]
7. Oh, K.; Oh, B.S.; Toh, K.A.; Yau, W.Y.; Eng, H.L. Combining sclera and periocular features for multi-modal identity verification. *Neurocomputing* **2014**, *128*, 185–198. [CrossRef]
8. Xiong, J.; Zhang, Z.; Wang, C.; Cen, J.; Wang, Q.; Nie, J. Pupil localization algorithm based on lightweight convolutional neural network. *Vis. Comput.* **2024**, 1–17. [CrossRef]
9. He, Z.; Tan, T.; Sun, Z.; Qiu, X. Toward accurate and fast iris segmentation for iris biometrics. *IEEE Trans. Pattern Anal. Mach. Intell.* **2008**, *31*, 1670–1684.
10. Lucio, D.R.; Laroca, R.; Severo, E.; Britto, A.S.; Menotti, D. Fully convolutional networks and generative adversarial networks applied to sclera segmentation. In Proceedings of the 2018 IEEE International Conference on Biometrics Theory, Applications and Systems (BTAS), Redondo Beach, CA, USA, 22–25 October 2018; pp. 1–7.
11. Vitek, M.; Rot, P.; Štruc, V.; Peer, P. A comprehensive investigation into sclera biometrics: A novel dataset and performance study. *Neural Comput. Appl.* **2020**, *32*, 17941–17955. [CrossRef]
12. Wu, Z.; Rajendran, S.; van As, T.; Zimmermann, J.; Badrinarayanan, V.; Rabinovich, A. EyeNet: A multi-task network for off-axis eye gaze estimation and user understanding. *arXiv* **2019**, arXiv:1908.09060.
13. Perry, J.; Fernandez, A. Minenet: A dilated cnn for semantic segmentation of eye features. In Proceedings of the IEEE/CVF International Conference on Computer Vision Workshops (ICCVW), Seoul, Republic of Korea, 27–28 October 2019; pp. 3671–3676.
14. He, K.; Zhang, X.; Ren, S.; Sun, J. Deep Residual Learning for Image Recognition. In Proceedings of the IEEE Conference on Computer Vision and Pattern Recognition (CVPR), Las Vegas, NV, USA, 27–30 June 2016; pp. 770–778.
15. Chaudhary, A.K.; Kothari, R.; Acharya, M.; Dangi, S.; Nair, N.; Bailey, R.; Kanan, C.; Diaz, G.; Pelz, J.B. Ritnet: Real-time semantic segmentation of the eye for gaze tracking. In Proceedings of the IEEE/CVF International Conference on Computer Vision Workshops (ICCVW), Seoul, Republic of Korea, 27–28 October 2019; pp. 3698–3702.
16. Luo, B.; Shen, J.; Cheng, S.; Wang, Y.; Pantic, M. Shape constrained network for eye segmentation in the wild. In Proceedings of the IEEE/CVF Winter Conference on Applications of Computer Vision (WACV), Snowmass Village, CO, USA, 1–5 March 2020; pp. 1952–1960.
17. Wang, Y.; Wang, J.; Guo, P. Eye-UNet: A UNet-based network with attention mechanism for low-quality human eye image segmentation. *Signal Image Video Process.* **2023**, *17*, 1097–1103.
18. Chaudhary, A.K.; Gyawali, P.K.; Wang, L.; Pelz, J.B. Semi-supervised learning for eye image segmentation. In Proceedings of the ACM Symposium on Eye Tracking Research and Applications, Stuttgart, Germany, 25–29 May 2021; pp. 1–7.
19. Hassan, B.; Hassan, T.; Ahmed, R.; Werghi, N.; Dias, J. SIPFormer: Segmentation of Multiocular Biometric Traits With Transformers. *IEEE Trans. Instrum. Meas.* **2022**, *72*, 1–14. [CrossRef]
20. Garbin, S.J.; Shen, Y.; Schuetz, I.; Cavin, R.; Hughes, G.; Talathi, S.S. Openeds: Open eye dataset. *arXiv* **2019**, arXiv:1905.03702.
21. Ronneberger, O.; Fischer, P.; Brox, T. U-Net: Convolutional Networks for Biomedical Image Segmentation. In Proceedings of the International Conference on Medical Image Computing and Computer-assisted Intervention, Munich, Germany, 5–9 October 2015; Springer: Berlin/Heidelberg, Germany, 2015; pp. 234–241.
22. Tan, M.; Le, Q. Efficientnetv2: Smaller models and faster training. In Proceedings of the International Conference on Machine Learning (ICML), Virtual, 18–24 July 2021; pp. 10096–10106.
23. Li, X.; Zhong, Z.; Wu, J.; Yang, Y.; Lin, Z.; Liu, H. Expectation-maximization attention networks for semantic segmentation. In Proceedings of the IEEE/CVF International Conference on Computer Vision (ICCV), Seoul, Republic of Korea, 27 October–2 November 2019; pp. 9167–9176.
24. Han, K.; Wang, Y.; Chen, H.; Chen, X.; Guo, J.; Liu, Z.; Tang, Y.; Xiao, A.; Xu, C.; Xu, Y.; et al. A survey on vision transformer. *IEEE Trans. Pattern Anal. Mach. Intell.* **2023**, *45*, 87–110. [CrossRef]
25. Dempster, A.P.; Laird, N.M.; Rubin, D.B. Maximum likelihood from incomplete data via the EM algorithm. *J. R. Stat. Soc. Ser. B Methodol.* **1977**, *39*, 1–22. [CrossRef]
26. Rot, P.; Emeršič, Ž.; Struc, V.; Peer, P. Deep multi-class eye segmentation for ocular biometrics. In Proceedings of the IEEE International Work Conference on Bioinspired Intelligence (IWOBI), San Carlos, Costa Rica, 18–20 July 2018; pp. 1–8.
27. Badrinarayanan, V.; Kendall, A.; Cipolla, R. Segnet: A deep convolutional encoder-decoder architecture for image segmentation. *IEEE Trans. Pattern Anal. Mach. Intell.* **2017**, *39*, 2481–2495. [CrossRef] [PubMed]
28. Osorio-Roig, D.; Rathgeb, C.; Gomez-Barrero, M.; Morales-González, A.; Garea-Llano, E.; Busch, C. Visible wavelength iris segmentation: A multi-class approach using fully convolutional neuronal networks. In Proceedings of the International Conference of the Biometrics Special Interest Group (BIOSIG), Darmstadt, Germany, 26–28 September 2018; pp. 1–5.
29. Proença, H.; Alexandre, L.A. The NICE. I: noisy iris challenge evaluation-part I. In Proceedings of the IEEE International Conference on Biometrics: Theory, Applications, and Systems (BTAS), Crystal City, VA, USA, 27–29 September 2007; pp. 1–4.
30. Long, J.; Shelhamer, E.; Darrell, T. Fully convolutional networks for semantic segmentation. In Proceedings of the IEEE Conference on Computer Vision and Pattern Recognition (CVPR), Boston, MA, USA , 7–12 June 2015; pp. 3431–3440.

31. Boutros, F.; Damer, N.; Kirchbuchner, F.; Kuijper, A. Eye-mms: Miniature multi-scale segmentation network of key eye-regions in embedded applications. In Proceedings of the IEEE/CVF International Conference on Computer Vision Workshops (ICCVW), Seoul, Republic of Korea, 27–28 October 2019.
32. Kansal, P.; Devanathan, S. Eyenet: Attention based convolutional encoder-decoder network for eye region segmentation. In Proceedings of the IEEE/CVF International Conference on Computer Vision Workshops (ICCVW), Seoul, Republic of Korea, 27–28 October 2019; pp. 3688–3693.
33. Hu, J.; Shen, L.; Sun, G. Squeeze-and-excitation networks. In Proceedings of the IEEE Conference on Computer Vision and Pattern Recognition (CVPR), Salt Lake City, UT, USA, 18–23 June 2018; pp. 7132–7141.
34. Woo, S.; Park, J.; Lee, J.Y.; Kweon, I.S. Cbam: Convolutional block attention module. In Proceedings of the European Conference on Computer Vision (ECCV), Munich, Germany, 8–14 September 2018; pp. 3–19.
35. Paszke, A.; Chaurasia, A.; Kim, S.; Culurciello, E. Enet: A deep neural network architecture for real-time semantic segmentation. *arXiv* **2016**, arXiv:1606.02147.
36. Iandola, F.; Moskewicz, M.; Karayev, S.; Girshick, R.; Darrell, T.; Keutzer, K. Densenet: Implementing efficient convnet descriptor pyramids. *arXiv* **2014**, arXiv:1404.1869.
37. Das, A.; Pal, U.; Ferrer, M.A.; Blumenstein, M.; Štepec, D.; Rot, P.; Emeršič, Ž.; Peer, P.; Štruc, V.; Kumar, S.A.; et al. SSERBC 2017: Sclera segmentation and eye recognition benchmarking competition. In Proceedings of the IEEE International Joint Conference on Biometrics (IJCB), Denver, CO, USA, 1–4 October 2017; pp. 742–747.
38. Sequeira, A.F.; Monteiro, J.C.; Rebelo, A.; Oliveira, H.P. MobBIO: A multimodal database captured with a portable handheld device. In Proceedings of the International Conference on Computer Vision Theory and Applications (VISAPP), Lisbon, Portugal, 5–8 January 2014; Volume 3, pp. 133–139.
39. Luo, B.; Shen, J.; Wang, Y.; Pantic, M. The iBUG Eye Segmentation Dataset. In Proceedings of the 2018 Imperial College Computing Student Workshop (ICCSW), London, UK, 20–21 September 2018; Volume 66, pp. 7:1–7:9. [CrossRef]
40. Perry, J.; Fernandez, A.S. EyeSeg: Fast and Efficient Few-Shot Semantic Segmentation. In Proceedings of the European Conference on Computer Vision Workshops (ECCVW), Glasgow, UK, 23–28 August 2020; Springer: Berlin/Heidelberg, Germany, 2020; pp. 570–582.
41. Naqvi, R.A.; Lee, S.W.; Loh, W.K. Ocular-net: Lite-residual encoder decoder network for accurate ocular regions segmentation in various sensor images. In Proceedings of the IEEE International Conference on Big Data and Smart Computing (BigComp), Busan, Republic of Korea, 19–22 February 2020; pp. 121–124.
42. Bowyer, K.W. The results of the NICE. II iris biometrics competition. *Pattern Recognit. Lett.* **2012**, *33*, 965–969. [CrossRef]
43. Test, B.I. CASIA.v4 Database. Available online: http://www.idealtest.org/dbDetailForUser.do?id=4 (accessed on 16 May 2024).
44. Lin, T.Y.; Dollár, P.; Girshick, R.; He, K.; Hariharan, B.; Belongie, S. Feature pyramid networks for object detection. In Proceedings of the IEEE Conference on Computer Vision and Pattern Recognition (CVPR), Honolulu, HI, USA , 21–26 July 2017; pp. 2117–2125.
45. Larsen, A.B.L.; Sønderby, S.K.; Larochelle, H.; Winther, O. Autoencoding beyond pixels using a learned similarity metric. In Proceedings of the International Conference on Machine Learning (ICML), New York, NY, USA, 20–22 June 2016; pp. 1558–1566.
46. Kothari, R.S.; Chaudhary, A.K.; Bailey, R.J.; Pelz, J.B.; Diaz, G.J. Ellseg: An ellipse segmentation framework for robust gaze tracking. *IEEE Trans. Vis. Comput. Graph.* **2021**, *27*, 2757–2767. [CrossRef]
47. Lee, C.Y.; Xie, S.; Gallagher, P.; Zhang, Z.; Tu, Z. Deeply-supervised nets. In Proceedings of the International Conference on Artificial Intelligence and Statistics, San Diego, CA, USA, 9–12 May 2015; pp. 562–570.
48. Zhao, X.; Jia, H.; Pang, Y.; Lv, L.; Tian, F.; Zhang, L.; Sun, W.; Lu, H. M^{2}SNet: Multi-scale in Multi-scale Subtraction Network for Medical Image Segmentation. *arXiv* **2023**, arXiv:2303.10894.
49. Seidel, R. Convex hull computations. In *Handbook of Discrete and Computational Geometry*; Chapman and Hall/CRC: Boca Raton, FL, USA, 2017; pp. 687–703.
50. Pihur, V.; Datta, S.; Datta, S. Weighted rank aggregation of cluster validation measures: A Monte Carlo cross-entropy approach. *Bioinformatics* **2007**, *23*, 1607–1615. [CrossRef] [PubMed]
51. Milletari, F.; Navab, N.; Ahmadi, S.A. V-net: Fully convolutional neural networks for volumetric medical image segmentation. In Proceedings of the International Conference on 3D Vision (3DV), Stanford, CA, USA, 25–28 October 2016; pp. 565–571.
52. Zhang, J.J.; Sun, G.M.; Zheng, K.; Li, Y.; Fu, X.H.; Ci, K.Y.; Shen, J.J.; Meng, F.C.; Kong, J.P.; Zhang, Y. ESLD: Eyes segment and landmark detection in the wild. *J. Image Graph.* **2022**, *27*, 2329–2343.
53. Vitek, M.; Das, A.; Pourcenoux, Y.; Missler, A.; Paumier, C.; Das, S.; De Ghosh, I.; Lucio, D.R.; Zanlorensi, L.A.; Menotti, D.; et al. Ssbc 2020: Sclera segmentation benchmarking competition in the mobile environment. In Proceedings of the IEEE International Joint Conference on Biometrics (IJCB), Houston, TX, USA, 28 September–1 October 2020; pp. 1–10.
54. Proença, H.; Filipe, S.; Santos, R.; Oliveira, J.; Alexandre, L.A. The UBIRIS. v2: A database of visible wavelength iris images captured on-the-move and at-a-distance. *IEEE Trans. Pattern Anal. Mach. Intell.* **2009**, *32*, 1529–1535. [CrossRef]
55. Teo, C.C.; Neo, H.F.; Michael, G.; Tee, C.; Sim, K. A robust iris segmentation with fuzzy supports. In Proceedings of the International Conference on Neural Information Processing: Neural Information Processing. Theory and Algorithms, Sydney, Australia, 21–25 November 2010; Springer: Berlin/Heidelberg, Germany, 2010; pp. 532–539.

56. Chen, L.C.; Zhu, Y.; Papandreou, G.; Schroff, F.; Adam, H. Encoder-decoder with atrous separable convolution for semantic image segmentation. In Proceedings of the European Conference on Computer Vision (ECCV), Munich, Germany, 8–14 September 2018; pp. 801–818.
57. Chen, J.; Lu, Y.; Yu, Q.; Luo, X.; Adeli, E.; Wang, Y.; Lu, L.; Yuille, A.L.; Zhou, Y. TransUNet: Transformers Make Strong Encoders for Medical Image Segmentation. *arXiv* **2021**, arXiv:2102.04306.

electronics

MDPI

Article

AffectiVR: A Database for Periocular Identification and Valence and Arousal Evaluation in Virtual Reality

Chaelin Seok [1], Yeongje Park [1], Junho Baek [1], Hyeji Lim [1], Jong-hyuk Roh [2], Youngsam Kim [2], Soohyung Kim [2] and Eui Chul Lee [3,*]

1 Department of AI & Informatics, Graduate School, Sangmyung University, Seoul 03016, Republic of Korea; 202334018@sangmyung.kr (C.S.); 202331043@sangmyung.kr (Y.P.); 202232029@sangmyung.kr (J.B.); 202232034@sangmyung.kr (H.L.)

2 Cyber Security Research Division Electronics and Telecommunications Research Institute (ETRI), Daejeon 34129, Republic of Korea; jhroh@etri.re.kr (J.-h.R.); kimzt@etri.re.kr (Y.K.); lifewsky@etri.re.kr (S.K.)

3 Department of Human-Centered Artificial Intelligence, Sangmyung University, Seoul 03016, Republic of Korea

* Correspondence: eclee@smu.ac.kr

Abstract: This study introduces AffectiVR, a dataset designed for periocular biometric authentication and emotion evaluation in virtual reality (VR) environments. To maximize immersion in VR environments, interactions must be seamless and natural, with unobtrusive authentication and emotion recognition technologies playing a crucial role. This study proposes a method for user authentication by utilizing periocular images captured by a camera attached to a VR headset. Existing datasets have lacked periocular images acquired in VR environments, limiting their practical application. To address this, periocular images were collected from 100 participants using the HTC Vive Pro and Pupil Labs infrared cameras in a VR environment. Participants also watched seven emotion-inducing videos, and emotional evaluations for each video were conducted. The final dataset comprises 1988 monocular videos and corresponding self-assessment manikin (SAM) evaluations for each experimental video. This study also presents a baseline study to evaluate the performance of biometric authentication using the collected dataset. A deep learning model was used to analyze the performance of biometric authentication based on periocular data collected in a VR environment, confirming the potential for implicit and continuous authentication. The high-resolution periocular images collected in this study provide valuable data not only for user authentication but also for emotion evaluation research. The dataset developed in this study can be used to enhance user immersion in VR environments and as a foundational resource for advancing emotion recognition and authentication technologies in fields such as education, therapy, and entertainment. This dataset offers new research opportunities for non-invasive continuous authentication and emotion recognition in VR environments, and it is expected to significantly contribute to the future development of related technologies.

Keywords: biometric authentication; head-mounted display; infrared periocular images; periocular dataset

1. Introduction

The global head-mounted display (HMD) market was valued at approximately USD 22.31 billion in 2022 and is expected to grow at a compound annual growth rate (CAGR) of 35.8% from 2023 to 2028 [1]. This growth indicates the accelerated adoption and technological advancements of HMDs across various fields such as virtual reality (VR), augmented reality (AR), gaming, medical applications, and military training. Immersion is a key element of VR experiences, playing a critical role in determining the quality of user experience. Higher immersion levels allow users to have more natural and realistic experiences in VR environments, significantly enhancing educational outcomes, therapeutic effects, and satisfaction in entertainment [2]. To increase immersion, various technical elements, including field of view, resolution, user recognition, and feedback, are crucial. These elements enhance interaction and realism in virtual environments, enabling deeper immersion. In particular, in order to maximize immersion, interaction in a VR environment must be natural and uninterrupted, and for this, implicit continuous authentication and emotion recognition play an important role.

Implicit continuous authentication is a method that allows authentication to occur naturally without the user being aware of the process, maintaining security without disrupting immersion in VR environments [3]. This approach continuously verifies user identity during a session, enhancing security and convenience by removing the need for repetitive actions like entering personal identification numbers(PINs). Periocular biometrics, which utilizes features around the eyes—such as eyelids, eyelashes, eyebrows, lacrimal glands, eye shape, and skin texture—holds significant potential for this in HMDs [4]. The periocular region offers high recognition accuracy with simple data acquisition [5]. In HMDs, the eye area remains fixed, making the process resilient to motion noise and ensuring consistent authentication. Emotion evaluation plays an important role in enhancing the realism of VR content. It helps develop better VR environments and uses the emotions felt by users as key data for evaluating VR content [6]. Emotion recognition enables VR systems to interact with users more naturally, creating environments that foster deeper immersion. For example, in educational VR content, emotion recognition monitors users' understanding or interest in real-time, allowing dynamic adjustments to the learning content, thereby maximizing learning effectiveness [7].

However, the development of technologies to enhance immersion still faces significant barriers due to a lack of suitable data. Most existing public datasets do not include periocular data obtained from VR devices, primarily relying on data captured by external cameras. Notable datasets like the CASIA Iris Database, IIT Delhi Dataset, and ND-Iris 0405 contain data collected with external equipment, not cameras embedded in headsets used in VR environments [8–10]. Thus, these datasets fail to reflect the specific conditions of VR, limiting their applicability in VR-based user authentication and emotion evaluation research. To overcome these limitations, this study collected data from 100 participants wearing VR devices. The high-resolution data accurately capture the features of the periocular region, providing essential material for user authentication and related research in VR environments. Additionally, participants watched seven emotion-inducing videos, with their emotions recorded according to Russell's emotion model, creating a dataset that can be used for future emotion evaluation in VR. This study presents a baseline for periocular biometric using the collected data, demonstrating the potential for its use in various future research areas.

2. Related Works

2.1. Dataset

Because it is difficult to acquire data in a VR environment, the data acquired in a VR environment are limited. Therefore, we compared our dataset with some existing datasets, including a periocular dataset that was not acquired in a VR environment. A comparison is presented in Table 1.

High-quality images are required for accurate periocular authentication. However, most public datasets have a low resolution of 640 × 480 or less, and among public datasets, high-resolution datasets have a low number of subjects. In addition, because most datasets obtained from VR environments were collected in the initial state of wearing VR, there is a lack of consideration of actual use environments, such as situations where the user takes off the VR device and puts it back on. However, in this study, we proceeded with the process of wearing the VR device again each time we watched each video. Therefore, a dataset was constructed taking into account changes in the eye position in the image depending on the device location.

Table 1. Comparison of periocular datasets.

Dataset	#Images	#Participants	Resolution	Camera/Sensor	Environment
CASIA-IrisV4 [8]	54,607	2800	640 × 480	-	Non-VR
IIT Delhi Iris Database [9]	1120	224	320 × 240	JIRIS, JPC1000, digital CMOS camera	Non-VR
ND-Iris 0405 [10]	64,980	356	640 × 480	LG 2200 iris imaging system	Non-VR
UBIRIS.v1 [11]	1877	241	300 × 300	Nikon E5700	Non-VR
UBIRIS.v2 [12]	11,002	261	72 × 72	Canon EOS 5D	Non-VR
MRL Eye Dataset [13]	84,898	37	640 × 480	Intel RealSense RS 300 sensor	Non-VR
			1280 × 1024	IDS Imaging sensor	Non-VR
			752 × 480	Aptina sensor	Non-VR
OpenEDS [14]	356,649	152	400 × 640	-	VR
VISA Dataset [15]	3501	100	640 × 480	IriSheild Camera	Non-VR
NVGaze [16]	7400	30	640 × 480	-	VR
OpenEDS2020 [17]	550,400	90	640 × 400	-	VR
Our Dataset	5,199,175	100	1920 × 1080	HTC Vive Binocular Add-on	VR

2.2. User Authentication Using Head-Mounted Display

Liebers et al. [18] proposed a research direction that utilizes behavior-based eye biometrics to enhance security in VR environments as more and more HMDs with built-in eye tracking functions are released to the market. Eye tracking technology must accurately track and analyze the user's eye movements or patterns. However, for some users, there may be issues with the accuracy and reliability of the authentication system because not all users respond comfortably to eye tracking technology. Luo et al. [19] pointed out that more and more personal and sensitive data are being generated due to the spread of VR and proposed a new biometric authentication method that adapts the human visual system (HVS) to the VR platform. OcuLock [20] is a system that combines an electro-oculography (EOG)-based HVS detection framework and a record comparison-based authentication scheme. This system considers the entirety of the HVS, including the eyelids, eye muscles, cells, and peripheral nerves, as well as eye movements. OcuLock achieved low equivalent error rates (EERs) of 3.55% and 4.97%. However, the OcuLock system uses EOG-based sensors to detect the HVS. Therefore, it has the disadvantage of requiring a separate sensor. Lohr et al. used the DenseNet architecture for end-to-end eye movement biometrics (EMBs) as a new method for user authentication in VR and AR devices. An EER of 3.66% was achieved using 5 s of registration and authentication. However, because this study relies on high-quality eye movement data, eye-tracking sensors in VR/AR devices may have lower signal quality than the data used in this study.

2.3. User Authentication Using Periocular Authentication

Oishi et al. [21] proposed a method to improve mobile device user authentication by combining iris and periocular authentication using a machine learning algorithm called AdaBoost. To overcome the limitations of low-quality cameras commonly installed in mobile devices, this paper proposed using peripheral authentication in combination with iris scanning. This method compensated for the loss of iris authentication accuracy caused by low-resolution cameras. However, the method of this study relies heavily on the quality of the camera built into the mobile device. Additionally, an excellent image sensor and lens are required to obtain high-quality iris images. Zhao et al. [22] proposed a new framework for efficient and accurate matching of automatically acquired periocular images in a less restricted environment. They explained that by using the SCNN framework for periocular recognition, it can be useful in situations where accurate iris recognition is difficult. As a result of experiments on four databases, higher accuracy and EER were achieved compared to existing state-of-the-art methods. However, in this study, real-world data can often be highly variable and noisy, so a dataset that does not require preprocessing for these cases was used.

3. Data Acquisition

3.1. Ethics Statement

This study was exempt from review by the Sangmyung University Institutional Review Board as it did not involve any direct interaction with human subjects or any procedures that posed more than minimal risk to participants (IRB Exemption Number: EX-2023-006). Prior to the experiment, participants were provided with a detailed explanation of the experimental procedure and precautions, and informed consent was obtained. All personal data (e.g., name, periocular images) were collected anonymously. Additionally, the consent form stated that participants could withdraw from the experiment at any time if they felt dizziness or discomfort.

3.2. Participants

Through the distribution of flyers within the university and utilizing social networks, we recruited a total of 101 participants. The eligibility criteria for participation were healthy adults aged 18 and above. Participants with suboptimal vision were allowed to wear transparent contact lenses or glasses. However, for individuals wearing glasses, the experiments were conducted twice (once with glasses on and once without glasses). During the experiments, one participant (P057) requested to discontinue the experiments, and consequently, the data from this participant were excluded from the final dataset.

3.3. Apparatus

For the playback of virtual reality content, the HTC Vive Pro was used, featuring dual active-matrix organic light emitting diode (AMOLED) 3.5″ displays with a resolution of 1440 × 1600, a refresh rate of 90 Hz, and a field of view of 110°. Inside the HMD, an infrared camera from Pupil Labs, the HTC Vive Binocular Add-on, was installed to capture eye movements. This camera boasts a resolution of 1920 × 1080, 30 fps, a field of view over 100°, and a camera latency of 8.5 ms. Each camera is equipped with five infrared light emitting diodes (LEDs) to capture images of the eyes in dark environments. The cameras are connected to a laptop via USB cable, which has a 10-core 2.80 GHz i7-1165G7 CPU, 16 GB memory, and Intel(R) Iris(R) Xe Graphics. To display augmented reality content, the HMD is connected to a more powerful laptop with a 14-core 2.7 GHz i7-12700H CPU, 32 GB memory, and an NVIDIA RTX 3080 Laptop GPU with 16 GB VRAM. Although the HTC Vive Pro has a refresh rate of 90 Hz, the images are captured at 30 fps, resulting in a mismatch of frame rates that introduces noise into the video.

3.4. Procedures

To consider variations in pupil size and position related to emotions, as well as changes in pupil size influenced by image brightness, seven distinct images were carefully chosen for the experimental set. These images encompassed a range of valence and arousal values and varying levels of brightness. The video employed in a previous study [23] was a 360° video designed for the VR environment, providing valence and arousal values associated with each video. Four videos, representing positive arousal, positive non-arousal, negative arousal, and negative non-arousal, were selected from the aforementioned study. However, it was judged that the videos that induced positive and negative arousal were not appropriate, so through an internal meeting, external positive and negative arousal videos were added. Additionally, to induce neutral emotions, a method involving the display of everyday objects on the screen was adopted—a recognized approach for inducing neutral emotions [24]. Consequently, a total of seven videos were chosen, and Table 2 outlines the valence and arousal values, video length, and triggering emotion of each video. For externally sourced videos, the anticipated valence and arousal values were provided. The video set comprised two positive arousal videos, two negative arousal videos, one negative non-arousal video, one positive non-arousal video, and one neutral video. Figure 1 illustrates a example from the experiment's video. The images were thoughtfully curated to encompass indoor and outdoor scenes, dark and bright environments, aiming to comprehensively consider changes in pupil size due to brightness.

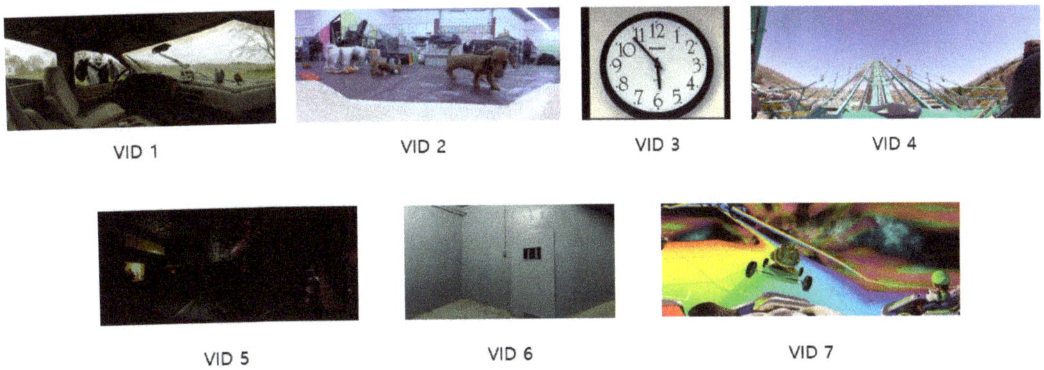

Figure 1. Example from the experiment's video.

Each video has a duration ranging from 70 (s) to 90 (s), followed by a 3 min break after its conclusion to alleviate any potential dizziness. During this break, participants underwent a self-assessment using the self-assessment manikin (SAM) to gauge emotional arousal [25]. SAM is a widely employed method for investigating an experimenter's emotional response to various stimuli. The SAM includes a positive–negative scale representing emotions and an arousal–non-arousal scale indicating the level of arousal, as depicted in Figure 2, with each scale having nine levels. In addition, because this dataset assumes an actual usage environment, the user's free movement and gaze movement are not controlled, and since the HMD is worn again for each video, there is variation in eye position for each video even though it is the same person.

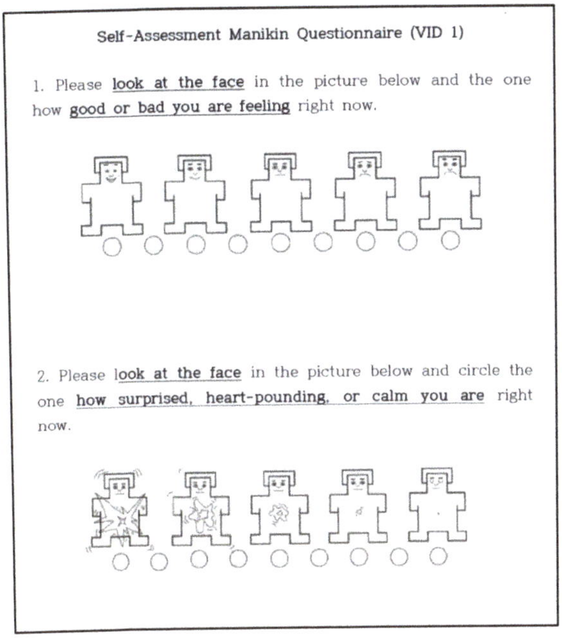

Figure 2. Self-assessment manikin questionnaire.

Table 2. Information about the video.

	VID 1	VID 2	VID 3	VID 4	VID 5	VID 6	VID 7
Valence	3.5 (expect)	7.47	5 (expect)	6.17	3.2	2.38	7 (expect)
Arousal	7 (expect)	5.35	3 (expect)	7.17	5.6	4.25	7.5 (expect)
Time (s)	90	70	90	90	90	90	90
Emotion	Negative arousal	Positive non-arousal	Neutral	Positive arousal	Negative arousal	Negative non-arousal	Positive arousal

3.5. Data Records

In this research, video acquisition was successfully completed for 100 out of the 101 participants, with one individual opting out of the experiment. Consequently, data for approximately 5,199,175 frames were obtained. The participants viewed seven videos designed to evoke emotions, and corresponding survey results were collected. The composition of the dataset is shown in Figure 3. Accordingly, the video data of each subject who participated in the experiment was structured to match the survey results for the video. During the experiment, information on whether lenses were worn and whether glasses were worn was also collected as metadata. In particular, whether the experiment was conducted first with glasses on or without them was expected to have a significant impact on emotion recognition, and the relevant information was recorded together. The resulting dataset was constructed by considering various aspects of the experiment and the reliability.

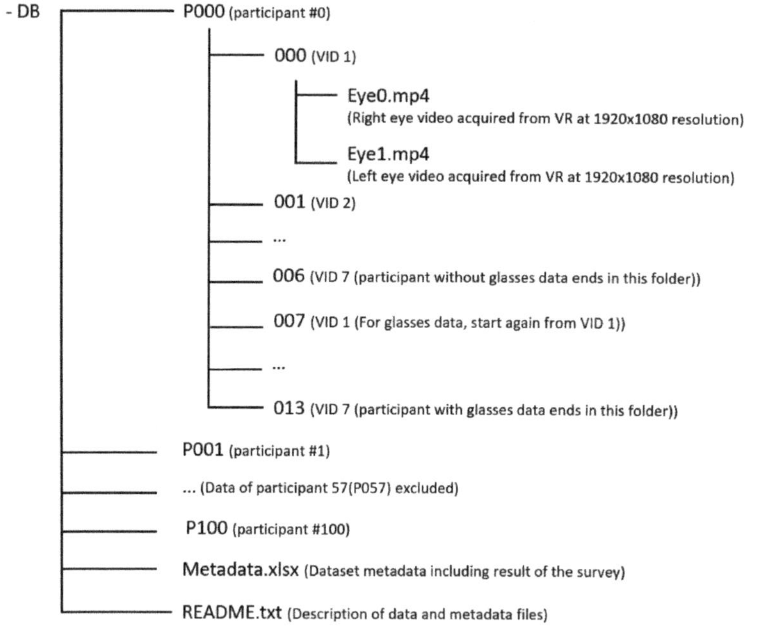

Figure 3. Composition of the dataset.

Figure 4 visually presents the data obtained through the experiment, and there is a change in the eye position of the same subject in each image. Furthermore, it clearly illustrates differences in periocular characteristics among subjects, including variations in eye shape, the presence or absence of double eyelids, and the shape of eyelashes. The observed distinctions in periocular features suggest the potential for subject identification based on these characteristics. It is worth noting that when subjects wear glasses, accurately locating the eye area may pose challenges due to the reflection of infrared light by the lenses. Addressing these challenges may require additional image processing technology or controlled lighting conditions.

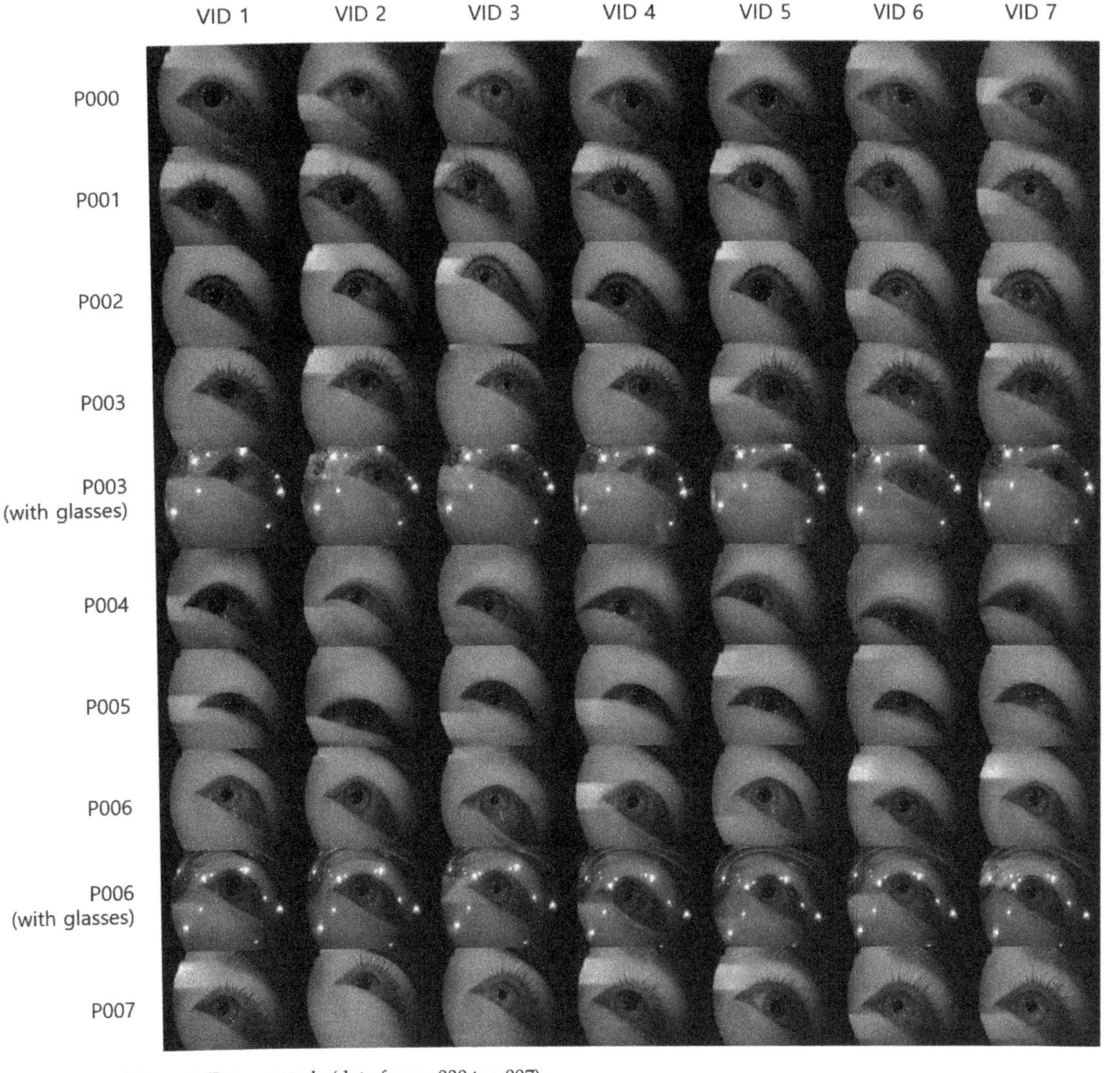

Figure 4. Data example (data from p000 to p007).

Figure 5 displays the image and histogram without glasses in (a) and with glasses in (b). In both cases, there is a substantial distribution of pixels with low brightness values (10–30) due to the VR-induced black borders around the eyes. Particularly in case (b), there is a significant increase in pixels with high brightness values (240 250) attributed to light reflecting from the glasses lens compared to (a). Moreover, the presence of glasses creates a shadow, and sporadic light-colored pixels exist due to dust or light reflection on the lenses, resulting in a distinctly different histogram. Additionally, in (a), distinct user features such as the iris and eyelashes are clearly visible in the center of the image, but in (b), these features are less evident as the pupils are notably positioned above the center due to the presence of glasses. However, in both dataset types, the diameter of the iris in the entire periocular frame is not sufficient, so these datasets may not be suitable for iris recognition.

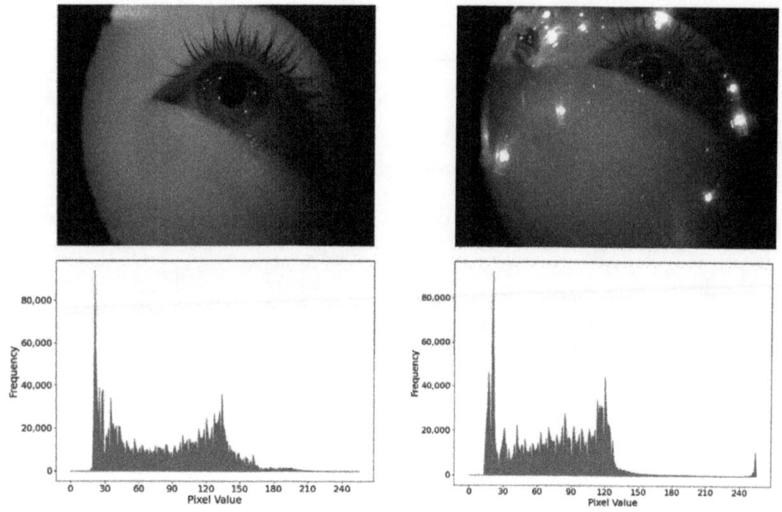

(a) (b)

Figure 5. Example image (P003) and histogram. (**a**) Image w/ glasses; (**b**) image w/o glasses.

Figure 6 provides a visual representation of the evaluation results for each video, while Figure 7 illustrates the valence and arousal values of each image in a box-and-whisker plot. In Figure 6, you can see that the distribution of emotional levels for each video allows for relative distinction. However, it is evident from Table 3 that the valence and arousal values are denser than anticipated. Particularly, even in videos designed to induce arousal, the arousal values appear to be distributed lower, and overall valence values are distributed higher. Observing Figure 7, it is evident that valence demonstrates an overall distribution of high values, whereas arousal values exhibit an overall distribution of low values. This observation can be attributed to two potential factors. Firstly, during the selection of experimental videos, it is conceivable that the videos were chosen to elicit an overall low arousal value, possibly to accommodate a broader audience. Secondly, the immersive nature of wearing a VR headset and experiencing a 360-degree video may have induced positive emotions in the subjects.

Table 3. Average of valence and arousal as a result of the survey.

VID 1		**VID 2**		**VID 3**		**VID 4**	
Valence	Arousal	Valence	Arousal	Valence	Arousal	Valence	Arousal
4.12	5.33	7.6	2.54	5.61	1.61	6.12	4.79
VID 5		**VID 6**		**VID 7**			
Valence	Arousal	Valence	Arousal	Valence	Arousal		
4.33	4.79	3.88	2.79	7.59	4.15		

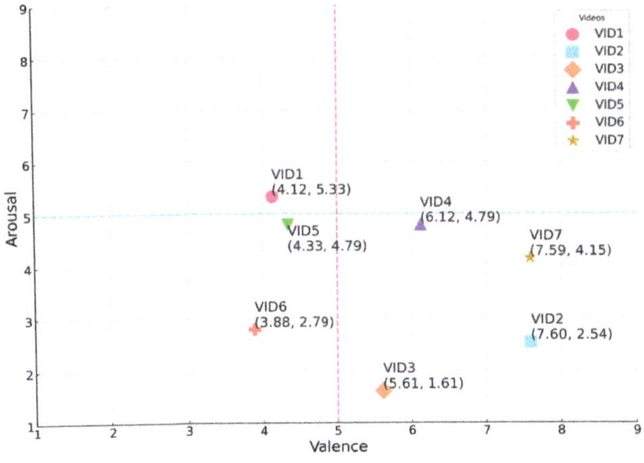

Figure 6. Survey results of valence and arousal distribution.

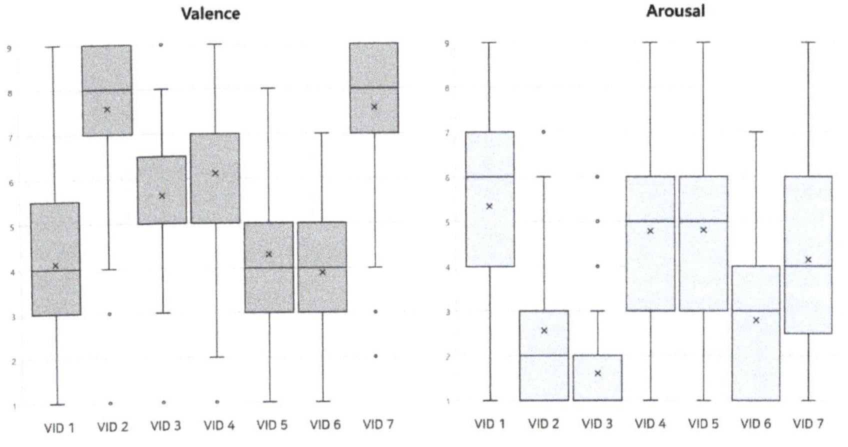

Figure 7. Box-and-whisker plot of valence and arousal as a result of the survey.

4. Method

4.1. Data Cleansing

Considering that the shape of both eyes is different for each person, only the right eye image was utilized in this study. Additionally, images featuring subjects wearing glasses were excluded from analysis due to the challenges posed by infrared light reflection on the lenses, making accurate eye area localization difficult. Moreover, images capturing closed or blinking eyes acquired during the experiment were omitted from consideration as they were deemed unsuitable for biometric recognition. The acquisition of eye images using infrared lights and cameras within the VR device introduce potential damage to iris images due to reflected infrared light in the iris area. To mitigate this, a process was implemented to remove reflected light present in the iris area. For the iris recognition task, an additional step involved converting the iris area into a square image using polar coordinate transformation. Given the dynamic nature of each user's eye position when wearing VR, a deep learning approach for accurate pupil extraction was deemed more effective than traditional algorithmic methods. Thus, a deep learning model based on Inception [26] was employed. Trained to detect and locate the pupil in real time within noisy images, this model consists of several inception blocks and reduction blocks, utilizing convolution filters and pooling layers of various sizes within each block. The model used was pretrained, and to exclude instances of closed or slightly closed eyes, eight frames of video were removed based on the absence of detected pupils during the extraction process. Figure 8 visually illustrates the functioning of the model, with white and red circles indicating the predicted pupil model generated by the pupil area detection model. Frames classified as having open eyes are represented by white circles, while frames identified as closed eyes are visualized as red circles.

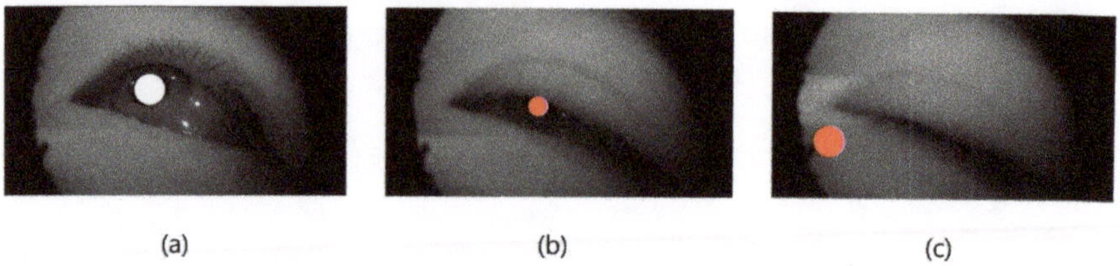

Figure 8. Examples of pupil extraction detection. A red dot indicates that the pupil was not detected in that frame, while a white dot indicates that the pupil was detected. Only frames where the pupil was detected were used for training the model. (**a**): When the eyes are open, (**b**) when eyes are half-open (in this case, it is classified as a frame with eyes closed), (**c**): when eyes are closed.

4.2. Dataset

For training the biometric recognition model, images were extracted and utilized from our dataset. Participants in this database viewed a total of seven videos, and from each, 15 images were randomly extracted for the training process. A total of 105 images were used per subject, and a total of 10,500 learning data for 100 subjects were constructed and model learning was performed. Considering the variability of the VR wearing environment, random parallel movement and brightness augmentation were applied to the images when learning the model. Additionally, considering that impostor pairs are more diverse than genuine pairs in an actual biometric authentication environment, the ratio of impostor pairs was increased when forming genuine and impostor pairs in 10,500 pieces of training data to enable robust comparison. The genuine and impostor matching tests were conducted using a dedicated test dataset, excluding the data utilized for training. Considering the relatively small number of subjects in the database, five-fold cross-validation performance was measured. The overall average performance was then calculated to evaluate the system.

4.3. Periocular Recognition Model

In this study, a Siamese-network-based deep learning model was utilized to compare and analyze the performance of biometric recognition models based on periocular data obtained from a VR environment. The Siamese network is a deep learning model structure that shares weights between CNN models. In the case of genuine image pairs, the feature values of the two images become closer, while in the case of impostor pairs, the feature values become further apart. The overall model structure is shown in Figure 9. In this study, the performance comparison was conducted by modifying the feature extraction network model based on the Siamese network. The three deep learning models used as feature extraction networks were MobileNetV3Large [27], EfficientNetB0 [28], and the Siamese-network-based deep learning model proposed by Hwang et al. [29]. Each model has its unique characteristics, covering a wide spectrum from lightweight models to high-performance models.

MobileNetV3 [27] is a lightweight deep learning model designed for efficient computational performance in mobile and embedded environments. The MobileNet series utilizes depthwise separable convolution, which reduces the number of parameters while optimizing the computation speed. MobileNetV3 further advances this by introducing the squeeze-and-excitation (SE) module and the hard swish activation function, striking a balance between performance and efficiency. It is evaluated as a model that consumes fewer computational resources, performs fast computations, yet still delivers respectable recognition performance. In this study, MobileNetV3Large was selected, considering the possibility of real-time processing on VR devices.

EfficientNet [28] is a model designed with a compound scaling strategy, which expands the network's depth, width, and resolution in a balanced way. EfficientNetB0 is the lightest version in this series, balancing performance and efficiency, making it a model that can be applied to various use cases. A key feature of EfficientNet is that it does not simply improve performance by increasing the model's size but achieves optimization in both performance and efficiency through compound scaling. EfficientNetB0's strength lies in its ability to deliver high performance even with limited data, making it suitable for the VR dataset, which was collected from a relatively small number of subjects.

The study by [29] argued that useful features for periocular biometrics might exist even at relatively lower layers in CNN-based models. As a result, the model was designed to utilize features extracted from intermediate layers of the deep learning model. Based on Deep-ResNet18, feature maps extracted from each stage are transformed into vectors using Global Average Pooling. These transformed vectors are then connected to a fully connected layer, mapping them to vectors of the same size. Consequently, one vector is generated for each convolutional layer stage, and the final feature vector is created by concatenating these vectors. This feature vector is used to perform periocular biometrics by comparing the two subjects.

The input images used for the model had a resolution of (240, 320). All models were trained using the TensorFlow and Keras libraries, and the Adam optimizer, which generally shows good performance, was used as the optimizer for training. The binary cross-entropy was employed as the loss function. To save the model with the best performance, the model parameters at the point where the validation loss was the lowest were saved. The batch size for training was set to 16, and the model was trained for a total of 10 epochs. Additionally, to prevent overfitting during training, the early stopping technique was applied, halting training if the validation loss did not improve for five consecutive epochs.

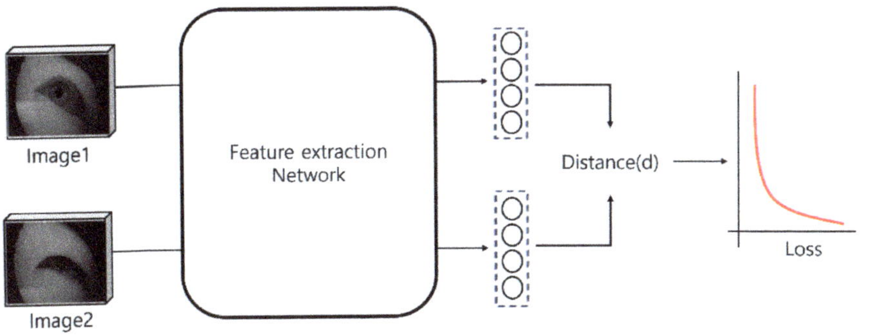

Figure 9. Siamese network structure for model training.

5. Results

In this study, we measured the false acceptance rate (FAR) and false rejection rate (FRR) based on similarity thresholds to compare the performance of the models and conducted receiver operating characteristic (ROC) curve and equal error rate (EER) analyses. A lower EER indicates a more robust biometric recognition system, and in most biometric systems, the threshold is typically set based on the value derived from the EER. In biometric recognition, minimizing the FAR, which is associated with the incorrect identification of others, is critical. Consequently, the FRR performance was evaluated under the condition that FAR remained below 1%. Table 4 summarizes the performance of the proposed biometric recognition models. As seen in the table, the performance of each model varies in terms of EER and FRR. MobileNetV3Large and EfficientNetB0 exhibited similar performances, with EERs of 7.11% and 6.55%, respectively. In contrast, the model proposed by

Hwang et al. [29] showed relatively lower performance with an EER of 10.76%. When comparing FRR at a FAR of less than 1%, MobileNetV3Large and EfficientNetB0 achieved similar performance, with FRRs of 24.90% and 25.37%, respectively, whereas the model proposed by Hwang et al. [29] displayed a lower performance with an FRR of 34.41%.

Table 4. Biometric recognition performance of different models.

Model	EER [%]	FRR (FAR < 1%) [%]
MobileNetV3Large	7.10	24.90
EfficientNetB0	6.55	25.36
Hwang et al. [29]	10.76	34.41

Figure 10 visualizes the ROC curves for each model. Through the analysis of each curve, it was found that the MobileNetV3Large model demonstrated an AUC of 0.98, which is very close to 1, indicating excellent performance. Similarly, the EfficientNetB0 model also showed an AUC of 0.98, exhibiting identical performance to MobileNetV3Large and demonstrating very high performance. Given that EfficientNetB0 has a lower EER than MobileNetV3Large, both models display similar overall performance, but EfficientNetB0 may slightly outperform MobileNetV3Large. On the other hand, the model proposed by Hwang et al. [29] achieved an AUC of 0.95, which, although slightly lower than the other two models, still maintains high performance.

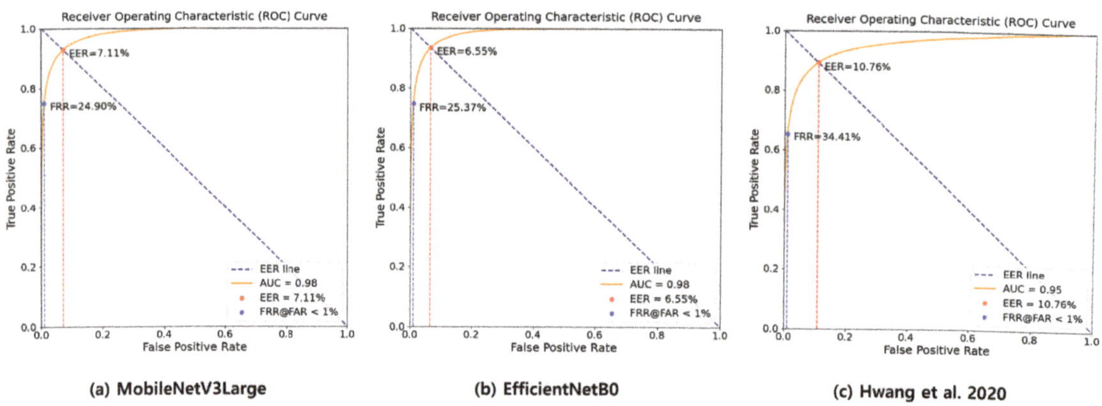

Figure 10. Comparison of ROC curves: (**a**) MobileNetV3Large; (**b**) EfficientNetB0; (**c**) Hwang et al. [29].

Figure 11 illustrates the genuine–impostor distribution of the models using the proposed dataset as input. The X-axis represents the distance between the feature vectors of two images, while the Y-axis represents the probability density at that distance. The closer the feature vector distance between two images, the higher the likelihood that the pair is genuine, and the further the distance, the higher the likelihood that the pair is an impostor. Typically, the distributions of genuine and impostor pairs each form two Gaussian distributions, and the smaller the overlapping region between the two distributions, the better the biometric recognition performance is considered to be. For the MobileNetV3Large model, genuine data are primarily located between Euclidean distances of 0.0 and 0.8. The distribution of the genuine data is very narrow and skewed to the left, indicating that genuine matches occur at very small distances. The impostor data are mainly positioned between Euclidean distances of 0.2 and 1.5 and follow a symmetric normal distribution. This suggests that the MobileNetV3Large model can effectively distinguish between genuine and impostor data, as the overlap between the two distributions is relatively small, indicating excellent performance. In contrast, the EfficientNetB0 model shows a broader distribution for genuine data compared to MobileNetV3Large, with the distribution spreading further to the right. The genuine data is primarily located between Euclidean distances of 0.0 and 1.0. And the impostor data is mainly positioned between Euclidean distances of 0.2 and 1.8 and follows a symmetric normal distribution. The impostor distribution also spreads more to the right, forming a symmetrical distribution. This model's broader distributions for both genuine and impostor data imply that the model includes more uncertainty, and the boundary between the two classes is relatively less distinct. Therefore, despite having the lowest EER, the EfficientNetB0 model suggests that its criteria for distinguishing between genuine and impostor pairs are not as clear as those of the MobileNetV3Large model. For the model proposed by Hwang et al. [29], the genuine distribution is more spread out compared to the previous two models, with a slightly asymmetrical normal distribution skewed to the left. The impostor distribution is similar to that of the EfficientNetB0 model but is skewed more to the left. The genuine data are spread between Euclidean distances of 0.2 and 1.5, and there is more overlap between the distributions of genuine and impostor data than in the previous two models. This indicates that the difference between genuine and impostor data is smaller, which contributes to the relatively lower performance of this model.

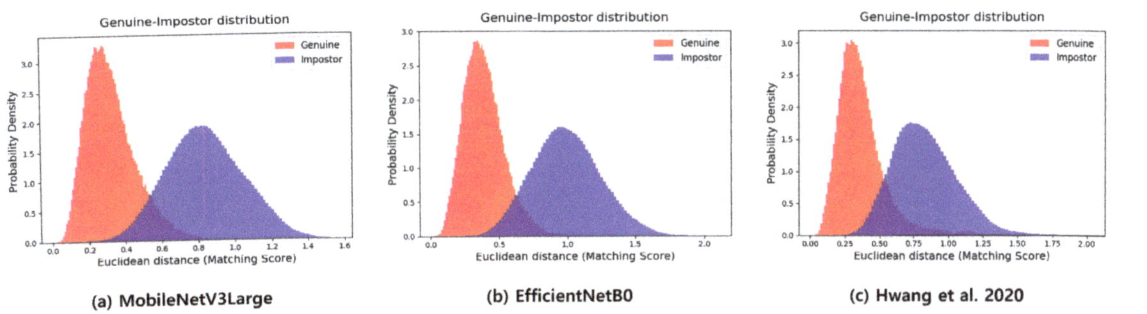

Figure 11. Comparison of genuine–impostor distribution: (**a**) MobileNetV3Large; (**b**) EfficientNetB0; (**c**) Hwang et al. [29].

6. Discussion

This study attempted to overcome the limitations of existing datasets by building a VR dataset recorded while subjects experienced actual VR content. Most existing public datasets were acquired from Westerners and were not suitable for VR research because they did not reflect the uniqueness of the VR environment by using data acquired from external cameras. Additionally, datasets captured in VR have a small number of subjects or low resolution. In contrast, this study collected high-resolution images using a camera attached to a VR device targeting Koreans and constructed a richer dataset through emotion-inducing videos. To induce emotions, the subjects watched seven videos, and after watching, the subjects checked the level of positive/negative and arousal/non-arousal through a self-assessment manikin questionnaire. The results of the questionnaire showed that the valence value was generally high, and the arousal value was generally distributed similarly across all videos. This may be because, during the selection process for the experimental videos, videos that generally induce low arousal values were included, which various subjects could watch. It is also possible that this resulted from cultural differences between Western and Eastern societies. It may also be because the experience of wearing VR and watching 360-degree videos itself induced positive emotions in the subjects. In the case of emotion recognition, it is feasible to predict the numerical values corresponding to emotions in the videos used in our constructed dataset through regression, using metrics such as mean absolute error, or to utilize each emotion as a category and use accuracy for prediction.

This study also presents a baseline for utilizing the dataset. Periocular biometric identification was performed using the constructed dataset. To improve the quality of the data, frames with eyes closed or blinking were removed, and frames with rapid changes in pupil size were filtered. This process improves the reliability and accuracy of biometrics, allowing the model to effectively learn the key features needed to distinguish between real and counterfeit. And the feature extraction network of the Siamese network was replaced with various models for comparative analysis. The results of this study highlight the comparative performance of three feature extraction networks—MobileNetV3Large, EfficientNetB0, and the model proposed by Hwang et al. (2020)—in terms of EER, FAR, and FRR. The models were evaluated using ROC curves and genuine–impostor distribution analysis to gauge their accuracy and ability to distinguish between genuine and impostor data. The analysis of the genuine–impostor distribution further illuminates the strengths and weaknesses of each model. The MobileNetV3Large model presents a compact and well-separated distribution of genuine and impostor data, with genuine data clustering tightly between Euclidean distances of 0.0 and 0.8. This narrow distribution, coupled with minimal overlap between the two classes, indicates that MobileNetV3Large can effectively distinguish between genuine and impostor matches, making it highly reliable for biometric recognition. In contrast, EfficientNetB0, despite its lower EER, shows a broader distribution of both genuine and impostor data. This broader spread suggests more uncertainty in the model's classification boundaries, making it less clear-cut in distinguishing between genuine and impostor data. The overlap between the distributions is larger than that of MobileNetV3Large, indicating that EfficientNetB0, while effective, may not be as confident in its predictions.

Also, balancing FAR and FRR is a critical challenge in biometric recognition systems. In this study, we evaluated FRR under the condition that FAR remained below 1%, as well as by analyzing the EER. However, there is a need for more detailed analysis of FRR performance at various FAR thresholds. Specifically, exploring methods to achieve an optimal FAR/FRR balance tailored to the needs of specific applications could be a key focus for future research. Also, no emotion rating data were used in the baseline, and images of glasses wearers were excluded from the analysis due to infrared reflection. Therefore, future research will expand the scope of application of the model by including various states such as glasses wearers, eye closure, and blinking and will contribute to expanding the use of periocular in more diverse fields through emotion classification, etc.

7. Conclusions

This study establishes a periocular dataset acquired in real VR usage environments, providing a crucial foundation for research in biometric recognition and emotion assessment. Existing datasets fail to reflect the unique characteristics of VR environments and often have limitations such as low resolution or a small number of subjects. In contrast, the dataset from this study includes high-resolution images captured using a camera attached to a VR device, specifically focusing on Korean subjects, making it more suitable for practical applications. The significance of this dataset is particularly highlighted in its potential to enable non-invasive continuous authentication and emotion assessment in VR environments. This opens possibilities for applications in fields where immersion is critical, such as education, therapy, and entertainment. The data collected alongside emotion-inducing videos can serve as a valuable resource for emotion recognition research, contributing to the development of more personalized and sophisticated VR environments. In conclusion, the dataset created in this study will serve as a key cornerstone for advancing technologies in user authentication and emotion recognition within VR environments. Based on this, the quality of user experiences can be enhanced, and safer, more reliable VR environments can be established. The expansion of such research lays the foundation for

VR technology to provide tangible value across various industries and make significant contributions to the future development of immersive technologies.

Author Contributions: Conceptulization—E.C.L.; Methodology—C.S.; Software—Y.P.; Validation—J.B.; Formal Analysis—C.S.; Investigation—J.-h.R., Y.K. and S.K.; Resources—C.S., Y.P., J.B. and H.L.; Data Curation—C.S.; Writing—Original Draft—C.S.; Writing—Review and Editing—E.C.L.; Visualization—C.S., Y.P. and J.B.; Supervision—E.C.L.; Project Administration—E.C.L.; Funding Acquisition—J.-h.R., Y.K. and S.K. All authors have read and agreed to the published version of the manuscript.

Funding: This work was supported by Institute of Information & communications Technology Planning & Evaluation (IITP) grant funded by the Korea government (MSIT) (RS-2023-00215700, Trustworthy Metaverse: blockchain-enabled convergence research).

Institutional Review Board Statement: Based on Article 13-1-1 and 13-1-2 of the Enforcement Regulations of the Act on Bioethics and Safety of the Republic of Korea, ethical review and approval were waived (IRB-SMU-C-2023-1-007) for this study by Sangmyung University's Institutional Review Board because this study uses only simple contact-measuring equipment or observation equipment that does not involve physical changes and does not include invasive procedures such as drug administration or blood sampling.

Informed Consent Statement: Informed consent was obtained from all subjects involved in the study. Written informed consent has been obtained from the subjects to publish this paper.

Data Availability Statement: All codes were released and shared at (https://github.com/schaelin/AffectiVR (accessed on 24 September 2024)). The code was written using Python 3.8.18, and how to use it is explained at (https://github.com/schaelin/AffectiVR (accessed on 24 September 2024)).

Conflicts of Interest: The authors declare no conflicts of interest.

References

1. Funk, M.; Marky, K.; Mizutani, I.; Kritzler, M.; Mayer, S.; Michahelles, F. Lookunlock: Using spatial-targets for user-authentication on hmds. In Proceedings of the Extended Abstracts of the 2019 CHI Conference on Human Factors in Computing Systems, Scotland, UK, 4–9 May 2019; pp. 1–6.
2. Rose, T.; Nam, C.S.; Chen, K.B. Immersion of virtual reality for rehabilitation-Review. *Appl. Ergon.* **2018**, *69*, 153–161. [CrossRef] [PubMed]
3. Kim, S.; Kim, S.; Jin, S. Trends in Implicit Continuous Authentication Technology. *Electron. Telecommun. Trends* **2018**, *33*, 57–67.
4. Kumari, P.; Seeja, K. Periocular biometrics: A survey. *J. King Saud Univ.-Comput. Inf. Sci.* **2022**, *34*, 1086–1097. [CrossRef]
5. Alonso-Fernandez, F.; Bigun, J. A survey on periocular biometrics research. *Pattern Recognit. Lett.* **2016**, *82*, 92–105. [CrossRef]
6. Joo, J.H.; Han, S.H.; Park, I.; Chung, T.S. Immersive Emotion Analysis in VR Environments: A Sensor-Based Approach to Prevent Distortion. *Electronics* **2024**, *13*, 1494. [CrossRef]
7. Petersen, G.B.; Petkakis, G.; Makransky, G. A study of how immersion and interactivity drive VR learning. *Comput. Educ.* **2022**, *179*, 104429. [CrossRef]
8. Li, S.; Yi, D.; Lei, Z.; Liao, S. The casia nir-vis 2.0 face database. In Proceedings of the IEEE Conference on Computer Vision and Pattern Recognition Workshops, Portland, OR, USA, 23–28 June 2013; pp. 348–353.
9. Kumar, A.; Passi, A. Comparison and combination of iris matchers for reliable personal authentication. *Pattern Recognit.* **2010**, *43*, 1016–1026. [CrossRef]
10. Bowyer, K.W.; Flynn, P.J. The ND-IRIS-0405 iris image dataset. *arXiv* **2016**, arXiv:1606.04853.
11. Proença, H.; Alexandre, L.A. UBIRIS: A noisy iris image database. In *Proceedings of the Image Analysis and Processing–ICIAP 2005: 13th International Conference, Cagliari, Italy, 6–8 September 2005*; Proceedings 13; Springer: Cagliari, Italy, 2005; pp. 970–977.
12. Proença, H.; Filipe, S.; Santos, R.; Oliveira, J.; Alexandre, L.A. The UBIRIS. v2: A database of visible wavelength iris images captured on-the-move and at-a-distance. *IEEE Trans. Pattern Anal. Mach. Intell.* **2009**, *32*, 1529–1535. [CrossRef] [PubMed]
13. Fusek, R. Pupil localization using geodesic distance. In *Proceedings of the Advances in Visual Computing: 13th International Symposium, ISVC 2018, Las Vegas, NV, USA, 19–21 November 2018*; Proceedings 13; Springer: Las Vegas, NV, USA, 2018; pp. 433–444.
14. Garbin, S.J.; Shen, Y.; Schuetz, I.; Cavin, R.; Hughes, G.; Talathi, S.S. Openeds: Open eye dataset. *arXiv* **2019**, arXiv:1905.03702.
15. Kagawade, V.C.; Angadi, S.A. VISA: A multimodal database of face and iris traits. *Multimed. Tools Appl.* **2021**, *80*, 21615–21650. [CrossRef]
16. Kim, J.; Stengel, M.; Majercik, A.; De Mello, S.; Dunn, D.; Laine, S.; McGuire, M.; Luebke, D. Nvgaze: An anatomically-informed dataset for low-latency, near-eye gaze estimation. In Proceedings of the 2019 CHI Conference on Human Factors in Computing Systems, Scotland, UK, 4–9 May 2019; pp. 1–12.
17. Palmero, C.; Sharma, A.; Behrendt, K.; Krishnakumar, K.; Komogortsev, O.V.; Talathi, S.S. Openeds2020: Open eyes dataset. *arXiv* **2020**, arXiv:2005.03876.

18. Liebers, J.; Schneegass, S. Gaze-based authentication in virtual reality. In Proceedings of the ACM Symposium on Eye Tracking Research and Applications, Stuttgart, Germany, 2–5 June 2020; pp. 1–2.
19. Luo, S.; Nguyen, A.; Song, C.; Lin, F.; Xu, W.; Yan, Z. OcuLock: Exploring human visual system for authentication in virtual reality head-mounted display. In Proceedings of the 2020 Network and Distributed System Security Symposium (NDSS), San Diego, CA, USA, 23–26 February 2020.
20. Lohr, D.; Komogortsev, O.V. Eye know you too: Toward viable end-to-end eye movement biometrics for user authentication. *IEEE Trans. Inf. Forensics Secur.* **2022**, *17*, 3151–3164. [CrossRef]
21. Oishi, S.; Ichino, M.; Yoshiura, H. Fusion of iris and periocular user authentication by adaboost for mobile devices. In Proceedings of the 2015 IEEE International Conference on Consumer Electronics (ICCE), Las Vegas, NV, USA, 9–12 January 2015; IEEE: Piscataway, NJ, USA, 2015; pp. 428–429.
22. Zhao, Z.; Kumar, A. Accurate periocular recognition under less constrained environment using semantics-assisted convolutional neural network. *IEEE Trans. Inf. Forensics Secur.* **2016**, *12*, 1017–1030. [CrossRef]
23. Li, B.J.; Bailenson, J.N.; Pines, A.; Greenleaf, W.J.; Williams, L.M. A public database of immersive VR videos with corresponding ratings of arousal, valence, and correlations between head movements and self report measures. *Front. Psychol.* **2017**, *8*, 2116. [CrossRef] [PubMed]
24. Trilla, I.; Weigand, A.; Dziobek, I. Affective states influence emotion perception: Evidence for emotional egocentricity. *Psychol. Res.* **2021**, *85*, 1005–1015. [CrossRef] [PubMed]
25. Lang, P.; Sidowski, J.; Johnson, J.; Williams, T. *Technology in Mental Health Care Delivery Systems*; Ablex Publishing Corporation: Norwood, NJ, USA, 1980.
26. Eivazi, S.; Santini, T.; Keshavarzi, A.; Kübler, T.; Mazzei, A. Improving real-time CNN-based pupil detection through domain-specific data augmentation. In Proceedings of the 11th ACM Symposium on Eye Tracking Research & Applications, Denver , CO, USA, 25–28 June 2019; pp. 1–6.
27. Howard, A.; Sandler, M.; Chu, G.; Chen, L.C.; Chen, B.; Tan, M.; Wang, W.; Zhu, Y.; Pang, R.; Vasudevan, V.; et al. Searching for mobilenetv3. In Proceedings of the IEEE/CVF International Conference on Computer Vision, Seoul, Republic of Korea, 27 October–2 November 2019; pp. 1314–1324.
28. Tan, M. Efficientnet: Rethinking model scaling for convolutional neural networks. *arXiv* **2019**, arXiv:1905.11946.
29. Hwang, H.; Lee, E.C. Near-infrared image-based periocular biometric method using convolutional neural network. *IEEE Access* **2020**, *8*, 158612–158621. [CrossRef]

electronics

MDPI

Article

Noise-Robust Biometric Authentication Using Infrared Periocular Images Captured from a Head-Mounted Display

Junho Baek [1,†], Yeongje Park [1,†], Chaelin Seok [1] and Eui Chul Lee [2,*]

1 Department of AI & Informatics, Graduate School, Sangmyung University, Seoul 03016, Republic of Korea
2 Department of Human-Centered Artificial Intelligence, Sangmyung University, Seoul 03016, Republic of Korea
* Correspondence: eclee@smu.ac.kr
† These authors contributed equally to this work.

Abstract: This study proposes a biometric authentication method using infrared (IR)-based periocular images captured in virtual reality (VR) environments with head-mounted displays (HMDs). The widespread application of VR technology highlights the growing need for robust user authentication in immersive environments. To address this, the study introduces a novel periocular biometric authentication system optimized for HMD usage. Ensuring reliable authentication in VR environments necessitates overcoming significant challenges, including flicker noise and infrared reflection. Flicker noise, caused by alternating current (AC)-powered lighting, produces banding artifacts in images captured by rolling-shutter cameras, obstructing biometric feature extraction. Additionally, IR reflection generates strong light glare on the iris surface, degrading image quality and negatively impacting the model's generalization performance and authentication accuracy. This study utilized the AffectiVR dataset, which includes noisy images, to address these challenges. In the preprocessing phase, iris reflections were removed, reducing the Equal Error Rate (EER) from 6.73% to 5.52%. Furthermore, incorporating a Squeeze-and-Excitation (SE) block to mitigate flicker noise and enhance model robustness resulted in a final EER of 6.39%. Although the SE block slightly increased the EER, it significantly improved the model's ability to suppress noise and focus on critical periocular features, ensuring enhanced robustness in challenging VR environments. Heatmap analysis revealed that the proposed model effectively utilized periocular features, such as the skin around the eyes and eye contours, compared to prior approaches. This study establishes a crucial groundwork for advancing robust biometric authentication systems capable of overcoming noise challenges in next-generation immersive platforms.

Keywords: biometric authentication; head-mounted display; infrared periocular images; noise reduction

1. Introduction

The rapid advancement of virtual reality (VR) and augmented reality (AR) technologies is accelerating the rise of the metaverse, creating new digital spaces that offer immersive experiences and realistic interactions for users [1,2]. These immersive experiences enable personalized services based on user data but also raise significant concerns regarding the security and privacy of the vast amounts of user data being collected [3]. Therefore, developing reliable authentication mechanisms for immersive platforms such as the metaverse has become an essential task.

Currently, VR and AR platforms primarily rely on traditional authentication methods such as personal identification numbers (PINs) or passwords [4]. However, these methods are not well suited to immersive environments and may detract from the user experience. Furthermore, in environments that require continuous authentication, existing methods reveal significant security vulnerabilities [5]. This highlights the urgent need for new authentication technologies that balance immersion with security.

One promising technology to address this challenge is periocular biometric authentication. This technology leverages unique biometric features around the eye, such as the iris, eyelids, and eyelashes, to identify users. It shows significant potential, especially for providing continuous and reliable authentication even while wearing a VR headset [6,7]. However, implementing this technology effectively in VR environments requires addressing several noise-related challenges.

One major noise issue in VR environments is flicker noise. This noise arises from brightness fluctuations caused by alternating current (AC)-powered lighting, producing banding artifacts in images captured by rolling-shutter cameras [8]. Flicker noise hinders the accurate extraction of iris and surrounding biometric features due to continuous brightness variations. Existing synchronization technologies and filtering algorithms aimed at mitigating this problem face challenges related to high technical complexity and cost, making practical application difficult [9,10]. Another significant obstacle is infrared (IR) reflection noise. IR reflections generated by VR headsets cause strong light reflections on the iris surface, distorting image details and introducing significant noise during model training. Furthermore, reflection patterns change dynamically with gaze shifts, negatively affecting the generalization performance of the model and the accuracy of authentication.

This study proposes a periocular biometric authentication method optimized for VR environments by utilizing the AffectiVR dataset [11], which contains images affected by flicker noise and IR reflection noise. Designed to overcome the limitations of existing authentication systems, this study specifically addresses major noise challenges in VR scenarios. The proposed process effectively removes IR reflections from the iris area, providing stable training data. Furthermore, the proposed model accurately captures detailed biometric features of the iris and surrounding tissues, enhancing the reliability of biometric authentication models. Despite realistic constraints such as flicker and reflection noise in immersive VR environments, the proposed process delivers highly reliable biometric authentication. This advancement significantly contributes to improving user experiences and strengthening security levels in next-generation digital platforms such as the metaverse. The key contributions of this study are as follows. First, the model's performance is enhanced by removing IR illumination reflections. Second, the model's reliability is ensured by mitigating the impact of flicker noise.

This manuscript is organized as follows: Section 2 reviews related works, highlighting previous studies on periocular biometrics and their limitations. Section 3 presents the proposed method, including dataset preprocessing, model architecture, and training procedures. Section 4 discusses experimental results and comparative analysis with baseline models. Finally, Sections 5 and 6 conclude the study with implications and future directions.

2. Related Works

2.1. Biometric Authentication Using Head-Mounted Display

Sivasamy et al. [12] proposed a novel system called VRCAuth for continuous user authentication in VR environments. To address the limitations of password or PIN-based initial authentication, which struggles to continuously verify user identity during VR usage, VRCAuth analyzes user head movements using VR headset sensors to provide seamless continuous authentication. The system leverages various machine-learning algorithms to identify users without disrupting their activities. However, since it relies solely on head movements, distinguishing attackers with similar patterns from legitimate user behavior may be challenging. Additionally, while the system achieves high accuracy with multiple classifiers, its training and updating processes may pose inefficiencies when handling real-time scenarios or large-scale datasets.

Bhalla et al. [13] explored user authentication using IMU (Inertial Measurement Unit) data collected from AR head-mounted displays and proposed a novel authentication system leveraging holographic headset sensor data as an auxiliary continuous behavioral biometric. A user study using Microsoft HoloLens collected unique motion samples, including head movements and hand gestures, from participants within an AR environment. The findings indicate that IMU data from head-mounted displays can effectively profile and authenticate users, demonstrating the potential for continuous authentication based on user interactions in AR environments. However, the study's sample size was limited to five subjects, posing challenges in generalizing findings to real-world applications.

Lohr et al. [14] employed the DenseNet architecture for end-to-end Eye Movement Biometrics (EMB) as a novel method for user authentication in VR and AR devices. Their study achieved an EER of 3.66% using 5 s of registration and authentication. However, since the method relies on high-quality eye movement data, the eye-tracking sensors in VR/AR devices may not match the signal quality of the data used in their research.

2.2. *Biometric Authentication Using Periocular Images*

Kumari et al. [15] proposed a novel periocular biometrics system for robust authentication in scenarios impacted by the COVID-19 pandemic. Addressing the limitations of contact-based biometrics like fingerprint systems or face biometrics affected by mask-wearing, the proposed method focuses on the periocular region as it remains visible and provides sufficient discriminative information. The system combines handcrafted features (e.g., HOG), non-handcrafted features from pretrained CNN models, and semantic information, such as gender, extracted through a custom CNN model. A feature fusion approach ensures robust performance across varied conditions, including eyeglasses, masked eye regions, and pose variations. Despite achieving high accuracy with feature fusion and multiclass SVM classifiers, the computational complexity of combining multiple feature types may limit real-time applicability or scalability for large datasets.

Zhang et al. [16] proposed a deep feature fusion approach for iris and periocular biometrics on mobile devices to address challenges like low-resolution images and limited computational resources. Using maxout CNNs for compact feature extraction and adaptive weights for multimodal fusion, the system optimizes joint representation, achieving high accuracy and outperforming traditional methods. They also introduced the CASIA-Iris-Mobile-V1.0 database, the largest NIR mobile iris dataset, to support further research.

Almadan et al. [17] attempted to solve the problem that, despite the high performance of the convolutional neural network (CNN) model for periocular image-based user authentication on mobile devices, it is difficult to deploy on mobile devices with limited resources because the model requires large space and has high computational complexity due to millions of parameters and calculations. To this end, they evaluated five neural network pruning methods and compared them with the knowledge distillation method to analyze the performance of CNN model inference and user biometric authentication using periocular images on mobile devices. However, this approach was tested on periocular images collected from mobile devices, and it presents the challenge of being difficult to implement in a head-mounted display environment.

Zou et al. [18] proposed a lightweight CNN that combines the attention mechanism and intermediate features, considering that although deep learning-based periocular biometric algorithms have made great progress, it is necessary to improve network performance with fewer parameters in practical applications. Experimental results using three public datasets and one self-collected periocular dataset demonstrate the effectiveness of the proposed network. However, it shares the disadvantage of being difficult to apply in a head-mounted display-wearing environment, as in the previous study.

Lohith et al. [19] proposed a multimodal biometric method using multiple biometric information to solve the problem that single-modal biometrics may deteriorate performance due to limitations such as intra-class variation and non-universality because it identifies users using one biometric information. In the paper, multimodality biometric authentication is proposed through feature-level fusion using biometric information from the face, ear, and periocular regions, and CNN is applied for feature representation. However, this approach necessitates additional inputs beyond the periocular region, which may limit its applicability.

3. Proposed Method

Figure 1 illustrates the periocular image-based biometric authentication system proposed in this study. The proposed method can be broadly divided into four processes, with the second process further comprising four subprocesses. Detailed explanations for each step are provided in the following. We used PyTorch and OpenCV libraries in our experiments, versions 2.5.3 and 4.2.0.34 respectively.

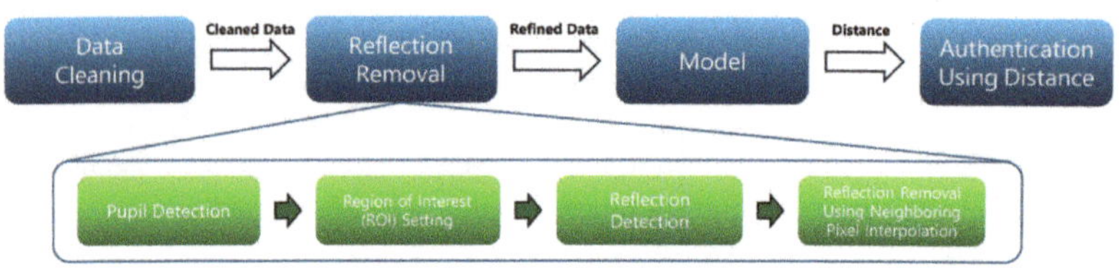

Figure 1. The periocular image-based biometric authentication system proposed in the study.

3.1. Dataset

In this study, the AffectiVR dataset [11] was used. This dataset contains data collected from 100 participants, and images around the eyes were recorded in a VR environment using the HTC Vive Pro and the 'HTC Vive Binocular Add-on'. During the dataset collection process, 360-degree videos were selected based on the study of [20], and 7 videos were selected considering changes in pupil size and eye movements of the participants. The videos included various lighting conditions, such as natural light, indoor lighting, and dark indoor environments, and reflected both static and dynamic viewpoints.

Each video played for approximately 90 s, and participants were able to freely control their movements and gaze directions. After watching the videos, a 3-minute break was provided to relieve fatigue caused by VR exposure. The data were recorded as a monocular video of each eye at 30 frames per second, 1920 × 1080 resolution, providing high-resolution data suitable for analyzing individual features such as skin texture around the eyes, eyelid shape, and eyelashes. This dataset contains a total of 5,199,175 frames of video data.

3.2. Data Preprocessing

Due to individual differences in the shape of the left and right eyes, this study utilized only the right eye's images. This approach was taken to maintain consistency in analysis and minimize variables that could arise from differences in the shape of both eyes. Additionally, frames unsuitable for biometric authentication, such as those depicting blinking, were excluded from the dataset acquired in this experiment. To remove frames where the eyes were closed, the following method was used: first, the pupil was extracted, and frames where the pupil was not captured, where the pupil's center suddenly moved significantly, or where the pupil's radius abruptly changed, were classified as frames with closed eyes. This process filtered out frames where the pupil was not clearly visible or displayed abnormal movement. Furthermore, in cases where the eyes were partially closed, it was likely that the frame was captured either during the act of opening or closing the eyes; thus, an additional eight frames surrounding the closed-eye frame were also removed. Through this method, we ensured that only images of open eyes were obtained. As a result, we secured periocular images exclusively in the open-eye state through a rigorous data filtering process, enhancing the reliability of the study and enabling accurate biometric authentication.

Additionally, reflections in the iris area typically have significantly higher brightness values compared to the surrounding regions, and this can act as noise during model training. To mitigate the impact of reflection noise, this study employed a method to remove reflections present in the iris. While eliminating reflections in the iris region can be problematic in iris authentication systems that directly rely on iris texture, we determined that this would not impact performance in our study, as we utilized periocular features in addition to the iris. The process of reflection removal proceeded as follows: the coordinates of the pupil center detected earlier were used to eliminate reflections. Since the size of the human iris does not exhibit significant variation between individuals, a circular region of interest (ROI) with a radius of 75 pixels was established around the detected pupil center. This ROI encompassed the iris area and served as the region for reflection detection. To detect reflections within this iris ROI, OpenCV was utilized, which identified the location and size of bright spots representing reflections. In this process, OpenCV's SimpleBlobDetector class was utilized and the minThreshold parameter was set to 190 to detect light reflection pixels. Once reflections were detected, the pixel values of a neighboring 7×7 region were analyzed to calculate the median value. The median value was used because it is less affected by outliers, allowing for more accurate interpolation. The calculated median value was then applied to the pixels containing reflections, effectively removing them. Through this interpolation process, a clean iris image with removed reflections was obtained. Figure 2 presents a comparison of images before and after reflection removal. In the image before reflection removal, noticeable reflections are present in the iris area; however, in the image after reflection removal, the reflections with higher values than the surrounding pixels are eliminated, resulting in a cleaner iris image. This can enhance the model's performance.

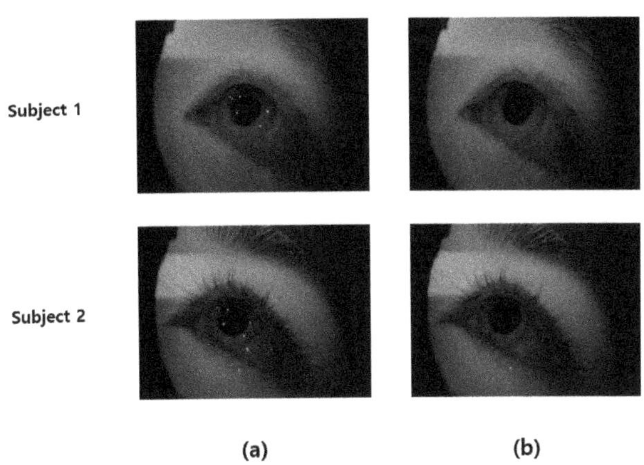

Figure 2. Example of removing reflective light (**a**): before removing reflective light, (**b**) after removing reflective light.

3.3. Model

To train the biometric authentication model, images were extracted from a dataset specifically constructed through experiments. To ensure an equal number of images per subject, 15 images were randomly selected from each subject's data for training. Ultimately, 105 images were compiled for each subject, resulting in a total of 10,500 training samples for 100 subjects, which were then used to train the model. To account for the variability in device positioning when wearing a VR headset, random horizontal translation and brightness adjustment were applied to the images during model training. Furthermore, recognizing that there are more impostor pairs than genuine pairs in real biometric authentication scenarios, the proportion of impostor pairs increased within the 10,500 training samples to create a robust comparison that closely mirrors actual conditions.

The base model structure utilized was a Siamese network-based deep learning model, as proposed in Hwang et al. [21]. The Siamese network is a deep learning model structure designed to learn the relationship between feature vectors of two images extracted from a convolutional neural network (CNN) model with shared weights. The goal is to minimize the distance between feature vectors for positive pair images while maximizing the distance for negative pairs. The Siamese network model structure is illustrated in Figure 3, while the feature extraction model structure is depicted in Figure 4.

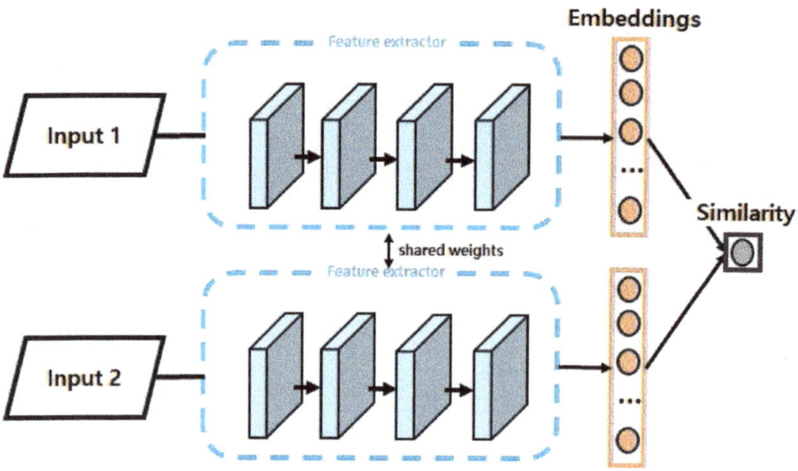

Figure 3. Siamese network architecture used for training.

In a CNN used for image feature extraction, shallow layers capture low-level features, while deeper layers extract high-level features. Typically, CNNs have multiple stacked layers, with the final output feature vector being utilized for further processing. However, Hwang et al. [21] suggested that useful features for biometric authentication based on eye images can also exist in the intermediate layers of CNN-based models. Thus, they designed the model to also utilize features extracted from the intermediate layers of the deep learning model. To achieve this, global average pooling is applied to the feature maps extracted from each layer to convert them into 1-dimensional vectors. These converted vectors are then connected to a fully connected layer to generate a unified 1-dimensional vector. As a result, one feature vector is generated for each convolutional layer, and the final feature vector is produced by merging them. These two feature vectors are then used to compare the two images, therefore performing biometric authentication based on the periocular image.

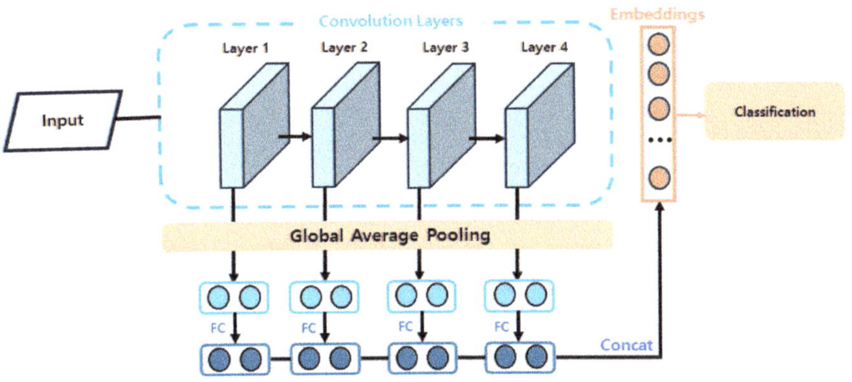

Figure 4. Structure of the feature extraction model proposed in the study by Hwang et al. [21].

The model employed in this experiment was based on the Deep-ResNet18 architecture introduced by Hwang et al. [21]. Additionally, the periocular images used as inputs for the model were downsampled from the original resolution of 1920 × 1080 to a lower resolution of 320 × 240. The detailed structure of the model used in this experiment is summarized in Table 1.

The dataset used for training the deep learning model contained noise manifested as thick horizontal lines in the images, as shown in Figure 5. This type of noise can be misinterpreted as a feature during model training. To mitigate this issue, we incorporated a Squeeze-and-Excitation (SE) block after the Residual block in our model. The SE block, commonly used in computer vision research to enhance image authentication performance, models the interdependence between channels to highlight significant features and suppress less relevant ones. It is a simple module that integrates seamlessly into various convolutional neural network (CNN) architectures and adds minimal additional parameters, therefore improving performance without substantially increasing model complexity. The Residual block structure with the SE block is illustrated in Figure 6.

For comparative performance evaluation, we modified the feature extraction model and conducted training under identical conditions. We selected two comparison models, MobileViT [22], and ResNet34 [23], to ensure a fair evaluation, particularly considering the need for continuous biometric authentication in practical environments. Models with excessive parameters were excluded from comparison to avoid undue complexity.

Training was performed using the Adam optimizer, known for its effectiveness, with binary cross-entropy as the loss function. To identify the best-performing model, we saved the model parameters corresponding to the lowest validation loss. The batch size was set to 16, and training was conducted for 10 epochs. To prevent overfitting, we employed early stopping, halting training if validation loss did not improve over 5 consecutive epochs. Performance evaluation involved splitting the dataset into training and testing sets at an 8:2 ratio and performing 5-fold cross-validation. The final performance metrics were calculated as the average across the five folds. The experiments were performed using Python 3.8.17 and CUDA 11.6, with TensorFlow 2.7.0 as the learning framework.

Table 1. Structure of the Deep-ResNet18 periocular image-based biometric authentication model proposed in the study by Hwang et al. [21].

Block	#Layer	Structure	#Channel
Block 1	1 2	Conv(7 × 7), stride = 2 Max Pooling(3 × 3), stride = 2	32
Block 2	3 4 5 6 7 8	Conv(3 × 3) Conv(3 × 3) Shortcut(2, 4) [1] Conv(3 × 3) Conv(3 × 3) Shortcut(5, 7) [1]	32
Block 3	9 10 11 12 13 14	Conv(3 × 3), stride = 2 Conv(3 × 3) Shortcut(8, 10) [1] Conv(3 × 3) Conv(3 × 3) Shortcut(11, 13) [1]	64
Block 4	15 16 17 18 19 20	Conv(3 × 3), stride = 2 Conv(3 × 3) Shortcut(14, 16) [1] Conv(3 × 3) Conv(3 × 3) Shortcut(17, 19) [1]	128
Block 5	21 22 23 24 25 26	Conv(3 × 3), stride = 2 Conv(3 × 3) Shortcut(20, 22) [1] Conv(3 × 3) Conv(3 × 3) Shortcut(24, 25) [1]	256
Pooling	27 28 29 30	Vector(8) [2] Vector(14) [2] Vector(20) [2] Vector(26) [2]	32 64 128 256
Concat	31	Concatenate(29, 30, 31, 32)	480

[1] Shortcut(x, y): A shortcut structure that performs element-wise addition operations on the x and y layers.
[2] Vector(x): Performs a fully connected layer operation with nodes of the same size as global average pooling for x.

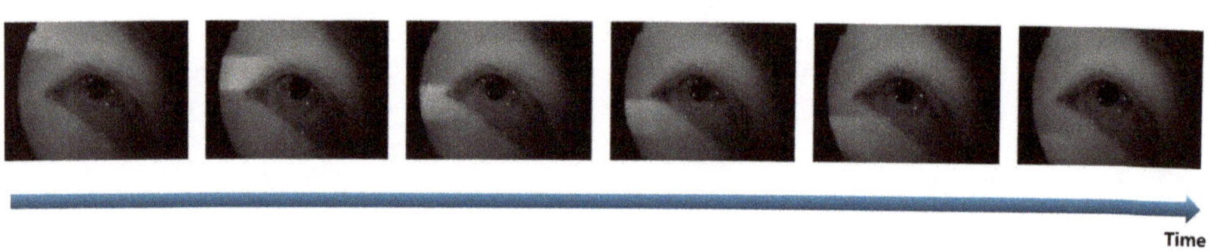

Figure 5. Noise observed in image data over time.

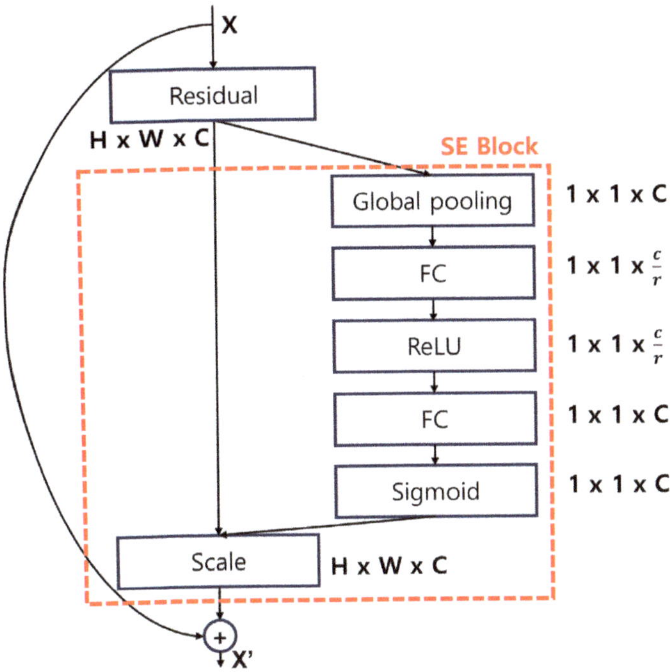

Figure 6. Residual block structure with SE block.

4. Results

4.1. Comparison of Results Before and After Reflective Noise Suppression

First, to compare the performance before and after reflection removal, the model was trained and evaluated with and without removing reflected light. Table 2 presents the biometric authentication performance based on whether reflection removal was applied. In biometric authentication, it is crucial to maintain a low False Acceptance Rate (FAR), which relates to the risk of incorrectly recognizing an impostor as a legitimate user. Therefore, we compared the False Rejection Rate (FRR) when the FAR was less than 1%. In this study, heatmap analysis was conducted to investigate the prediction results of the biometric authentication model. This technique visualizes the significant regions in the model's output and has been widely used in recent computer vision-based studies, such as object detection and image classification. Many of these studies have employed the gradient-weighted class activation mapping (Grad-CAM) method [24]. Grad-CAM evaluates the gradient of each pixel concerning the model's output, reflecting the degree of influence each pixel has on the final result. Pixels that are more influential are represented in red on the heatmap, indicating their importance.

Figure 7 illustrates the results of a heatmap analysis conducted to assess the impact of reflection removal on model performance. As seen in Figure 7, the influence of specular light pixels is significant in images that have not undergone reflection removal. This suggests that specular light features are heavily relied upon during the biometric authentication process. However, in the images where reflection removal was applied, it is evident that the model focuses more on features related to the shape of the eyes and the surrounding skin rather than on specular light. Thus, it can be concluded that the model was trained to prioritize specific periocular features over specular light using the images applied to reflection removal. Figures 8 and 9 display the Genuine–Impostor distribution and the receiver operating characteristic (ROC) curve, respectively, for the model when evaluated with the AffectiVR dataset used in this study. The x-axis of Figure 8 represents the distance between the feature vectors of the two images input into the model. Typically, the Genuine–Impostor distribution forms two Gaussian curves with some separation, and the less overlap there is between these distributions, the better the biometric authentication performance. According to the performance evaluation, training the model with the data after reflection removal led to improvements in both the Equal Error Rate (EER) and the False Rejection Rate (FRR) when the False Acceptance Rate (FAR) was less than 1%.

Table 2. Comparison of Biometric Authentication Performance with and without Reflection Removal.

Performance (%)	Before Reflection Removal	After Reflection Removal
EER	6.73	5.52
FRR (FAR < 1%)	23.70	19.28

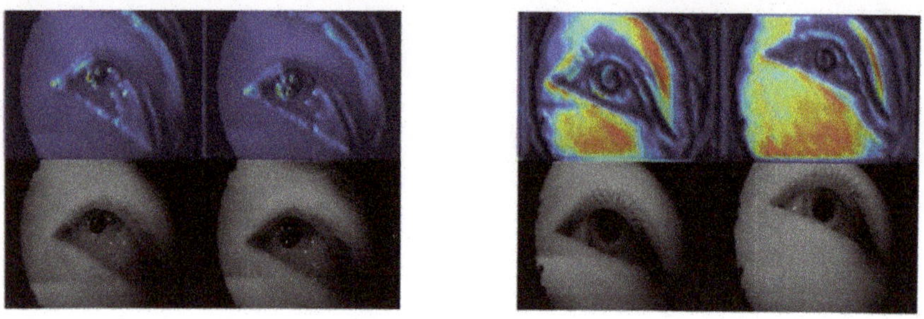

(a) (b)

Figure 7. Heatmap images according to reflection removal; (**a**) before reflection removal, (**b**) after reflection removal. Red on the heatmap indicates a higher value, while blue indicates a lower value.

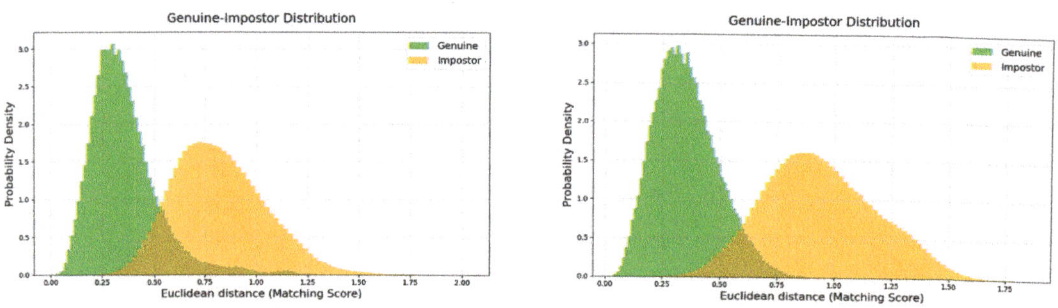

(a) (b)

Figure 8. Comparison of Genuine—Impostor distribution graphs according to reflection removal; (**a**) before reflection removal, (**b**) after reflection removal.

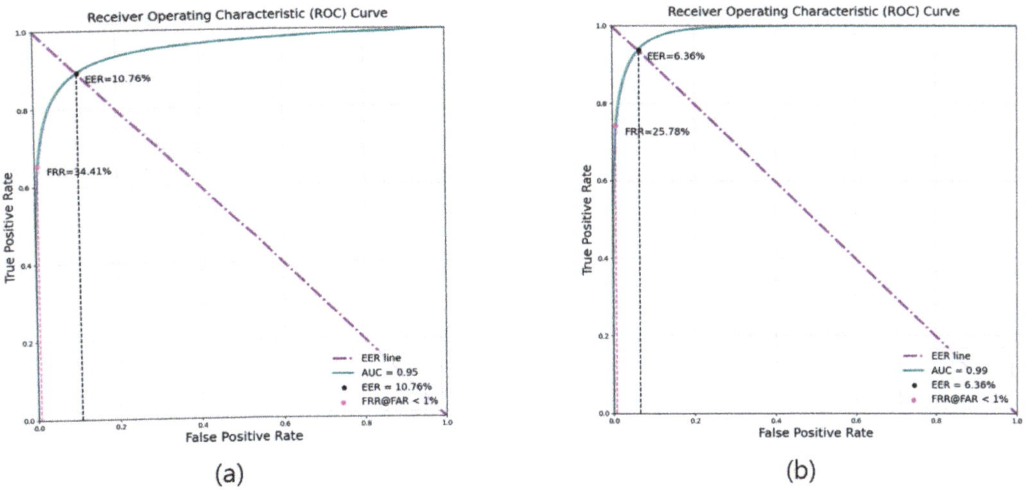

Figure 9. Comparison of ROC curves according to reflection removal; (**a**) before reflection removal, (**b**) after reflection removal.

4.2. Comparison of Results Before and After Using SE Block

In order to compare the performance before and after utilizing the SE block structure, models before and after introducing the SE block structure were trained. Table 3 shows the biometric authentication performance depending on whether the SENet structure was reflected. Figure 10 shows the Genuine–Impostor distribution and ROC curve of the model predicted using the AffectiVR dataset in this study as input, and Figure 11 shows the Genuine—Impostor distribution and ROC curve of the model trained by integrating the SENet structure into the model. The x-axis in Figure 10b is the distance between the feature vectors of two images used as inputs of the model. According to the performance measurement results, when the model was trained using the data after introducing the SENet structure, it was confirmed that the performance slightly decreased in both measures of EER and FRR.

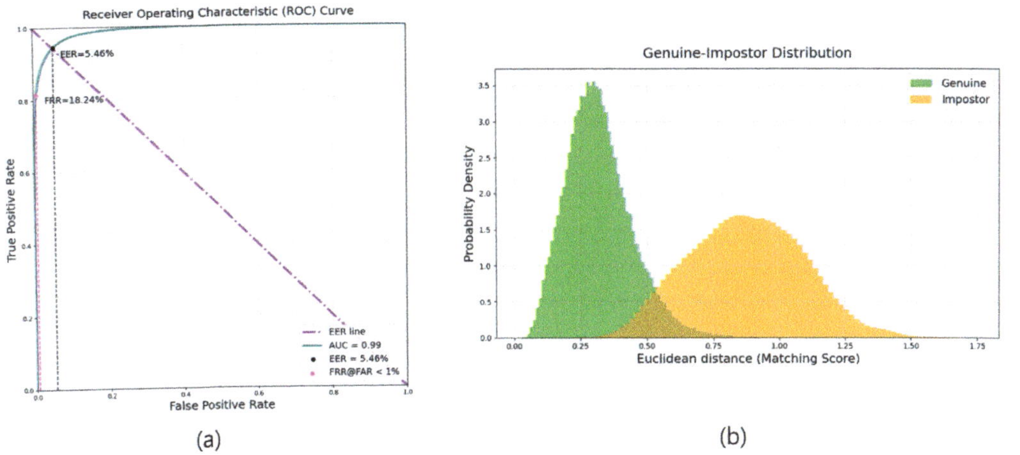

Figure 10. Biometric authentication performance results before reflecting SENet structure. (**a**) ROC curve, (**b**) Genuine—Impostor distribution.

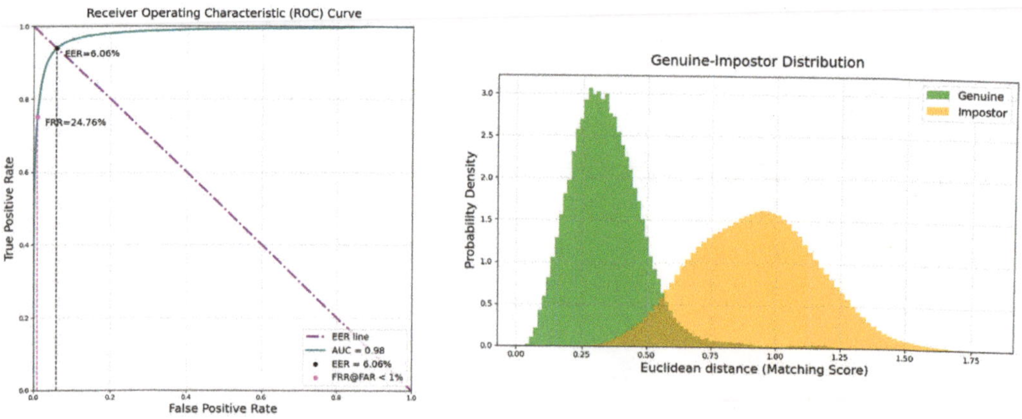

(a) (b)

Figure 11. Biometric authentication performance results after reflecting SENet structure. (**a**) ROC curve, (**b**) Genuine—Impostor distribution.

Table 3. Comparison of performance results depending on whether SENet structure is reflected or not.

Model	EER	FRR (FAR < 1%)
Deep-ResNet [21]	5.52	19.28
Deep-SE-ResNet	6.39	24.52

Through Figure 12, we can see that the preprocessed image mainly utilizes the features around the eyes related to the skin around the eyes and the shape of the eyes instead of the power noise. Therefore, we can conclude that by incorporating the SENet structure into the model, the performance decreased, but the model was trained to emphasize the specific features around the eyes rather than the power noise.

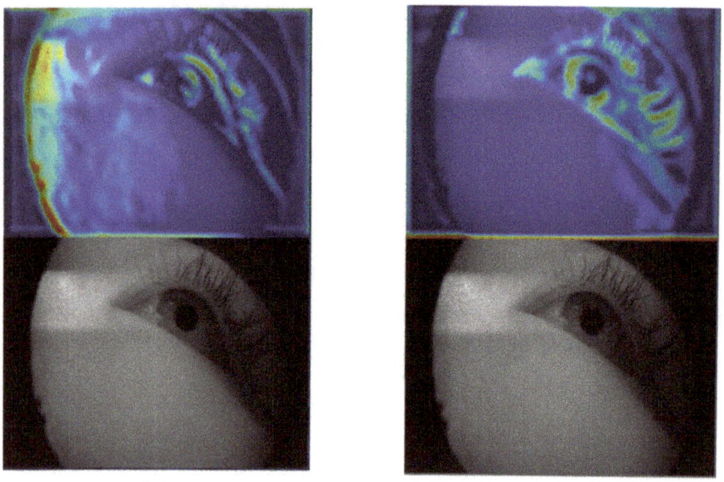

(a) (b)

Figure 12. Heatmap images according to whether the SENet structure is integrated or not. (**a**) Image before integration, (**b**) image after integration. Red on the heatmap indicates a higher value, while blue indicates a lower value.

4.3. Additional Model Training and Performance Comparison

In this study, to compare models suitable for the dataset environment, two additional models were trained by changing only the feature extraction network while maintaining the same environment. This experiment aimed to compare the performance of a deeper model within the same architecture and the performance of a model incorporating an attention mechanism. To this end, ResNet34 [23] and MobileViT [22] were additionally trained.

The choice of MobileViT over vanilla ViT was driven by the requirement for real-time performance in user biometric authentication systems, particularly in head-mounted display (HMD) environments. MobileViT offers a more lightweight structure, which is crucial for maintaining real-time processing capabilities while achieving high accuracy. The performance evaluation of each model is presented in Table 4.

Table 4. Comparison of biometric authentication performance according to the number of parameters of several backbone models.

Model	Parameters	EER	FRR (FAR < 1%)
ResNet34 [23]	5.7 M	5.61	18.44
MobileViT [22]	2.3 M	6.39	30.33
Deep-SE-ResNet	3.2 M	6.39	24.52

5. Discussion

In this study, when comparing the performance before and after integrating the SENet structure, the EER of the model slightly decreased from 5.52% to 6.39% and the FRR (FAR < 1%) slightly decreased from 19.28% to 24.52% after introducing the SENet structure. In a performance comparison with the ResNet34 model and the MobileViT model, the ResNet34 model achieved the best performance with an EER of 5.61% and an FRR of 18.44%, while the MobileViT model had the poorest performance with an EER of 9.74% and an FRR of 30.33%. These results show that the performance of the Deep-SE-ResNet model slightly decreased after the introduction of the SE block, but the heatmap analysis results show that the model with the SE block introduced learns only specific and meaningful periocular features better. This indicates that the model has shifted towards more effectively suppressing abnormal features such as power noise and more clearly extracting periocular features, which are crucial for biometric authentication. Power noise was recognized as a major feature in the previous model, but with the introduction of the SE block, these abnormal features were suppressed, and instead, specific features such as the skin around the eyes and the shape of the eyes were highlighted as major features. Our study used periocular images that are not front-facing like those used in prior research, and they contain power noise. Considering that the SE block suppresses noise and emphasizes crucial features, we expect that performance could be further improved if noise-free data were utilized. In particular, the SE block models the interdependence between channels to emphasize important features and suppress less important features, so the model was trained in a direction that enables more reliable biometric authentication. Based on these results, the model that introduced the SE block is significant in that the model was changed to extract only the features of the meaningful part of the data.

Therefore, despite a slight decrease in performance, the introduction of the SE block contributed to extracting more reliable features for biometric authentication by suppressing abnormal features such as power noise and emphasizing periocular-specific features. This suggests an important direction for future research on user biometric authentication in VR environments, and it is expected that the dataset and model of this study will play an important role in increasing the applicability in real-world environments.

These findings underscore the unique advantage of using SE blocks and reflective noise suppression in environments where maintaining specific feature fidelity is critical. By actively down-weighting noise-prone areas and highlighting periocular features, this approach enables the model to be more resilient to variations that can compromise authentication accuracy. Such robustness is crucial for VR environments, where environmental noise and lighting inconsistencies are common. Thus, our method lays the groundwork for creating authentication systems that are both adaptive and precise in real-time applications.

In addition, as a result of experiments using multiple models, the Deep-SE-ResNet18 model showed the most effective performance relative to the number of model parameters. This suggests that the Deep-SE-ResNet18 model can achieve high performance even with relatively few parameters, considering the relationship between the dataset size and the number of model parameters. These results emphasize the necessity and practicality of lightweight models in biometric authentication research in virtual reality environments and show that they can increase the applicability in environments that require real-time performance.

6. Conclusions

In this study, we utilized the AffectiVR dataset for user authentication in a virtual reality head-mounted display environment and presented a biometric authentication model using it. We utilized the AffectiVR dataset, which was acquired from virtual reality devices and is therefore suitable for real environments. This dataset is essential for user authentication research in a virtual reality environment and can also contribute to improving biometric authentication performance with high-resolution images. Additionally, we removed reflected light from the iris, which can act as noise, to enhance the model's ability to learn features around the eyes. Through this preprocessing, we improved the performance from the existing 6.73% to 5.52% EER.

The dataset used in this study contained noise in the form of horizontal lines. Upon analyzing the heatmap of the existing model, we observed that the heatmap was centered around this noise. To reduce the impact of this noise, we introduced the SE block structure, resulting in a slightly higher EER of 6.39%. However, further heatmap analysis revealed that the model with the SE block focused on biometric features around the eyes rather than the noise. This study also compared various models and presented a benchmark that will be valuable for future research.

Given the limited research on periocular biometrics in virtual reality environments, this study offers several significant advantages. First, it provides an opportunity to develop and verify a more realistic biometric authentication model using data collected in an actual virtual reality device usage environment. Second, this study successfully trained a model that is robust to power noise, which can occur in a VR environment, using the SE block structure. This can serve as an important reference for developing models that consider similar environments in future studies. Finally, by comparing various models and presenting a benchmark, this study makes an academic contribution that researchers can use to develop more effective biometric authentication systems in the future. Finally, by comparing various models and presenting a benchmark, this study makes an academic contribution that researchers can use to develop more effective biometric authentication systems in the future.

In future studies, we will optimize machine-learning algorithms to enable faster and more accurate real-time authentication. Moreover, we anticipate that extracting the iris from the image and combining it with periocular biometrics to perform multi-biometric authentication will yield even better performance. Iris authentication technology, known for its high accuracy and security, combined with existing eye image-based authentication, could establish a dual security system, ensuring high reliability even in a virtual reality environment. We expect that this multi-biometric authentication system will further strengthen security by analyzing various biometric characteristics such as the user's eye blinking and gaze movements.

In addition, incorporating SE blocks into the model demonstrated robustness to noise in Grad-CAM qualitative evaluations. This indicates the potential to develop models less influenced by noise, addressing one of the major challenges in learning with the AffectiVR dataset. In other words, this suggests that the model could demonstrate strong generalization capabilities when applied to other datasets without the noise present in the AffectiVR dataset. Therefore, future research will focus on improving performance by integrating SE blocks and conducting evaluations on data collected from various head-mounted devices.

Author Contributions: Conceptualization, E.C.L.; Data curation, C.S.; Formal analysis, J.B. and C.S.; Investigation, Y.P., J.B. and C.S.; Methodology, J.B. and Y.P.; Project administration, E.C.L.; Resources, C.S., Y.P. and J.B.; Software, Y.P. and J.B.; Supervision, E.C.L.; Validation, J.B. and Y.P.; Visualization, C.S.; Writing—original draft, J.B. and Y.P.; Writing—review and editing, E.C.L., Y.P. and J.B. All authors have read and agreed to the published version of the manuscript.

Funding: This research was funded by a 2024 Research Grant from Sangmyung University (2024-A000-0086).

Institutional Review Board Statement: Based on Article 13-1-1 and 13-1-2 of the Enforcement Regulations of the Act on Bioethics and Safety of the Republic of Korea, ethical review and approval were waived (IRB-SMU-C-2023-1-007) for this study by Sangmyung University's Institutional Review Board because this study uses only simple contact-measuring equipment or observation equipment that does not involve physical changes and does not include invasive procedures such as drug administration or blood sampling.

Informed Consent Statement: Informed consent was obtained from all subjects involved in the study. Written informed consent has been obtained from the subjects to publish this paper.

Data Availability Statement: The dataset used in this study is available for academic purposes only. To access the dataset, permission must be requested via email at eclee@smu.ac.kr. All codes were released and shared at (https://github.com/schaelin/AffectiVR (accessed on 24 September 2024)). The code was written using Python 3.8.18, and how to use it is explained at (https://github.com/schaelin/AffectiVR (accessed on 24 September 2024)).

Conflicts of Interest: The authors declare no conflicts of interest.

References

1. Wang, Y.; Su, Z.; Zhang, N.; Xing, R.; Liu, D.; Luan, T.H.; Shen, X. A survey on metaverse: Fundamentals, security, and privacy. *IEEE Commun. Surv. Tutor.* **2022**, *25*, 319–352. [CrossRef]
2. Mystakidis, S. Metaverse. *Encyclopedia* **2022**, *2*, 486–497. [CrossRef]
3. Zhao, R.; Zhang, Y.; Zhu, Y.; Lan, R.; Hua, Z. Metaverse: Security and privacy concerns. *J. Metaverse* **2023**, *3*, 93–99. [CrossRef]
4. George, C.; Khamis, M.; von Zezschwitz, E.; Burger, M.; Schmidt, H.; Alt, F.; Hussmann, H. *Seamless and Secure vr: Adapting and Evaluating Established Authentication Systems for Virtual Reality*; NDSS: San Diego, CA, USA, 2017.
5. Boutros, F.; Damer, N.; Raja, K.; Ramachandra, R.; Kirchbuchner, F.; Kuijper, A. Fusing iris and periocular region for user verification in head mounted displays. In Proceedings of the 2020 IEEE 23rd International Conference on Information Fusion (FUSION), Rustenburg, South Africa, 6–9 July 2020; pp. 1–8.
6. Kumari, P.; Seeja, K. Periocular biometrics: A survey. *J. King Saud Univ.-Comput. Inf. Sci.* **2022**, *34*, 1086–1097. [CrossRef]
7. Alonso-Fernandez, F.; Bigun, J.; Fierrez, J.; Damer, N.; Proença, H.; Ross, A. Periocular biometrics: A modality for unconstrained scenarios. *Computer* **2024**, *57*, 40–49. [CrossRef]
8. Lin, X.; Li, Y.; Zhu, J.; Zeng, H. DeflickerCycleGAN: Learning to detect and remove flickers in a single image. *IEEE Trans. Image Process.* **2023**, *32*, 709–720. [CrossRef] [PubMed]

9. Nadernejad, E.; Mantel, C.; Burini, N.; Forchhammer, S. Flicker reduction in LED-LCDs with local backlight. In Proceedings of the 2013 IEEE 15th International Workshop on Multimedia Signal Processing (MMSP), Pula, Sardinia, Italy, 30 September–2 October 2013; pp. 312–316.
10. Castro, I.; Vazquez, A.; Arias, M.; Lamar, D.G.; Hernando, M.M.; Sebastian, J. A review on flicker-free AC–DC LED drivers for single-phase and three-phase AC power grids. *IEEE Trans. Power Electron.* **2019**, *34*, 10035–10057. [CrossRef]
11. Seok, C.; Park, Y.; Baek, J.; Lim, H.; Roh, J.h.; Kim, Y.; Kim, S.; Lee, E.C. AffectiVR: A Database for Periocular Identification and Valence and Arousal Evaluation in Virtual Reality. *Electronics* **2024**, *13*, 4112. [CrossRef]
12. Sivasamy, M.; Sastry, V.; Gopalan, N. VRCAuth: Continuous authentication of users in virtual reality environment using head-movement. In Proceedings of the 2020 5th International Conference on Communication and Electronics Systems (icces), Coimbatore, India, 10–12 June 2020; pp. 518–523.
13. Bhalla, A.; Sluganovic, I.; Krawiecka, K.; Martinovic, I. MoveAR: Continuous biometric authentication for augmented reality headsets. In Proceedings of the 7th acm on Cyber-Physical System Security Workshop, Virtual, 7 June 2021; pp. 41–52.
14. Lohr, D.; Komogortsev, O.V. Eye know you too: Toward viable end-to-end eye movement biometrics for user authentication. *IEEE Trans. Inf. Forensics Secur.* **2022**, *17*, 3151–3164. [CrossRef]
15. Kumari, P.; Seeja, K.R. A novel periocular biometrics solution for authentication during COVID-19 pandemic situation. *J. Ambient. Intell. Humaniz. Comput.* **2021**, *12*, 10321–10337. [CrossRef] [PubMed]
16. Zhang, Q.; Li, H.; Sun, Z.; Tan, T. Deep feature fusion for iris and periocular biometrics on mobile devices. *IEEE Trans. Inf. Forensics Secur.* **2018**, *13*, 2897–2912. [CrossRef]
17. Almadan, A.; Rattani, A. Compact cnn models for on-device ocular-based user recognition in mobile devices. In Proceedings of the 2021 IEEE Symposium Series on Computational Intelligence (SSCI), Virtual, 5–7 December 2021; pp. 1–7.
18. Zou, Q.; Wang, C.; Yang, S.; Chen, B. A compact periocular recognition system based on deep learning framework AttenMidNet with the attention mechanism. *Multimed. Tools Appl.* **2023**, *82*, 15837–15857. [CrossRef]
19. Lohith, M.; Manjunath, Y.S.K.; Eshwarappa, M. Multimodal biometric person authentication using face, ear and periocular region based on convolution neural networks. *Int. J. Image Graph.* **2023**, *23*, 2350019. [CrossRef]
20. Li, B.J.; Bailenson, J.N.; Pines, A.; Greenleaf, W.J.; Williams, L.M. A public database of immersive VR videos with corresponding ratings of arousal, valence, and correlations between head movements and self report measures. *Front. Psychol.* **2017**, *8*, 2116. [CrossRef]
21. Hwang, H.; Lee, E.C. Near-infrared image-based periocular biometric method using convolutional neural network. *IEEE Access* **2020**, *8*, 158612–158621. [CrossRef]
22. Mehta, S.; Rastegari, M. Mobilevit: Light-weight, general-purpose, and mobile-friendly vision transformer. *arXiv* **2021**, arXiv:2110.02178.
23. He, K.; Zhang, X.; Ren, S.; Sun, J. Deep residual learning for image recognition. In Proceedings of the IEEE Conference on Computer Vision and Pattern Recognition, Las Vegas, NV, USA, 27–30 June 2016; pp. 770–778.
24. Selvaraju, R.R.; Cogswell, M.; Das, A.; Vedantam, R.; Parikh, D.; Batra, D. Grad-cam: Visual explanations from deep networks via gradient-based localization. In Proceedings of the IEEE International Conference on Computer Vision, Venice, Italy, 22–29 October 2017; pp. 618–626.

electronics

MDPI

Article

Enhancing Web Application Security: Advanced Biometric Voice Verification for Two-Factor Authentication

Kamil Adam Kamiński [1,2,*], Andrzej Piotr Dobrowolski [3], Zbigniew Piotrowski [3] and Przemysław Ścibiorek [4]

1 Institute of Optoelectronics, Military University of Technology, 2 Kaliski Street, 00-908 Warsaw, Poland
2 BITRES Sp. z o.o., 9/2 Chałubiński Street, 02-004 Warsaw, Poland
3 Faculty of Electronics, Military University of Technology, 2 Kaliski Street, 00-908 Warsaw, Poland; andrzej.dobrowolski@wat.edu.pl (A.P.D.); zbigniew.piotrowski@wat.edu.pl (Z.P.)
4 POL Cyber Command, 2 Buka Street, 05-119 Legionowo, Poland; przemyslaw.scibiorek@wat.edu.pl
* Correspondence: kamil.kaminski@wat.edu.pl

Abstract: This paper presents a voice biometrics system implemented in a web application as part of a two-factor authentication (2FA) user login. The web-based application, via a client interface, runs registration, preprocessing, feature extraction and normalization, classification, and speaker verification procedures based on a modified Gaussian mixture model (GMM) algorithm adapted to the application requirements. The article describes in detail the internal modules of this ASR (Automatic Speaker Recognition) system. A comparison of the performance of competing ASR systems using the commercial NIST 2002 SRE voice dataset tested under the same conditions is also presented. In addition, it presents the results of the influence of the application of cepstral mean and variance normalization over a sliding window (WCMVN) and its relevance, especially for voice recordings recorded in varying acoustic tracks. The article also presents the results of the selection of a reference model representing an alternative hypothesis in the decision-making system, which significantly translates into an increase in the effectiveness of speaker verification. The final experiment presented is a test of the performance achieved in a varying acoustic environment during remote voice login to a web portal by the test group, as well as a final adjustment of the decision-making threshold.

Keywords: speaker recognition; biometrics (access control); authentication; cepstral analysis; Gaussian mixture model; genetic algorithms; system verification

1. Introduction

The two-factor login method described in this article using a voice biometrics system is implemented in the novel PicWATermark system for user verification and authentication. This is implemented, among other things, by means of voice biometrics but also by means of a marking method using a watermark as an identifier contained in the digital material [1,2]. In addition, the module will have in-built copyright protection mechanisms for the creators of the digital material, e.g., to identify the digital images taken.

The voice biometrics system that is the subject of this article provides convenient functionality for the user using the PicWATermark system, enhancing not only login convenience but also security. In addition, in this era of the prevailing SARS-CoV-2 virus pandemic, it allows the PicWATermark system to be used efficiently without the need to remove a protective mask or gloves, which would be necessary when using facial biometrics or a fingerprint as a second login component. It is also important to remember that the human voice, as a biometric, does not require additional passwords to be remembered or other sensitive data to be entered, and every user has it with them at all times. This represents a significant advantage over the use of additional passwords, which are becoming increasingly difficult to remember due to the complexity required.

The implementation of the voice biometrics module is shown in Figure 1. Voice authentication is one of the three possible two factor authentication (2FA) methods in the PicWATermark system (alongside photo and PIN authorization). The voice authentication module in the system exists as a Docker container that communicates with the user authentication module via a REST API. The BIO module, which is part of the voice authorization module, consists of two submodules. The first is the learning submodule, which is used in the creation of the user voice model. The testing submodule, on the other hand, is used in biometric verification mode, during which the characteristic features of the voice are compared with a previously created model of the user's voice.

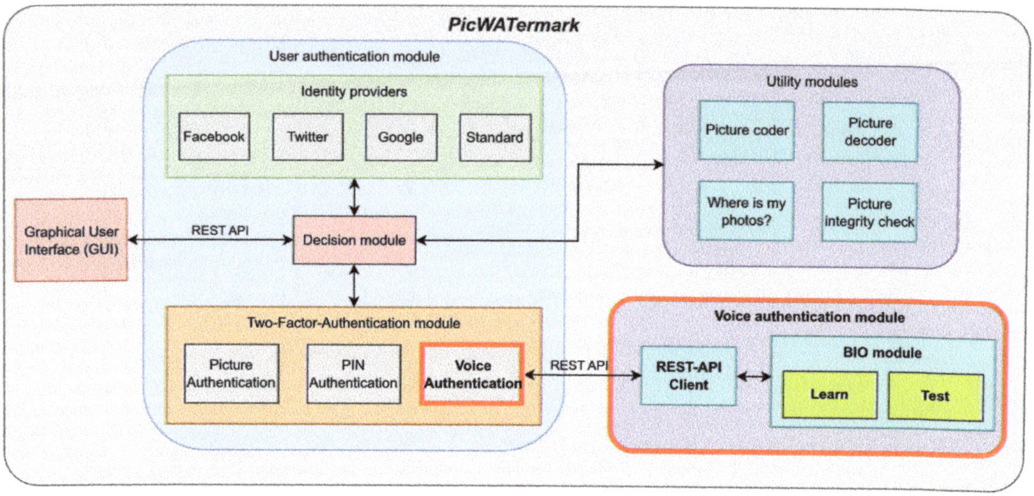

Figure 1. Implementation diagram for the user authentication module in the PicWATermark system.

User login to the PicWATermark system using the voice authorization module must be preceded by the activation of two-factor authorization in the user account. During this operation, the user is asked to provide a 25 s voice sample, through which a voice model will be created. Once the model has been successfully generated, the user can log into the system using their voice. To do this, in addition to the standard login data (username and password), the user must record a 5 s voice sample, which is then analyzed by the testing submodule of the voice biometrics module (BIO). After successful verification of the login and password and a voice sample, the user is granted access to the PicWATermark system.

The aforementioned architecture of the voice biometrics system has been further elaborated upon in Section 3. Secure login constitutes a daily challenge faced by nearly every computer or smartphone user in the contemporary world. Therefore, in response to this issue, the authors have attempted to create a voice biometric system and subsequently integrate it into a two-factor authentication system.

2. Related Works

In this section, an analysis of the latest scientific publications in the areas of 2FA and voice biometrics is presented.

In the first instance, the authors will focus on presenting the most commonly used components of 2FA. As research demonstrates, the utilization of the second factor of authentication has become a socially prevalent phenomenon [3–5]. Only 21% of users employ single-factor authentication, while as many as 72% utilize a second factor of authentication to enhance its security.

In Table 1, the authors have compiled popular authentication factors constituting 2FA [6–12]. They have subjected them to comparison based on the following parameters:

– *Universality*—every individual should possess the considered factor;
– *Uniqueness*—the factor should ensure a high degree of differentiation among individuals;
– *Collectability*—the factor should be measurable through practical means;
– *Performance*—determines the potential for achieving accuracy, speed, and reliability;
– *Acceptability*—society should not have reservations about the use of technology employed by the specific factor.
– *Spoofing*—indicates the level of difficulty in intercepting and falsifying a sample of data from the respective factor.

Table 1. Comparison of individual factors for 2FA: H—high; M—medium; L—low; n/a—unavailable [8,10].

Factor	Universality	Uniqueness	Collectability	Performance	Acceptability	Spoofing
Password	n/a	L	H	H	H	H
Token	n/a	M	H	H	H	H
Voice	M	L	M	L	H	H
Facial	H	L	M	L	H	M
Ocular-based	H	H	M	M	L	H
Fingerprint	M	H	M	H	M	H
Hand geometry	M	M	M	M	M	M
Location	n/a	L	M	H	M	H
Vein	M	M	M	M	M	M
Thermal image	H	H	L	M	H	H
Behavior	H	H	L	L	L	L
Beam-forming	n/a	M	L	L	L	H
OCS [1]	n/a	L	L	L	L	M
ECG [2]	L	H	L	M	M	L
EEG [3]	L	H	L	M	L	L
DNA	H	H	L	H	L	L

[1]—Occupant Classification Systems (OCS); [2]—Electrocardiographic (ECG) Recognition; [3]—Electroencephalographic (EEG) Recognition.

Subsequently, the authors conducted a review of currently employed voice biometrics methods. The vast majority of authors use the cesptral method to create a unique vector of discriminant features, as well as mel-scale summation filters to create so-called *mel-frequency cepstrum coefficients (MFCCs)* [13–23]. Additional distinctive features are also used, such as *T-phase* features [3] or features based on the method of *Linear Predictive Coding (LPC)* [13,16,19–21].

Another essential element of the architecture of speaker recognition systems is an effective classifier. A popular and effective classification method is the *Gaussian mixture model with Universal Background Model (GMM-UBM)* method or its various modifications. Using a high number of Gaussian distributions per voice model [13–15]. In recent years, there has also been a trend towards the use of *Deep Neural Networks (DNN)* [17,18,24], including *Convolutional Neural Networks (CNN)* [19], as well as so-called *Long Short-Term Memory Networks (LSTM)* [16,20,21]. Another type of neural network is the *Time Delay Neural Network (TDNN)* [21–25], as well as the *Sequence-to-Sequence Attentional Siamese Neural Network (Seq2Seq-ASNN)* [26].

The authors of this paper use mel-cepstral features and weighted cepstral features during the generation of discriminant features, as well as a GMM classifier with a few Gaussian distributions, providing memory-saving processing, which is importance for the implementation of the voice biometric system. For a detailed description of the various processing steps, see Section 3. It should be noted that cross-comparing speaker recognition systems is not the easiest thing to do. This is because there are a number of commercial voice datasets that are used to test the effectiveness of *Automatic Speaker Recognition (ASR)* systems. Nevertheless, it can be concluded that, depending on the speech processing methods used and the voice base used, the above-mentioned authors achieve an *equal error rate (EER)* of between 16.09% and 0.73%.

The voice biometrics system described in this paper performs at a very good level relative to its competitors, taking additionally into account the fact that the experiments presented were carried out under real-world conditions using a cloud implementation of the ASR system. The individual test results are presented in Section 4 of the article.

Furthermore, it should be noted that most of the voice biometric systems described in the literature lack practical aspects and attempts at their real-world implementation. The authors of this article have taken on the challenge of developing and implementing a practical voice biometrics system that, considering Table 1, is excellently suited for use in 2FA systems. The utilization of voice biometrics for this purpose represents an innovative idea and a significant contribution to existing research, especially in comparison to commonly used additional security measures such as passwords, facial recognition, or fingerprint scans. Moreover, this approach is highly secure, as demonstrated in Section 4.

3. Methods

The structure of the ASR system described in this article is shown in Figure 2. The remainder of this section describes the individual modules of the ASR system in more detail, starting with the speech acquisition and signal pre-processing processes and the associated proprietary methods for selecting the processed speech frames. Another element of the operation of the presented voice biometrics system is the process of extracting, selecting, and normalizing the unique characteristics of the speaker's voice. The process involved cepstral analysis of the speech signal as well as a genetic algorithm. This is followed by a presentation of the classifier used, using Gaussian mixture models, which is a memory-efficient and individually information-rich classification method. The next stage of processing is the decision-making process and the normalization of the final speaker verification result.

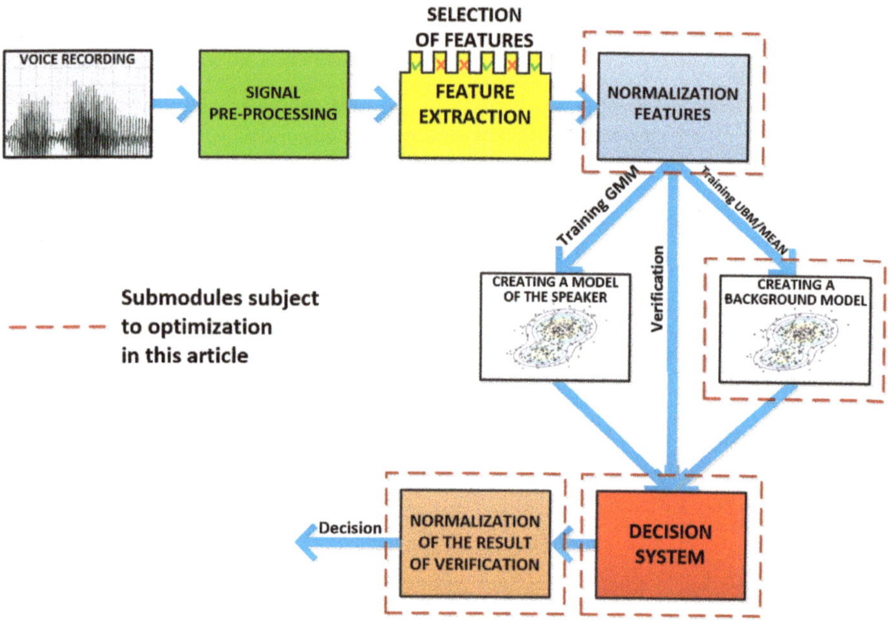

Figure 2. Operating diagram of the voice user verification module.

3.1. Signal Acquisition

The first stage of the ASR system is the acquisition of voice signals. We are talking about signals subject to verification as well as signals that are training material for the creation of voice models. During acquisition, the quality of the acoustic track used, as well as the conditions in which the voice recordings were made, are important considerations. In the presented implementation of the ASR system, the stability of the Internet connection is also of importance due to the need to upload the recorded speech fragment to the PicWATermark server.

3.2. Signal Pre-Processing

During the pre-processing of the speech signal, several operations are carried out to prepare the signal for feature extraction, thereby minimizing the impact of the recording device on system performance.

The first of the processes implemented is the clipping of silences, which are a typical part of almost every vocal utterance. This operation makes it possible to reduce the number of signal frames processed, which increases the speed of voice recognition and, above all, the efficiency of correct speaker verification, as only the frames relevant to speaker recognition are analyzed. In the presented implementation of the system, silence clipping is implemented twice. The first "rough" clipping of silence is carried out by the *front-end* using *Voice Activity Detection*. Thanks to this approach, a selection of signal frames containing speech is already made during recording, which saves both time and the transfer of data sent by the user to the PicWATermark server. Further "fine" selection of ASR-relevant frames is carried out in further signal pre-processing.

Another operation performed on the processed speech signal, already taking place on the PicWATermark server, is its normalization, where two actions are performed, i.e., removal of the mean value and scaling. The removal of the mean value from the digital speech signal is due to imperfections in the acquisition process. A speech signal in physical terms is nothing more than variations in sound pressure, so its average value can be assumed to be zero. In the practical implementation of digital speech signal processing, this value is almost always non-zero. This is due to the processing of speech fragments of finite length. The second action performed on the signal is scaling, which compensates for the mismatch between the speech signal and the range of the transducer. This allows quietly recorded parts of speech to be amplified. In the case of an ASR system designed for speaker verification independent of speech content, it is not necessary to preserve the energy relations occurring between the individual signal fragments. Therefore, in the present system, scaling is implemented relative to the maximum value of the signal to avoid distortions and make maximum use of the available number representation.

The next stage is signal filtering, known as *pre-emphasis*. It aims to compensate for the phenomenon found in the speech signal of lower amplitudes of higher frequency components relative to lower frequency components [27]. The aforementioned filtering is of greatest importance for frequencies above 3 kHz [28], so in the presented implementation of the ASR system, which processes signals with a maximum frequency of 4 kHz, its importance is minor.

The next step in the pre-processing of the speech signal is filtering in the frequency domain to reduce the components of the sound that are inaudible to humans. For this purpose, a high-pass filter with the amplitude characteristics shown in Figure 3 was used. The filter parameters were selected through an optimization process.

The speech signal processed in this way is then divided into short (quasi-stationary) fragments called frames. Each processed frame is analyzed separately and used in the creation of a separate distinctive feature vector.

Associated with the segmentation process is the windowing operation, i.e., the multiplication of the signal by an assumed time window with a width that determines the length of the frame. The time window is moved along the time axis with a specific increment. To minimize the phenomenon of so-called spectrum leakage, i.e., strong artifacts present in the processed signal. The ASR system presented here uses a Hamming window with low sidelight levels.

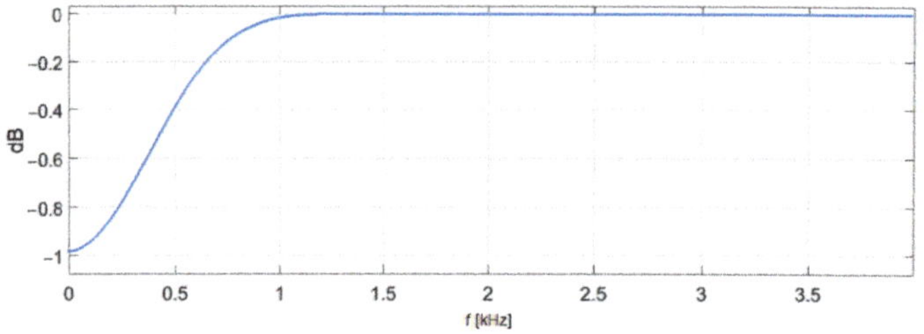

Figure 3. Amplitude characteristics of a 22-order Chebyshev filter of type II [29].

The final element of speech signal pre-processing is the selection of signal frames relevant to the ASR system. The aforementioned silence clipping function is the first "coarse" element to eliminate silence for longer parts of speech. In the presented implementation of the ASR system, three additional mechanisms are used to allow more accurate selection of signal frames.

The first is implemented to extract only voiced parts of speech, carrying information about the laryngeal tone. In the voiced frames, there are maxima in the frequency domain in a regular manner, which cannot be said for the voiceless fragments of processed speech, which resemble more of a noise signal. Using the autocorrelation function allows the sonority of the signal frame under consideration to be determined. The highest value of the autocorrelation function is obtained for zero offset; however, the bar is related to the energy of the signal, which is why the second maximum of the autocorrelation function is considered when looking for sonorous frames, which should be juxtaposed with the empirically determined sonority threshold [29].

Another criterion used to select representative signal frames is the re-detection of frames containing only the speech signal. This time with the elimination of shorter fragments of silence. The assumed minimum length of the cut frame of silence and the applied offset are of the same size as those used in the extraction of individual features in this ASR system. The process of selecting a threshold value for this criterion was also subject to optimization [29].

The final stage of frame selection is carried out on the basis of checking their noise level. This is made possible by determining the fundamental frequency using independent methods—autocorrelation F_{0ac} and cepstral F_{0c}. These two methods of determining F_0 have different resistance to signal noise. Proper use of this property makes it possible to determine which signal frames do not meet the accepted quality criterion (1) [30]. According to the literature, the autocorrelation method of determining the fundamental frequency is considered more accurate than the cepstral method; however, it is less robust to the noise of the signal under consideration. Therefore, the smaller the difference occurring between the fundamental frequency determined by these methods, the more the frame of the signal under consideration can be considered less noisy [29].

$$|F_{0c} - F_{0ac}| \leq p_f \min(F_{0c}, F_{0ac}) \quad (1)$$

where p_f represents the optimized threshold value [29].

3.3. Extraction of Distinctive Features

Another essential module of two-factor login using a voice biometrics system is the generation of speakers' personal characteristics. This stage is particularly important because errors and shortcomings therein reduce the discriminatory capacity of speakers' voices, which, in the later stages of the system's operation, can no longer be made up for. The main objective of the parameterization is to transform the temporal input waveform in such a way as to obtain a possibly small number of descriptors containing the most relevant information about the speaker's voice, thus minimizing their sensitivity to signal variation that is irrelevant to this system, i.e., dependent on the content of the speech or the parameters of the acoustic track used during acquisition.

Due to the redundancy of the signal in the time domain, it is much more efficient from the point of view of this voice biometrics system to analyze it further in the frequency domain. One of the reasons for this approach is inspired by the functioning of the sense of hearing, which, in the course of evolution, has been adapted to interpret the amplitude-frequency envelope of the speech signal appropriately [31].

The frequency form of the speech signal is the initial element in the subsequent parameterization. In the presented voice biometrics system, two types of descriptors requiring further mathematical transformations of the amplitude spectrum have been used, namely *weighted cepstral features* and *mel-cepstral features.*

For the generation of weighted cepstral features, the next process is the logarithmization of the amplitude spectrum, whereby the multiplicative relationship between the slow-variable component and the amplitudes of the individual stimulus-derived pulses is converted into an additive relationship. By subjecting such a signal to an inverse Fourier transform, the slow-variable waveforms associated with the transmittance of the vocal tract are placed close to zero on the cepstral time axis, called pseudo-time, while the pulses associated with the laryngeal sound start approximately within the period of the laryngeal signal and repeat every period. The final step in the generation of weighted cepstral features is to multiply the resulting signal in the pseudo-time domain by a summation filter bank that takes into account not only the maximum amplitudes of the bands in the cepstrum but also the values surrounding them, which also carry individual information about the speaker's voice.

During mel-cesptral feature generation, the Mel-Frequency Cepstrum Coefficients (MFCC) method was used [32]. It works by multiplying the amplitude Fourier spectrum after transformation through a mel filter bank, which mimics the human auditory organ and its non-linear sensitivity to stimuli from different frequency ranges, resulting in improved perception. Figure 4 illustrates this feature for 30 filters and a maximum signal frequency of 4 kHz.

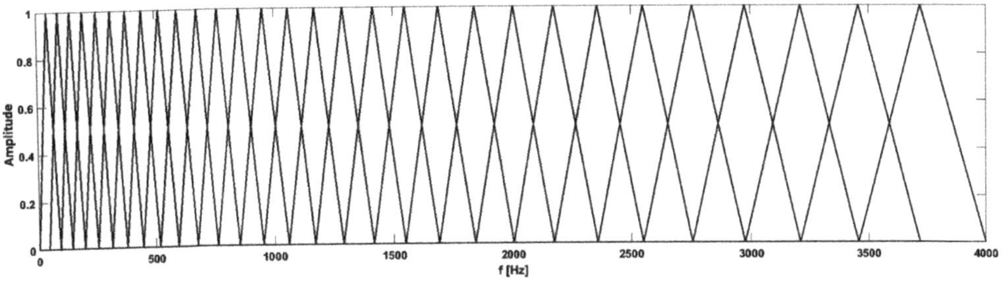

Figure 4. Distribution of 30 mel filters in the frequency range up to 4 kHz [29].

The processed signal is then logarithmized, similar to the weighted cepstral features. The final step in mel-cepstral feature generation is subjecting the signal to a cosine transformation for feature decorrelation.

3.4. *Selection of Distinctive Features*

Worldwide research shows that using the maximum set of features does not always produce the best results [33–36]. Feature selection often offers the possibility of obtaining higher or the same classification accuracy for a reduced feature vector, which in turn translates into reduced computation time.

When assessing feature quality, some features may be in the form of measurement noise, degrading the ability to recognize a given pattern, while others may be highly correlated with each other, resulting in the dominance of these features over the others and usually adversely affecting the quality of the classification.

An important element is the choice of feature selection method. A wide variety of selection methods, ranging from fast ranking methods to time-consuming methods incorporating complex classifiers, are available in the literature. The best-known quality measures and feature selection methods include the *Fisher coefficient*, *t-statistics*, *cross-correlation*, *sequential forward selection*, *genetic algorithms*, and *linear discriminant analysis*.

In the system presented here, the authors used a genetic algorithm to select the most representative features of the speaker's voice. This method takes into account the synergy of the features and makes it possible to obtain an optimal set of them; however, it is time-consuming. The working principle of the implemented feature classifier using a genetic algorithm is shown in Figure 5. In contrast, a detailed description of the genetic feature selector created by the authors is described in the article [34].

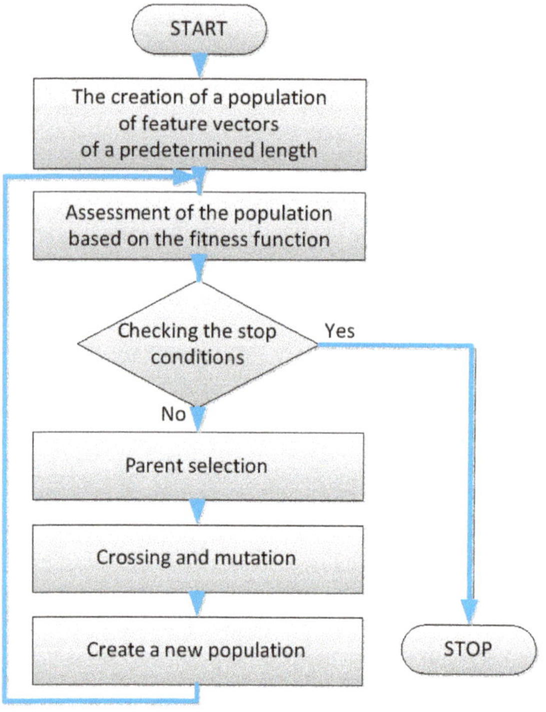

Figure 5. Flowchart of feature selection using a genetic algorithm [34].

3.5. Normalization of Distinctive Features

In the presented voice biometrics system, the normalization of distinctive features is realized using the mean value of a given feature and its standard deviation in the processed signal frame (*cepstral mean and variance normalization over a sliding window*—WCMVN) [28]. Norming is perfomed according to the following formula:

$$\hat{x}_t(i) = \frac{x_t(i) - \mu_t(i)}{\delta_t(i)} \quad (2)$$

where $x_t(i)$ and $\hat{x}_t(i)$ are the *i*-th components of the feature vectors in the considered frame before and after normalization, respectively, while μ_t and δ_t are respectively the mean value and standard deviation at time *t* for the feature vectors adopted during normalization [28].

3.6. Creation of Voice Models

Classification in the presented voice biometrics system is implemented based on a linear combination of Gaussian distributions. By making appropriate use of the distinctive features that constitute the learning data for the classifier, it is possible to create memory-efficient, rich in individual information, voice models called *Gaussian mixture model.*

During the operation of the classifier, the models iteratively adjust their parameters, i.e., expectation values, covariance matrices, and distribution weights, to the learning data according to the *Expectation Maximization* (EM) algorithm.

The operation of the EM algorithm involves the iterative repetition of two steps. The first is the *estimation* of the *a posteriori* probability value of the current model occurrence for the observations of the considered learning data. In contrast, the second step is *maximization*, allowing the parameters of the new model to be determined [37], maximizing the aforementioned probability function. Each subsequent step uses the quantities calculated in the previous step. The model learning process ends when there is no adequate increment in the reliability function or if the maximum number of iterations is reached.

During the speaker identification process, a decision is made as to which of the speakers represented by the λ_k voice models (for $k = 1, \ldots, N$, where *N* is the number of voices in the considered dataset) is most likely to belong to the recognized fragment of the voice signal represented by the set of personal feature vectors X. The discrimination function then takes the form [37].

$$g_k(X) = p(X|\lambda_k) \tag{3}$$

The selection of the most likely voice model is carried out by ranking according to the criterion [37].

$$k^* = \arg\max g_k(X) \tag{4}$$

In order to convert the multiplicative relationship between consecutive observations into an additive one, in a practical implementation, the logarithmic value of the reliability function (*log-likelihood*) is determined, and the criterion is Equation (5) [37].

$$lk^* = \arg\max_{1 \le k \le N} \sum_{t=1}^{T} \log p(x_t|\lambda_k) \tag{5}$$

where the probability $p(x_t \mid \lambda_k)$ is the weighted sum of the Gaussian distributions for a single observation *t*.

Also associated with the classification process using GMM is the *Universal Background Model (UBM)*, which is created using learning data from different classes [38,39].

The model has two main uses. The first is to use it as initiating data in the process of creating models of specific speakers. With this approach, the model can be trained in fewer iterations as it does not start with strongly outlying initial data. The GMM-UBM algorithm has been more extensively described and tested in earlier studies by the authors [39,40].

The universal voice model can also be used in a decision-making system to determine the alternative hypothesis proving that the signal comes from another speaker in the population [41,42].

3.7. Decision-Making System

In the decision-making system of the speaker verification system, there are two hypotheses about the probability of unique features of a recognized utterance in a given statistical model of the speaker. The hypotheses can be formulated as follows:

– H_0 (null hypothesis)—the voice signal *X* comes from speaker *k*,

– H_1 (alternative hypothesis)—the voice signal X comes from another speaker ~k from the population.

Deciding whether a voice signal X comes from speaker k or comes from another speaker ~k depends on the relationship between the null and alternative hypothesis probabilities and the juxtaposition with the detection threshold θ. If we assume that the null hypothesis is represented by the λ_{hyp} model and the alternative hypothesis by the λ_{hyp} model, this relationship can be described by Equation (6):

$$\Lambda(X) = \frac{p\left(X \middle| \lambda_{hyp}\right)}{p\left(X \middle| \lambda_{hyp}\right)} > \theta \tag{6}$$

The above equation is called the *likelihood ratio test (LRT)* or *Neyman-Pearsonar test* [28,42]. The likelihood quotient (6) is also often given in the logarithmic Equation (7)

$$\Lambda(X) = log\left(\frac{p\left(X \middle| \lambda_{hyp}\right)}{p\left(X \middle| \lambda_{hyp}\right)}\right) = logp(X|\lambda_{hyp}) - logp(X|\lambda_{hyp}) > \theta \tag{7}$$

As the null hypothesis, the result obtained from Equation (5) can be taken as the null hypothesis, where the GMM classifier created by the authors looks for the maximum value of the sum of the logarithms of the probability densities telling the occurrence of the feature x_t vector in the speaker model λ_k. Accordingly, this relationship can be presented as follows:

$$logp(X|\lambda_{hyp}) = \max_{1 \le k \le N} \sum_{t=1}^{T} \log p(x_t|\lambda_k) \tag{8}$$

where: N is the number of all voices in the dataset and T is the number of personal feature vectors extracted from the recognized speech signal. Determining the value of the logarithm of the plausibility of the alternative hypothesis $logp(X|\lambda_{hyp})$ in the system presented here is performed by directly using the logarithm of the plausibility obtained by the UBM universal voice model created (described in Section 4.2).

$$logp(X|\lambda_{hyp}) = logp(X|\lambda_{UBM}) \tag{9}$$

3.8. Normalizing the Outcome of the Verification

The final processing step in this voice biometrics system is the normalization of the user verification result. For this purpose, the authors used the C-normalization (*combined normalization*) method—a combination of Z-normalization (*zero normalization*) and T-normalization (*test normalization*), assuming that the results of Z and T normalization are independent random variables. During its implementation, the results were subject to transformation according to the formula [43]:

$$C = \frac{T + Z}{2} \sim N\left(\frac{\mu_Z + \mu_T}{2} \frac{\delta_Z^2 + \delta_T^2}{4}\right) \tag{10}$$

where μ_Z and μ_T are successively the averages resulting from the Z- and T-normalizations, and δ_Z and δ_T are the standard deviations of these normalizations. The first component of formula (10) (T-normalization) is implemented at test time (online), the test recording is checked against the declared speaker model and a group of other cohort models, and then the speaker under consideration is assigned the mean and variance of these scores. In the case of the other component of Equation (10) (Z-normalization), the model is checked against initial statements of which the modeled speaker is not the author, and then the speaker under consideration is assigned the mean and variance from these results.

In addition, an important element of this normalization is the proper selection of the models included in the cohort involved in determining the components of Equation (10).

4. Results

This section contains experimental results illustrating the optimization process of selected elements of the voice biometrics system that have not been investigated before in the authors' previous research [44,45]. The first part of the section presents a proposal to improve the performance of the decision-making system, and the second part presents the impact of feature normalization and verification score normalization on the effectiveness of voice biometrics in a multisession voice dataset. In contrast, the last part of the section provides the results of the optimization of the adopted decision threshold.

4.1. Impact of the Normalization of Distinctive Features on the Effectiveness of the ASR System

The first experiment conducted was to verify the speaker verification results obtained using a multisession voice dataset consisting of recordings of 50 speakers recorded on 10 independent acoustic tracks at a sampling rate of 8 kS/s [46]. This allows the performance of voice biometrics to be tested in a varied acoustic environment, making the presented results more realistic (red markings in Figure 6). An attempt was also made to additionally normalize the signal's distinctive features by including the mean value of a feature and its standard deviation in the processed signal frame WCMVN [28] (blue markings in Figure 6). The results also include two options for how to test the ASR system. The first allows the system to be tested using the same acoustic tracks that were used to create the voice models (indicated by the circles in Figure 6). The other (more complex) requirement, on the other hand, requires that different acoustic tracks are used when testing the ASR system than those used when creating the voice models (indicated by the triangles in Figure 6).

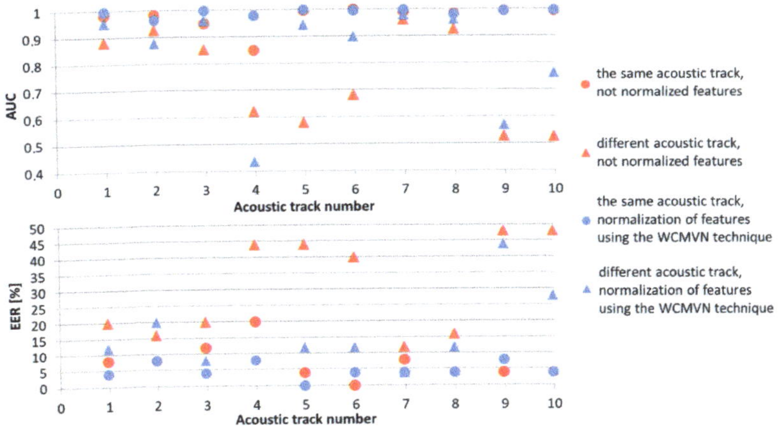

Figure 6. Results of speaker verification in the multisession voice dataset.

As the results in Figure 6 show, it is appropriate to use additional normalization of distinctive features, which has a direct impact on increasing the effectiveness of speaker verification. This increase is particularly noticeable for the more difficult testing option of using different acoustic tracks when creating voice models and testing the ASR system. This option is an extremely difficult situation, but it may occasionally occur in a real-life situation when using an ASR system.

4.2. Optimization of the Adopted Alternative Hypothesis in the Decision-Making System

In subsequent experiments, a series of studies were carried out using the NIST 2002 SRE commercial voice dataset, which contained recordings of 330 voices (191 female,

139 male) [47]. The recordings were resampled to a sampling rate of 8 kS/s, similar to telephony conditions. The aim of the research was to test the impact of varying the selection of the alternative hypothesis $\lambda_{\overline{hyp}}$ of the reliability quotient used to make a decision during speaker vetting.

The first approach assumed the determination of $\lambda_{\overline{hyp}}$, by means of the mean of the logarithms of the reliability *M* of the population models, which are not also the declared models (Figure 7). A test of this solution is shown later in this section.

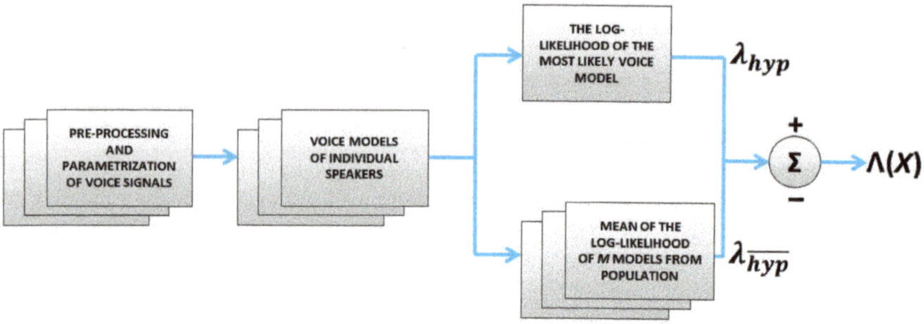

Figure 7. Diagram for determining the credibility quotient for the alternative hypothesis, derived from the average of the logarithms of credibility from M population models.

The other option involved the determination of an alternative hypothesis using a universal voice model (UBM), for which *M* speakers' learning data was used. Figure 8 shows a diagram of the proposed solution. A test of this solution is shown in Figure 9 (blue lines).

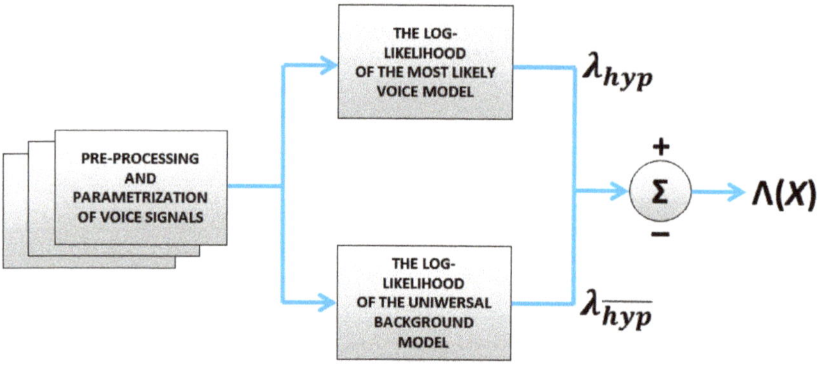

Figure 8. Diagram for determining the credibility quotient for the alternative hypothesis, derived from the logarithm of the credibility of the universal voice model.

For experiments requiring speaker identity (user/intruder), half of the voice models and all test signals were used. The results presented in Figure 9 illustrate the impact of the number of voices included in the reference model (necessary to determine the alternative hypothesis) on the quality of the classification. The options adopted mirror the solutions presented in Figures 7 and 8, but are enriched by varying the selection of the nearest voice models.

The first option involves selecting the closest voices from the dataset to the speech fragment to be verified (*online*), which will then be used to create a reference model $\lambda_{\overline{hyp}}$. The second (*offline*) option, on the other hand, involves selecting the closest voices to the speaker model created during learning and then creating a reference model based on this

λ_{hyp}. In addition, results for a UBM created from randomly selected voices from the base (green line) are also presented.

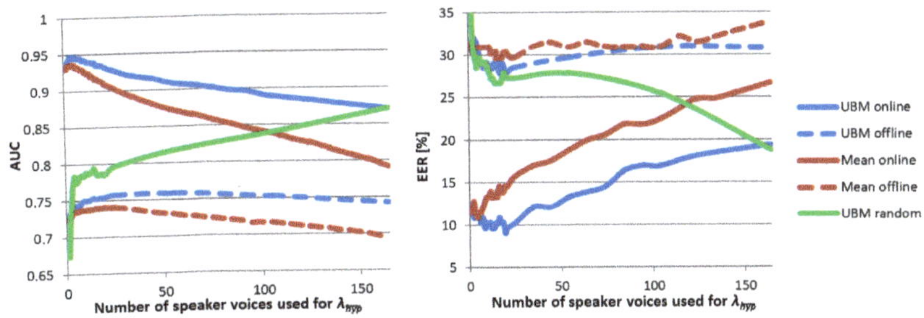

Figure 9. Performance results of the ASR system depending on the reference model used, obtained from the NIST 2002 SRE voice dataset.

As can be seen from the above experiments, the best of the proposed options for the reference model is to use a universal voice model (UBM), created from the most similar voice models against the test (*online*) recording. The number of votes used for λ_{hyp}, chosen by the authors, is 8, which is primarily due to the lowest EER value obtained.

Figure 10 shows an illustration of the operational curve (ROC) and the detection error trade-off (DET) curve for the most favorable option. In addition, the exact values of the area under the curve (AUC) and the equal error rate (EER) are presented.

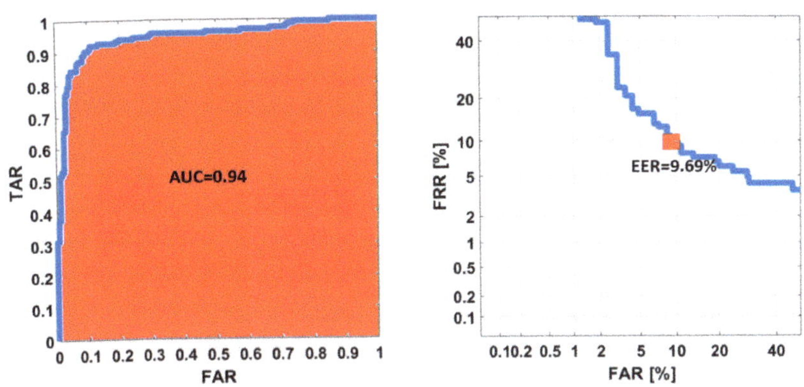

Figure 10. Results of speaker verification of the most favorable alternative hypothesis selection option in the NIST 2002 SRE voice dataset using the ROC curve and DET curve.

4.3. Optimization of the Decision Threshold

For the final verification of the implemented voice biometrics module in the PicWATermark system, a series of tests were carried out, and a group of speakers were invited to perform them. The tests were conducted in three groups. The first involved 21 testers, who carried out the process of teaching and testing the voice biometrics module. Each speaker created their voice model on the first of the two available audio tracks. The first audio track consisted of the following: a Trust GXT 232 MANTIS microphone with USB connector and a Dell Latitude 5285 tablet with integrated sound card. The other track, in turn, consisted of a Trust MC-1300 microphone with a 3.5 mm jack connector and a Lenovo Y510p notebook with an integrated sound card. In the next sequence, each speaker performed a login test for their own account on both audio tracks. In further illustrations, a more complex variant of testing the system was used, i.e., logging in to the account from a different device than the user voice model. In addition, a series of potential attempts were made to hack into another user's account using both acoustic tracks, logging into the account of the next person on the user list. This approach allows the dataset to make *n* voices, *n* attempts to log the right users, and *n* attempts to log potential intruders.

Subsequent voice biometrics tests in the PicWATermark system were performed in two rounds (10 and 24 participants). These experiments were already taking place during the COVID-19 outbreak, forcing them to be conducted entirely remotely. After creating their voice model, each tester was asked to attempt to log in to their own account and to the account of the next speaker on the list. It should be noted at this point that each speaker logged in from a completely independent acoustic track, which makes the voice verification results obtained significantly more realistic.

A total of 55 speakers were experimented with in three rounds, allowing the results of 110 logins to be collected (55 to their own account and 55 to another user's account as an intruder). Figure 11 provides an illustration of the reliability quotient results obtained when trying to log in to one's own account (green circles) and another user's account (red circles). The experiments were carried out with a fixed decision threshold of "0" (blue line), resulting in an *accuracy* (ACC) classification score of 91.82% from 110 logins to the system.

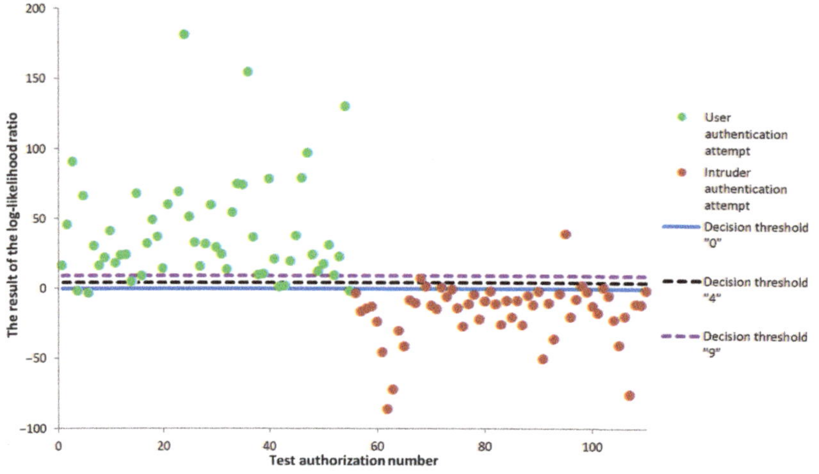

Figure 11. Summary illustration of the speaker verification results obtained by the group of speakers testing the voice biometrics module.

A selection of decision threshold values (Figure 12) was also made, which resulted in a significantly higher classification accuracy of 93.64% for decision thresholds "4" (black point) and "9" (purple point).

The final evidence of the correct operation of the implemented speaker verification system are the depictions of the operational curve (ROC) and detection error trade-off (DET) curve shown in Figure 13. In addition, the area under the curve (AUC) and the equilibrium error rate (EER) were determined, which quantify the quality of the decision-making system. The results presented in Figure 13 are based on a sample of 110 speaker logins in the PicWATermark system.

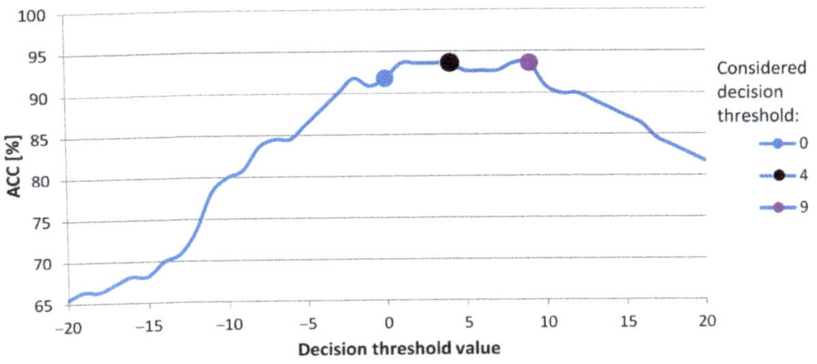

Figure 12. Optimization of the decision threshold of a speaker recognition system based on 110 verifications.

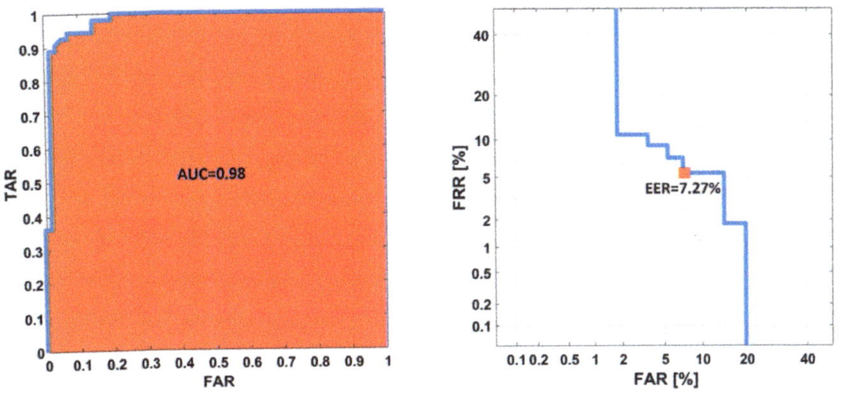

Figure 13. Evaluation of a voice biometrics classifier based on the ROC curve and DET curve in a dataset of 110 speaker logins in the PicWATermark system.

Given these results and the fact that they were carried out on numerous independent acoustic tracks, it seems reasonable to adjust the decision threshold in further implementations of the PicWATermark system. As the choice of an appropriate decision threshold represents a trade-off between the convenience of logging into one's own account and the danger of intrusion by an intruder, the authors adopted trials at level "9" in further implementations of the system. This approach allows for an increase in the achievable value of the ACC and increases the safety of the system.

4.4. Comparison with other Speaker Verification Methods

To test the validity of using the Gaussian mixture model method for speaker classification, the authors compared the results obtained with other available methods. The classification method based on Gaussian mixture models is not one of the latest trends in the field of voice biometrics, but nevertheless, in a situation where we have a small representation of data for a given class, it performs excellently. In order to confirm this thesis, the authors conducted independent tests using the commercial voice dataset NIST 2002 SRE [47] described in Section 4.2. The same test conditions were used, i.e., the voice recordings were divided into a 25 s training fragment and a 5 s test fragment. The experiment used all 330 available voices, which were resampled to a sampling rate of 8 kS/s. The authors compared the ASR system presented in this paper, using the author's feature set and optimized GMM classifier, with two other available systems whose implementation allowed them to be downloaded and tested for performance on their own [48,49]. The need to independently test other speaker classification systems was due to the fact that results described by other authors are often difficult to compare. This is because of the different voice datasets used to test the system, as well as because of the different ways in which the experiments were conducted, among other things, the different lengths of recordings used to train and test the system.

The first of the alternative speaker verification methods that were compared is the I-vector method [48], which aims to model the overall variability of the training data and compress the information into a low-dimensional vector. The used classifier was pre-trained using the LibriSpeech dataset of approximately 10,000 h of speech corpora [50]. The details of the operation of this method are beyond the scope of the article and are presented in the publication [51].

The second speaker verification method that was compared is the YAMNET (Yet Another Mixture of Experts Network) method, which is a neural network model developed by Google for classifying various audio sounds [49]. It has been trained on a large base of different categories of sounds, including animal noises, music, and environmental sounds, among others. For the purposes of this article, a transfer learning technique was used to apply the YAMNET network to speaker verification. Implementation details of the YAMNET network are presented in the article [52,53].

Table 2 presents a summary of the obtained EER values for the 3 methods of speaker verification, i.e., optimized author's GMM, I-vector, and YAMNET.

Table 2. Results of speaker verification method comparison using the NIST 2002 SRE dataset, which consists of 330 speakers.

Name of the Speaker Verification Method	Optimized Custom GMM	I-Vector	YAMNET
Number of features	23	60	64 *
EER	9.69%	10.91%	11.21%

* 64 is the number of mel bands in the mel septrogram.

5. Conclusions

The web-based implementation of the voice biometrics system presented in this article has undergone extensive optimization and operational testing. The high speaker verification results obtained demonstrate that voice biometrics can be successfully used as a 2FA component. Tests were performed using commercial and in-house voice datasets. For example, in the light of research based on the NIST 2002 SRE dataset [13], the results achieved by the authors are at least satisfactory, achieving a 6.4% lower EER.

However, the most valuable experiment was the testing of the implemented voice biometrics system by speakers logging in remotely to their accounts from independent acoustic tracks. The tests resulted in an EER value of 7.27% when sampling 110 system logins by 55 testers. This is the closest to real-world use of the voice biometrics module in the PicWATermark system.

In addition, the authors conducted independent tests of other implementations of voice biometric systems based on the I-vector method and YAMNET. The tests were conducted under the same system testing conditions. The ASR system presented in the paper achieved a lower EER of 1.22% than the I-vector classifier [48] and 1.52% lower than the YAMNET classifier [49]. This demonstrates the superior ability of the presented ASR system to classify speakers compared to other systems. The relatively low EER obtained compared to other methods is due, among other things, to well-chosen discriminative features, appropriately optimized GMMs, and small data representations for given classes, for which GMMs perform excellently in data generalization.

Furthermore, it is important to note that the practical implementation of the present voice biometrics system in the context of 2FA, as presented in the article, opens new avenues for the utilization of this type of biometrics in security systems. The objective set forth by the authors, which aimed at creating an effective voice biometrics system and implementing it in a practical 2FA setting, has been successfully achieved.

Certainly, the developed voice biometrics system needs to be further improved and address the current threats facing voice biometrics, such as increasing the system's resilience against impersonation attempts, including using deepfake technology, which, together with the development of artificial intelligence, could pose a major challenge to voice biometrics in the future. Nevertheless, this work is a significant contribution to the practical applications of voice biometrics in 2FA systems, highlighting the difficulties and challenges faced by the authors of similar systems, which include, among others, the system's resistance to the diversity of voice recording devices as well as the scalability of the system architecture that allows for efficient handling of large user bases.

Author Contributions: Conceptualization, K.A.K., A.P.D. and Z.P; methodology, A.P.D. and K.A.K.; software, K.A.K. and P.Ś; validation, A.P.D.; formal analysis, K.A.K. and A.P.D.; investigation, K.A.K. and A.P.D.; resources, K.A.K.; data curation, K.A.K. and P.Ś.; writing—original draft preparation, K.A.K.; writing—review and editing, A.P.D. and Z.P.; visualization, K.A.K.; supervision, A.P.D. and Z.P.; project administration, Z.P.; funding acquisition, Z.P. All authors have read and agreed to the published version of the manuscript.

Funding: This research work was supported and funded by The National Centre for Research and Development, grant no. CyberSecIdent/381319/II/NCBR/2018 for the implementation and financing of a project implemented on behalf of state defense and security as part of the program "Cyberse-curity and e-Identity" as well as by the Military University of Technology under research project no. UGB/22-864/2023 on "Methods of watermark embedding and extraction and methods of aggregation and spectral analysis with the use of neural networks".

Institutional Review Board Statement: Not applicable.

Informed Consent Statement: Not applicable.

Data Availability Statement: Not applicable.

Conflicts of Interest: The authors declare no conflict of interest.

References

1. Piotrowski, Z.; Lenarczyk, P.P. Blind Image Counterwatermarking—Hidden Data Filter. *Multimed Tools Appl.* **2017**, *76*, 10119–10131. [CrossRef]
2. Kaczmarek, P.; Piotrowski, Z. Desigining a mobile application on the example of a system for digital photos watermarking. In Proceedings of the Radioelectronic Systems Conference 2019, Jachranka, Poland, 20–21 November 2019; SPIE: Bellingham, WA, USA, 2020; Volume 11442, pp. 272–279. [CrossRef]
3. Hossain, M.N.; Zaman, S.F.U.; Khan, T.Z.; Katha, S.A.; Anwar, M.T.; Hossain, M.I. Implementing Biometric or Graphical Password Authentication in a Universal Three-Factor Authentication System. In Proceedings of the 2022 4th International Conference on Computer Communication and the Internet, ICCCI, Chiba, Japan, 1–3 July 2022; pp. 72–77. [CrossRef]
4. Two-Factor Authentication (2FA) Security Adoption Surges- | ChannelE2E. Available online: https://www.channele2e.com/news/two-factor-authentication-2fa-adoption-surges (accessed on 1 September 2023).
5. The 2021 State of the Auth Report: 2FA Climbs, While Password Managers and Biometrics Trend | Duo Security. Available online: https://duo.com/blog/the-2021-state-of-the-auth-report-2fa-climbs-password-managers-biometrics-trend (accessed on 1 September 2023).
6. Nogia, Y.; Singh, S.; Tyagi, V. Multifactor Authentication Schemes for Multiserver Based Wireless Application: A Review. In Proceedings of the ICSCCC 2023-3rd International Conference on Secure Cyber Computing and Communications, Jalandhar, India, 26–28 May 2023; pp. 196–201. [CrossRef]
7. Fujii, H.; Tsuruoka, Y. SV-2FA: Two-Factor User Authentication with SMS and Voiceprint Challenge Response. In Proceedings of the 2013 8th International Conference for Internet Technology and Secured Transactions, ICITST 2013, London, UK, 9–12 December 2013; pp. 283–287. [CrossRef]
8. The '123' of Biometric Technology | Semantic Scholar. Available online: https://www.semanticscholar.org/paper/The-%E2%80%98-123-%E2%80%99-of-Biometric-Technology-Yau-Yun/b2f539d1face23a018b8e2824a898a8fee3ac77c (accessed on 1 September 2023).
9. Mairaj, M.; Khan, M.S.A.; Agha, D.E.S.; Qazi, F. Review on Three-Factor Authorization Based on Different IoT Devices. In Proceedings of the 2023 Global Conference on Wireless and Optical Technologies, GCWOT 2023, Malaga, Spain, 24–27 January 2023. [CrossRef]

10. Ometov, A.; Bezzateev, S.; Mäkitalo, N.; Andreev, S.; Mikkonen, T.; Koucheryavy, Y. Multi-Factor Authentication: A Survey. *Cryptography* **2018**, *2*, 1. [CrossRef]
11. Alomar, N.; Alsaleh, M.; Alarifi, A. Social Authentication Applications, Attacks, Defense Strategies and Future Research Directions: A Systematic Review. *IEEE Commun. Surv. Tutor.* **2017**, *19*, 1080–1111. [CrossRef]
12. Bezzateev, S.; Fomicheva, S. Soft Multi-Factor Authentication. In Proceedings of the Wave Electronics and its Application in Information and Telecommunication Systems, WECONF-Conference Proceedings, St. Petersburg, Russia, 1–5 June 2020. [CrossRef]
13. Gandhi, A.; Patil, H.A. Feature Extraction from Temporal Phase for Speaker Recognition. In Proceedings of the 2018 International Conference on Signal Processing and Communications (SPCOM), Bangalore, India, 16–19 July 2018; pp. 382–386. [CrossRef]
14. Dustor, A. Speaker Verification with TIMIT Corpus-Some Remarks on Classical Methods. In Proceedings of the Signal Processing-Algorithms, Architectures, Arrangements, and Applications Conference Proceedings, SPA 2020, Poznan, Poland, 23–25 September 2020; pp. 174–179. [CrossRef]
15. Kang, W.H.; Kim, N.S. Adversarially Learned Total Variability Embedding for Speaker Recognition with Random Digit Strings. *Sensors* **2019**, *19*, 4709. [CrossRef] [PubMed]
16. Xu, Q.; Wang, M.; Xu, C.; Xu, L. Speaker Recognition Based on Long Short-Term Memory Networks. In Proceedings of the 2020 IEEE 5th International Conference on Signal and Image Processing (ICSIP), Nanjing, China, 23–25 October 2020; pp. 318–322. [CrossRef]
17. Hu, Z.; Fu, Y.; Xu, X.; Zhang, H. I-Vector and DNN Hybrid Method for Short Utterance Speaker Recognition. In Proceedings of the 2020 IEEE International Conference on Information Technology, Big Data and Artificial Intelligence (ICIBA), Chongqing, China, 6–8 November 2020; pp. 67–71. [CrossRef]
18. Lin, W.; Mak, M.-M.; Li, N.; Su, D.; Yu, D. Multi-Level Deep Neural Network Adaptation for Speaker Verification Using MMD and Consistency Regularization. In Proceedings of the ICASSP 2020-2020 IEEE International Conference on Acoustics, Speech and Signal Processing (ICASSP), Barcelona, Spain, 4–8 May 2020; pp. 6839–6843. [CrossRef]
19. Jagiasi, R.; Ghosalkar, S.; Kulal, P.; Bharambe, A. CNN Based Speaker Recognition in Language and Text-Independent Small Scale System. In Proceedings of the 2019 Third International conference on I-SMAC (IoT in Social, Mobile, Analytics and Cloud) (I-SMAC), Palladam, India, 12–14 December 2019; pp. 176–179. [CrossRef]
20. Devi, K.J.; Thongam, K. Automatic Speaker Recognition from Speech Signal Using Bidirectional Long-Short-Term Memory Recurrent Neural Network. *Comput. Intell.* **2023**, *39*, 170–193. [CrossRef]
21. Moumin, A.A.; Kumar, S.S. Automatic Speaker Recognition Using Deep Neural Network Classifiers. In Proceedings of the 2021 2nd International Conference on Computation, Automation and Knowledge Management (ICCAKM), Dubai, United Arab Emirates, 19–21 January 2021; pp. 282–286. [CrossRef]
22. Hong, Q.-B.; Wu, C.-H.; Wang, H.-M.; Huang, C.-L. Statistics Pooling Time Delay Neural Network Based on X-Vector for Speaker Verification. In Proceedings of the ICASSP 2020-2020 IEEE International Conference on Acoustics, Speech and Signal Processing (ICASSP), Barcelona, Spain, 4–8 May 2020; pp. 6849–6853. [CrossRef]
23. Wang, S.; Yang, Y.; Wu, Z.; Qian, Y.; Yu, K. Data Augmentation Using Deep Generative Models for Embedding Based Speaker Recognition. *IEEE/ACM Trans. Audio Speech Lang. Process.* **2020**, *28*, 2598–2609. [CrossRef]
24. Bykov, M.M.; Kovtun, V.V.; Kobylyanska, I.M.; Wójcik, W.; Smailova, S. Improvement of the Learning Process of the Automated Speaker Recognition System for Critical Use with HMM-DNN Component. In Proceedings of the Photonics Applications in Astronomy, Communications, Industry, and High-Energy Physics Experiments 2019, Wilga, Poland, 25 May–2 June 2019; SPIE: Bellingham, WA, USA, 2019; Volume 11176, pp. 588–597. [CrossRef]
25. Zhang, C.; Yu, M.; Weng, C.; Yu, D. Towards Robust Speaker Verification with Target Speaker Enhancement. In Proceedings of the ICASSP 2021-2021 IEEE International Conference on Acoustics, Speech and Signal Processing (ICASSP), Toronto, ON, Canada, 6–11 June 2021; pp. 6693–6697. [CrossRef]
26. Zhang, Y.; Yu, M.; Li, N.; Yu, C.; Cui, J.; Yu, D. Seq2Seq Attentional Siamese Neural Networks for Text-Dependent Speaker Verification. In Proceedings of the ICASSP 2019-2019 IEEE International Conference on Acoustics, Speech and Signal Processing (ICASSP), Brighton, UK, 12–17 May 2019; pp. 6131–6135. [CrossRef]
27. Madisetti, V.; Williams, D.B. *Digital Signal Processing Handbook*; CRC Press, LLC: Boca Raton, FL, USA, 1999.
28. Makowski, R. *Automatyczne Rozpoznawanie Mowy-Wybrane Zagadnienia*; Oficyna Wydawnicza Politechniki Wrocławskiej: Wrocław, Poland, 2011; ISBN 978-83-7493-615-6.
29. Kamiński, K. System Automatycznego Rozpoznawania Mówcy Oparty na Analizie Cepstralnej Sygnału Mowy i Modelach Mieszanin Gaussowskich. Ph.D. Thesis, Military University of Technology, Warsaw, Poland, 2018.
30. Ciota, Z. *Metody Przetwarzanie Sygnałów Akustycznych w Komputerowej Analizie Mowy*; EXIT: Warsaw, Poland, 2010; ISBN 978-83-7837-531-9.
31. Pawłowski, Z. *Foniatryczna Diagnostyka Wykonawstwa Emisji Głosu Śpiewaczego i Mówionego*; Impuls Press: Cracow, Poland, 2005; ISBN 978-83-7850-295-1.
32. Davis, S.B.; Mermelstein, P. Comparison of parametric representations for monosyllabic word recognition in continuously spoken sentations. *IEEE Trans. ASSP* **1980**, *28*, 357–366. [CrossRef]

33. Harrag, A.; Saigaa, D.; Boukharouba, K.; Drif, M. GA-based feature subset selection Application to Arabic speaker recognition system. In Proceedings of the 2011 11th International Conference on Hybrid Intelligent Systems (HIS), Malacca, Malaysia, 5–8 December 2011; pp. 383–387. [CrossRef]
34. Kamiński, K.; Dobrowolski, A.; Majda, E. Selekcja cech osobniczych sygnału mowy z wykorzystaniem algorytmów genetycznych. *Inżynieria Bezpieczeństwa Obiektów Antropog.* **2019**, *1–2*, 8–16. [CrossRef]
35. Osowski, S. *Metody i Narzedzia Eksploracji Danych*; BTC: Warsaw, Poland, 2013; ISBN 978-83-60233-92-4.
36. Zamalloa, M.; Bordel, G.; Rodriguez, L.J.; Penagarikano, M. Feature Selection Based on Genetic Algorithms for Speaker Recognition. In Proceedings of the 2006 IEEE Odyssey—The Speaker and Language Recognition Workshop, San Juan, PR, USA, 28–30 June 2006; pp. 1–8. [CrossRef]
37. Tran, D.; Tu, L.; Wagner, M. Fuzzy Gaussian mixture models for speaker recognition. In Proceedings of the International Conference on Spoken Language Processing ICSLP 1998, Sydney, Australia, 30 November–4 December 1998; p. 798.
38. Janicki, A.; Staroszczyk, T. Klasyfikacja mówców oparta na modelowaniu GMM-UBM dla mowy o różnej jakości. *Prz. Telekomun. —Wiadomości Telekomun.* **2011**, *84*, 1469–1474.
39. Kamiński, K.; Dobrowolski, A.P.; Majda, E. Evaluation of functionality speaker recognition system for downgraded voice signal quality. *Prz. Elektrotechniczny* **2014**, *90*, 164–167. [CrossRef]
40. Kaminski, K.; Majda, E.; Dobrowolski, A.P. Automatic Speaker Recognition Using a Unique Personal Feature Vector and Gaussian Mixture Models. In Proceedings of the 2013 Signal Processing: Algorithms, Architectures, Arrangements, and Applications (SPA), Poznan, Poland, 26–28 September 2013; IEEE: Piscataway, NJ, USA, 2013; pp. 220–225.
41. Reynolds, D.A.; Quatieri, T.F.; Dunn, R.B. Speaker Verification Using Adapted Gaussian Mixture Models. *Digit. Signal Process.* **2000**, *10*, 19–41. [CrossRef]
42. Kamiński, K.; Dobrowolski, A.P.; Majda, E. Voice identification in the open set of speakers. *Prz. Elektrotechniczny* **2015**, *91*, 206–210. [CrossRef]
43. Büyük, O.; Arslan, M.L. Model selection and score normalization for text-dependent single utterance speaker verification. *Turk. J. Electr. Eng. Comput. Sci.* **2012**, *20*, 1277–1295. [CrossRef]
44. Kamiński, K.A.; Dobrowolski, A.P. Automatic Speaker Recognition System Based on Gaussian Mixture Models, Cepstral Analysis, and Genetic Selection of Distinctive Features. *Sensors* **2022**, *22*, 9370. [CrossRef] [PubMed]
45. Dobrowolski, A.P.; Majda, E. Application of homomorphic methods of speech signal processing in speakers recognition system. *Prz. Elektrotechniczny* **2012**, *88*, 12–16.
46. Kamiński, K.; Dobrowolski, A.P.; Majda, E.; Posiadała, D. Optimization of the automatic speaker recognition system for different acoustic paths. *Prz. Elektrotechniczny* **2015**, *91*, 89–92. [CrossRef]
47. Martin, A.; Przybocki, M. *2002 NIST Speaker Recognition Evaluation LDC2004S04*; Linguistic Data Consortium: Philadelphia, PA, USA, 2004. [CrossRef]
48. Pretrained Speaker Recognition System-MATLAB SpeakerRecognition. Available online: https://www.mathworks.com/help/audio/ref/speakerrecognition.html (accessed on 3 July 2023).
49. YAMNet Neural Network-MATLAB Yamnet. Available online: https://www.mathworks.com/help/audio/ref/yamnet.html (accessed on 17 July 2023).
50. Panayotov, V.; Chen, G.; Povey, D.; Khudanpur, S. Librispeech: An ASR Corpus Based on Public Domain Audio Books. In Proceedings of the ICASSP, IEEE International Conference on Acoustics, Speech and Signal Processing-Proceedings 2015, South Brisbane, QLD, Australia, 19–24 April 2015; pp. 5206–5210. [CrossRef]
51. Matějka, P.; Glembek, O.; Castaldo, F.; Alam, M.J.; Plchot, O.; Kenny, P.; Burget, L.; Černocky, J. Full-Covariance UBM and Heavy-Tailed PLDA in i-Vector Speaker Verification. In Proceedings of the ICASSP, IEEE International Conference on Acoustics, Speech and Signal Processing-Proceedings, Prague, Czech Republic, 22–27 May 2011; pp. 4828–4831. [CrossRef]
52. Gemmeke, J.F.; Ellis, D.P.W.; Freedman, D.; Jansen, A.; Lawrence, W.; Moore, R.C.; Plakal, M.; Ritter, M. Audio Set: An Ontology and Human-Labeled Dataset for Audio Events. In Proceedings of the ICASSP, IEEE International Conference on Acoustics, Speech and Signal Processing-Proceedings 2017, New Orleans, LA, USA, 5–9 March 2017; pp. 776–780. [CrossRef]
53. Hershey, S.; Chaudhuri, S.; Ellis, D.P.W.; Gemmeke, J.F.; Jansen, A.; Moore, R.C.; Plakal, M.; Platt, D.; Saurous, R.A.; Seybold, B.; et al. CNN Architectures for Large-Scale Audio Classification. In Proceedings of the ICASSP, IEEE International Conference on Acoustics, Speech and Signal Processing-Proceedings 2017, New Orleans, LA, USA, 5–9 March 2017; pp. 131–135. [CrossRef]

electronics

MDPI

Article

Identity Recognition System Based on Multi-Spectral Palm Vein Image

Wei Wu *, Yunpeng Li, Yuan Zhang and Chuanyang Li

School of Information Engineering, Shenyang University, Shenyang 110044, China;
liyunpeng121991@163.com (Y.L.); zhangyuan3519@163.com (Y.Z.); lichuanyang6@163.com (C.L.)
* Correspondence: wuwei2017@syu.edu.cn

Abstract: A multi-spectral palm vein image acquisition device based on an open environment has been designed to achieve a highly secure and user-friendly biometric recognition system. Furthermore, we conducted a study on a supervised discriminative sparse principal component analysis algorithm that preserves the neighborhood structure for palm vein recognition. The algorithm incorporates label information, sparse constraints, and local information for effective supervised learning. By employing a robust neighborhood selection technique, it extracts discriminative and interpretable principal component features from non-uniformly distributed multi-spectral palm vein images. The algorithm addresses challenges posed by light scattering, as well as issues related to rotation, translation, scale variation, and illumination changes during non-contact image acquisition, which can increase intra-class distance. Experimental tests are conducted using databases from the CASIA, Tongji University, and Hong Kong Polytechnic University, as well as a self-built multi-spectral palm vein dataset. The results demonstrate that the algorithm achieves the lowest equal error rates of 0.50%, 0.19%, 0.16%, and 0.1%, respectively, using the optimal projection parameters. Compared to other typical methods, the algorithm exhibits distinct advantages and holds practical value.

Keywords: palm vein recognition; multispectral image; feature extraction; dimensionality reduction

1. Introduction

Palm vein recognition technology appeared in 1991 [1], and it utilizes the uniqueness and long-term stability of palm vein distribution for identity authentication [2,3]. It attracted people's attention because of its high security, liveness detection, user acceptability [4], and convenience. Traditional palm vein recognition requires users to place their palms inside an image acquisition box to avoid interference from visible light. To enhance recognition accuracy, contact-based captures with hand immobilization devices are used, imposing significant constraints on users. Non-contact palm vein acquisition in open environments is more user-friendly, but it introduces interference from visible light on near-infrared imaging. The non-transparency, non-uniformity, and heterogeneity of tissues surrounding the palm vein result in the scattering of near-infrared light used for palm vein illumination [3]. The presence of visible light in open environments exacerbates scattering, increases noise, and leads to un-clear imaging and poor image quality, reducing the amount of useful information. This is the fundamental reason affecting the recognition performance of palm vein images. Furthermore, the non-contact acquisition method enlarges intra-class differences due to rotations, translations, scaling, and changes in illumination during multiple captures of the same sample. These two dilemmas make palm vein recognition highly challenging.

Palm vein recognition technology has developed four main approaches based on feature extraction methods: texture-based methods, structure-based methods, deep learning-based methods, and sub-space-based methods [3].

Texture-based methods, such as double Gabor orientation Weber local descriptor (DG-WLD) [5], multi-scale Gabor orientation Weber local descriptors (MOGWLD) [6], difference of block means (DBM) [7], democratic voting down-sampling (DVD) [8], and various local binary pattern [9] (LBP) variants mentioned in [10], extract information about the direction, frequency, and phase of palm vein texture as features for matching and recognition. However, these methods are limited by the inadequate richness and clarity of texture information in palm vein images, which can result in decreased recognition performance.

Structure-based methods, such as the speeded-up robust feature (SURF) operator [11], histogram of oriented gradient (HOG) [12], and maximum curvature direction feature (MCDF) [13], extract point- and line-based structural features to represent palm veins. Recognition performance may be adversely affected in cases of poor image quality, as certain point and line features might be lost.

Deep learning-based methods employ various neural networks to automatically extract features and perform classification and recognition, overcoming the limitations of traditional feature extraction methods. For instance, Wu et al. [1] selectively emphasize classification features using the SER model and weaken less useful features, thereby addressing issues related to rotation, translation, and scaling. Similarly, Wei et al. [14] applied neural architecture search (NAS) techniques to overcome the drawbacks of manually designed CNNs, expanding the application of NAS technology in palm vein recognition. However, these methods may require large palm vein databases, limiting their applicability.

Sub-space-based methods, such as two-dimensional principal component analysis (2D-PCA) [15], neighborhood-preserving embedding (NPE) [16], two-dimensional Bhattacharyya bound linear discriminant analysis [17], and variants [18–20] of classical methods such as PCA, treat palm vein images as high-dimensional vectors or matrices. These methods transform the palm vein images into low-dimensional representations through projection or mathematical transformations for image matching and classification. Subspace methods offer advantages, such as high recognition rates and low system resource consumption, compared to other approaches. However, due to their disregard for the texture features of the images, they may exhibit a certain degree of blindness in the dimensionality reduction process. This could lead to the omission of some discriminative features that are crucial for classification, particularly in non-contact acquisition methods in open environments, where the impact on recognition performance becomes more pronounced.

Non-contact palm vein image acquisition in open environments has garnered significant research attention due to its hygienic and convenient nature, offering promising prospects for various applications. Nevertheless, the scarcity of non-contact acquisition devices and publicly available datasets in open environments has impeded progress in non-contact palm vein image recognition research. Consequently, this study focuses on three key contributions: Firstly, the proposal of a multi-spectral palm vein image acquisition device specifically designed for open environments. Secondly, the establishment of a non-contact palm vein image dataset utilizing the developed acquisition device. Finally, addressing the existing challenges in the field, the study introduces a supervised discriminative sparse principal component analysis algorithm with a preserved neighborhood structure (SDSPCA-NPE) for palm vein recognition. As a sub-space method, this approach combines supervised label information with sparse constraints, resulting in discriminative and highly interpretable palm vein features. It mitigates issues related to un-clear imaging and poor texture quality, expands the inter-class distance of projected data, and enhances discriminability among different palm vein samples. During projection, the concept of neighborhood structure information, commonly employed in non-linear dimensionality reduction methods, is introduced. Robust neighborhood selection techniques are utilized to preserve similar local structures in palm vein samples before and after projection. This approach captures the non-uniform distribution of palm vein images and improves the drawbacks arising from increased image variations within the same class due to rotation, scaling, translation, and lighting changes. Experimental evaluations conducted on self-built palm vein databases and commonly used public multi-spectral palm vein databases, including the CASIA (Institute of Automation, Chinese Academy of Sciences) database [21], the Tongji University database, and the Hong Kong Polytechnic

University database [22], demonstrate the superior performance of the proposed method compared to current typical methods.

The remaining sections of this paper are organized as follows: Section 2 introduces the self-developed acquisition device; Section 3 presents the proposed algorithm; Section 4 describes the experiments and results analysis; and Section 5 concludes the paper.

2. Multi-Spectral Image Capture Device

When near-infrared light (NIR) in the range of 720–1100 nm penetrates the palm, the different absorption rates of NIR radiation by various components of biological tissues result in a high absorption rate of blood hemoglobin (including oxygenated and deoxygenated hemoglobin). This leads to the formation of observable shadows, allowing the identification of vein locations and the generation of palm vein images [3]. Due to the reflection, scattering, or fluorescence in different tissues of the palm, the optical penetration depth varies from 0.5 mm to 5 mm. Vein acquisition devices [2] can only capture superficial veins, and palm vein images are typically obtained using a reflection imaging approach. To improve user acceptance and enhance comfort during palm vein recognition, open environment capture is employed, which un-avoidably introduces visible light (390–780 nm) illuminating the palm and entering the imaging system, resulting in the acquisition of multi-spectral palm vein images. As shown in Figure 1, visible light entering the skin increases light scattering, thereby interfering with clear palm vein imaging [22].

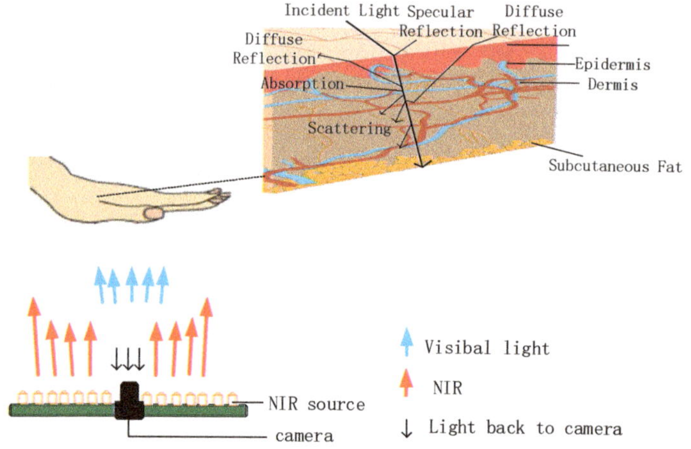

Figure 1. Palm vein image schematic diagram.

The self-developed non-contact palm vein image acquisition device in an open environment is shown in Figure 2. To enhance the absorption of near-infrared light by palm veins and minimize interference from visible light, the device employs two CST brand near-infrared linear light sources, model BL-270-42-IR, with a wavelength of 850 nm. These light sources are equipped with an intensity adjustment controller. The device uses an industrial camera, model MV-VD120SM, for image capture. The captured images are grayscale with a resolution of 1280 pixels × 960 pixels and 8 bits.

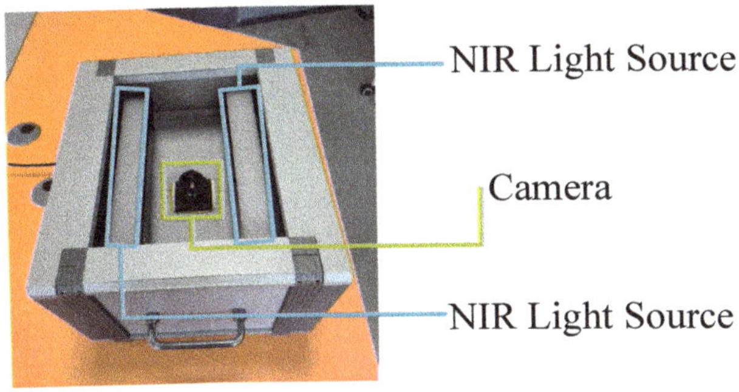

Figure 2. Device for self-built palm vein database collection.

3. Method

The proposed methodology consists of the following steps: (1) image pre-processing, (2) feature extraction (SDSPCA-NPE), and (3) feature matching and recognition.

3.1. Image Pre-Processing

The most important issue in image pre-processing is the localization of the region of interest (ROI). ROI extraction normalizes the feature area of different palm veins, significantly reducing computational complexity. In this study, the ROI localization method proposed in reference [2] was adopted. This method identifies stable feature points on the palm, namely the valleys between the index and middle fingers and between the ring finger and little finger. Through ROI extraction, it partially corrects image rotation, translation, and scaling issues caused by non-contact imaging.

The ROI extraction process is illustrated in Figure 3. Firstly, the original image (Figure 3a) is denoised using a low-pass filter. Then, the image is binarized, and the palm contour is extracted using binary morphological dilation, refining it to a single-pixel width. Vertical line scanning is performed from the right side to the left side of the image, and the number of intersection points between the palm contour and the scan line is counted. When there are 8 intersection points, it indicates that the scan line passes through four fingers, excluding the thumb. From the second intersection point, p2, to the third intersection point, p3, the palm contour is traced to locate the valley point, point A, between the index finger and the middle finger (Figure 3c), using the disk method [2]. Similarly, between p6 and p7, the valley point, point B, between the ring finger and the little finger is located. Points A and B are connected, forming a square ABCD on the palm with the side length equal to the length of AB, denoted as d. This square is then grayscale normalized and resized to a size of 128 pixels × 128 pixels, resulting in the desired ROI, as shown in Figure 3d.

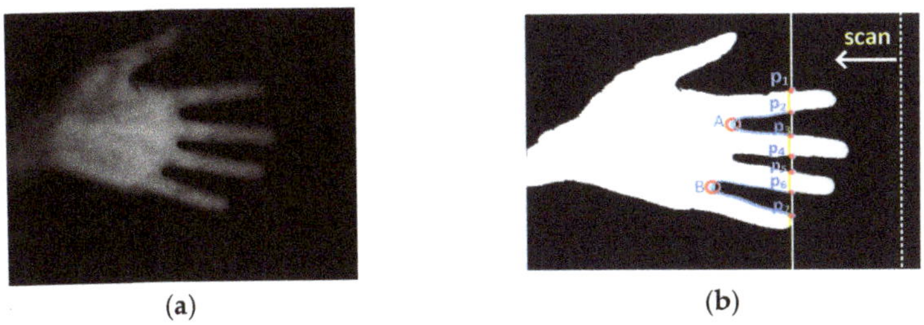

Figure 3. *Cont.*

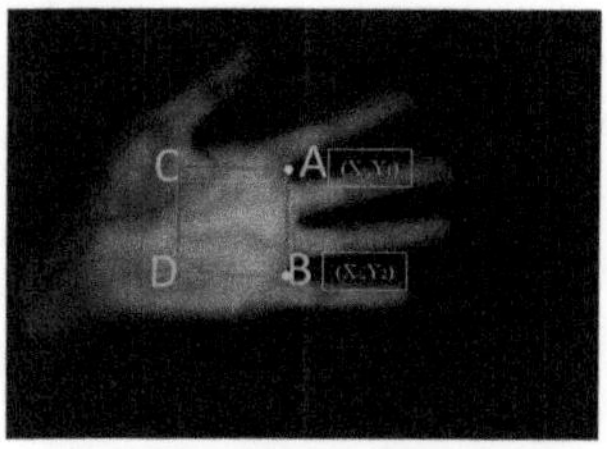

(c)

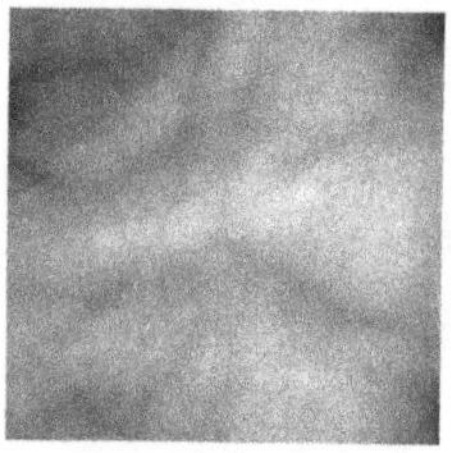

(d)

Figure 3. Flow chart of palm vein image ROI extraction: (**a**) denoising; (**b**) determine the cross point; (**c**) determine the valley point; and (**d**) extract the ROI region.

3.2. Feature Extraction (SDSPCA-NPE)

Palm vein images often encounter interference in the form of partial noise and deformation during the non-contact acquisition process. These disturbances not only increase the difficulty of processing palm vein data but also pose challenges to dimensionality reduction and classification, which hinder palm vein image recognition. To address these unique characteristics of palm vein images, this study employs supervised discriminative sparse principal component analysis (SDSPCA) [23] for dimensionality reduction and recognition. SDSPCA combines supervised discriminative information and sparse constraints into the PCA model [15], enhancing interpretability and mitigating the impact of high inter-class ambiguity in palm vein image samples. By projecting palm vein images using SDSPCA, the integration of sparse constraints and supervised learning achieves more effective dimensionality reduction for classification tasks, ultimately improving the recognition performance of palm vein images. The SDSPCA model is depicted below:

$$\begin{gathered}\min_{\mathbf{Q}} \| \mathbf{X}-\mathbf{Q}\mathbf{Q}^{\mathrm{T}}\mathbf{X} \|_{\mathrm{F}}^{2}+\alpha \| \mathbf{Y}-\mathbf{Q}\mathbf{Q}^{\mathrm{T}}\mathbf{Y} \|_{\mathrm{F}}^{2}+\beta \| \mathbf{Q} \|_{2,1} \\ \text{s.t. } \mathbf{Q}^{\mathrm{T}}\mathbf{Q}=\mathbf{I}_{\mathrm{k}}\end{gathered} \tag{1}$$

Optimize as follows [23]:
Step 1:

$$\begin{aligned}&\|\mathbf{X}-\mathbf{Q}\mathbf{Q}^{\mathrm{T}}\mathbf{X}\|_{\mathrm{F}}^{2}\\ &=\mathrm{Tr}\left(\left(\mathbf{X}-\mathbf{Q}\mathbf{Q}^{\mathrm{T}}\mathbf{X}\right)^{\mathrm{T}}\left(\mathbf{X}-\mathbf{Q}\mathbf{Q}^{\mathrm{T}}\mathbf{X}\right)\right)\\ &=\mathrm{Tr}\left(\mathbf{X}^{\mathrm{T}}\mathbf{X}-\mathbf{X}^{\mathrm{T}}\mathbf{Q}\mathbf{Q}^{\mathrm{T}}\mathbf{X}\right)\\ &=\mathrm{Tr}\left(\mathbf{X}^{\mathrm{T}}\mathbf{X}\right)-\mathrm{Tr}\left(\mathbf{Q}^{\mathrm{T}}\mathbf{X}\mathbf{X}^{\mathrm{T}}\mathbf{Q}\right)\end{aligned}$$

$\mathrm{Tr}\left(\mathbf{X}^{\mathrm{T}}\mathbf{X}\right)$ as a fixed value, independent of the final minimization problem solution.
Step 2:

$$\min_{\mathbf{Q}}\|\mathbf{X}-\mathbf{Q}\mathbf{Q}^{\mathrm{T}}\mathbf{X}\|_{\mathrm{F}}^{2}=\min_{\mathbf{Q}}-\mathrm{Tr}\left(\mathbf{Q}^{\mathrm{T}}\mathbf{X}\mathbf{X}^{\mathrm{T}}\mathbf{Q}\right)$$

By simple algebraic calculation [24], the above equation can be optimized as follows:

$$\begin{gathered}\min_{\mathbf{Q}} \| \mathbf{X}-\mathbf{Q}\mathbf{Q}^{\mathrm{T}}\mathbf{X} \|_{\mathrm{F}}^{2}+\alpha \| \mathbf{Y}-\mathbf{Q}\mathbf{Q}^{\mathrm{T}}\mathbf{Y} \|_{\mathrm{F}}^{2}+\beta \| \mathbf{Q} \|_{2,1}\\ =\min_{\mathbf{Q}}-\mathrm{Tr}\left(\mathbf{Q}^{\mathrm{T}}\mathbf{X}\mathbf{X}^{\mathrm{T}}\mathbf{Q}\right)-\alpha\mathrm{Tr}\left(\mathbf{Q}^{\mathrm{T}}\mathbf{Y}\mathbf{Y}^{\mathrm{T}}\mathbf{Q}\right)+\beta\mathrm{Tr}\left(\mathbf{Q}^{\mathrm{T}}\mathbf{D}\mathbf{Q}\right)\\ =\min_{\mathbf{Q}}\mathrm{Tr}\left(\mathbf{Q}^{\mathrm{T}}\left(-\mathbf{X}\mathbf{X}^{\mathrm{T}}-\alpha\mathbf{Y}\mathbf{Y}^{\mathrm{T}}+\beta\mathbf{D}\right)\mathbf{Q}\right)\\ \text{s.t. } \mathbf{Q}^{\mathrm{T}}\mathbf{Q}=\mathbf{I}_{\mathrm{k}}\end{gathered} \tag{2}$$

In the proposed method, α and β are weight parameters. The training data matrix is $\mathbf{X} = [\mathbf{x}_1, \ldots, \mathbf{x}_n]^T \in \mathbb{R}^{n \times d}$, where n is the number of training samples, and d is the feature dimension. Using $\mathbf{Y} = [\mathbf{y}_1, \ldots, \mathbf{y}_n]^T \in \mathbb{R}^{n \times c}$ as the label matrix of the dataset $\mathbf{X}$, $\mathbf{Y}$ is constructed as follows:

$$\mathbf{Y}_{i,j} = \begin{cases} 1, & if c_j = i, j = 1,2\ldots,n, i = 1,2,\ldots,c \\ 0, & otherwise \end{cases} \tag{3}$$

where c represents the number of classes in the training data, and $c_j \in \{1, \ldots, c\}$ represents the class labels. The optimal Q consists of k-tail eigenvectors of $\mathbf{Z} = -\mathbf{X}\mathbf{X}^{\mathrm{T}} - \alpha\mathbf{Y}\mathbf{Y}^{\mathrm{T}} + \beta\mathbf{D}$, where $\mathbf{D} \in \mathbb{R}^{n \times n}$ is a diagonal matrix, and the i-th diagonal element is:

$$\mathrm{D}_{\mathrm{ii}} = \frac{1}{2\sqrt{\Sigma_{\mathrm{j}=1}^{\mathrm{k}} \mathrm{Q}_{\mathrm{ij}}^2 + \epsilon}} \tag{4}$$

where ε is a small positive constant to avoid dividing by zero.

SDSPCA has achieved good performance in palm vein recognition. However, when faced with partially low-quality palm vein images, the method exhibits a performance decline. The underlying reason lies in the sparse characteristics of palm vein images, where the effective information often occupies only a few dimensions in the high-dimensional space. This effective information exhibits inherent structures and features among palm vein images, providing a certain level of correlation and similarity among data points in high-dimensional space. These correlations and similarities result in the formation of a low-dimensional manifold in the high-dimensional space for the palm vein dataset, which is essential for dimensionality reduction-based recognition. However, palm vein images captured in open environments suffer from image quality degradation due to the scattering of palm veins under near-infrared illumination. This leads to un-clear imaging of some palm vein patterns and poor image quality. Additionally, within the same sample, variations in rotation, scale, translation, and lighting conditions during multiple captures further increase image differences. Under the influence of these factors, effective information is reduced and interfered with, leading to interactions in high-dimensional space. As a result, palm vein images exhibit an un-evenly distributed low-dimensional manifold with high inter-class similarity and large intra-class differences. Therefore, as SDSPCA is a linear dimensionality reduction method that performs linear projection on the entire dataset, it has limitations in capturing the un-even non-linear geometric structure of the palm vein dataset in high-dimensional space. Consequently, palm vein samples cannot be well distributed in the final linear projection space, limiting the classification capability.

In order to address the aforementioned issue, previous researchers have utilized several non-linear dimensionality reduction methods, such as locally preserving projection (LPP) [25], locally linear embedding (LLE) [26], and neighborhood preserving embedding (NPE). However, although these methods have achieved non-linear dimensionality reduction, their classification capability is limited. Therefore, this paper proposes a supervised discriminative sparse PCA algorithm, named SDSPCA-NPE, that preserves the neighborhood structure. This algorithm inherits the advantages of SDSPCA in enlarging the inter-class distance through supervised learning while overcoming its limitations. By incorporating the constraints of NPE, the proposed method introduces local structural information to capture the non-linear geometric structure of the palm vein dataset. As a result, the projected palm vein data exhibits an improved distance distribution, enhancing the classification performance of palm vein data. The model for NPE is presented as follows:

$$\begin{aligned} &\min \textstyle\sum_i \| \mathbf{x}_\mathrm{i} - \sum_\mathrm{j} \mathrm{W}_{\mathrm{ij}} \mathbf{x}_\mathrm{j} \|^2 \\ &= \min_{\mathbf{W}} \mathrm{Tr}\left(\mathbf{X}^\mathrm{T}(\mathbf{I} - \mathrm{W})^\mathrm{T}(\mathbf{I} - \mathrm{W})\mathbf{X}\right) \\ &= \min_{\mathbf{W}} \mathrm{Tr}\left(\mathbf{X}^\mathrm{T}\mathbf{M}\mathbf{X}\right) \\ &\text{s.t. } \mathbf{X}^\mathrm{T}\mathbf{X} = \mathbf{I}_\mathrm{k} \end{aligned} \tag{5}$$

M is the result of multiplying the transpose matrices of $(\mathbf{I}-\mathrm{W})$ and $(\mathbf{I}-\mathrm{W})$. W_{ij} represents a matrix consisting of distance weight coefficients between X_i and X_j in the original space. The construction process of W_{ij} is described here first. If X_i and X_j is a k-nearest neighbor relationship, then the following heat kernel function calculation is used. In the following equation, if it is not a k-nearest neighbor relationship, then W_{ij} is equal to 0.

$$W_{ij} = e^{-\frac{\|x_i - x_j\|^2}{t}} \tag{6}$$

The 't' represents the bandwidth parameter used in the computation of the heat kernel matrix [27].

NPE, in essence, aims to preserve the local linear relationships among palm vein data samples during dimensionality reduction. It directly approximates a non-linear projection space that satisfies the implicit low-dimensional manifold of palm vein data while striving to retain the relative proximity relationships between data points. This ensures the connectivity of the same samples during dimensionality reduction of low-dimensional manifolds, thereby reducing the impact of noise and outliers.

Specifically, NPE performs linear reconstruction on palm vein samples within local regions, typically using a k-nearest neighbor approach. By minimizing the reconstruction error in the dimensionality reduction process, the local structure is preserved in the projection space. This yields a complex non-linear low-dimensional embedding space within the high-dimensional manifold, consequently reducing the intra-class distance after projection and achieving optimal dimensionality reduction. Figure 4 illustrates the schematic diagram of the NPE principle.

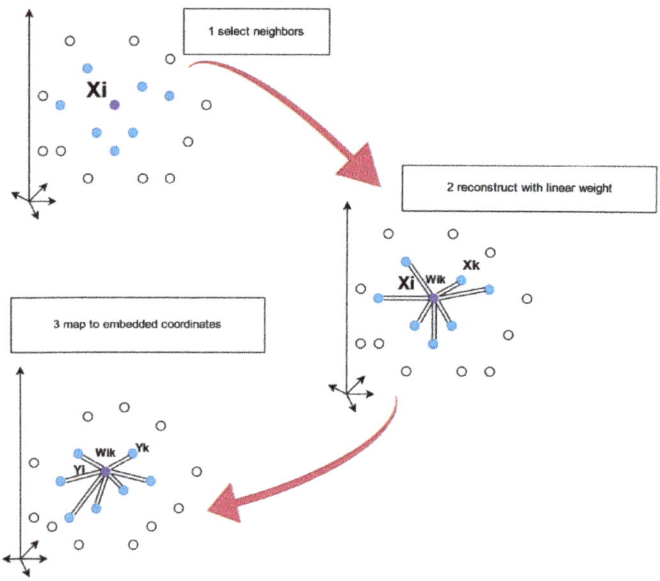

Figure 4. Flowchart of the NPE.

The neighborhood preserving embedding (NPE) technique employed in our proposed method allows for capturing the non-linear and non-uniform distribution of the palm vein dataset in high-dimensional space. This capability enables the method to mitigate the effects of variations, such as rotation, scaling, translation, and changes in lighting conditions, which often lead to increased differences in palm vein images of the same class across multiple captures. Moreover, it helps reduce the interference caused by outliers present in the palm vein samples. In the context of palm vein recognition, when the original palm vein data exhibits a non-uniform distribution within a class due to the influence of outliers, linear dimensionality reduction methods that seek the final projection space through global linear transformations often fail to preserve the non-linear and non-uniform distribution structure of the high-dimensional palm vein dataset. Consequently, they demonstrate low tolerance towards outliers during dimensionality reduction, resulting in the misclassification of such samples. In contrast, by applying NPE's non-linear mapping and utilizing robust neighborhood selection techniques, the method encompasses the outliers within the neighborhood range. This allows the outliers to be pulled closer to samples of the same class during the dimensionality reduction process, ultimately resulting in a more compact distribution of palm vein samples within the low-dimensional space for the same class and larger separations from samples of other classes.

The proposed method is as follows:

$$\begin{aligned} &\min_{\mathbf{Q}} \| \mathbf{X} - \mathbf{Q}\mathbf{Q}^{\mathrm{T}}\mathbf{X} \|_{\mathrm{F}}^2 + \alpha \| \mathbf{Y} - \mathbf{Q}\mathbf{Q}^{\mathrm{T}}\mathbf{Y} \|_{\mathrm{F}}^2 + \beta \| \mathbf{Q} \|_{2,1} + \delta \textstyle\sum_{\mathrm{i}} \| \mathbf{x}_{\mathrm{i}} - \sum_{\mathrm{j}} \mathrm{W}_{\mathrm{ij}} \mathbf{x}_{\mathrm{j}} \|^2 \\ &= \min_{\mathbf{Q}} - \mathrm{Tr}\left(\mathbf{Q}^{\mathrm{T}}\mathbf{X}\mathbf{X}^{\mathrm{T}}\mathbf{Q}\right) - \alpha \mathrm{Tr}\left(\mathbf{Q}^{\mathrm{T}}\mathbf{Y}\mathbf{Y}^{\mathrm{T}}\mathbf{Q}\right) + \beta \mathrm{Tr}\left(\mathbf{Q}^{\mathrm{T}}\mathbf{D}\mathbf{Q}\right) + \delta \mathrm{Tr}\left(\mathbf{Q}^{T}\mathbf{X}\mathbf{X}^{T}\mathbf{M}\mathbf{X}\mathbf{X}^{T}\mathbf{Q}\right) \\ &= \min_{\mathbf{Q}} \mathrm{Tr}\left(\mathbf{Q}^{\mathrm{T}}\left(-\mathbf{X}\mathbf{X}^{\mathrm{T}} - \alpha \mathbf{Y}\mathbf{Y}^{\mathrm{T}} + \beta \mathbf{D} + \delta \mathbf{X}\mathbf{X}^{T}\mathbf{M}\mathbf{X}\mathbf{X}^{T}\right)\mathbf{Q}\right) \\ &\text{s.t. } \mathbf{Q}^{\mathrm{T}}\mathbf{Q} = \mathbf{I}_{\mathrm{k}} \end{aligned} \tag{7}$$

The optimal $\mathbf{Q}$ consists of k-tail eigenvectors of $\mathbf{Z} = -\mathbf{X}\mathbf{X}^{\mathrm{T}} - \alpha \mathbf{Y}\mathbf{Y}^{\mathrm{T}} + \beta \mathbf{D} + \delta \mathbf{X}\mathbf{X}^{T}\mathbf{M}\mathbf{X}\mathbf{X}^{T}$. We initialize the $\mathbf{Q}$, and we calculate $\mathbf{D}$ based on a given formula, and obtain Z. With Z and D at hand, we proceed to update the $\mathbf{Q}$ values through this iterative process, ultimately arriving at the optimal $\mathbf{Q}$ [23].

The proposed method, SDSPCA-NPE, is a supervised learning variant of PCA that inherits the advantages of SDSPCA. The approach utilizes sparse-constrained principal component analysis, which not only extracts and condenses the main components of palm vein images, but also reduces the ambiguity associated with PCA dimensionality reduction. Additionally, class labels are incorporated into the algorithm model, preserving the category information of palm vein images. This constraint influences the extraction of principal components by approximating the given label information through linear transformations. As a result, the similarity of feature vectors projected from different classes of palm vein samples is reduced. The final method extracts highly interpretable and well-classifiable principal component features from palm vein images while mitigating the performance interference caused by poor image quality due to lighting variations. This makes it more suitable for palm vein recognition.

The final proposed method, SDSPCA-NPE, introduces local structural information to address the limitations of SDSPCA, which only considers global and class information in supervised learning. By incorporating sparse constraints and class information, the resulting feature vectors exhibit strong interpretability and sensitivity to class information, effectively reducing the impact of lighting variations in palm vein images and improving the problem of high inter-class similarity. This leads to better inter-class distances. Additionally, the method preserves the local structural information of the data during projection, maintaining certain neighborhood relationships from the original palm vein data. This enhances tolerance for non-uniformly distributed outliers and reduces intra-class distances. As a result, the final palm vein feature vectors demonstrate improved classification performance, with increased inter-class distances and decreased intra-class distances in terms of distance distribution. Figure 5 provides an overview of the proposed method.

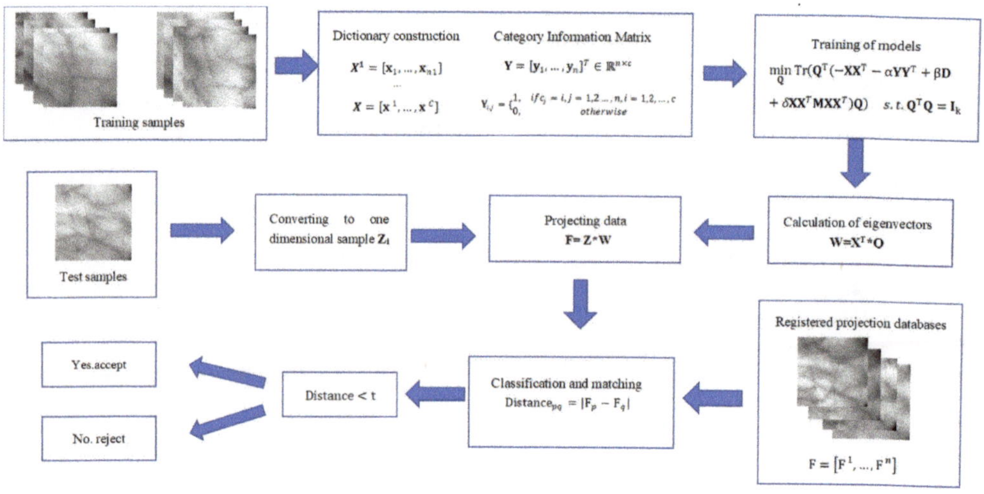

Figure 5. Flowchart of the proposed method.

3.3. Feature Matching and Recognition

By projecting the ROI image onto the projection matrix, a set of coordinates representing the position of the image in the sub-space can be obtained, serving as the basis for classification. After feature extraction, the image p yields a set of positional coordinates, F_p, in the sub-space, which are used as the matching feature vectors. Firstly, the within-class and between-class thresholds, t, are calculated based on the distribution curves of matching within the training set. Within-class matching refers to matching different images from the same palm, while between-class matching refers to matching images from different palms [2]. The matching distance is computed as the Euclidean distance between the feature vectors F_p of image p and F_q of image q, denoted as:

$$Distance_{pq} = |F_p - F_q| \quad (8)$$

Intra-class and inter-class matching curves are drawn, and the Euclidean distance corresponding to the intersection of the two curves is the threshold t.

Figure 6 shows the distribution of the Euclidean distances between the feature vectors of the palm vein images for intra- and inter-class matching. The solid line is the intra-class distance distribution, and the dashed line is the inter-class distance distribution. The t-value corresponding to the intersection point is 0.165, representing a matching threshold of t = 0.165. The threshold 't' is subject to variation, and it may differ for different databases.

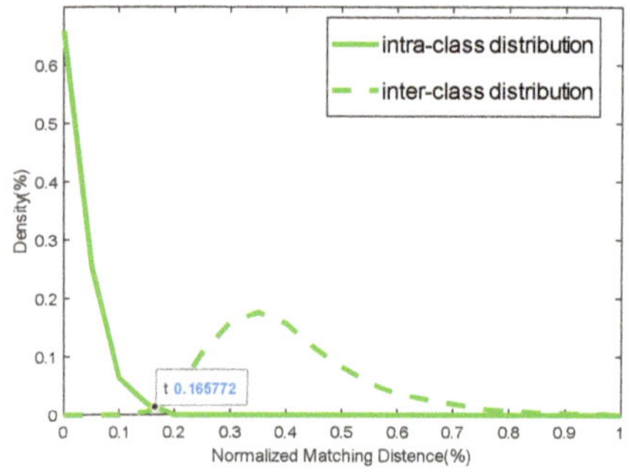

Figure 6. Curves of matching distribution for intra-class and inter-class.

For matching, the two image feature vectors in the test set are computed to calculate the Euclidean distance if they satisfy the following:

$$\text{Distance} < t \tag{9}$$

It is considered to belong to the same person and is accepted; otherwise, it is rejected.

4. Experimental Results and Analysis

The proposed algorithm was validated for its feasibility through experiments conducted on a self-built image database, the image database of the Institute of Automation, the Chinese Academy of Sciences, the image database of Hong Kong Polytechnic University, and the image database of Tongji University.

4.1. Feature Matching and Recognition

Four palm vein databases collected by heterogeneous devices under different conditions are considered to evaluate the proposed method's recognition accuracy.

(1) Self-built image databases: The self-developed device for palm vein image acquisition shown in Figure 2 was used for shooting, and the acquisition environment is shown in Figure 7. Two hundred and sixty-five palm images of the left and right hands of 265 people were collected. The left and right hands of the same person were regarded as different samples. In total, 530 palms were captured, with 10 images taken for each hand, resulting in a total of 5300 images. In the scope of the 5300 images we collected, the FTE rate of our device is 0%.

(2) CASIA (Chinese Academy of Sciences Institute of Automation) databases: Multi-spectral Palm Vein Database V1.0 contains 7200 palm vein images collected from 100 different hands. Its palmprint images taken at 850 nm wavelength can clearly show the palm veins, making it a universal palm vein atlas.

(3) Hong Kong Polytechnic University databases (PolyU): The PolyU multi-spectral database collects palmprint images under blue, green, red, and near-infrared (NIR) illumination. The CCD camera and high-power halogen light source form a contact device for contact collection. Palm vein samples are extracted from palmprint images collected under near-infrared illumination. It contains 250 palm vein images collected by users under a near-infrared light source, and 6000 images were collected.

(4) Tongji University databases: Tongji University's non-contact collection of palm vein galleries has a light source wavelength of 940 nm. It contains 12,000 palm vein image samples from individuals between 20 and 50. These images were captured using proprietary non-contact acquisition devices. The data were collected in two stages, including 600 palms, and each palm had 20 palm vein images.

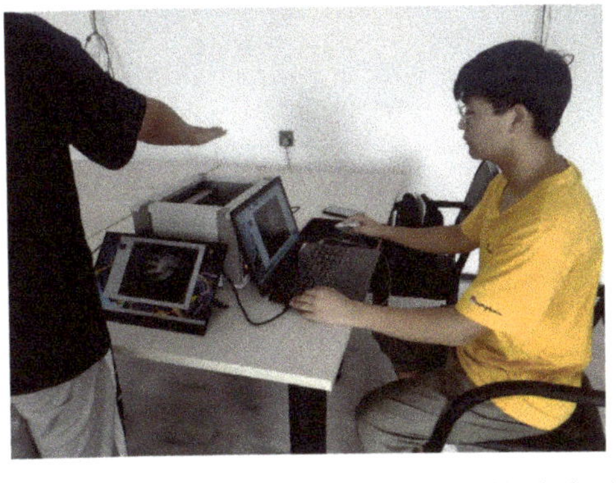

Figure 7. Acquisition environment of the self-built database.

Figures 8–11 show the basic situation of each database sample. As shown in the figure, the collected images are affected by the palm vein itself and external factors, and there are different degrees of blurring.

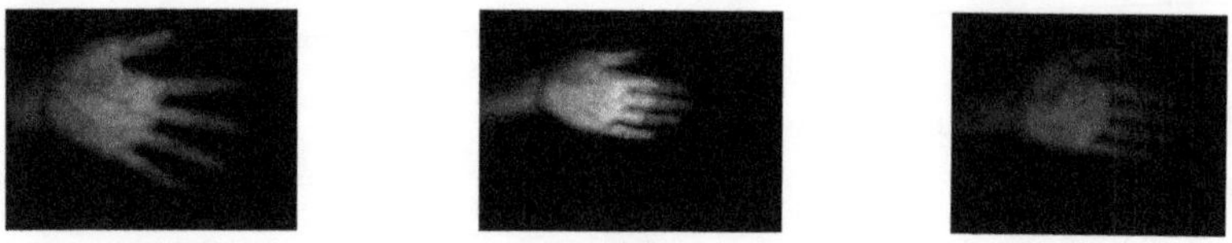

(a) (b) (c)

Figure 8. Self-built database samples: (**a**) Sample 1; (**b**) Sample 2; and (**c**) Sample 3.

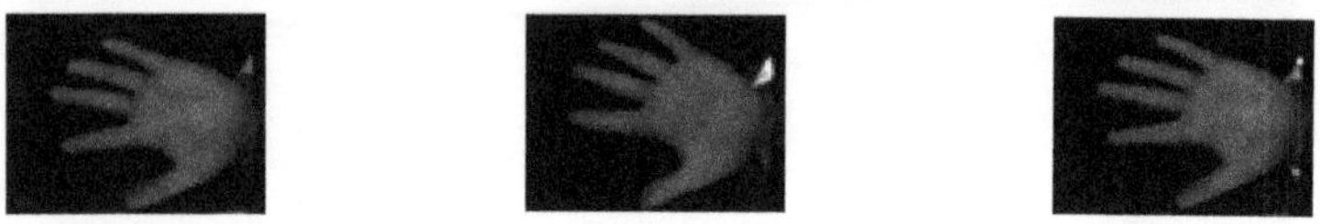

(a) (b) (c)

Figure 9. CASIA database samples: (**a**) Sample 1; (**b**) Sample 2; and (**c**) Sample 3.

(a) (b) (c)

Figure 10. PolyU database samples: (**a**) Sample 1; (**b**) Sample 2; and (**c**) Sample 3.

(a) (b) (c)

Figure 11. Tongji database samples: (**a**) Sample 1; (**b**) Sample 2; and (**c**) Sample 3.

4.2. Performance Evaluation and Error Indicators

Each of the databases consists of 100 classes, with six images per class. For each class, the first four images are used for training, while the remaining two images are used for testing. After feature extraction, a total of 40,000 matches are performed among the 200 test palm vein images. Among these matches, 400 matches are performed for samples of the same class, while 39,600 matches are performed for samples of different classes [2]. The threshold value 't' is determined based on the distribution curve of intra-class and inter-class samples in the training set. The performance of the recognition system is evaluated using the following metrics: false rejection rate (FRR), false acceptance rate (FAR), correct recognition rate (CRR), and recognition time.

$$FRR = \frac{NFR}{NAA} \times 100\% \tag{10}$$

$$FAR = \frac{NFA}{NIA} \times 100\% \tag{11}$$

NAA and NIA are the total numbers of attempts by legitimate and fake (illegal) users, respectively; NFR and NFA are the number of false rejects and false acceptances, respectively. CRR is defined as:

$$CRR = \frac{Number\ of\ correct\ identification}{Total\ number\ of\ identification} \times 100\% \quad (12)$$

As an error indicator, the equivalent error rate (EER) and receiver operating characteristic (ROC) curves are used, as they are the most commonly used indicators for reporting the accuracy of biometric systems in verification mode.

4.3. Parameter Adjustment and Sensitivity Analysis

By adjusting the parameters of the SDSPCA-NPE method, we tested their impact on the final recognition performance in order to determine the optimal parameter combination. In the SDSPCA-NPE method, the weight parameters significantly influence the recognition effectiveness of palm vein features. During the training stage of SDSPCA-NPE, there are three parameters: α, β, and δ. These parameters primarily determine the influence factors for class information, regularization, and local structure.

Taking Figure 12a as an example, we conducted numerous experiments with different values of k to find the optimal setting that ensures a good trade-off between performance and computational efficiency. Setting k to be too large can lead to the curse of dimensionality, resulting in computational challenges and potential over-fitting. Conversely, selecting k to be too small may lead to insufficient information representation and decreased performance. After determining the optimal value for k, we kept α constant and made changes to β and δ. The performance of these parameters was recorded in four different databases, and the results are presented in Figure 12.

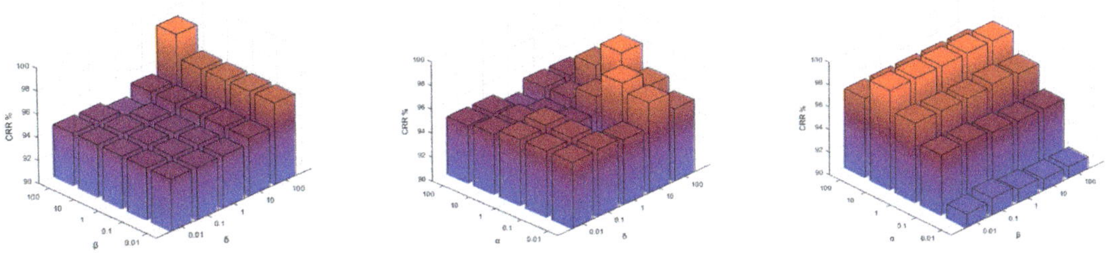

(a) **(b)** **(c)**

Figure 12. Performance index and parameter relationship: (**a**) β and δ; (**b**) α and δ; (**c**) α and β. The blue to red gradient represents the CRR from low to high.

The conclusion drawn is that SDSPCA-NPE is robust to β within the range of [0.01, 100], but sensitive to α and δ. Specifically, within a certain range, the weights assigned to class information and local information have a significant impact on the classification ability.

4.4. Ablation Experiments

In the experiment, the proposed method integrates global information, category information (supervised), and local information, aiming to verify the performance improvement achieved by combining these pieces of information. To validate this, individual experiments were conducted using the NPE, SDSPCA, and SDSPCA-NPE algorithms on the same image database. The specific performance results can be found in Figure 13.

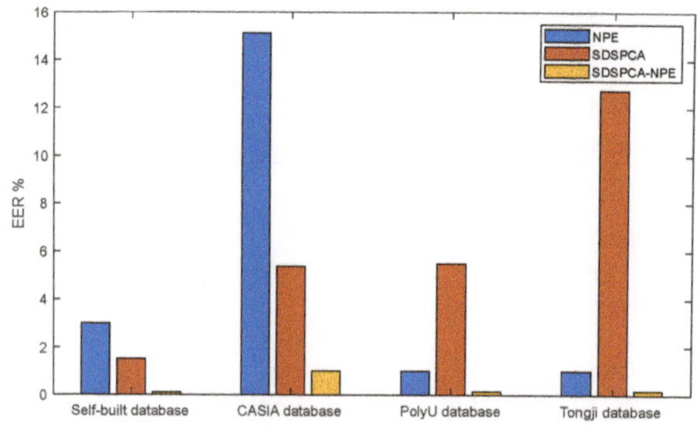

Figure 13. Performance of different components in the database.

From Figure 13, it can be observed that the proposed method, EER, demonstrates superior performance across all four datasets. Furthermore, NPE and SDSPCA exhibit the expected performance differences when applied to datasets that adhere to their respective dimensionality reduction principles. In conclusion, the SDSPCA-NPE algorithm combines the strengths of each individual algorithm, effectively integrating class-specific, global, and local information. It exhibits better applicability compared to SDSPCA and NPE alone, resulting in more desirable performance outcomes.

4.5. Performance Comparison

A comparison of our proposed algorithm with several typical algorithms is presented here, evaluating their performance on four databases. Table 1 displays the performance results (CRR/EER) of different algorithms. The corresponding ROC curves are illustrated in Figure 14.

Here are some introductions to these used algorithms:

(1) PCA: This method extracts the main information from the data, avoiding the comparison of redundant dimensions in palm vein images. However, it may result in data points being mixed together, making it difficult to distinguish between similar palm vein image samples, leading to sub-par performance.

(2) NPE: NPE retains the local information structure of the data, ensuring that the projected palm vein data maintains a close connection among samples of the same class. It effectively reduces the intra-class distance of similar palm vein samples. However, this method assumes the effective existence of local structures within the palm vein samples. It lacks robustness for samples that do not satisfy this data characteristic, such as palm vein images with significant deformation.

(3) SDSPCA: SDSPCA incorporates class information and sparse regularization into PCA. It exhibits a certain resistance to anomalous samples (e.g., blurry or deformed images) in palm vein images. However, its classification capability still cannot overcome the inherent limitations of PCA, resulting in the loss of certain components crucial for classification and un-satisfactory performance, especially for similar palm vein image samples.

(4) DBM: DBM utilizes texture features extracted from divided blocks, offering a simple structure, easy implementation, and fast speed. However, its performance is significantly compromised when dealing with low-quality or deformed palm vein images. Nevertheless, it performs reasonably well on high-quality palm vein data.

(5) DGWLD: DGWLD consists of an improved differential excitation operator and dual Gabor orientations. It better reflects the local grayscale variations in palm vein images, enhancing the differences between samples of different classes. However, it still struggles with sample rotation and deformation issues in non-contact palm vein images, and it incurs higher computational costs.

(6) MOGWLD: MOGWLD builds upon the dual Gabor framework by extracting multi-scale Gabor orientations and improving the original differential excitation by considering grayscale differences in multiple neighborhoods. This method enhances the discriminative power for distinguishing between samples from different classes. However, despite the improvement over the previous method, it increases the computational time and does not fundamentally enhance the classification ability for blurry and deformed samples within the same class.
(7) JPCDA: JPCDA incorporates class information into PCA, effectively reducing inter-class ambiguity. However, it does not perform well with non-linear palm vein data.

From Table 1 and Figure 14, it can be observed that sub-space methods, such as the SDSPCA-NPE algorithm, outperform other texture-based methods in terms of time efficiency. In terms of specific performance, the algorithm achieves superior results across four databases, with the best CRR and EER performance. It also exhibits better time complexity compared to the majority of methods. However, it should be noted that certain methods show lower time complexity and even better EER performance on individual image databases. Nonetheless, these algorithms lack universality and are not applicable for distinguishing palm vein images, especially when dealing with non-uniformly distributed palm vein databases.

Table 1. Performance of different algorithms in a database.

Algorithms	Database	EER (%)	Times(10^{-4} s)
PCA [15]	Self-built	0.28	19.59
	CASIA	2.38	19.77
	PolyU	1.5	19.45
	Tongji	6	19.58
DBM [7]	Self-built	5.01	521.54
	CASIA	22.53	522.52
	PolyU	2.31	525.16
	Tongji	5.66	549.56
DGWLD [5]	Self-built	8.26	2020.56
	CASIA	22.85	2066.15
	PolyU	7.21	2058.94
	Tongji	3.66	2054.89
MOGWLD [6]	Self-built	10.26	24,645.82
	CASIA	19.70	24,645.92
	PolyU	5.13	24,645.79
	Tongji	2.73	24,659.23
NPE [16]	Self-built	0.50	13.81
	CASIA	7.50	13.90
	PolyU	1	14.19
	Tongji	9.6	14.11
SDSPCA [23]	Self-built	1.50	13.56
	CASIA	15.39	13.89
	PolyU	5.50	13.57
	Tongji	10.75	13.63
JPCDA [28]	Self-built	0.13	24.56
	CASIA	0.72	24.39
	PolyU	0.50	24.77
	Tongji	0.55	24.96
SDSPCA-NPE	Self-built	0.10	19.77
	CASIA	0.50	38.50
	PolyU	0.16	19.75
	Tongji	0.19	19.69

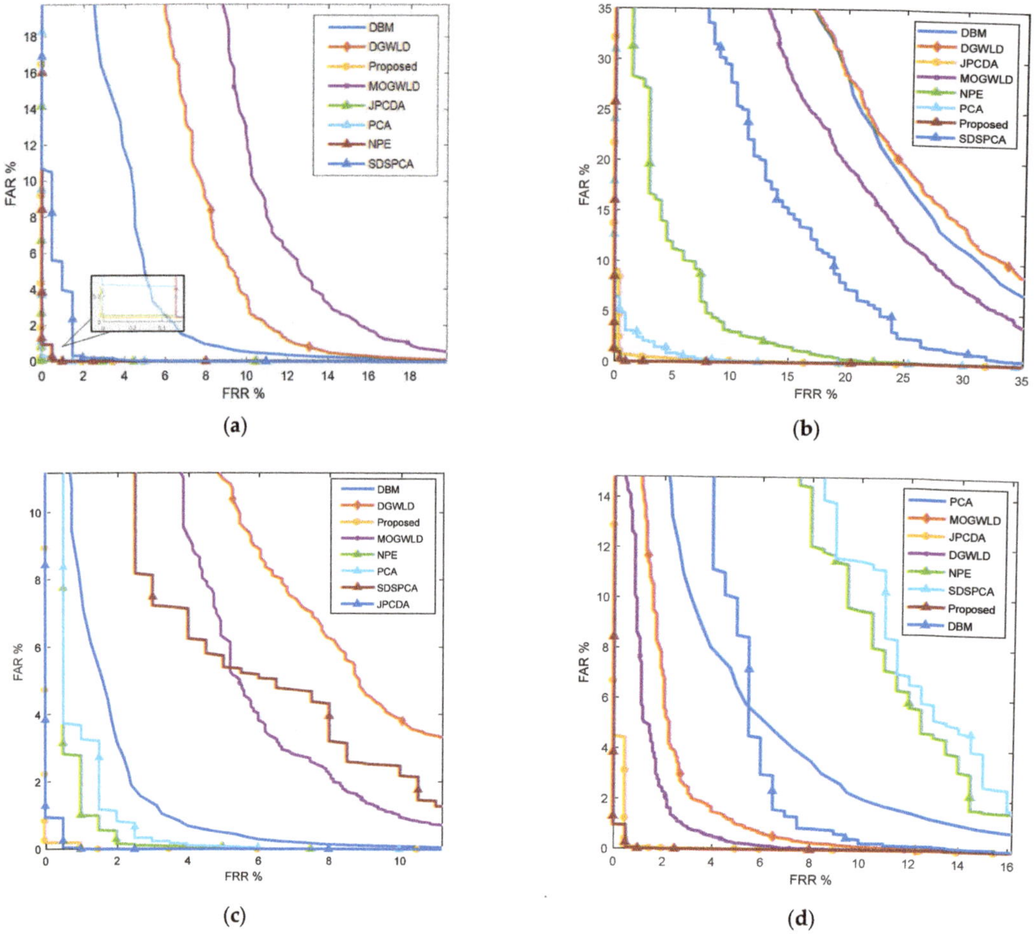

Figure 14. ROC curves. (**a**) Self-built database. (**b**) CASIA database. (**c**) PolyU database. (**d**) Tongji database.

It can be concluded that SDSPCA-NPE, as a supervised algorithm, effectively combines local structural information and global information for dimensionality reduction, yielding better overall performance than other algorithms across the four databases.

5. Conclusions

We have designed an open-environment palm vein image acquisition device based on multi-spectral imaging to achieve a high-security palm vein recognition system. Additionally, we have established a non-contact palm vein image dataset. In this study, we propose a supervised discriminative sparse principal component analysis (SDSPCA-NPE) algorithm that preserves the neighborhood structure to improve recognition performance. By utilizing sparse constraints in supervised learning, the SDSPCA-NPE algorithm obtains interpretable principal component features that contain class-specific information. This approach reduces the impact of issues such as un-clear imaging and low image quality during the acquisition process. It expands the inter-class distance and enhances the discriminability between different palm vein samples. Moreover, we introduce the neighborhood structure information into the projection step using robust neighborhood selection techniques, which ensure the preservation of similar local structures in the palm vein samples before and after projection. This technique captures the un-even distribution of palm vein images and addresses the drawbacks of increased image differences within the same class caused by rotation, scale variation, translation, and illumination changes. Experimental results demonstrate the effectiveness of the proposed method on three self-built databases, the CASIA database, the Hong Kong Polytechnic University database, and the Tongji University database. The equal error rates achieved are 0.10%, 0.50%, 0.16%, and 0.19%, respectively. Our approach outperforms other typical methods in terms of recognition accuracy. The system achieves real-time performance with an identification time of approximately 0.0019 s, indicating its practical value. Future work will focus on miniaturizing the palm vein acquisition device and developing recognition algorithms to accommodate large-scale palm vein databases.

Author Contributions: Conceptualization, W.W.; methodology, W.W.; software, W.W.; validation, W.W.; formal analysis, W.W.; investigation, Y.L. and Y.Z.; resources, Y.L.; data curation, Y.Z. and C.L.; writing—original draft preparation, Y.L.; writing—review and editing, Y.L.; visualization, Y.L.; supervision, W.W.; project administration, W.W.; funding acquisition, W.W. All authors have read and agreed to the published version of the manuscript.

Funding: This research received no external funding the National Natural Science Foundation of China (61903358), the China Postdoctoral Science Foundation (2019M651142), and the Natural Science Foundations of Liaoning Province (2023-MS-322).

Data Availability Statement: The dataset presented in this study is available. All data used in the study can be obtained from publicly available databases and emails from the author's mailbox.

Conflicts of Interest: The authors declare no conflict of interest.

References

1. MacGregor, P.; Welford, R. Veincheck: Imaging for security and personnel identification. *Adv. Imaging* **1991**, *6*, 52–56.
2. Wu, W.; Wang, Q.; Yu, S.; Luo, Q.; Lin, S.; Han, Z.; Tang, Y. Outside Box and Contactless Palm Vein Recognition Based on a Wavelet Denoising Resnet. *IEEE Access* **2021**, *9*, 82471–82484. [CrossRef]
3. Wu, W.; Elliott, S.J.; Lin, S.; Sun, S.; Tang, Y. Review of Palm Vein Recognition. *IET Biom.* **2019**, *9*, 1–10. [CrossRef]
4. Lee, Y.P. Palm vein recognition based on a modified (2D)2LDA. *Signal Image Video Process.* **2013**, *9*, 229–242. [CrossRef]
5. Wang, H.B.; Li, M.W.; Zhou, J. Palmprint recognition based on double Gabor directional Weber local descriptors. *Electron. Inform.* **2018**, *40*, 936–943.
6. Li, M.W.; Liu, H.Y.; Gao, X.J. Palmprint recognition based on multiscale Gabor directional Weber local descriptors. *Prog. Laser Optoelectron.* **2021**, *58*, 316–328. [CrossRef]
7. Almaghtuf, J.; Khelifi, F.; Bouridane, A. Fast and Efficient Difference of Block Means Code for Palmprint Recognition. *Mach. Vis. Appl.* **2020**, *31*, 1–10. [CrossRef]
8. Leng, L.; Yang, Z.; Min, W. Democratic Voting Downsampling for Coding-based Palmprint Recognition. *IET Biom.* **2020**, *9*, 290–296. [CrossRef]
9. Karanwal, S. Robust Local Binary Pattern for Face Recognition in Different Challenges. *Multimed. Tools Appl.* **2022**, *81*, 29405–29421. [CrossRef]
10. El Idrissi, A.; El Merabet, Y.; Ruichek, Y. Palmprint Recognition Using State-of-the-art Local Texture Descriptors: A Comparative Study. *IET Biom.* **2020**, *9*, 143–153. [CrossRef]
11. Kaur, P.; Kumar, N.; Singh, M. Biometric-Based Key Handling Using Speeded Up Robust Features. In *Lecture Notes in Networks and Systems*; Springer Nature: Singapore, 2023; pp. 607–616.
12. Kumar, A.; Gupta, R. Futuristic Study of a Criminal Facial Recognition: A Open-Source Face Image Dataset. *Sci. Talks* **2023**, *6*, 100229. [CrossRef]
13. Yahaya, Y.H.; Leng, W.Y.; Shamsuddin, S.M. Finger Vein Biometric Identification Using Discretization Method. *J. Phys. Conf. Ser.* **2021**, *1878*, 012030. [CrossRef]
14. Jia, W.; Xia, W.; Zhao, Y.; Min, H.; Chen, Y.-X. 2D and 3D Palmprint and Palm Vein Recognition Based on Neural Architecture Search. *Int. J. Autom. Comput.* **2021**, *18*, 377–409. [CrossRef]
15. Rida, I.; Al-Maadeed, S.; Mahmood, A.; Bouridane, A.; Bakshi, S. Palmprint Identification Using an Ensemble of Sparse Representations. *IEEE Access* **2018**, *6*, 3241–3248. [CrossRef]
16. Sun, S.; Cong, X.; Zhang, P.; Sun, B.; Guo, X. Palm Vein Recognition Based on NPE and KELM. *IEEE Access* **2021**, *9*, 71778–71783. [CrossRef]
17. Guo, Y.-R.; Bai, Y.-Q.; Li, C.-N.; Bai, L.; Shao, Y.-H. Two-Dimensional Bhattacharyya Bound Linear Discriminant Analysis with Its Applications. *Appl. Intell.* **2021**, *52*, 8793–8809. [CrossRef]

18. Jolliffe, I.T. Principal Component Analysis and Factor Analysis. In *Principal Component Analysis*; Springer: New York, NY, USA, 1986; pp. 115–128.
19. Liu, J.-X.; Xu, Y.; Gao, Y.-L.; Zheng, C.-H.; Wang, D.; Zhu, Q. A Class-Information-Based Sparse Component Analysis Method to Identify Differentially Expressed Genes on RNA-Seq Data. *IEEE/ACM Trans. Comput. Biol. Bioinform.* **2016**, *13*, 392–398. [CrossRef] [PubMed]
20. Multilinear Principal Component Analysis. In *Multilinear Subspace Learning*; Chapman and Hall/CRC: Boca Raton, FL, USA, 2013; pp. 136–169.
21. Al-jaberi, A.S.; Mohsin Al-juboori, A. Palm Vein Recognition, a Review on Prospects and Challenges Based on CASIA's Dataset. In Proceedings of the 2020 13th International Conference on Developments in eSystems Engineering (DeSE), Virtual Conference, 14–17 December 2020.
22. Salazar-Jurado, E.H.; Hernández-García, R.; Vilches-Ponce, K.; Barrientos, R.J.; Mora, M.; Jaswal, G. Towards the Generation of Synthetic Images of Palm Vein Patterns: A Review. *Inf. Fusion* **2023**, *89*, 66–90. [CrossRef]
23. Feng, C.-M.; Xu, Y.; Liu, J.-X.; Gao, Y.-L.; Zheng, C.-H. Supervised Discriminative Sparse PCA for Com-Characteristic Gene Selection and Tumor Classification on Multiview Biological Data. *IEEE Trans. Neural Netw. Learn. Syst.* **2019**, *30*, 2926–2937. [CrossRef]
24. Jiang, B.; Ding, C.; Luo, B.; Tang, J. Graph-Laplacian PCA: Closed-Form Solution and Robustness. In Proceedings of the 2013 IEEE Conference on Computer Vision and Pattern Recognition, Portland, OR, USA, 23–28 June 2013.
25. Feng, D.; He, S.; Zhou, Z.; Zhang, Y. A Finger Vein Feature Extraction Method Incorporating Principal Component Analysis and Locality Preserving Projections. *Sensors* **2022**, *22*, 3691. [CrossRef]
26. Wang, X.; Yan, W.Q. Human Identification Based on Gait Manifold. *Appl. Intell.* **2022**, *53*, 6062–6073. [CrossRef]
27. Roweis, S.T.; Saul, L.K. Nonlinear Dimensionality Reduction by Locally Linear Embedding. *Science* **2000**, *290*, 2323–2326. [CrossRef] [PubMed]
28. Zhao, X.; Guo, J.; Nie, F.; Chen, L.; Li, Z.; Zhang, H. Joint Principal Component and Discriminant Analysis for Dimensionality Reduction. *IEEE Trans. Neural Netw. Learn. Syst.* **2020**, *31*, 433–444. [CrossRef] [PubMed]

electronics

Article

Real-Time Human Movement Recognition Using Ultra-Wideband Sensors

Minseong Noh [1], Heungju Ahn [2] and Sang C. Lee [2,*]

1 Department of Computer Engineering, Daegu Gyeongbuk Institute of Science and Technology, Daegu 42988, Republic of Korea; noms4694@dgist.ac.kr
2 College of Transdisciplinary Studies and Jimbo Robotics, Daegu Gyeongbuk Institute of Science and Technology, Daegu 42988, Republic of Korea; heungju@dgist.ac.kr
* Correspondence: sclee@dgist.ac.kr; Tel.: +82-10-4506-4556

Abstract: This study introduces a methodology for the real-time detection of human movement based on two legs using ultra-wideband (UWB) sensors. Movements were primarily categorized into four states: stopped, walking, lingering, and the transition between sitting and standing. To classify these movements, UWB sensors were used to measure the distance between the designated point and a specific point on the two legs in the human body. By analyzing the measured distance values, a movement state classification model was constructed. In comparison to conventional vision/laser/LiDAR-based research, this approach requires fewer computational resources and provides distinguished real-time human movement detection within a CPU environment. Consequently, this research presents a novel strategy to effectively recognize human movements during human–robot interactions. The proposed model effectively discerned four distinct movement states with classification accuracy of around 95%, demonstrating the novel strategy's efficacy.

Keywords: ultra-wideband sensor; human-following robot; human movement pattern; classification

1. Introduction

In recent years, the rapid advancements and innovations in robotics have led to the increased integration of robots into daily life, work environments, and various industries [1–5]. As a part of this integration, the ability for robots to perceive human movements and behaviors accurately and respond appropriately has become increasingly important [6–8]. This capability is not only vital for the robot's stability but also in improving the user convenience and work efficiency [9,10]. Therefore, a smooth response system between humans and robots has become one of the primary research topics in robotics [11,12]. To establish an effective response system, it is essential for robots to first discern and understand the current human movements. Addressing this challenge, this paper presents a methodology by which robots can perceive human movements.

In the domain of robotics, the accurate perception of user movement is paramount in enhancing the interaction between humans and robots. Currently, there is vigorous research in the fields of vision and laser sensing aimed at achieving this objective [13–26]. Vision-based systems are advantageous for their ability to capture detailed imagery, enabling the analysis of complex human postures with high accuracy. This is complemented by the richness of the visual information available, such as color and texture, which aids in the precise interpretation of human actions. Laser sensing, on the other hand, offers precision in distance measurement and is capable of tracking movements accurately, even under varied environmental conditions. However, methods utilizing vision or lasers come with the drawback of requiring large computational resources [27,28]. Additionally, vision and laser sensing faces challenges when temporary occlusions occur, such as when an obstacle momentarily obscures the person, making it difficult to discern their posture [29,30].

Contrary to these approaches, this study proposes a methodology that simply adds an additional UWB sensor to an existing UWB-based human-following robot [31,32]. This method enables the real-time classification of human movement using minimal CPU operations, without using deep learning tools. Additionally, by relying on the distance metrics between sensors, this technique can offer superior reliability in detecting human movement states over vision- or laser-based methods, particularly in situations where temporary visual obstructions of the user occur. Additionally, the robustness of the UWB sensors facilitates the robot's ability to track movements with a reasonable degree of accuracy, even when the user is performing cornering maneuvers [32]. This means that the robot can effectively follow a person moving around corners, maintaining the tracking performance despite the user being momentarily beyond direct sight. This capability demonstrates the potential for the robot's operational effectiveness in complex environments, where obstacles frequently obstruct the line of sight.

In this study, while dealing with human movements, movements initiated by both legs were especially focused on. The reason for focusing on the movement of both legs was as follows. In most situations, human locomotion is primarily carried out via the movement of the two legs. From this perspective, if a mobile robot can understand the actions of a person's two legs, the robot will be able to actively respond to human movement.

In the case of huma-following robots, which utilize UWB sensors, it is especially important to discern the movements of both human legs. Traditional human-following robots [31–33] employing ultra-wideband (UWB) sensor technology ascertain the position of a user through bilateration, calculating the distance from the robot to the person. These systems typically follow the user based on their location. However, this approach is limited to only identifying the user's position and does not provide any information on how the user is moving. As a result, this limitation leads to several challenges and issues. For instance, if a user simply sits down and stands up in the same spot, this action can result in distance change, causing the robot to mistakenly interpret it as a positional shift, leading to unintended movements. Similarly, if a worker stops and moves slightly to perform a simple task, the robot might perceive these minor movements as positional changes, reacting continuously and behaving in a manner inconsistent with the user's intention. However, if the robot understands not only the user's positional information but also the type of movement, the mobile robot can deal with the various situations appropriately.

In order to address the aforementioned challenges, this paper introduces a novel methodology that involves attaching an additional UWB sensor to the human body, thereby enabling the acquisition of distance measurements for both human legs. By observing the changes in distance values corresponding to both legs, this study discerned user movements, thereby revealing insights into the movements of the human legs, which was previously unattainable through conventional methods. In addition, to accurately interpret user movements, human movement states were initially categorized into four distinct states: stopped, walking, lingering, and sitting/standing. For each category, patterns in the distance values corresponding to the different movements were analyzed. Based on these patterns, a movement classification model was subsequently developed. The classification of each movement was conducted in the following three stages. First, a binary classification was performed to distinguish between stopped and non-stopped (walking, lingering, sitting/standing) states based on velocity and acceleration values derived from the distance data. A simple threshold was established for this purpose. Second, among the non-stopped movements, a further binary classification was conducted to differentiate walking from non-walking (lingering, sitting/standing) movements. To achieve this, human walking patterns were modeled, and the characteristics of these patterns were identified using the Fast Fourier Transform (FFT) and cosine similarity, facilitating movement classification. Third, the classification between lingering and sitting/standing was made by comparing the slope of the acceleration values of both legs over a specific period. Through these three stages, the user's movements were comprehensively classified into the four specified states.

This paper initially introduces a methodology that prioritizes the classification of human movement states into four categories, focusing on the changes in the user's location. Following this, it validates the suitability of attaching sensors to both legs of the user, based on the modeling of the human walking sequence. Subsequently, the paper analyzes patterns in the sensor data corresponding to the previously defined four states and proposes a model to classify these states based on the analyzed patterns. The paper concludes with an analysis of the experimental results.

Designed in the structured manner shown in Figure 1, the study not only presents a novel approach to understanding and classifying human movements but also significantly contributes to the field of robotics by providing a comprehensive framework to enhance human–robot interaction. Through the meticulous application of this methodology, the paper aims to offer insights that pave the way for more intuitive and efficient human-following robots, thereby marking a step forward in the integration of robotic systems into human-centric environments.

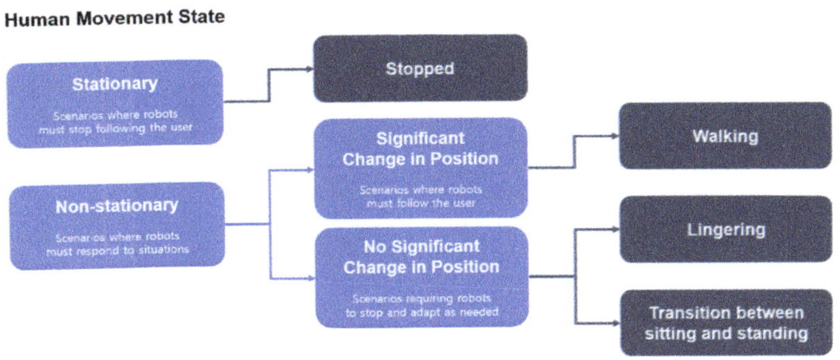

Figure 1. Definition of human movement states.

2. Definition of Human Movement State

In prior research, the study of human movement typically focuses on the direction and speed of a person's travel or on classifying a more diverse array of movements, including walking, jumping, jogging, lying down, standing, sitting, stair climbing, and falling. These studies are conducted to understand pedestrian gait states, to detect accidents such as falls during daily activities, and to quantify and define human movements for applications in kinesiology, biomechanics, and biomedicine. Tools such as soft-robotic-stretch (SRS) sensors, video cameras, piezoelectric accelerometers, pyroelectric infrared (PIR) sensors, Mica2 sensors, and IMU sensors have been utilized for these purposes [34–40].

In contrast to these existing studies, this research focuses on the movements exhibited by users in a working environment when interacting with a human-following robot. In scenarios wherein a robot is following a person, especially a worker, uncommon movements such as jumping or lying down are beyond the scope of this research and thus not considered. Instead, this model is specialized for scenarios that are probable during work-related activities.

In this study, human movements are categorized into four principal categories for the purpose of robot detection. To categorize movements associated with human locomotion, three main classifications were initially identified: stationary states, movements resulting in a change in location, and movements without a significant change in location. In a human-following robot, it is essential for the robot to categorize human movements into stationary and non-stationary states. Furthermore, it is crucial to subdivide the non-stationary states of human movement into those involving significant positional changes and those that do not.

The necessity to classify human movements into stationary and non-stationary states arises from the inherent sensor inaccuracies present in real-world robotic applications.

Sensors attached to both the robot and the human subject are prone to errors, which can lead to false interpretations of user motion; a stationary human may be perceived as moving due to these errors, increasing the likelihood of the robot malfunctioning. In the context of a worker-following robot, which often involves carrying heavy loads and closely trailing a user, the ability to accurately discern the user's stationary and mobile states becomes crucial. If the robot were to respond to error values while the user is stationary, this could lead to accidents within the working environment. Therefore, it is important to ensure precise differentiation for the safety of operational environments [9].

The reason for distinguishing between non-stationary human states that involve a change in position and those that do not is as follows. In cases of movements involving significant positional changes, such as walking, it is crucial for the robot to classify these as situations where it should follow the human's shifting location. For movements that do not result in significant positional changes, such as lingering or transitions between sitting and standing, the robot should recognize that alterations in sensor-detected distances do not necessitate adjustments in response to the human's location changes.

In this study, movements that do not result in a significant change in location are categorized as lingering and transitions between sitting and standing. In scenarios whereby workers need to squat to access materials from the robot's payload, it is important that the robot does not misconstrue this action as a change in the worker's position, which would otherwise lead to the unnecessary movement of the robot, potentially complicating the worker's task or even causing a collision risk. Additionally, in a working environment, workers are likely to take occasional brief pauses to manage tasks. If a worker-following robot were to respond to every instance of such lingering, it would decrease the robot's operational efficiency and similarly elevate the risk of accidents. Hence, for both efficiency and safety in robotic operations, it is imperative that robots discern lingering and sitting/standing behaviors and respond appropriately to each [9].

Therefore, within the scope of this study, human movements are systematically classified into three broad categories: a stationary state, movements resulting in a change in location, and movements without a significant change in location. Under this classification scheme, a stopped state corresponds to a stationary state in this paper. A walking state corresponds to movements that result in a location change. A lingering state and sitting/standing state correspond to movements without significant location changes. Consequently, human movement within the context of this research is categorized into four distinct types: stopped, walking, lingering, and sitting/standing.

3. Human Walking Sequence Modeling

Prior to developing a model for the classification of human movement states, this research first sought to establish the validity of using UWB sensors for movement classification and to determine the optimal placement of sensors for the accurate assessment of human motion. In order to achieve this objective, this section focused on modeling the walking state, identified as the most complex and characteristic among the four defined movements. By abstracting the human walking sequence and comparing it with actual experimental data, efforts were made to pinpoint the sensor placement that best captured the intricacies of the walking pattern.

Considering the inherent error margin of approximately 10 centimeters in UWB sensors, this research conducted a series of experiments to identify the optimal leg position for sensor attachment [41]. When the sensors are positioned at the upper part of the leg, close to the waist, the variation between the legs during walking is minimal, making it difficult to discern the characteristics of the human gait due to the inherent measurement error of approximately 10 centimeters associated with UWB sensors. Therefore, placing UWB sensors in proximity to the waist region proved to be inappropriate to capture the characteristics of the human gait. Conversely, positioning the sensors too low, beneath the knee, resulted in an increase in measurement errors due to the proximity of the UWB sensors to the ground, which is a characteristic limitation of UWB sensors, thus complicating the acquisition of clean patterns [42]. Considering these factors, the sensors were affixed slightly above the knee, and it was experimentally observed that the gait patterns derived from the measured distances at this location were more distinct compared to previous trials.

Therefore, to demonstrate that sensor placement slightly above the knee yielded clear and consistent gait patterns during walking, preliminary modeling was conducted to determine how the UWB sensor distance readings would manifest in ideal walking scenarios. For a visual representation, Figure 2 illustrates the trajectory of the sensors positioned directly above the knee during a human walking sequence. In Figure 2, the dark orange segment represents the left leg, while the light orange segment indicates the right leg. In the visualized patterns, it can be observed that, during the walking phase, the supporting leg maintains a straight alignment, largely unaffected by the movement of the knee joint. Concurrently, the hip point near the waist of the supporting leg serves as the pivot, enabling the opposite thigh to execute a circular motion, propelling forward. Considering these assumptions, the movement of the human legs during walking is represented by a combination of sine and cosine functions as follows.

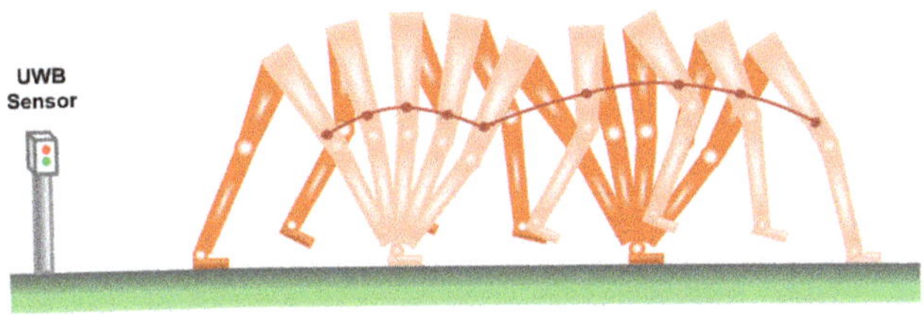

Figure 2. Human walking sequence. The light orange area represents the right leg of the subject, while the dark orange area indicates the left leg. The red points denote specific points above the knees, highlighting the locations where the UWB sensors are attached on the legs. The red curved lines connecting these points illustrate the trajectory during walking.

$$x_1 = r_1 \cos(\theta_1), \quad y_1 = r_1 \sin(\theta_1) \tag{1}$$

$$x_2 = (r_1 + r_2)\cos(\theta_1), \quad y_2 = (r_1 + r_2)\sin(\theta_1) \tag{2}$$

$$x_3 = (r_1 + r_2)\cos(\theta_1) + r_2\cos(\theta_2), \quad y_3 = (r_1 + r_2)\sin(\theta_1) + r_2\sin(\theta_2) \tag{3}$$

Initially, the distance from the heel to a point slightly above the knee is defined as r_1. Given the angle, θ_1, created by the supporting leg with the ground, the location directly above the knee can be depicted as (x_1, y_1), as detailed in Equation (1). The distance from this point to the waist is marked as r_2. The position of the waist corresponds to Equation (2). Using these parameters, the position above the knee for the opposite leg can be denoted as (x_3, y_3). When the opposite thigh forms an angle, θ_2, with the ground, it aligns with Equation (3).

To compare the distance value data evident in the ideal walking pattern with the actual measured values, a simulation environment representing ideal conditions was conceptualized. To obtain a clean pattern, the values of r_1 and r_2 in the proposed equation were set to 0.5, analogous to the experimenter, and the maximum angle of leg separation during walking was established at 60 degrees. In the actual experimental environment, the distance from the robot's UWB sensor to the UWB sensors on the person's legs is measured. To reflect this, the simulation environment recorded the distances from the point $(-2, 0.5)$ to the recurring patterns of (x_1, y_1) and (x_3, y_3) throughout the simulation. The specific point $(-2, 0.5)$ was chosen in the simulation to mirror the actual experimental setup where the height of the UWB sensors on the robot's legs from the ground was similar to the height of the UWB sensors on the experimenter's legs from the ground. Consequently, in the simulation, the r_1 value and the y-coordinate of the specific point were set to be equal to maintain consistency with the experimental conditions. Furthermore, in actual situations, smoother transitions between both legs are expected to occur compared to the model constructed with the above equations. Therefore, a moving average was applied, as demonstrated in the ideal conditions represented in Figure 3.

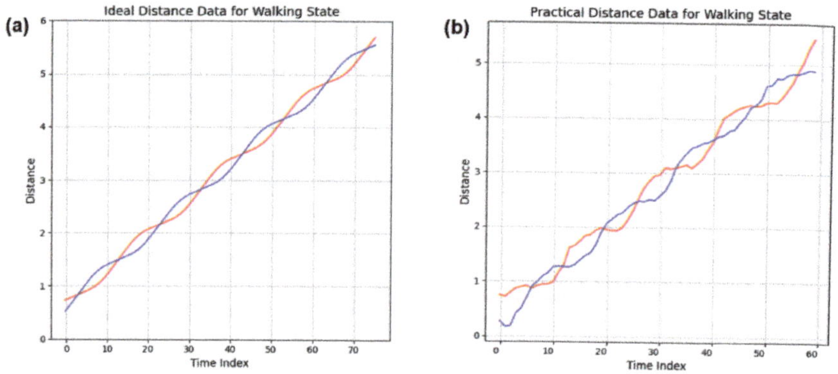

Figure 3. Trajectories of distance values from a fixed point to both legs during a walking scenario. In the graph, the red line represents the right leg, while the blue line signifies the left leg. (**a**) modeled ideal conditions; (**b**) practically measured values.

Subsequently, an experiment was conducted to compare the ideal gait pattern with the practical pattern obtained from attaching UWB sensors to the legs. As observed in Figure 3, which displays the results of the experiment, the designed gait model closely mimics the actual walking pattern. This similarity suggests that when UWB sensors are attached slightly above the knees, they can effectively capture the characteristic crossing of the legs, thereby lending credibility to the use of UWB sensor measurements for the classification of complex gait patterns. This foundational understanding serves as the basis for the more in-depth analysis of human movement patterns in the subsequent sections of this paper.

4. Human Movement Pattern Analysis

In this study, user movements were classified into four distinct categories, stopped, walking, lingering, and sitting/standing, as per the definitions provided earlier. The analysis predominantly utilized distance measurements acquired from ultra-wideband (UWB) sensors attached to both legs of the human, which were used to calculate the distance to the robot.

In Figure 4, a brief overview of the ultra-wideband (UWB) sensors employed in this study is provided prior to proceeding with the analysis. Two sensors were affixed to the robot, functioning as anchors, with the primary purpose of determining the user's position through the process of bilateration. Although a single UWB sensor could suffice for position identification, two UWB sensors were attached to the user in this study. This configuration was chosen not only to precisely pinpoint the user's location but also to leverage the movement data obtained from both legs, thereby accurately determining various user movements.

To implement this, the distance information of the two legs was represented as shown in Figure 5. If there are two UWB sensors on the robot and two on the person, a total of four distance values are generated. Among these values, the relevant distance is the one from the center of the robot to the user. Utilizing Stewart's theorem [43], a well-known result in geometry, values L and R were derived as shown in Equation (4). Notably, the distance between the two UWB sensors on the robot was 0.6 m in the experiments.

$$L = \sqrt{\frac{d_1^2 + d_2^2}{2} - 0.3^2}, \quad R = \sqrt{\frac{d_3^2 + d_4^2}{2} - 0.3^2} \tag{4}$$

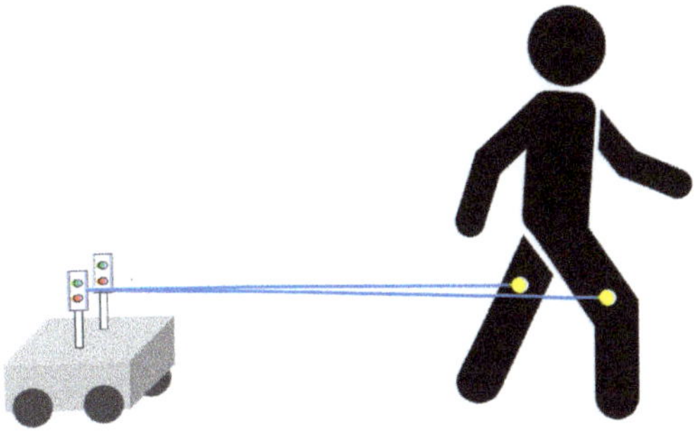

Figure 4. Schematic of a human-following robot using two UWB sensors.

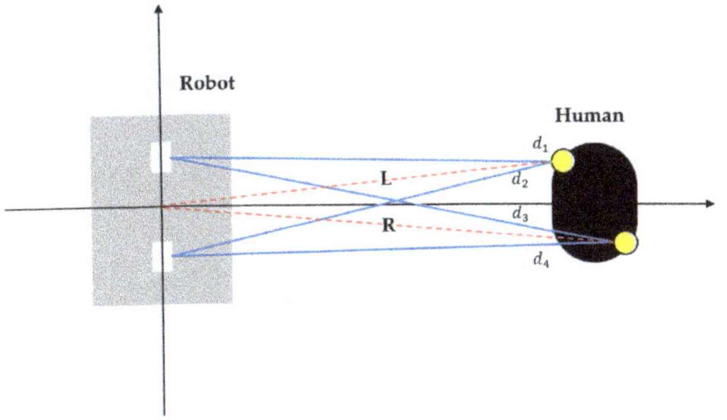

Figure 5. Top view of human and robot.

Utilizing the distance value L obtained from the left leg and the distance value R from the right leg, experiments were conducted for the four movement states previously defined. The experimental results are illustrated in Figure 6. Upon the detailed examination of the scenarios presented in Figure 6, a notable characteristic became apparent. In the walking scenario, the legs exhibited an alternating movement pattern with the distance values progressively increasing. In contrast, the other movement scenarios displayed synchronized motion of both legs, with the distance values exhibiting minimal fluctuations and remaining within a stable range.

This observation highlights a clear relationship between the legs' movement patterns and their distance values from a specific point. Utilizing this relationship allows for the precise identification of the user's activity. To enhance the visibility of these distinctive characteristics and to extract meaningful features from each movement pattern, a series of data processing steps were employed.

Initially, the raw data underwent a smoothing process via a moving average technique, which helped to reduce the inherent measurement errors of the UWB sensors. This was followed by first-order differentiation to highlight the rate of change in the distance values. Another round of moving average smoothing was applied to refine the data further. Subsequently, second-order differentiation was conducted to calculate the acceleration values, providing insights into the rapidity of movement changes. To emphasize the variations in movement patterns, these acceleration values were once again smoothed using a moving average. These processing steps led to the distinct separation of the various movement patterns, as illustrated in Figure 7. This enhanced clarity enables a more precise and insightful analysis of the user's activities.

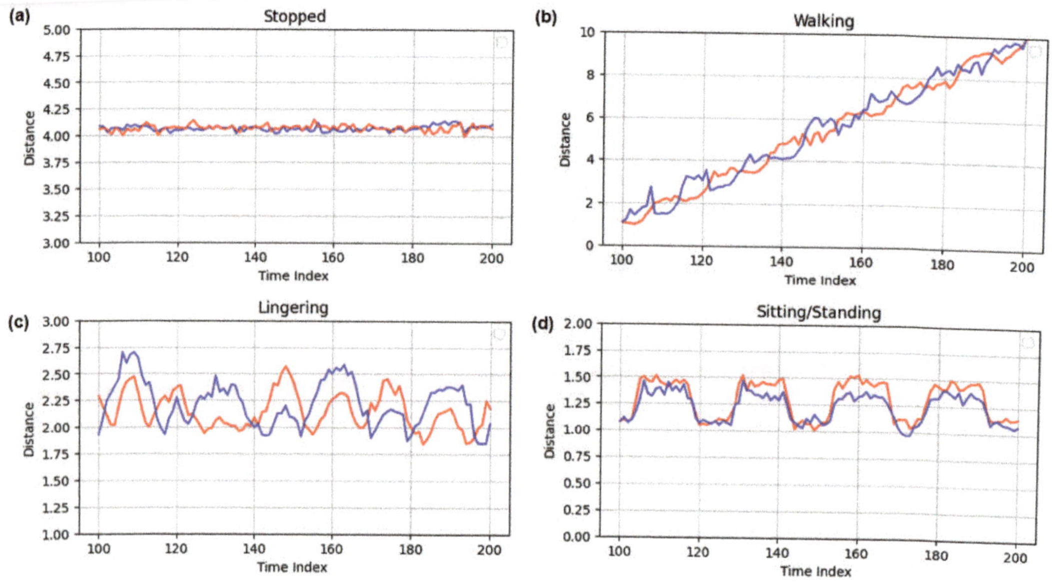

Figure 6. Representative distance data for four types of human movement. In the graph, the red line represents the right leg, while the blue line signifies the left leg. (**a**) distance fluctuations recorded while the subject remains stationary; (**b**) distance changes measured between the legs while walking; (**c**) variations in the distance between the legs when the subject is lingering in place; (**d**) distance alterations observed between the legs during repeated transitions from sitting to standing.

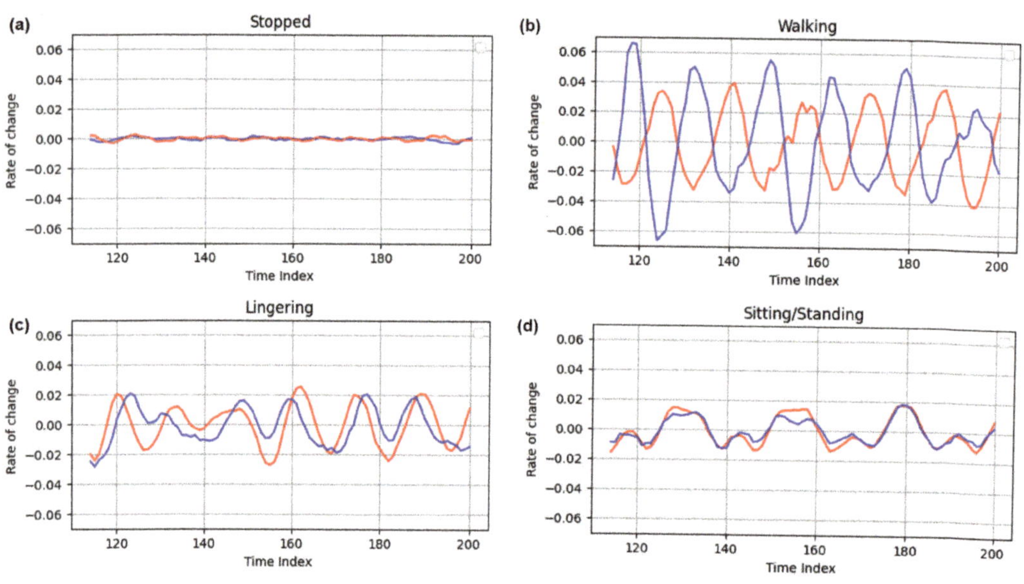

Figure 7. Processed acceleration data for four distinct movement types. In the graph, the red line represents the right leg, while the blue line signifies the left leg. (**a**) smoothed acceleration changes while the subject is stationary; (**b**) smoothed acceleration data measured from the legs during walking; (**c**) smoothed acceleration fluctuations of the legs when the subject is lingering; (**d**) smoothed acceleration variations of the legs during repeated sitting-to-standing transitions.

Upon analyzing the acceleration data presented in Figure 7, significant characteristics are revealed. In the case of the walking movement, each leg operated autonomously, intersecting at specific instances. At these intersection points, the velocity of the supporting leg was reduced to a minimum, while the opposing leg simultaneously achieved its maximum velocity. As a result, the acceleration values approached zero at these intersection points. Additionally, due to the distinct movement patterns exhibited by each leg, their acceleration values tended to progress in opposite directions. This characteristic uniquely distinguished the walking state from other types of movement.

Conversely, during the lingering and sitting/standing states, the movement patterns generated by each leg exhibit pronounced similarities to one another. This resulted in the acceleration values following a parallel trajectory rather than diverging. The recognition and utilization of these observed differences in movement patterns played a crucial role in accurately classifying each specific type of movement state in subsequent analyses.

5. Human Moving Pattern Classification Method

In this section, the methodology used to classify individual states based on the previously established human movement state is presented, utilizing distance measurements taken by the robot from both legs of the user. This paper leverages a tree-structured algorithm, as defined in Figure 1, categorizing human movements efficiently in a CPU environment without the necessity for pattern classification methods such as deep learning. When classifying user movements using computer vision methods with deep learning, models such as VGG-16, ResNet-50, and GoogleNet are employed, which require the use of approximately 138 million, 25 million, and 7 million parameters, respectively, leading to considerable computational demands [44–46]. Contrastingly, the tree-structured algorithm proposed in this study is designed for computational efficiency, requiring fewer than 100 computations to effectively categorize human movements. This marked difference highlights the superior efficiency of our approach over deep learning methodologies, which rely on millions of parameters and extensive training periods.

As depicted in Figure 8, the initial step in this methodology is to ascertain whether the individual is moving or stopped. This differentiation is crucial as it not only enhances the operational efficiency of the robot but also presents clear demarcation from other movement patterns, justifying its placement at the top of the priority list. Following this, the walking state, which significantly influences changes in the user's position, is identified and segregated. This is crucial because, in the case of a human-following robot, there must be a responsive system to detect changes in a person's position and subsequently follow them, provided that they are not in a stationary state. Subsequent classifications are made for movements such as lingering and sitting/standing, which contribute to an enhanced user experience and increased stability in the robot's operations. A variety of methods, including velocity and acceleration value comparisons, Fourier transformations, cosine similarity measures, and gradient change observations, are employed for these classifications.

Additionally, the rationale behind dividing the classification modeling process into three distinct steps is rooted in performance considerations. Specifically, if the Fourier transformation, utilized in Step 2, were to be employed as the sole method for the differentiation of all movement types, certain classifications would become challenging. For instance, the walking state can be identified due to the independent movement of each leg, resulting in crossing patterns in the distance value graphs of the legs, as previously explained. However, other states, such as stopped, sitting/standing, and lingering, are more difficult to distinguish using this method alone, as these involve less independent leg movements and more similar motion patterns. Similarly, if only the gradient difference comparison method used in Step 3 were to be applied, the stopped and sitting/standing states, wherein both legs move or remain still together, would show gradient differences close to zero. In contrast, walking and lingering, where the legs move independently, would exhibit larger gradient differences, making it challenging to accurately classify all four states using this method alone. Therefore, this paper initially proposes a basic model that classifies movements according to a tree structure in three steps. Subsequently, to further enhance the performance, an enhanced method is introduced. As a reference, the UWB sensor values are refreshed every 0.2 s. The velocity and acceleration values referenced herein are derived from the simple subtraction of consecutive sensor readings, without division by 0.2 s.

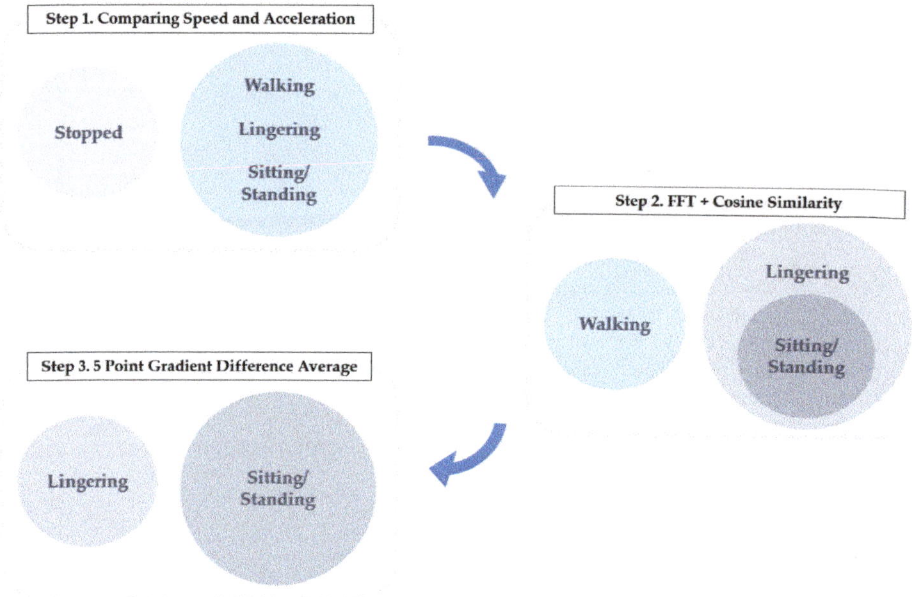

Figure 8. Steps for classification of 4 human movement states.

5.1. Step 1—Method to Distinguish between Stopped and Non-Stopped States

To accurately determine whether the current user's state is stopped or non-stopped, it is imperative to comprehend the characteristics of the UWB sensor. The UWB sensor exhibits a distance measurement error of ±0.1 m. Consequently, even when a user is stationary, the sensor's margin of error may cause it to mistakenly interpret the user as being in motion, potentially leading the robot to act in a manner that does not align with the user's intentions.

Theoretically, a stationary user could exhibit a velocity of up to $0.1 - (-0.1) = 0.2$ and acceleration of $0.2 - (-0.2) = 0.4$ due to this sensor error. However, empirical tests with the UWB sensor attached to a person's body demonstrated that the velocity magnitude seldom surpasses 0.02 when in a stopped state, and the acceleration magnitude consistently stays below 0.004. These findings indicate that the sensor error does not abruptly oscillate between its minimum and maximum values. Rather, it progressively increases or decreases, providing the rationale for the observed data and ensuring reliability in distinguishing between stopped and non-stopped states.

Given these observations, a velocity threshold of 0.02 and an acceleration threshold of 0.004 were set to distinguish between the stopped and non-stopped states. These thresholds effectively encompass all instances of the stopped state while ensuring that other movement states do not breach these boundaries. Within these thresholds, both velocity and acceleration tend to converge towards 0. For other movement states, such as walking, lingering, and sitting and stopping, the values consistently fall outside these thresholds. In all conditions except the stopped state, when the velocity approaches zero, acceleration takes on positive or negative values outside the established threshold. Conversely, if the acceleration approaches zero, the velocity exhibits positive or negative values outside the established threshold. Therefore, only in the stopped state do both the velocity and acceleration values appear within the established threshold limits.

5.2. Step 2—Method to Distinguish between Walking and Non-Walking States

To effectively distinguish between walking, lingering, and the states of sitting/standing, it is crucial to comprehend the characteristic patterns of the walking state manifested in repetitive waves. Figures 6 and 7 provide clarity on this issue, illustrating the patterns of the distance values and smoothed acceleration values, respectively.

In the instance of walking, there is continuous movement as each leg alternates, leading to persistent changes in the user's position. Analyzing the acceleration data reveals a fascinating pattern: the acceleration graphs for each leg consistently intersect, moving in opposite directions. This phenomenon, where the graph of one leg moves inversely to the other, can be aptly described as demonstrating reduced similarity between the graphs.

Conversely, during lingering, there is not any distinct or systematic pattern. Rather, the motion exhibits a degree of randomness. Upon closely examining the acceleration values for both legs, it becomes apparent that the movement patterns do not follow exact opposite directions. Instead, the patterns of movement seem to be mirrored, creating an impression of one leg appearing to chase the other.

For sitting/standing activities, distance values provide key insights. When a user sits, the UWB sensor's relative distance increases sharply. Similarly, when the user stands up, there is a marked decline in the distance value. The simultaneous movement of both legs, as they fold during sitting or extend during standing, results in high similarity between the acceleration graphs of the two legs.

Based on the observed patterns, the similarity of the smoothed acceleration graphs generated by each leg serves as a classification tool. Lower similarity between the graphs of both legs suggests a walking state, while higher similarity indicates a lingering state or a sitting/standing state. To quantify the similarity between these graphs, the acceleration values over a specific period underwent decomposition into periodic components through the application of the Discrete Fourier Transform (DFT), as expressed in Equation (6). Cosine similarity was then applied to these components for comparison. Considering the need for real-time application, the Fast Fourier Transform (FFT) was chosen instead of the conventional Discrete Fourier Transform (DFT). The components obtained from the FFT for each graph were subsequently used to calculate the cosine similarity, as outlined in Equation (9). It is important to note that the similarity values range from -1 to 1, where a value closer to -1 indicates low similarity (characteristic of walking), and values near +1 denote high similarity, aligning with other types of movement.

Based on the observed patterns, the similarity of the smoothed acceleration graphs generated by each leg serves as a classification tool. Lower similarity between the graphs of both legs suggests a walking state, while higher similarity indicates a lingering state or a sitting/standing state. To quantify the similarity between these graphs, the acceleration values over a specific period underwent decomposition into periodic components through the application of the Fourier Transform (FT):

$$F(\omega) = \int_{-\infty}^{\infty} f(t)e^{-j\omega t}\,dt \tag{5}$$

In this study, due to the discrete nature of the sensor values, the Discrete Fourier Transform (DFT) was specifically utilized:

$$f_k = \sum_{n=0}^{N-1} x_n e^{-\frac{2\pi i}{N}kn} \quad \text{for } k = 0, \ldots, N-1 \tag{6}$$

Considering the need for real-time application, the Fast Fourier Transform (FFT) was chosen instead of the conventional Discrete Fourier Transform (DFT):

$$F[k] = F_{\text{even}}[k] + e^{-j\frac{2\pi}{N}k} \cdot F_{\text{odd}}[k] \quad \text{for} \quad k = 0, \ldots, \frac{N}{2} - 1 \tag{7}$$

$$F[k + \frac{N}{2}] = F_{\text{even}}[k] - e^{-j\frac{2\pi}{N}k} \cdot F_{\text{odd}}[k] \quad \text{for} \quad k = 0, \ldots, \frac{N}{2} - 1 \tag{8}$$

The components obtained from the FFT for each graph were subsequently used to calculate the cosine similarity, as outlined in Equation (9). It is important to note that the similarity values range from -1 to 1, where a value closer to -1 indicates low similarity (characteristic of walking), and values near +1 denote high similarity, aligning with other types of movement.

$$\text{similarity}(A, B) = \cos(\theta) = \frac{A \cdot B}{\|A\|\|B\|} \tag{9}$$

5.3. Step 3—Method to Distinguish between Lingering and Sitting/Standing

To discern the scenarios of lingering and sitting/standing, the differential gradient of the acceleration values obtained from each leg was utilized. Relying solely on the FFT and cosine similarity methodologies depicted in Section 5.2 posed challenges in distinguishing between these two movement states due to their almost identical graphical representations, often yielding similarity values close to 1. Nevertheless, upon meticulous analysis, a distinct pattern emerged: during transitions into sitting or standing positions, the legs exhibited nearly synchronous movements, resulting in almost identical acceleration profiles. This distinctive pattern sharply differentiates it from the lingering scenario, providing a solid foundation for categorization.

For sitting/standing, any sudden increase or decrease in acceleration corresponds to the act of sitting or standing, respectively. During these actions, the acceleration graphs for both left and right legs show striking similarities, leading to a gradient difference close to zero. In contrast, the lingering scenario reveals noticeable gradient differences between two consecutive points. To enhance the reliability of this method, rather than considering only two points, an average gradient difference across five points was computed and utilized as a threshold for classification. For this analysis, let the coordinates of the left leg acceleration vector be denoted as $(a_1, b_1), \ldots, (a_5, b_5)$ and those of the right leg as $(c_1, d_1), \ldots, (c_5, d_5)$. By formulating Equation (10), all possible gradients across these five points can be computed. The average of these values was termed as the 5-point gradient difference average in this study.

$$\text{Gradient difference} = \frac{1}{10} \sum_{l=2}^{5} \sum_{k=1}^{l-1} \left| \frac{b_l - b_k}{a_l - a_k} - \frac{d_l - d_k}{c_l - c_k} \right| \tag{10}$$

5.4. Enhanced Method for Human Moving Pattern Classification

In Step 2, by leveraging the FFT results, most of the data related to walking, lingering, and sitting/standing motions were effectively classified using cosine similarity. Furthermore, the approach used in Step 3, which compared the gradient difference in the acceleration data between lingering motion and sitting/standing motion, was effective for the majority of the data sets. However, despite the effectiveness of these methods, some specific data points were not precisely classified.

To elucidate the observed phenomena, Figure 9 is presented as an example. Figure 9 graphically depicts the acceleration values for both walking and lingering situations. In Figure 9, the green sections depict instances where the graph aligns with the intended pattern, while the red sections represent deviations from the expected trajectory. In the walking scenario, represented by the green regions, the graphs trend in opposing directions, leading to diminished similarity between the two graphs. Conversely, during lingering situations, the graphs derived from both legs adhere to a complementary pattern, exhibiting increased similarity. However, the red sections reveal anomalies. In walking scenarios, the gradient differences between consecutive points nearly converge to zero, enhancing their similarity. The lingering scenario, highlighted in the red region, diverges from its typical pattern, with the two graphs briefly intersecting, mimicking the walking pattern. This transient intersection arises because, during lingering, the patterns of the two legs momentarily shift, mirroring aspects of the walking pattern.

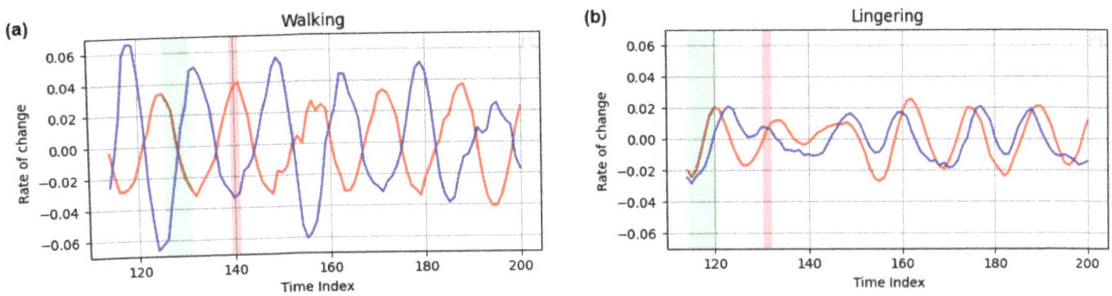

Figure 9. Analysis of the observed anomalie. In the graph, the red line represents the right leg, while the blue line signifies the left leg. (**a**) examples of data acquired during walking, illustrating desired outcomes within the green box and undesired deviations within the red box; (**b**) instances of data captured while lingering, showing preferred directional results in the green box and non-preferred anomalies in the red box.

For this reason, while most scenarios manifest as intended, akin to the green region, there are sporadic occurrences of unintended situations resembling the red region. To address these inconsistencies, a straightforward and effective approach was implemented. While the majority of the data are classified correctly, transient misjudgments arise at specific points due to the inherent characteristics of human movement. In instances where making a decision at a particular point proves challenging, the system is designed to reference the immediately preceding data. It retains classification details from the last five instances, spanning a 1-s duration, and adopts the state most frequently identified during that interval. This method effectively manages such outlier scenarios.

6. Experiments and Results

To evaluate the accuracy of the human moving pattern classification method proposed in this study, experiments were conducted across four distinct human movement scenarios: stopped, walking, lingering, and sitting/standing. Subsequently, after carrying out experiments for each of these scenarios, composite scenarios were designed and tested to demonstrate how the method discerned human actions in real-world situations. This involved setting up experiments that mimicked real-life conditions by combining elements from the initial four scenarios, thereby obtaining results that showcased the method's effectiveness in accurately classifying human movements in complex and variable environments. Beginning with the experimental setup, Decawave's ultra-wideband sensor was utilized. Specifically, as shown in Table 1, the model used wasDWM1001-DEV, boasting an operating frequency of 6.5 GHz and a detection frequency of 5 Hz, with sensor accuracy of ±10 cm [47].The equipment was sourced from Decawave, a part of Qorvo, from Dublin, Ireland. Two UWB sensors were mounted on the experimental robot at a distance of 60 cm apart. For human subjects, two sensors were affixed slightly above the knees on both legs, allowing for the acquisition of a total of four distance values from the robot to the person. To ensure the stability of the sensors' positions on the legs during the experiments, they were securely fixed using velcro straps. The experimental setup can be seen in Figure 10.

For this experiment, the authors of this paper conducted the tests personally. To validate the experimental methodology, the four situations were initially modeled as depicted in Figure 11. The participant was then instructed to act according to these models.

By monitoring the participant's actions, it was ensured that the data collected closely matched the modeled behaviors. During the experiment, the distance from the ground to the sensors on the participant's legs was set at 0.6 m, and the distance from the sensors located on the participant's legs to the waist was 0.4 m. The following details the four experimental scenarios.

Table 1. Parameters and specifications of the UWB sensor and human movement.

Parameter	Value
Device	DW1001-DEV (UWB sensor)
Operating Frequency	6.5 GHz
Detection Frequency	5 Hz
Detection Error	±0.1 m
Distance between Two Robot Sensors	0.6 m
Robot Sensor-to-Ground Distance	0.5 m
Walking Speed	~1 m/s
Lingering Speed	~0.5 m/s
Sitting/Standing Speed	~0.5 m/s

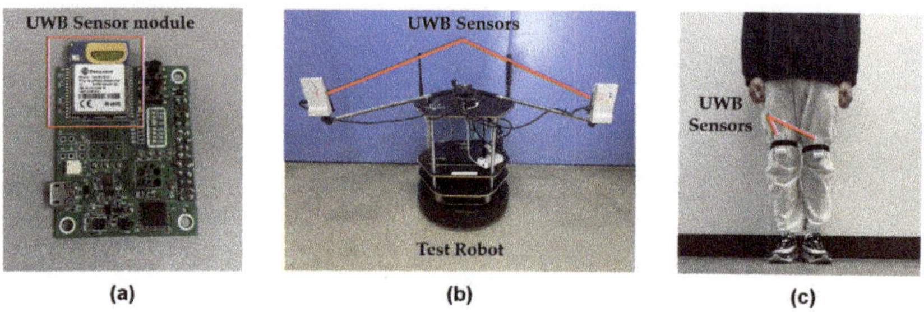

Figure 10. Experimental setup with test robot and participant outfitted with UWB sensors: (**a**) the ultra-wideband (UWB) sensor module used for the experiment; (**b**) overall view of the autonomous robot equipped with UWB sensors; (**c**) participant's legs fitted with UWB sensors in a real-world setting.

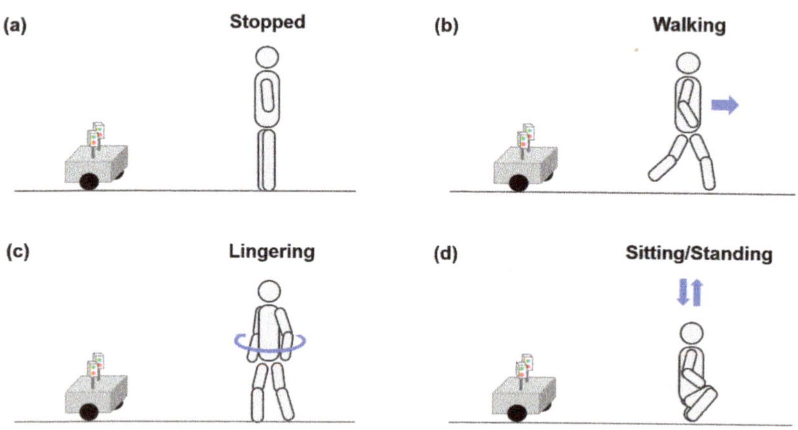

Figure 11. Schematic representations of participant scenarios for different states in the experiment: (**a**) the participant in a stationary state; (**b**) the participant walking towards the robot; (**c**) the participant in a lingering state; (**d**) the participant transitioning between sitting and standing positions.

- Stopped Scenario

In this scenario, UWB sensors were attached to both legs of the user, maintaining a stationary position. Instead of attaching the UWB sensors to a static object, the decision was made to attach them to the body and minimize movement to capture information about human immobility. This approach was adopted to obtain data relevant to the stopped state.

- Walking Scenario

As elaborated in the Methods section under human walking sequence modeling, walking was executed in a manner whereby the cross movement of both legs was distinctly visible. The experiment was conducted with an average walking speed of 0.5–1 m/s. It was assumed that the walker would move in the direction facing the sensor for this experiment.

- Lingering Scenario

This scenario was designed with the assumption that one leg would be the primary mover, while the other would remain largely stationary. The primary leg briefly steps forward and returns to its original position. The other leg, although displaying minor directional shifts or movements in response to the motion of the primary leg, showed no other significant movement during the experiment.

- Sitting and Standing Scenario

After modeling the typical motions of sitting and standing, a scenario was conceived whereby both legs simultaneously descended as the user sat and rose as the user stood in place. This approach was designed to clearly delineate the actions of sitting down and standing up.

Based on the provided scenarios, experiments were conducted as depicted in Figure 12. Using these experiments, distance data were acquired from the UWB sensors on the robot to the UWB sensors on both legs of the participant in each respective situation. During this process, the modeled motions for each scenario were repeated to consecutively collect 100 data points for each, yielding a total of 400 data points. Subsequently, these distance data were utilized to perform classification.

For a precise analysis, the distance data were stored in the form of a CSV (Comma-Separated Values) file. The data were imported into Python, followed by the execution and visualization of Steps 1, 2, and 3. Specifically, for Step 1, which was the classification of the stopped state, classification was done simply through designating speed and acceleration thresholds. Due to this straightforward approach, visualization was not conducted for this step, and only an accuracy evaluation was performed.

Following Step 2, the cosine similarity values were obtained as results. These results were then represented over time steps using Python. Additionally, to observe the distribution of results for each movement state, visualizations of the histogram and kernel density estimation were carried out for the cosine similarity outcomes as depicted in Figure 13. Consequently, in the walking scenario, since the acceleration values of both legs proceeded in opposite directions, the cosine similarity values were observed to be predominantly close to -1. For the lingering and sitting/standing situations, since both legs moved similarly, the cosine similarity values largely appeared to be close to 1.

In Step 3, the outcome was derived using the slope differences of the acceleration values from the previous five points. Similarly, histograms and kernel density estimations were conducted to understand the distribution of outcomes for each movement state, as depicted in Figure 14. For the lingering state, as both legs moved somewhat independently, the histogram clearly showed a significant deviation in the slope differences of their acceleration values from 0. In the sitting/standing state, as the experiment was based on a scenario wherein both legs moved down and up simultaneously, the histogram revealed that the slope difference of the acceleration values between the legs was closely aligned to 0.

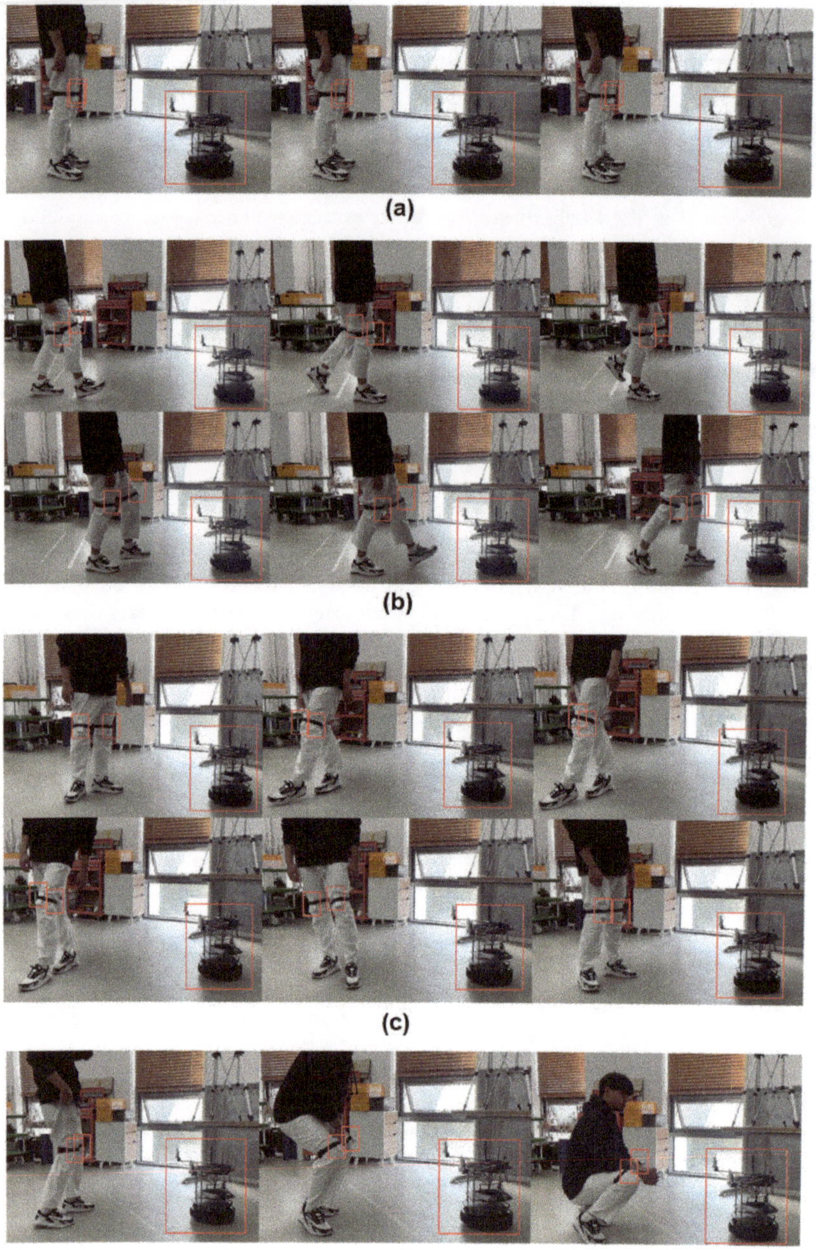

(a)

(b)

(c)

(d)

Figure 12. Actual experimental setup. In the image, the large red box indicates the location of the robot, while the small red box denotes the position of the UWB sensor attached to the body. (**a**) actual experimental process of a stopped motion scenario; (**b**) actual experimental process of a walking motion scenario; (**c**) actual experimental process of a lingering motion scenario; (**d**) actual experimental process of a sitting/standing motion scenario.

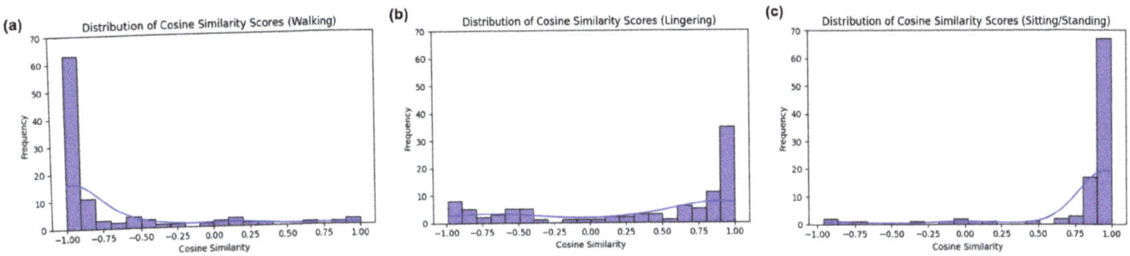

Figure 13. Results utilizing FFT and cosine similarity from Step 2: (**a**) histogram and kernel density estimation of cosine similarity scores derived from the walking scenario dataset; (**b**) histogram and kernel density estimation of cosine similarity scores derived from the lingering scenario dataset; (**c**) histogram and kernel density estimation of cosine similarity scores derived from the sitting/standing scenario dataset.

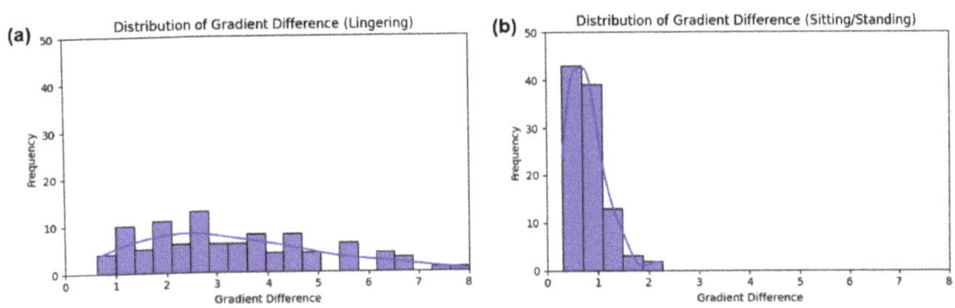

Figure 14. Gradient difference analysis from Step 3: (**a**) histogram and kernel density estimation of gradient differences for the lingering scenario; (**b**) histogram and kernel density estimation of gradient differences for the sitting/standing scenario.

Following the thresholds mentioned in the Methods section, the data were classified. The classification accuracy results for each step can be observed in Table 2. For the basic model, Step 1 showed an impeccable 100% accuracy across all movement states: stopped, walking, lingering, and sitting/standing. Subsequently, in Step 2, the walking state exhibited accuracy of 84%, the lingering state had 78%, and the sitting/standing state demonstrated high accuracy of 96%. In Step 3, where the classification was conducted for the lingering and sitting/standing states, the accuracy rates were 87% and 91%, respectively. While the basic model showcased high accuracy, there were instances in which it failed to classify certain values correctly. To address these limitations, an advanced model for human movement classification, proposed in this paper, was implemented. Compared to the basic model, the advanced model in Step 1 maintained 100% accuracy for movement states. In Step 2, the accuracy for the walking state improved from 84% to 97%, the lingering state from 78% to 92%, and the sitting/standing state reached a perfect score of 100%. Moreover, in Step 3, the accuracy for the lingering state surged from 87% to 95%, and, for the sitting/standing state, it increased slightly from 91% to 93%. This resulted in average overall accuracy of approximately 95%.

Additionally, to illustrate the outcomes in real-world settings when individuals engage in complex movements, further experiments were conducted. These experiments were designed considering a human-following robot environment, wherein a scenario was simulated with the user loading items onto the human-following robot and moving. The scenario unfolded as follows: the user approached the robot by walking, came to a stop in front of the robot, and then sat down to retrieve items from the robot; then, they stood up again and finally moved away from the robot. This complex scenario encompassed walking, stopping, and transitions between sitting and standing. The distance measurements obtained from this experiment, along with the calculated speed and acceleration values, are presented in Figure 15.

Table 2. Classification accuracy for different human moving states.

Human State	Step 1		Step 2		Step 3	
Method	**Basic**	**Advanced**	**Basic**	**Advanced**	**Basic**	**Advanced**
Stopped	100	100	-	-	-	-
Walking	100	100	84	97	-	-
Lingering	100	100	78	92	87	95
Sitting/Standing	100	100	96	100	91	93

Note: A dash (-) indicates that classification did not occur for the movement at the respective stage.

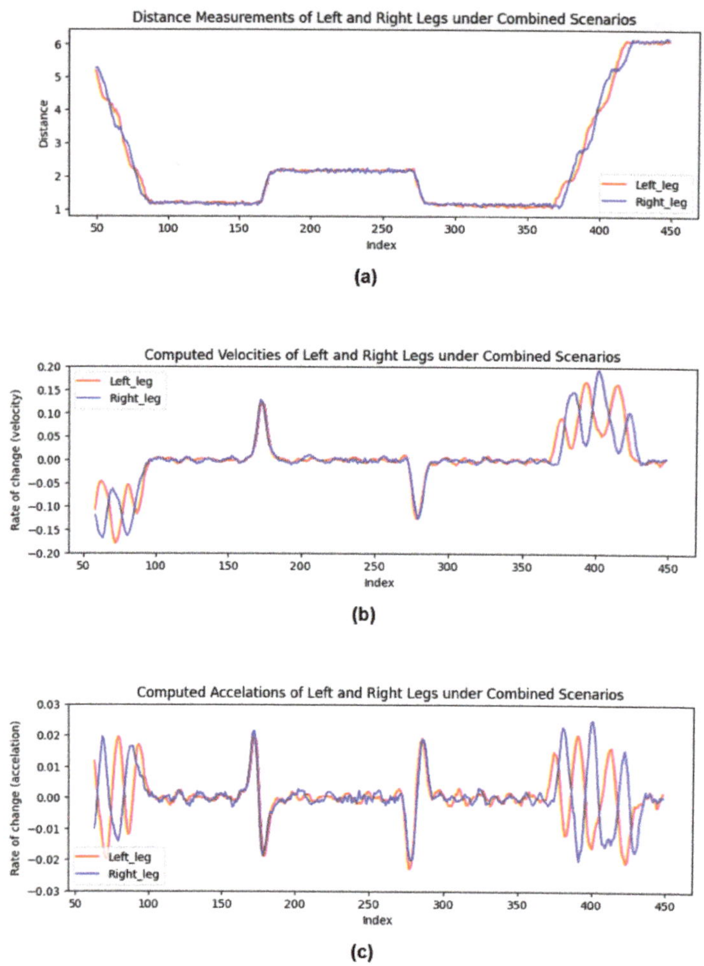

Figure 15. Measured outcomes under a composite scenario, considering a real-world human-following robot context. The scenario simulated a user approaching the robot, stopping, sitting to pick up an item, standing, and then moving away from the robot. (**a**) Variation in measured distances; (**b**) changes in computed velocities after smoothing with a moving average; (**c**) changes in computed accelerations after smoothing with a moving average.

As illustrated in the results visualized in Figure 15, the data exhibited distinct movement states throughout the experiment. From the 50th to the 90th index, the subject is in a walking state. This is followed by a stopped state from the 90th to the 170th index. A transition between sitting and standing is observed from the 170th to the 180th index. The subject returns to a stopped state from the 180th to the 270th index, followed by another transition between sitting and standing from the 270th to the 280th index. The subject remains in a stopped state from the 280th to the 370th index, transitions back to a walking state from the 370th to the 420th index, and ultimately exhibits a stopped state again from the 420th to the 450th index. These segments effectively demonstrate the capability of the proposed method to classify complex human movements within a dynamic human-following robot environment.

For the speed and acceleration values, a moving average smoothing technique was applied to correct the values, resulting in a slight shift in the indices compared to the initial distance measurements. Despite this shift, the application of the previously mentioned three phases allowed for the clean classification of movement states. Due to the moving average, there was a mismatch between the indices of the actual measured distances and the calculated speed/acceleration values. Therefore, the fine adjustment of the indices was performed to account for this delay, and the experimental results were processed through the three-step methodology.

The final classification of movement states achieved accuracy of 95% for the stopped state, approximately 83% for the walking state, and 90% for transitions between sitting and standing. Overall, the method demonstrated accuracy of 92%, closely mirroring the individual measurement accuracy of 95%. This consistency underscores the model's effectiveness in real-world scenarios, confirming its robust performance across different states of movement.

7. Conclusions

In this study, the focus was on enhancing human–robot interaction by allowing a robot equipped with UWB sensors to detect human movements in real time. The study presented an enhanced approach extending beyond the traditional method that utilized a pair of UWB sensors on a robot and a single UWB sensor on a person to derive two distance measurements and ascertain the person's location through bilateration. This advancement involves affixing UWB sensors to each of the individual's legs, thereby not only pinpointing the user's location but also discerning their movement states, including sitting, walking, lingering, and transitioning between sitting and standing. These movement states, crucial in a workspace setting, were defined to aid the robot in recognizing and adapting to the human's activities. By recognizing these behaviors, the robot is better equipped to support and interact with workers, thereby fostering a more collaborative environment.

In this study, distinct patterns for each movement state were elucidated using distance data between UWB sensors on robots and humans, based on distance measurements, velocity, and smoothed acceleration values. A three-stage classification method was proposed. In Step 1, velocity and acceleration thresholds were utilized to differentiate the stopped state from others. Step 2 employed the FFT and cosine similarity to distinguish walking motions from lingering and sitting/standing motions. In Step 3, the five-point gradient difference method introduced in the paper effectively differentiated between lingering motion and sitting/standing motion. The study's three-step classification method demonstrated high efficacy in identifying human movement states, with the initial step perfectly distinguishing stationary states. Subsequent steps showed substantial accuracy, with improvements observed when an enhanced method incorporating brief historical data was applied. This approach yielded near-perfect accuracy rates across all movement states, achieving overall average accuracy of approximately 95%.

The final constructed model demonstrates that, with minimal computation in a CPU environment, it can effectively recognize and classify four types of movements with approximate accuracy of 95%. Additionally, in experiments simulating composite motion scenarios that considered real-world environments, the model achieved overall accuracy of 92%. This experimental outcome evidences the considerable success of the classification algorithm, offering a novel approach to detecting human movements in the field of robotics to enhance human–robot interaction. The methodology proposed in this paper addresses a significant challenge in follower robots utilizing UWB sensors. It not only tracks the location of a person but also understands and responds to their current behaviors, thereby improving both the safety and convenience of follower robots in work environments. In conclusion, the experimental methodologies and classification models introduced in this study are expected to make a significant impact on the field of robotics. By enabling robots to accurately interpret human intentions and behaviors, the research extends beyond follower robots with UWB sensors to a multitude of sectors, such as industrial safety, medical assistance, and personalized service robotics. This paves the way for enhanced service coordination and support, marking the advent of a new era of synergy between humans and robots across various operational environments.

Author Contributions: Conceptualization, M.N.; methodology, M.N.; software, M.N.; validation, M.N.; formal analysis, S.C.L.; data curation, M.N.; writing—original draft preparation, M.N.; writing—review and editing, H.A.; visualization, M.N.; project administration, H.A. and S.C.L. All authors have read and agreed to the published version of the manuscript.

Funding: Technology Development Program of the Ministry of SMEs and Startups: RS-2022-00141837; Daegu Gyeongbuk Institute of Science and Technology (DGIST) Research and Development Program of the Ministry of Science: 23-DPIC-13.

Institutional Review Board Statement: The study was approved by the Institutional Review Board of Daegu Gyeongbuk Institute of Science and Technology (DGISTIRB-2024-008-01 and 03/25/2024).

Informed Consent Statement: Informed consent was obtained from all subjects involved in the study.

Data Availability Statement: The data supporting the results reported in this study were collected through experiments conducted by the authors themselves. These data can be made available upon request for the purposes of ensuring the transparency and reproducibility of the research. The authors are prepared to provide the relevant data within a reasonable scope if requested. Currently, there are no specific privacy or ethical restrictions on these data, allowing interested researchers to directly contact the authors for access to them.

Conflicts of Interest: The authors declare no conflicts of interest.

References

1. Bayram, B.; İnce, G. Advances in Robotics in the Era of Industry 4.0. In *Industry 4.0: Managing the Digital Transformation*; Springer International Publishing: Cham, Switzerland, 2018; pp. 187–200.
2. Demir, K.A.; Döven, G.; Sezen, B. Industry 5.0 and Human-Robot Co-working. *Procedia Comput. Sci.* **2019**, *158*, 688–695. [CrossRef]
3. Vysocky, A.; Novak, P. Human-robot collaboration in industry. *Sci. J.* **2016**, *9*, 903–906. [CrossRef]
4. Heyer, C. Human-robot interaction and future industrial robotics applications. In Proceedings of the 2010 IEEE/RSJ International Conference on Intelligent Robots and Systems, Taipei, Taiwan, 18–22 October 2010; pp. 4749–4754.
5. Rawassizadeh, R.; Sen, T.; Kim, S.J.; Meurisch, C.; Keshavarz, H.; Mühlhäuser, M.; Pazzani, M. Manifestation of Virtual Assistants and Robots into Daily Life: Vision and Challenges. *CCF Trans. Pervasive Comput. Interact.* **2019**, *1*, 163–174. [CrossRef]
6. Haddadin, S.; Albu-Schaffer, A.; De Luca, A.; Hirzinger, G. Collision Detection and Reaction: A Contribution to Safe Physical Human-Robot Interaction. In Proceedings of the 2008 IEEE/RSJ International Conference on Intelligent Robots and Systems, Nice, France, 22–26 September 2008; pp. 3356–3363.
7. Maurice, P.; Malaisé, A.; Amiot, C.; Paris, N.; Richard, G.-J.; Rochel, O.; Ivaldi, S. Human movement and ergonomics: An industry-oriented dataset for collaborative robotics. *Int. J. Robot. Res.* **2019**, *38*, 1529–1537. [CrossRef]
8. Geravand, M.; Flacco, F.; De Luca, A. Human-robot physical interaction and collaboration using an industrial robot with a closed control architecture. In Proceedings of the 2013 IEEE International Conference on Robotics and Automation, Karlsruhe, Germany, 6–10 May 2013; pp. 4000–4007.
9. Hägele, M.; Schaaf, W.; Helms, E. Robot assistants at manual workplaces: Effective co-operation and safety aspects. In Proceedings of the 33rd ISR (International Symposium on Robotics), Stockholm, Sweden, 7–11 October 2002; p. 97.
10. Fryman, J.; Matthias, B. Safety of Industrial Robots: From Conventional to Collaborative Applications. In Proceedings of the ROBOTIK 2012: 7th German Conference on Robotics, Munich, Germany, 21–22 May 2012; pp. 1–5.

11. Galin, R.R.; Meshcheryakov, R.V. Human-Robot Interaction Efficiency and Human-Robot Collaboration. In *Robotics: Industry 4.0 Issues & New Intelligent Control Paradigms*; Kravets, A.G., Ed.; Springer International Publishing: Cham, Switzerland, 2020; pp. 55–63.
12. Thrun, S. Toward a Framework for Human-Robot Interaction. *Hum.-Comput. Interact.* **2004**, *19*, 9–24. [CrossRef]
13. Poppe, R. Vision-based human motion analysis: An overview. *Comput. Vis. Image Underst.* **2007**, *108*, 4–18. [CrossRef]
14. Moeslund, T.B.; Hilton, A.; Krüger, V. A survey of advances in vision-based human motion capture and analysis. *Comput. Vis. Image Underst.* **2006**, *104*, 90–126. [CrossRef]
15. Chang, C.-C.; Tsai, W.-H. Vision-based tracking and interpretation of human leg movement for virtual reality applications. *IEEE Trans. Circuits Syst. Video Technol.* **2001**, *11*, 9–24. [CrossRef]
16. Sung, Y.; Chung, W. Human tracking of a mobile robot with an onboard LRF (Laser Range Finder) using human walking motion analysis. In Proceedings of the 2011 8th International Conference on Ubiquitous Robots and Ambient Intelligence (URAI), Incheon, Republic of Korea, 23–26 November 2011; pp. 366–370.
17. Zheng, C.; Wu, W.; Chen, C.; Yang, T.; Zhu, S.; Shen, J.; Kehtarnavaz, N.; Shah, M. Deep Learning-Based Human Pose Estimation: A Survey. *ACM Comput. Surv.* **2023**, *56*, 11. [CrossRef]
18. Luo, Y.; Ren, J.; Wang, Z.; Sun, W.; Pan, J.; Liu, J.; Pang, J.; Lin, L. LSTM Pose Machines. In Proceedings of the IEEE Conference on Computer Vision and Pattern Recognition (CVPR), Salt Lake City, UT, USA, 18–23 June 2018; pp. 5207–5215.
19. Wei, S.-E.; Ramakrishna, V.; Kanade, T.; Sheikh, Y. Convolutional Pose Machines. In Proceedings of the IEEE Conference on Computer Vision and Pattern Recognition (CVPR), Las Vegas, NV, USA, 27–30 June 2016; pp. 4724–4732.
20. Sun, M.; Savarese, S. Articulated Part-Based Model for Joint Object Detection and Pose Estimation. In Proceedings of the 2011 International Conference on Computer Vision, Barcelona, Spain, 6–13 November 2011; pp. 723–730.
21. Tian, Y.; Zitnick, C.L.; Narasimhan, S.G. Exploring the Spatial Hierarchy of Mixture Models for Human Pose Estimation. In Proceedings of the European Conference on Computer Vision (ECCV), Florence, Italy, 7–13 October 2012; Springer: Berlin/Heidelberg, Germany, 2012; pp. 256–269.
22. Chen, Y.; Tian, Y.; He, M. Monocular human pose estimation: A survey of deep learning-based methods. *Comput. Vis. Image Underst.* **2020**, *192*, 1–20. [CrossRef]
23. Yan, Q.; Xu, W.; Huang, J.; Cao, S. Laser and force sensors based human motion intent estimation algorithm for walking-aid robot. In Proceedings of the 2015 IEEE International Conference on Cyber Technology in Automation, Control, and Intelligent Systems (CYBER), Shenyang, China, 8–12 June 2015; pp. 1858–1863.
24. Dimitrievski, M.; Veelaert, P.; Philips, W. Behavioral Pedestrian Tracking Using a Camera and LiDAR Sensors on a Moving Vehicle. *Sensors* **2019**, *19*, 391. [CrossRef] [PubMed]
25. Roche, J.; De-Silva, V.; Hook, J.; Moencks, M.; Kondoz, A. A Multimodal Data Processing System for LiDAR-Based Human Activity Recognition. *IEEE Trans. Cybern.* **2022**, *52*, 10027–10040. [CrossRef] [PubMed]
26. Koide, K.; Miura, J.; Menegatti, E. A portable three-dimensional LIDAR-based system for long-term and wide-area people behavior measurement. *Int. J. Adv. Robot. Syst.* **2019**, *16*, 1729881419841532. [CrossRef]
27. Bakhtiarnia, A.; Zhang, Q.; Iosifidis, A. Single-layer vision transformers for more accurate early exits with less overhead. *Neural Netw.* **2022**, *153*, 461–473. [CrossRef]
28. Goel, A.; Tung, C.; Lu, Y.-H.; Thiruvathukal, G.K. A Survey of Methods for Low-Power Deep Learning and Computer Vision. In Proceedings of the IEEE 6th World Forum on Internet of Things (WF-IoT), New Orleans, LA, USA, 2–16 June 2020; pp. 1–6.
29. Rathnayake, T.; Khodadadian Gostar, A.; Hoseinnezhad, R.; Tennakoon, R.; Bab-Hadiashar, A. On-Line Visual Tracking with Occlusion Handling. *Sensors* **2020**, *20*, 929. [CrossRef] [PubMed]
30. Zhu, L.; Menon, M.; Santillo, M.; Linkowski, G. Occlusion Handling for Industrial Robots. In Proceedings of the 2020 IEEE/RSJ International Conference on Intelligent Robots and Systems (IROS), Las Vegas, NV, USA, 25–29 October 2020; pp. 10663–10668.
31. Feng, T.; Yu, Y.; Wu, L.; Bai, Y.; Xiao, Z.; Lu, Z. A Human-Tracking Robot Using Ultra Wideband Technology. *IEEE Access* **2018**, *6*, 42541–42550. [CrossRef]
32. Dang, C.V.; Ahn, H.; Kim, J.-W.; Lee, S.C. Collision-Free Navigation in Human-Following Task Using a Cognitive Robotic System on Differential Drive Vehicles. *IEEE Trans. Cogn. Dev. Syst.* **2023**, *15*, 78–87. [CrossRef]
33. Ahn, H.; Dang, C.V.; Lee, S.C. Complex-Valued Function Modeling of Bilateration and its Applications. *IEEE Access* **2023**, *11*, 92913–92925. [CrossRef]
34. Yun, J.; Lee, S.-S. Human Movement Detection and Identification Using Pyroelectric Infrared Sensors. *Sensors* **2014**, *14*, 8057–8081. [CrossRef] [PubMed]
35. Lugade, V.; Fortune, E.; Morrow, M.; Kaufman, K. Validity of Using Tri-Axial Accelerometers to Measure Human Movement—Part I: Posture and Movement Detection. *Med. Eng. Phys.* **2014**, *36*, 169–176. [CrossRef] [PubMed]
36. Li, C.; Lin, M.; Yang, L.T.; Ding, C. Integrating the Enriched Feature with Machine Learning Algorithms for Human Movement and Fall Detection. *J. Supercomput.* **2014**, *67*, 854–865. [CrossRef]
37. Chander, H.; Burch, R.F.; Talegaonkar, P.; Saucier, D.; Luczak, T.; Ball, J.E.; Turner, A.; Kodithuwakku Arachchige, S.N.K.; Carroll, W.; Smith, B.K.; et al. Wearable Stretch Sensors for Human Movement Monitoring and Fall Detection in Ergonomics. *Int. J. Environ. Res. Public Health* **2020**, *17*, 3554. [CrossRef] [PubMed]

38. Darko, F.; Denis, S.; Mario, Z. Human Movement Detection Based on Acceleration Measurements and k-NN Classification. In Proceedings of the EUROCON 2007—The International Conference on "Computer as a Tool", Warsaw, Poland, 9–12 September 2007; pp. 589–594.
39. Del Rosario, M.B.; Redmond, S.J.; Lovell, N.H. Tracking the Evolution of Smartphone Sensing for Monitoring Human Movement. *Sensors* **2015**, *15*, 18901–18933. [CrossRef] [PubMed]
40. De, P.; Chatterjee, A.; Rakshit, A. Regularized K-SVD-Based Dictionary Learning Approaches for PIR Sensor-Based Detection of Human Movement Direction. *IEEE Sens. J.* **2021**, *21*, 6459–6467. [CrossRef]
41. Wang, M.; Chen, Z.; Zhou, Z.; Fu, J.; Qiu, H. Analysis of the Applicability of Dilution of Precision in the Base Station Configuration Optimization of Ultrawideband Indoor TDOA Positioning System. *IEEE Access* **2020**, *8*, 225076–225087. [CrossRef]
42. Malik, W.Q.; Stevens, C.J.; Edwards, D.J. Multipath Effects in Ultrawideband Rake Reception. *IEEE Trans. Antennas Propag.* **2008**, *56*, 507–514. [CrossRef]
43. Altshiller-Court, N. Stewart's Theorem. In *College Geometry: A Second Course in Plane Geometry for Colleges and Normal Schools*, 2nd ed.; Barnes and Noble: New York, NY, USA, 1952; pp. 152–153.
44. Simonyan, K.; Zisserman, A. Very Deep Convolutional Networks for Large-Scale Image Recognition. *arXiv* **2015**, arXiv:1409.1556.
45. He, K.; Zhang, X.; Ren, S.; Sun, J. Deep Residual Learning for Image Recognition. *arXiv* **2015**, arXiv:1512.03385.
46. Szegedy, C.; Liu, W.; Jia, Y.; Sermanet, P.; Reed, S.; Anguelov, D.; Erhan, D.; Vanhoucke, V.; Rabinovich, A. Going Deeper with Convolutions. *arXiv* **2014**, arXiv:1409.4842.
47. Decawave. DWM1001C Data Sheet. Available online: https://www.qorvo.com/products/d/da007950 (accessed on 23 October 2023).

electronics

MDPI

Article

A Weakly Supervised Crowd Counting Method via Combining CNN and Transformer

Yuhang Cai and De Zhang *

School of Electrical and Information Engineering, Beijing University of Civil Engineering and Architecture, Beijing 100044, China; 201806050103@stu.bucea.edu.cn
* Correspondence: zhangde@bucea.edu.cn

Abstract: During the past five years, there has been an increasing trend of weakly supervised crowd counting methods being developed since such methods just rely on count-level annotations and avoid a laborious labeling process. But, the existing weakly supervised methods usually fail to achieve comparable counting performance to the fully supervised methods. To improve the accuracy of crowd counting tasks, we propose to combine the convolutional neural network (CNN) and Transformer frameworks. Since CNN focuses on capturing local detail information and Transformer can effectively extract global context information, we believe that the combination of CNN and Transformer could learn more efficient feature representations for crowd images. Our proposed framework is named CrowdCCT (Crowd Counting via CNN and Transformer), and it is composed of a CNN feature extraction part, a Transformer feature extraction part, and a counting regression part. In the CNN part, we utilize DenseNet121 to learn rich semantic features with its inherent dense connection structure. In the Transformer part, we introduce two attention modules, Multi-Scale Dilated Attention (MSDA) and Location-Enhanced Attention (LEA), working together to extract more expressive features. The output features are then fed into the regression part to generate the predicted counting results. Experiments on four crowd counting benchmark datasets demonstrate that our proposed CrowdCCT can achieve superior performance. Also, the experimental results validate the feasibility and effectiveness of combining CNN and Transformer for weakly supervised counting tasks. Our work could be expected to promote further combination research on CNN and Transformer.

Keywords: crowd counting; weakly supervised; transformer; CNN

1. Introduction

Crowd counting is an important task in the analysis of crowd scenes, aiming to automatically estimate the number of people in an image or video frame [1]. With the growth in population and the growing trend of urbanization, there are frequent occurrences of crowds gathering in public places. So, crowd counting currently plays an essential role in many scenarios, such as public safety, traffic management, urban planning, and abnormal situation warning [2,3].

In the last decade, deep-learning-based approaches have been developed rapidly and proven to be effective for many computer vision tasks, including crowd counting. Typical crowd counting methods usually take advantage of the powerful feature extraction capability of convolutional neural networks (CNNs) and have achieved excellent performance in recent years [1,4–7]. Researchers have also succeeded in designing complex networks to handle various challenges in crowd counting, such as large-scale variation, perspective distortion, and occlusions. For example, Zhang et al. [1] proposed a multi-column convolutional neural network (MCNN) to capture the scale variation in individuals in a crowd. He et al. [7] designed a joint attention network including a multi-order scale attention module and a multi-pooling relational channel attention module, which can be used to obtain more scale information and reduce the impact of background occlusion, respectively. However, these methods belong to the fully supervised category, and they obtain the total number of people in a crowd image by regressing a density map. Thus, they require point-level annotations as prior information. Point-level annotation requires marking the human head position of each individual in the crowd, which is laborious and time-consuming. Especially in congested scenes, as shown in Figure 1, completing the annotation for a single image requires over 10,000 points of the human head position, which demands significant labeling effort.

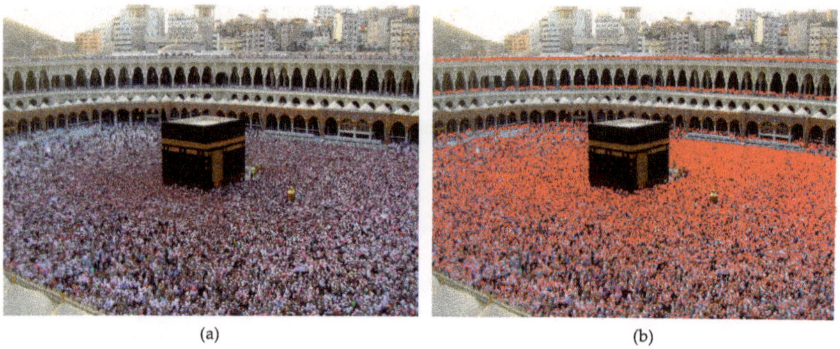

Figure 1. Illustration of the laborious point annotations for a dense crowd image. (**a**) An example image from UCF-QNRF dataset. (**b**) The corresponding annotation results with red points marked on each head.

Different from fully supervised methods, weakly supervised counting methods only require count-level annotation information, which is the total number of humans in a crowd scene and can be acquired with much less annotation effort. Therefore, methods based on weakly supervised learning have gained increasing attention in recent years. CNN and Transformer are two commonly used frameworks in the existing weakly supervised methods. Lei et al. [8] proposed to use a small number of point-level annotations and a large number of count-level annotations during the CNN training process. They pointed out that the total number of persons can be obtained economically in real crowd scenes. Yang et al. [9] proposed a soft-label sorting network to help CNN backbone enhance its counting ability. However, CNN-based weakly supervised methods cannot achieve satisfactory performance due to the limited receptive fields of convolutional kernels, which weaken their ability to capture the global context information in the crowd images.

To overcome this limitation, Transformer-based weakly supervised methods have been proposed. The Transformer architecture can capture long-range dependencies effectively due to its global receptive fields [10]. The Transformer architecture can overcome the shortcomings of CNN. Transformer-based methods have achieved superior counting performance. Specifically, Transformer-based methods split input images into patches and then arrange these patches into sequences of linear embeddings. These embeddings are then taken as the inputs of the Transformer encoder. Liang et al. [11] applied the Vision Transformer (ViT) [12] as the backbone network to extract the crowd features and regressed the predicted counts directly. However, ViT is limited in extracting multi-scale features. Considering the scale variation problem in crowd counting, hierarchical Transformer architectures have been introduced in this task recently [13–15]. Tian et al. [16] proposed the CCTrans model based on pyramid Transformer Twins [13]. Li et al. [17] proposed the CCST model based on Swin Transformer [15] and customized an adaptive fusion regression head. All these methods are striving to handle scale variation in human heads well.

For weakly supervised crowd counting methods, severe scale variation is still a challenge regarding improving the counting accuracy. An efficient feature representation can play a critical role in improving crowd counting performance. Generally, a CNN can be derived to be more concentrated on extracting the local semantic features and Transformer could capture a global feature representation to build long-range dependency relationships. Hence, we propose the CrowdCCT model by combining the CNN and Transformer architectures to extract effective crowd features, which takes advantage of CNN and Transformer to improve the counting accuracy. Specifically, we utilize DenseNet, a powerful CNN model, to extract abundant local feature information by utilizing its special dense connection. Then, the output feature maps are transferred into the Transformer framework. To solve the scale variation problem, a Multi-Scale Dilated Attention (MSDA) module is introduced, in which different dilation rates are arranged for different heads to learn an effective multi-scale feature representation. Moreover, a Location-Enhanced Attention (LEA) module is designed to help locate the positions of persons and distinguish foreground objects from complex background aspects more accurately.

To summarize, the main contributions of this paper are as follows:

(1) For the weakly supervised crowd counting problem, we propose CrowdCCT, an effective joint framework that combines CNN and Transformer. This joint learning framework can take advantage of both CNN and Transformer to achieve highly efficient feature representations.
(2) In the Transformer part, we develop two valuable attention modules called MSDA and LEA. MSDA is designed to overcome the challenge presented by the scale variations in human heads by mining the semantic correlations among different crowd regions. LEA can help to reduce background noise via enhancing the location information of individuals.
(3) Extensive experiments on multiple benchmark datasets show that the proposed CrowdCCT outperforms pure CNN-based and pure Transformer-based weakly supervised methods. In addition, our method is very competitive compared with some fully supervised methods.

The rest of this paper is organized as follows. Section 2 introduces the related works on crowd counting. Section 3 presents the details of the proposed CrowdCCT. In Section 4, we describe the experimental settings and compare our results with other state-of-the-art methods. Finally, Section 5 concludes this work.

2. Related Works

In this section, we briefly review some mainstream related works on crowd counting and present them, mainly with CNN-based and Transformer-based classifications.

2.1. CNN-Based Crowd Counting

Convolutional neural networks (CNNs) have been successfully applied in the field of computer vision [18,19]. With the rapid development of CNNs, density-map-based counting methods generated by deep learning have become a research hotspot for the task of crowd counting.

Previously, Fu et al. [20] pioneered the application of CNNs in crowd counting by introducing a model that utilizes a cascade of two CNN classifiers. Thereby, the accuracy and speed of density estimations have been significantly enhanced. Zhang et al. [1] proposed the multi-column CNN (MCNN) structure that utilizes filters with various receptive field sizes to extract features. Thus, the CNN model can adapt scale variation caused by changes in viewing perspective. Moreover, MCNN promoted the development of the multi-scale strategy applied in crowd counting. Afterwards, Cheng et al. [21] formulated a multi-column mutual learning (MCML) method to further improve the learning ability of the multi-scale CNN model. Liu et al. [22] proposed a novel scale-aware and global contextual network (SGCNet) that utilizes multi-scale attention mechanisms to selectively enhance features at different scales. Wang et al. [23] introduced a multi-scale features fused network with a multi-level supervised path to generate high-quality density maps.

Researchers also investigated the applications of the pyramid architecture. Sindagi et al. [24] explored a contextual pyramid CNN (CP-CNN) and employed this model to encode the local and global context into the density estimation process. Liang et al. [25] established residual pyramid dilated convolution modules with different dilated rates. In addition, exploiting other useful information could help to improve the model performance. Shi et al. [26] introduced a perspective-aware CNN (PACNN) to predict perspective maps and incorporate them as perspective-aware weighting layers into the network model. Liu et al. [27] developed a novel LibraNet in which they formulate crowd counting as a sequential decision problem and implement it as scale weighing. Song et al. [28] proposed a purely point-based framework, aiming to handle the crowd counting and individual localization tasks simultaneously.

Due to laborious annotation costs regarding crowd counting, weakly supervised counting methods have been developed. Yang et al. [9] introduced a soft-label sorting strategy working in conjunction with the counting CNN model. Lei et al. [8] proposed a novel multiple auxiliary task training (MATT) approach in which both the primary branch and the auxiliary branch could generate density maps to encode more accurate position information. Although these approaches mitigate the dependence on costly point-level annotations to some extent, CNN-based weakly supervised techniques still face inherent challenges, especially the limitation of global context modeling capability. Therefore, these methods cannot achieve satisfactory performance.

2.2. Transformer-Based Crowd Counting

Modeling context information is critical for crowd counting and density estimation. The Transformer framework has the advantage of capturing long-range dependencies. For fully supervised crowd counting, Bai et al. [29] introduced CounTr, a novel end-to-end Transformer approach for crowd counting and density estimation. Liu et al. [30] treated crowd counting as a decomposable point querying process and built a point query Transformer model.

With the development of weakly supervised counting methods, Liang et al. [11] introduced ViT into the task of crowd counting and first proposed a Transformer-based weakly supervised crowd counting method, TransCrowd. It demonstrated that a Transformer-based model could effectively extract the semantic crowd information more effectively than a CNN-based model. Then, Tian et al. [16] developed the CCTrans method by adopting pyramid Transformer backbone Twins [13] and also constructed a pyramid feature aggregation module. Savner et al. [31] proposed CrowdFormer to simulate the human's top-down visual perception mechanism by utilizing overlap patching Transformer blocks. Deng et al. [32] introduced a unified Transformer-based framework to implement weakly supervised crowd counting and crowd localization tasks. Chen et al. [33] developed a novel hybrid lightweight weakly supervised crowd counting network. GhostNet is utilized as the backbone, but Swin Transformer blocks are incorporated to mitigate the requirement of global context information.

Based on the aforementioned literature, researchers have also started to construct a combination framework by exploiting the advantages of both CNN and Transformer. For fully supervised crowd counting, Liu et al. [34] proposed a pyramid Transformer CNN network (PTCNet) that employs pyramid ViT [14] to extract multi-level global context information of crowds and then utilizes three CNN branches to learn the features of various scales. For weakly supervised crowd counting, Li et al. [35] designed a hypergraph association crowd counting (HACC) framework. The backbone of HACC is based on Swin Transformer and multi-scale dilated pyramid CNN. Moreover, a novel hypergraph association module was proposed to handle the problem of uneven distribution of crowd density.

To the best of our knowledge, there are currently few studies on weakly supervised crowd counting based on combining CNN and Transformer. How to effectively combine these two different frameworks in complex crowd counting tasks remains a key research challenge. This work aims to establish a joint CNN and Transformer network model and achieve better counting performance under weakly supervised settings.

3. Methods

In this section, we outline the framework of CrowdCCT and provide a detailed introduction of its components. CrowdCCT, as illustrated in Figure 2, is composed of three main components: CNN part, Transformer part, and regression part.

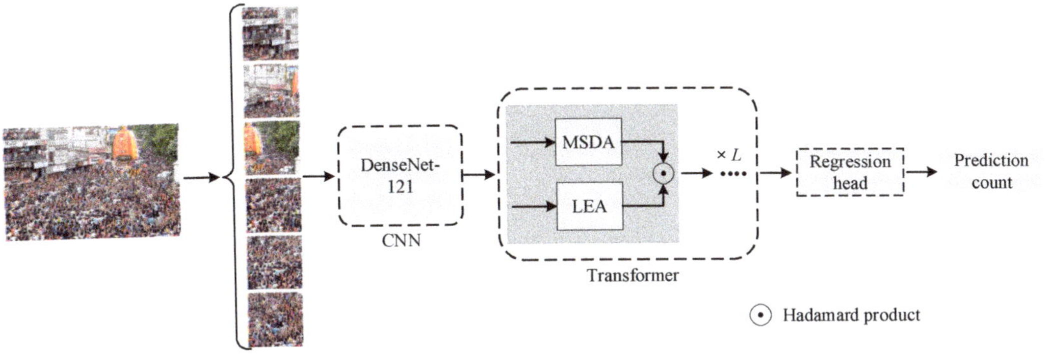

Figure 2. An overview of the proposed CrowdCCT.

In this model, we utilize a three-phased processing flow for efficient crowd counting. Initially, each image is divided into fixed-size patches and a corresponding image sequence is composed of these patches. Then, the image sequences are taken as the input of the CNN part. This phase aims to learn the semantic features of the crowd in the image and provides a foundation for further analysis. Next, the output of the CNN part is optimized. Specifically, the number of channels in the feature map is reduced from 1024 to 768 via a series of convolutional layer operations. This step helps to reduce the number of parameters while maintaining the expressive ability of the features and contributes to the lightweighting and efficiency of the model. Subsequently, the optimized feature maps are fed into the Transformer part. At this phase, the feature vectors pass through the MSDA and LEA modules. The MSDA module aims to extract and integrate the semantic information at multiple scales, which can enhance the representation ability of the features. Conversely, the LEA module serves to improve the accuracy of counting through enhancing the attention at specific locations. Thus, it can assist the model to focus on key areas in the image, such as crowded areas. The outputs of these two modules are then passed to a Hadamard product operation for further processing of the feature vectors. Here, Hadamard product is the operation of element-wise multiplication of two matrices of the same dimension. Ultimately, the Transformer part reconstructs the output into a two-dimensional feature map, containing rich information of crowd distribution. Then, a counting regression operation is applied to convert the feature map information into an accurate crowd counting prediction. Through this structured and hierarchical processing approach, our model can not only extract key features from images but also predict the number of people in a crowd image accurately.

3.1. CNN Part

A pure Transformer processes images by passing them into the Transformer block directly. However, effectively extracting both global and local features is crucial in weakly supervised counting tasks. As pure Transformers struggle to extract local features directly and effectively, CNN is introduced to assist with the procedure of feature extraction. With a multi-layered structure, CNN can learn representations of image features, evolving from simple to complex. At lower levels, CNN captures basic visual patterns like edges and textures. At higher levels, CNN can recognize more complex shapes and object features. This hierarchical processing of feature extraction is essential for understanding crowds and person distributions in crowd images.

Since DenseNet121 [36] excels regarding high performance in many computer vision tasks, such as object detection and classification, the CNN part adopts it for feature extraction in crowd counting and uses the extracted features as the input of the Transformer part. DenseNet121 utilizes a dense connectivity scheme that connects each layer to every other layer in a feed-forward manner, in which each layer takes the feature maps of the previous layer as input and passes its own feature maps to all subsequent layers. The network is organized with multiple tightly connected dense blocks, as shown in Figure 3. The DenseNet121 used in our experiments consists of three dense blocks, which have the same number of layers. To enrich the feature information while minimizing the number of model parameters, we remove the final pooling layer and the fully connected layer of DenseNet121. For an input image $I \in R^{H \times W \times 3}$, where H and W represent the height and width, 3 is the number of channels, and the operation of the CNN part can be defined as below:

$$R_f = F_{dense} \tag{1}$$

where R_f represents the result of feature extraction and F_{dense} denotes the calculation process of DenseNet121. In this way, the CNN part can extract features with rich semantic information, which ensures the effectiveness of feature extraction. It also helps our model to generate high-resolution feature maps, thus improving the accuracy of crowd counting.

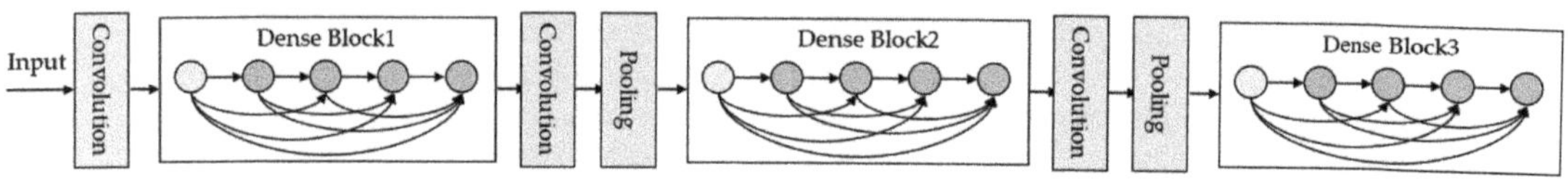

Figure 3. The DenseNet with three dense blocks used in the CNN part. The layers between two adjacent blocks are referred to as transition layers, and they change the size of feature maps via convolution and pooling operation.

3.2. *Transformer Part*

As shown in Figure 2, the Transformer part consists of two key modules: the Multi-Scale Dilated Attention (MSDA) and the Location-Enhanced Attention (LEA). The two modules work together to enhance the expressiveness of features.

Initially, the Transformer part takes the output from the CNN part as its input. The output of the CNN part offers rich contextual information and provides a foundation for further Transformer processes. Especially, MSDA and LEA in the Transformer part process the input data separately. Then, a Hadamard product operation is conducted with the output results of these two attention modules in order to integrate the features from both modules and enhance the feature expression ability. The whole process can be expressed by the following three formulas:

$$x_1 = F_{MSDA}(x_{in}) \tag{2}$$

$$x_2 = F_{LEA}(x_{in}) \tag{3}$$

$$x_{out} = x_1 \odot x_2 \tag{4}$$

where x_1 denotes the feature passing through the MSDA module, x_2 denotes the feature passing through the LEA module, and $\odot$ is the Hadamard product.

3.2.1. Multi-Scale Dilated Attention (MSDA)

Based on the locality and sparsity observed in the global attention of shallow layers in vanilla Vision Transformers [11], we develop the operation of sliding window dilated attention (SWDA). Compared to traditional sliding window computations, SWDA does not perform self-attention computation for all keys and values. Instead, it selects keys and values within a sliding window centered on the query patch sparsely. Only a portion of the positions within the window participate in the self-attention computation for the current query block, while the other positions are ignored. Formally, the SWDA can be described as follows:

$$X = \mathrm{SWDA}(Q,\ K,\ V,\ r) \tag{5}$$

where Q, K, and V represent the query matrix, key matrix, and value matrix, respectively. Each row of the three matrices indicates a single query/key/value feature vector.

We use (i, j) to represent the position coordinates of a query patch in the feature map. By taking (i, j) as the center of the query patch, a window with size $\omega \times \omega$ slides over the feature map. Furthermore, we define a dilation rate r to control the degree of sparsity. Through the SWDA operation, keys and values are sparsely selected within this window for self-attention computation. For any position (i, j) in the feature map, the corresponding component of the output X from SWDA operation can be formulated as below:

$$x_{ij} = \mathrm{Attention}(q_{ij}, K_r, V_r) = \mathrm{Softmax}(\frac{q_{ij}K_r^T}{\sqrt{d_k}})V_r,\ 1 \le i \le W,\ 1 \le j \le H \tag{6}$$

where H and W denote the height and width of the feature map, respectively. The conditions of $1 \le i \le W,\ 1 \le j \le H$ ensure that computations are performed for every position in the feature map. d_k denotes the dimensionality of the keys. K_r and V_r are sparse selections from the K and V feature maps, respectively.

As shown in Figure 4, we use a 3×3 kernel size with dilation rates $r = (1,\ 2,\ 3)$ for different heads. Also, the sizes of receptive fields utilized in different heads are $3 \times 3, 5 \times 5$, and 7×7. Given the query positioned at (i, j), keys and values located in the set $(i',\ j')$ of coordinates, defined as below, will be selected for performing self-attention operation.

$$\{(i',\ j')i' = i + p \times r,\ j' = j + q \times r\},\ -\frac{\omega}{2} \le p,\ q \le \frac{\omega}{2} \tag{7}$$

where ω is the window size as mentioned above; p and q are control variables for calculating each point in the set $(i',\ j')$.

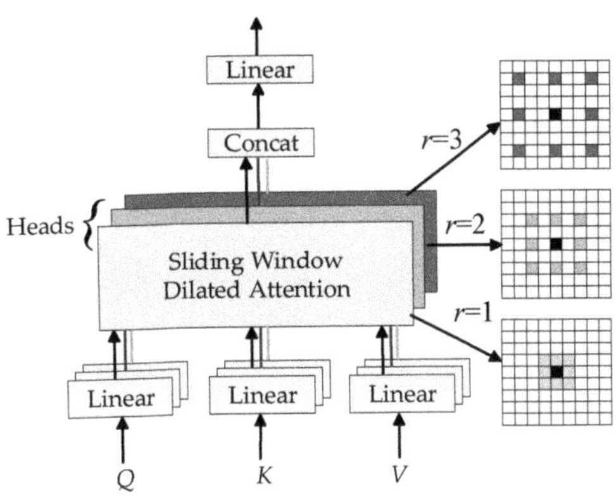

Figure 4. Flow chart of MSDA module.

The SWDA conducts the self-attention operation for all query patches via sliding window. For query patches located at the edges of the feature map, we adopt the zero-padding strategy. Then, based on SWDA operation, the MSDA module is designed to employ different dilation rates for different heads, where each dilation rate corresponds to a different window size. Different heads have different attention window sizes; thus, each head serves to extract information from different scales. The combination of the attention results from different scales can be helpful in the capture of rich information across scales, thereby enhancing the overall performance of the network. The MSDA module is explicitly provided with the properties of locality and sparsity by sparsely selecting keys and values around the center of a query patch. It can model long-range dependencies in the global context effectively, even under sparse selection.

As shown in Figure 4, MSDA module begins with a given feature map X, which initially undergoes linear projection to extract the corresponding query (Q), key (K), and value (V) matrices. The feature map X is then partitioned into n different heads; each head calculates the self-attention independently on a subsegment of the feature map. For each head h_i, attention is calculated by multi-scale SWDA with unique dilation rates r_i. Specifically, the MSDA can be formulated as below:

$$h_i = \text{SWDA}(Q_i, K_i, V_i, r_i),\ 1 \leq i \leq n \tag{8}$$

$$X = \text{Linear}(\text{Concat}[h_i, \ldots, h_n]) \tag{9}$$

where h_i represents the dilation rate for head h_i and Q_i, K_i, and V_i are the feature map slices of head h_i. The outputs for $\{h_i\}_{i=1}^{n}$ are concatenated together and finally fed into a linear layer for feature aggregation. The dilation rate of the head h_i determines the sparsity and receptive field size when executing SWDA. By setting different dilation rates for different heads, MSDA effectively aggregates semantic information at various scales within the attended receptive field.

3.2.2. Location-Enhanced Attention (LEA)

Traditional self-attention mechanism takes global context information into consideration during computation but encounters shortcomings when dealing with local details. To further improve the discriminative ability of local features, we develop LEA module with a position encoding block to enhance self-attention mechanism. In simple terms, we combine the output of self-attention with the local enhanced position encoding, resulting in an enhanced output. As shown in Figure 5, the working flow of position encoding can be found in the dotted box.

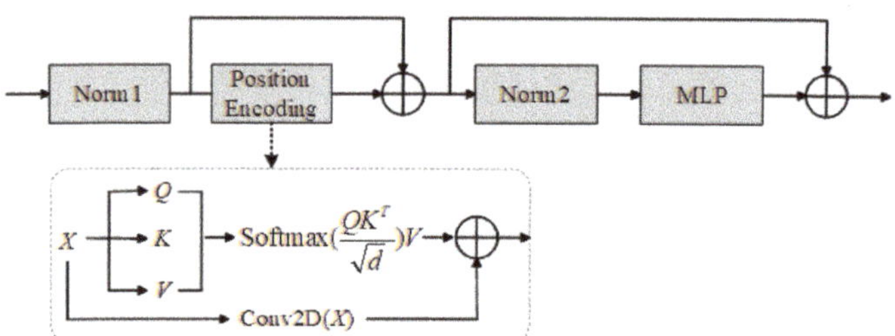

Figure 5. The specific diagram of LEA module.

Both Norm1 and Norm2 are normalization layers, which are used to standardize input features. The MLP (multi-layer perceptron) is capable of performing nonlinear transformations on input data to extract complex feature relationships. Positional encoding can generate position-related encodings by depth-wise convolution and actually contains the order information of the sequence. Since the input sequences are constructed with image patches, the order information implies the spatial location information in the original images. Hence, positional encoding helps to enhance the model's ability of perceiving local spatial structures combined with adding the related information to each feature map.

In the position encoding block, we map the input tensors into three matrices, query, key, and value, and calculate the attention scores via dot product. Specifically, for the input tensor $X \in R^{H \times W \times C}$, we can obtain the query, key, and value matrices by linear transformations shown below:

$$Q,\ K,\ V = XW^Q,\ XW^K,\ XW^V \tag{10}$$

where W^Q, W^K, and W^V are the learnable parameter matrices. Subsequently, the similarity between the query and the key is calculated via dot product and adjusted with the scaling factor $\sqrt{d}$.

$$A = \text{Softmax}(\frac{QK^T}{\sqrt{d}}) \tag{11}$$

Then, we take A as the attention weight and multiply A by the value matrix V to obtain the self-attention output.

$$X_1 = AV \tag{12}$$

To enrich the local semantic information in the above output, we introduce position encoding into the self-attention mechanism. Specifically, we process the input tensor with a depth-wise convolution operation to capture positional encoding within the local neighborhood. Given the input tensor X, we first rearrange it into a suitable format for convolution operations and then apply depth-wise convolution. The operation of position encoding can be represented as below:

$$X_{PE} = \text{Conv2D}(X) \tag{13}$$

where Conv2D is the depth-wise convolution operation and X_{PE} refers to the result of position encoding. Such encoding can capture the position information of the input tensor within the local area, which is helpful to enhance the model's sensitivity to background noise and foreground people.

Finally, we add the position encoding result to the attention output to enhance the local information. This enhanced information is then projected and regularized by a linear layer and a dropout layer. The specific process can be expressed as the following formula:

$$X = \text{Dropout}(\text{Linear}(X_1 + X_{PE})) \tag{14}$$

By introducing local enhancement with positional encoding, as LEA module takes the global context into consideration while enhancing the representation of local features, it is beneficial for the counting task, which requires fine spatial dependencies.

3.3. Regression Part and Loss Function

The regression part serves as the final count prediction. After feature extraction and fusion in the previous parts, the necessary rich information for regression is learned. As shown in Figure 6, the regressor used in our model mainly contains two fully connected layers, two activation layers based on ReLU, and a dropout layer with the ratio of 0.8. The first layer reduces the feature dimensions, and the parameters of subsequent layers decrease accordingly. The final layer outputs the predicted crowd counts.

$$x = \text{FC2}(\text{Dropout}(\text{ReLU}(\text{FC1}(\text{ReLU}(x_f))), p)) \tag{15}$$

where x_f denotes the final features obtained from CNN and Transformer parts and p is the dropout ratio [37].

Figure 6. Diagram of the regression part.

We utilize L_1 loss, also known as the mean absolute error, to measure the difference between the predicted value and the ground-truth value. L_1 calculates the average of the absolute differences across all data points to provide a robust measure of prediction accuracy, which is more efficient than other loss functions, such as L_2 loss (mean squared error). L_1 loss can be expressed as

$$L_1 = \frac{1}{M}\sum_{i=1}^{M}|P_i - G_i| \tag{16}$$

where P_i and G_i represent the predicted count and the corresponding ground truth for the ith image. M denotes the batch size of the training images.

4. Experiments and Results

To evaluate the performance of our proposed CrowdCCT, we conduct experiments on four widely used crowd counting datasets. In the following, we sequentially present the implementation details, datasets, the evaluation metrics, the comparative results, the visualization of feature maps, and ablation studies.

4.1. Implementation Details

Our experiments are carried out on the platform of PyTorch 2.0 with a NVIDIA V100 GPU. For the CNN part, we adopt DenseNet121 as the feature extraction network. Specifically, we remove the final pooling layer and the fully connected layer. For the Transformer part, the backbone is similar to ViT [12], including 12 Transformer layers. The number of heads is also set to 12. In the MSDA module, the window size is set to 32.

During the training phase, several widely used data augmentation strategies are utilized, such as random flipping and gray scaling. According to TransCrowd [11], we resize all original images to 1152 × 768 (landscape) or 768 × 1152 (portrait) and then crop each image into 6 patches of size 384 × 384. The number of people in each patch is calculated by the location annotation in the image. Pretrained weights from ImageNet are used to initialize the Transformer encoder. Adam optimizer is utilized with the learning rate of 1×10^{-5} and weight decay of 1×10^{-4} to train the whole model. In addition, the batch size is set to 16s.

4.2. Datasets

ShanghaiTech Dataset [1]: This dataset consists of 1198 images with a total of 330,165 instances. The dataset is divided into two parts based on density: Part_A and Part_B. Part_A contains 482 images with densely populated crowds. The training set includes 300 images, and the test set includes 182 images. Part_B contains 716 images with sparsely populated crowds. The training set includes 400 images, and the test set includes 316 images.

UCF_CC_50 Dataset [38]: The UCF_CC_50 dataset is the first challenging large-scale crowd counting dataset. It was created with web images from public lectures. To capture diverse scenes, the images were collected with different labels, such as concerts, protests, stadiums, marathons, etc. It contains 50 images, with an average of 1280 individuals per image and a total of 63,075 instances across all images. The number of individuals per image ranges from 94 to 4543.

UCF-QNRF Dataset [39]: This dataset includes 1535 challenging images with 1.25 million instances. The minimum and maximum object counts per image are 49 and 12,865, respectively. Images are sorted based on count. Every 5th image is selected for testing, resulting in 1201 images for training and 334 images for testing. This large-scale dataset covers various locations, viewpoints, perspectives, and time periods of day.

JHU-CROWD++ Dataset [40]: This dataset consists of 4372 images and 1.51 million instances, with an average resolution of 910 × 1430. The dataset contains some scenes under severe weather and lighting conditions, such as snow, rain, and haze, and provides rich crowd head location annotations.

4.3. Evaluation Metrics

To evaluate the accuracy of our approach, the mean absolute error (MAE) and the mean squared error (MSE) are adopted as metrics. Specifically, MAE and MSE are defined as below:

$$\mathrm{MAE} = \frac{1}{n}\sum_{i=1}^{n} |x_i - \overline{x}_i| \tag{17}$$

$$\mathrm{MSE} = \frac{1}{n}\sum_{i=1}^{n} (x_i - \overline{x}_i)^2 \tag{18}$$

where n represents the number of images in the test set, x_i represents the ground-truth count of the ith image, and $\overline{x}_i$ is the estimated number of pedestrians in the ith image. A smaller MAE indicates better accuracy of the network, while a smaller MSE indicates better robustness of the network.

4.4. Comparison to Existing Methods

The effectiveness of the proposed CrowdCCT is demonstrated through detailed comparisons with state-of-the-art methods on these datasets mentioned above. As shown in Table 1, the quantitative results from the ShanghaiTech, UCF_CC_50, and UCF-QNRF datasets are listed for comparison. We compare our method with some advanced fully supervised methods and weakly supervised methods. The best results for weakly supervised methods are indicated in bold font, and the second-best are indicated with underline. It can be observed from Table 1 that our method can achieve comparable performance with early fully supervised methods, such as MCNN [1], Switching-CNN [41], PACNN [26], S-DCNet [42], and so on. Compared to weakly supervised methods, including the pure CNN network proposed by Yang et al. [9], MATT [8], and pure Transformer architectures like TransCrowd [11], CrowdFormer [31], MSPT-Net [43], and SR2 [44], our method presents superior performance.

Table 1. Performance comparison regarding ShanghaiTech, UCF_CC_50, and UCF-QNRF datasets.

Method	SHTech Part_A		SHTech Part_B		UCF_CC_50		UCF-QNRF	
	MAE	MSE	MAE	MSE	MAE	MSE	MAE	MSE
MCNN [1]	110.2	173.2	26.4	41.3	377.6	509.0	277.0	426.0
CMTL [45]	101.3	152.4	20.0	31.1	322.8	397.9	252.0	514.0
Switching-CNN [41]	90.4	135.4	21.6	33.4	318.1	439.2	228.0	445.0
CP-CNN [24]	73.6	106.4	20.1	30.1	295.0	320.9	-	-
ACSCP [46]	75.7	102.7	17.2	27.4	291.0	404.6	-	-
PACNN [26]	66.3	106.4	8.9	13.5	267.9	357.8	-	-
S-DCNet [42]	58.3	95.0	6.7	10.7	204.2	301.3	104.4	176.1
LibraNet [27]	55.9	97.1	7.3	11.3	-	-	88.1	143.7
P2PNet [28]	52.7	85.1	6.3	9.9	172.7	256.2	85.3	154.5
Sorting-Net [9]	104.6	145.2	12.3	21.2	-	-	-	-
MATT [8]	80.1	129.4	11.7	17.5	355.0	550.2	97.2	168.5
CCTrans [16]	64.4	<u>95.4</u>	**7.0**	**11.5**	245.0	343.6	92.1	158.9
TransCrowd-T [11]	66.1	105.1	10.6	19.7	288.9	407.6	98.9	176.2
TransCrowd-G [11]	66.1	105.1	9.3	16.1	272.2	395.3	97.2	168.5
CrowdFormer [31]	<u>63.5</u>	107.7	7.7	12.8	<u>233.3</u>	**336.6**	<u>91.5</u>	166.9
MSPT-Net [43]	65.5	97.1	7.8	12.8	-	-	94.3	162.7
SR2 [44]	63.9	99.6	8.4	14.0	-	-	96.5	**153.1**
CrowdCCT (ours)	**63.4**	**94.4**	<u>9.1</u>	<u>12.5</u>	**211.3**	<u>337.2</u>	**91.1**	<u>161.8</u>

The best results are in bold, and the second-best are indicated with underline.

As shown in Table 1, our proposed model significantly improves both MAE and MSE metrics on these datasets. The ShanghaiTech Part_A dataset contains images from a wide range of scenes with large variations in crowd density, so accurately estimating the number of people is very challenging. Our proposed method, CrowdCCT, achieves the best MAE of 63.4 and the best MSE of 94.4. Compared to the earlier CNN-based fully supervised method ACSCP [46] and PACNN [26] (MAE of 66.3), our method makes encouraging progress. Compared to earlier CNN-based weakly supervised method MATT [8] (MAE of 80.1), our model achieves superior results by a large margin. Moreover, compared to advanced methods CCTrans [16], TransCrowd [11], and CrowdFormer [31], our model still presents the best performance. These results indicate that combining CNN and Transformer could adapt to different densities better, while the regression head could learn optimal ratios from large-scale datasets. On the ShanghaiTech Part_B dataset, our model obtains the results of MAE 9.1 and MSE 12.5. Compared to the latest models, our model exhibits slightly lower performance. But, compared to TransCrowd [11], the first Transformer-based weakly supervised method, our model demonstrates an improvement in counting accuracy and a relatively large decrease in MSE. It can also be seen that all models achieve excellent results on the Part_B dataset because, compared to other datasets, the crowd density of Part_B is relatively low and there exist very few occlusions.

UCF_CC_50 dataset has only 50 images and all of them contain highly dense crowds. We use five-fold cross-validation to train our model for this dataset. Compared with other weakly supervised methods, our method achieves the best MAE of 211.3 and the second-best MSE of 337.2. Particularly, when compared to TransCrowd, we can see the obvious improvements on both MAE and MSE metrics. The reason may be that the combination of CNN and Transformer integrates local and global information effectively, which can inject strong robustness into our model when facing highly dense scenarios.

For the experimental results on the UCF-QNRF dataset, we can observe that the proposed CrowdCCT reaches first place regarding MAE with 91.1 and third place regarding MSE with 161.8. We also find that CCTrans [16] and CrowdFormer [31] present comparable performance on this dataset with MAE values of 92.1 and 91.5, respectively. These two methods both utilize the pyramid-structured ViT to extract multi-scale features. Differently, we propose to use a Multi-Scale Dilated Attention module in the ViT backbone to capture multi-scale features. Moreover, we develop a Location-Enhanced Attention module to recognize foreground people more precisely. Hence, from an overall viewpoint, our proposed CrowdCCT can perform better than CCTrans [16] and CrowdFormer [31].

To further verify the generalization ability of our proposed model, we have conducted experiments on the JHU-CROWD++ dataset. The experimental results are listed in Tables 2 and 3. "Low", "Medium", and "High" indicate the sub-categories in JHU-CROWD++ dataset based on different degrees of crowd density. The best results are indicated in bold font, and the second-best are indicated with underline. In our experiments, we use a validation set to assess the performance of different models and select the best one, and then test it on the test set.

Table 2. Performance comparison regarding validation set of JHU-CROWD++.

Method	Low		Medium		High		Overall	
	MAE	MSE	MAE	MSE	MAE	MSE	MAE	MSE
MCNN [1]	90.6	202.9	125.3	259.5	494.9	856.0	160.6	377.7
CMTL [45]	50.2	129.2	88.1	170.7	583.1	986.5	138.1	379.5
SANet [47]	13.6	26.8	50.4	78.0	397.8	749.2	83.1	272.6
SFCN [48]	11.8	19.8	39.3	73.4	297.3	620.4	59.3	229.3
BL [49]	6.9	10.3	39.7	85.2	279.8	620.4	59.3	229.2
CG-DRCN [40]	17.1	44.7	40.8	71.2	317.4	719.8	67.9	262.1
TransCrowd-T [11]	7.1	10.7	<u>33.3</u>	<u>54.6</u>	302.5	557.4	58.4	201.1
TransCrowd-G [11]	<u>6.7</u>	<u>9.5</u>	34.5	55.8	285.9	532.8	56.8	193.6
CrowdFormer [31]	8.9	26.0	34.2	55.4	**251.6**	**501.5**	<u>53.4</u>	<u>183.3</u>
CrowdCCT (ours)	**5.6**	**8.1**	**31.4**	**48.3**	<u>260.3</u>	<u>528.1</u>	**51.6**	**182.1**

The best results are in bold, and the second-best are indicated with underline.

Table 3. Performance comparison regarding test set of JHU-CROWD++.

Method	Low		Medium		High		Overall	
	MAE	MSE	MAE	MSE	MAE	MSE	MAE	MSE
MCNN [1]	97.1	192.3	121.4	191.3	618.6	1166.7	188.9	483.4
CMTL [45]	58.5	136.4	81.7	144.7	635.3	1225.3	157.8	490.4
SANet [47]	17.3	37.9	46.8	69.1	397.9	817.7	91.1	320.4
SFCN [48]	16.5	55.7	38.1	59.8	341.8	758.8	77.5	297.6
BL [49]	10.1	32.7	34.2	54.5	352.0	768.7	75.0	299.9
CG-DRCN [40]	19.5	58.7	38.4	62.7	367.3	837.5	82.3	328.0
TransCrowd-T [11]	8.5	23.2	33.3	71.5	368.3	816.4	76.4	319.8
TransCrowd-G [11]	7.6	16.7	34.8	73.6	354.8	752.8	74.9	295.6
CrowdFormer [31]	10.6	37.4	**30.4**	**50.5**	**301.3**	680.4	65.4	265.9
CrowdCCT (ours)	**5.5**	**16.5**	34.9	53.9	302.3	**585.2**	**63.5**	**227.2**

The best results are in bold, and the second-best are indicated with underline.

According to Tables 2 and 3, our method can achieve superior performance compared to some mainstream fully supervised methods, such as MCNN [1], SFCN [48], CG-DRCN [40], and so on. Compared with Transformer-based weakly supervised methods, our method performs better than classical TransCrowd and obtains competitive results on both MAE and MSE metrics with CrowdFormer. It can be seen from Tables 2 and 3 that our method demonstrates superior performance, with lower MAE and MSE values on the overall evaluation of validation set and test set than CrowdFormer. Hence, based on the results listed in Tables 1–3, CrowdCCT obtains satisfactory counting accuracy, and thus the effectiveness of combining CNN and Transformer for the task of crowd counting is verified.

The computation cost of a model is also a crucial factor, and we present the comparison results with several recent studies in Table 4. As can be observed, the overall computational cost of our proposed CrowdCCT is relatively larger than other single CNN or Transformer models. Hence, it is unavoidable to produce a greater parameter quantity by combining CNN and Transformer. But, the comparison result of GFLOPs could be acceptable, which benefits from the design of our MSDA module in the Transformer part. Our model just needs to perform the self-attention calculations selectively in MSDA module. Therefore, how to reduce the parameters of the combination model is the focus of our subsequent research.

Table 4. Comparison of the computation costs of different methods.

Method	Resolution	Backbone	Params (M)	GFLOPs
P2PNet [28]	384 × 384	CNN	19.2	58.8
BL [49]	384 × 384	CNN	21.6	45.7
TransCrowd-T [11]	384 × 384	Transformer	86.8	46.4
TransCrowd-G [11]	384 × 384	Transformer	90.4	46.7
CCTrans [16]	384 × 384	Transformer	104.2	50.3
CrowdCCT (ours)	384 × 384	CNN + Transformer	128.3	54.6

To demonstrate the robustness of our model across various scenarios, we choose some example images randomly and present the corresponding prediction results in Figure 7. The first row illustrates the model's adaptability to different crowd densities, varying from sparse to dense. The second row displays images under various lighting conditions. The third row demonstrates the adaptability of our model under severe weather conditions. The experimental results show minimal discrepancies between ground-truth and predicted values for these images consistently, proving that our model could still perform well under challenging environments.

Figure 7. Examples of crowd counting estimation under different conditions.

4.5. Visualization

To further validate the effectiveness of the proposed CrowdCCT, we visualize the results of final convolutional layer with heat maps. Figure 8 shows several examples of the JHU-CROWD++ dataset. Although only being trained with weakly supervised count-level annotations, our model can still effectively distinguish foreground persons from background and pay more attention to the crowd region in the images. It is also noted that there are still a few crowd regions not being afforded attention due to the lack of individual person annotations.

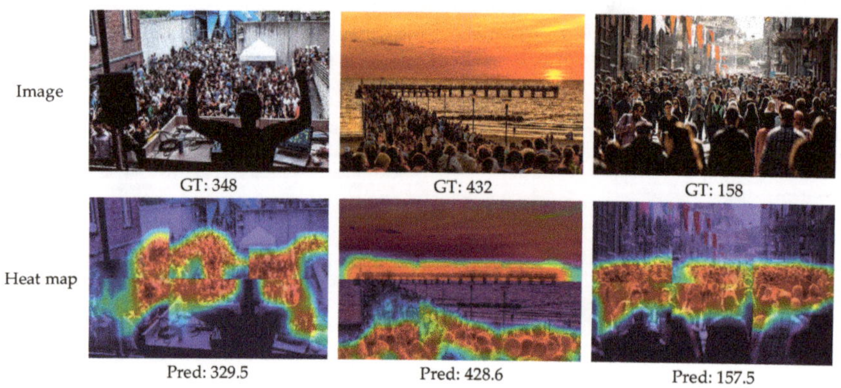

Figure 8. Visualization examples of feature maps.

4.6. Ablation Study

We conducted various ablation experiments on the CrowdCCT model to verify the contribution of each component and to justify the reasoning behind it. Tables 5 and 6 present the ablation study results on the ShanghaiTech dataset. Since our MSDA module divides the feature map into three different heads, each of which calculates the self-attention independently on a subsegment of the feature map, it uses the dilation rates to control feature extraction. To verify the effect of different dilation rate combinations on feature extraction, we designed three different combinations of dilation rate values to verify their contribution. Table 5 shows that different combinations of dilation rates produce different impacts.

Table 5. Ablation study for different dilation rates on MSDA.

Dilation Rates	SHTech Part_A		SHTech Part_B	
	MAE	MSE	MAE	MSE
1, 1, 2	67.7	108.5	17.5	37.9
2, 2, 4	68.1	115.2	18.2	39.5
1, 2, 3	63.4	94.4	9.1	12.5

Table 6. Ablation study for different components in our model.

CNN Part	Transformer Part		SHTech Part_A		SHTech Part_B	
	MSDA	LEA	MAE	MSE	MAE	MSE
√			71.5	136.8	12.5	23.7
	√		148.9	230.8	48.7	87.9
		√	132.8	213.7	38.1	65.2
	√	√	126.4	201.2	24.6	61.1
√	√		68.1	113.5	11.7	23.7
√		√	67.5	112.1	11.1	20.1
√	√	√	63.4	94.4	9.1	12.5

As shown in Table 5, the model performs best when the dilation rates are set with $r = (1, 2, 3)$. With this combination, the model can capture both local details and context information due to the progressively increasing dilation rates and expanding receptive field.

When $r = (1, 1, 2)$, the first two heads use the same dilation rate $r = 1$, which makes the heads focus on a smaller receptive field, while the third head expands the receptive field slightly with $r = 2$. This combination aims to study the effect of multiple heads operating at the same scale and compare it with combinations regarding different dilation rates across three heads. The results show that this configuration reduces the ability to capture multi-scale information.

For $r = (2, 2, 4)$, the first two heads use the same dilation rate $r = 2$, resulting in a medium receptive field, while the third head extends the large receptive field. This combination allows us to study the effect of using larger receptive fields, especially when multiple heads focus on capturing broader contextual information. The results indicate that setting the receptive field too large will lead to the loss of crucial information, resulting in slightly lower overall performance.

We can draw the conclusion that our ablation experiments reveal the contribution of different dilation rate combinations to the model performance. In particular, a combination of progressively increasing dilation rates $r = (1, 2, 3)$ is able to capture multi-scale features effectively, resulting in the best performance.

We also explored the roles of parts in CrowdCCT. According to Table 6, it is observed that the CNN part and MSDA and LEA modules in the Transformer part can provide their corresponding progressive improvements to the whole model. This trend is consistent across both the Part_A and Part_B datasets.

Specifically, on the Part_A dataset, the CNN part obtains the evaluation metrics with MAE of 71.5 and MSE of 136.8. The MSDA module achieves MAE of 148.9 and MSE of 230.8, and the LEA module can reach 132.8 on MAE and 213.7 on MSE. When utilizing MSDA and LEA simultaneously in the Transformer part, our model can achieve an obvious performance improvement with MAE of 126.4 and MSE of 201.2. Hence, the combination of these two attention modules in the Transformer part also plays an important role.

Additionally, we observe that that LEA has superior performance compared to MSDA. The possible reason is that LEA incorporates local enhanced positional encoding, which enables it to capture and utilize spatial information and pinpoint crowd information more precisely. Therefore, LEA can integrate location-based context more efficiently, leading to improved accuracy in crowd counting. On the other hand, MSDA utilizes a multi-scale dilated mechanism by sparsely selecting features. Although this module is designed to focus on the most relevant features at various scales, the process of sparse selection might inevitably overlook certain critical information.

As shown in Table 6, the CNN part contributes a great deal to the improvements regarding both the MAE and MSE metrics. This phenomenon suggests CNN's proficiency in capturing intricate patterns that other modules might overlook. CNN can effectively capture and extract local features, which are essential for the counting task. Moreover, the DenseNet used in the CNN part has the ability of retaining and exploiting information at different levels of dense connectivity and enables each layer to receive features from all previous layers directly. MSDA and LEA, as ViT attention modules, also play crucial roles in enhancing the model's overall performance. They are superior at capturing global context and dependencies within the data, which can complement the local feature extraction capabilities of DenseNet. This synergy between local and global feature extraction helps the model to be more robust and predict more accurately.

In summary, the joint model of CNN and Transformer achieves superior performance. The proposed model combination effectively extracts both global-level features and location information, empowering the model to learn multi-scale information from key areas. We also experimentally verify the reasonableness of the model parameter selection.

5. Conclusions

This paper proposes a novel network architecture named CrowdCCT, in which Transformer is utilized as the backbone and combined with CNN for feature extraction to address the challenges of weakly supervised crowd counting tasks. The proposed CrowdCCT consists of three main parts. The CNN part is responsible for extracting visual features of crowds from input images. The Transformer part learns global contextual information using self-attention mechanisms and captures contrasting features between the foreground and background, and the counting regression part uses features extracted from the previous two parts to predict crowd counts. Through extensive experiments and visual analysis, we verify the effectiveness and superior performance of CrowdCCT in weakly supervised crowd counting tasks.

The limitation of our model is the large number of parameters, making it undesirable for practical applications currently. In the near future, we will explore a deeper integration approach between CNN and Transformer for the crowd counting task while lessening the model size.

Author Contributions: Methodology, Y.C.; Formal analysis, D.Z.; Investigation, D.Z.; Writing—original draft, Y.C. All authors have read and agreed to the published version of the manuscript.

Funding: This work was supported in part by the National Natural Science Foundation of China (No. 62271035) and Beijing Municipal Natural Science Foundation (No. 4232021).

Data Availability Statement: The raw data supporting the conclusions of this article will be made available by the authors on request.

Conflicts of Interest: The authors declare no conflicts of interest.

References

1. Zhang, Y.Y.; Zhou, D.S.; Chen, S.; Gao, S.; Ma, Y. Single-Image Crowd Counting via Multi-Column Convolutional Neural Network. In Proceedings of the IEEE Conference on Computer Vision and Pattern Recognition, Las Vegas, NV, USA, 27–30 June 2016.
2. Li, D.; Zhang, H.J.; Ji, Y.Z.; Ding, Y.X. Crowd Counting by Using Multi-Level Density-Based Spatial Information: A Multi-Scale CNN Framework. *Inf. Sci.* **2020**, *528*, 79–91.
3. Jing, S.; Kang, K.; Loy, C.C.; Wang, X.G. Deeply Learned Attributes for Crowded Scene Understanding. In Proceedings of the IEEE Conference on Computer Vision and Pattern Recognition, Boston, MA, USA, 7–12 June 2015.

4. Xu, C.F.; Qiu, K.; Fu, J.; Bai, S.; Xu, Y.C.; Bai, X. Learn to Scale: Generating Multipolar Normalized Density Maps for Crowd Counting. In Proceedings of the IEEE/CVF International Conference on Computer Vision, Seoul, Republic of Korea, 27 October–2 November 2019.
5. Tripathi, G.; Singh, K.; Vishwakarma, D.K. Convolutional Neural Networks for Crowd Behavior Analysis: A Survey. *Vis. Comput.* **2019**, *35*, 753–776. [CrossRef]
6. Wang, S.Z.; Lu, Y.; Zhou, T.; Di, H.; Lu, L.; Zhang, L. SCLNet: Spatial Context Learning Network for Congested Crowd Counting. *Neurocomputing* **2020**, *404*, 227–239. [CrossRef]
7. He, Y.Q.; Xia, Y.F.; Wang, Y.Z.; Yin, B.Q. Jointly Attention Network for Crowd Counting. *Neurocomputing* **2022**, *487*, 157–171. [CrossRef]
8. Lei, Y.J.; Liu, Y.; Zhang, P.; Liu, L. Towards Using Count-Level Weak Supervision for Crowd Counting. *Pattern Recognit.* **2020**, *109*, 107616. [CrossRef]
9. Yang, T.F.; Li, G.R.; Wu, Z.; Su, L.; Huang, Q.M.; Sebe, N. Weakly-Supervised Crowd Counting Learns from Sorting Rather Than Locations. In *Computer Vision–ECCV 2020: 16th European Conference, Glasgow, UK, 23–28 August 2020, Proceedings, Part VIII 16*; Lecture Notes in Computer Science 2020; Springer International Publishing: Berlin/Heidelberg, Germany, 2020; Volume 12353, pp. 1–17.
10. Ashish, V.; Noam, S.; Niki, P.; Jakob, U.; Llion, J.; Aidan, N.G.; Lukasz, K.; Illia, P. Attention is All You Need. In Proceedings of the Advances in Neural Information Processing Systems, Long Beach, CA, USA, 4–9 December 2017.
11. Liang, D.K.; Chen, X.W.; Xu, W.; Zhou, Y.; Bai, X. TransCrowd: Weakly-Supervised Crowd Counting with Transformers. *Sci. China Inf. Sci.* **2022**, *65*, 160104. [CrossRef]
12. Dosovitskiy, A.; Beyer, L.; Kolesnikov, A.; Weissenborn, D.; Zhai, X.H.; Unterthiner, T.; Dehghani, M.; Minderer, M.; Heigold, G.; Gelly, S.; et al. An Image Is Worth 16×16 Words: Transformers for Image Recognition at Scale. In Proceedings of the International Conference on Learning Representations, Virtual, 26 April–1 May 2020.
13. Chu, X.X.; Tian, Z.; Wang, Y.Q.; Zhang, B.; Ren, H.B.; Wei, X.L.; Xia, H.X.; Shen, C.H. Twins: Revisiting the Design of Spatial Attention in Vision Transformers. In Proceedings of the 35th International Conference on Neural Information Processing Systems, Online, 6–14 December 2021; Volume 34, pp. 9355–9366.
14. Wang, W.H.; Xie, E.; Li, X.; Fan, D.P.; Song, K.; Liang, D.; Lu, T.; Luo, P.; Shao, L. PVTv2: Improved Baselines with Pyramid Vision Transformer. *Comput. Vis. Media* **2022**, *8*, 415–424. [CrossRef]
15. Liu, Z.; Lin, Y.T.; Cao, Y.; Hu, H.; Wei, Y.X.; Zhang, Z.; Lin, S.; Guo, B. Swin Transformer: Hierarchical Vision Transformer Using Shifted Windows. In Proceedings of the IEEE International Conference on Computer Vision, Montreal, QC, Canada, 10–17 October 2021.
16. Tian, Y.; Chu, X.X.; Wang, H.P. CCTrans: Simplifying and Improving Crowd Counting with Transformer. *arXiv* **2021**, arXiv:2109.14483.
17. Li, B.; Zhang, Y.; Xu, H.H.; Yin, B. CCST: Crowd Counting with Swin Transformer. *Vis. Comput.* **2023**, *39*, 2671–2682. [CrossRef]
18. Teng, Q.; Sun, S.; Song, W.; Bei, J.; Wang, C. Deep Convolutional Neural Network for Indoor Regional Crowd Flow Prediction. *Electronics* **2024**, *13*, 172. [CrossRef]
19. Sowmya, B.P.; Supriya, M.C. Convolutional Neural Network (CNN) Fundamental Operational Survey. *Learn. Anal. Intell. Syst.* **2021**, *21*, 245–258.
20. Fu, M.; Xu, P.; Li, X.D.; Liu, Q.; Ye, M.; Zhu, C. Fast Crowd Density Estimation with Convolutional Neural Networks. *Eng. Appl. Artif. Intell.* **2015**, *43*, 81–88. [CrossRef]
21. Cheng, Z.Q.; Li, J.X.; Dai, Q.; Wu, X.; He, J.Y.; Hauptmann, A.G. Improving the Learning of Multi-Column Convolutional Neural Network for Crowd Counting. In Proceedings of the 27th ACM International Conference on Multimedia, Nice, France, 21–25 October 2019.
22. Liu, Q.; Guo, Y.Q.; Sang, J.; Tan, J.H.; Wang, F.S.; Tian, S. SGCNet: Scale-Aware and Global Contextual Network for Crowd Counting. *Appl. Intell.* **2022**, *52*, 12091–12102. [CrossRef]
23. Wang, Y.J.; Zhang, W.; Huang, D.X.; Liu, Y.Y.; Zhu, J.H. Multi-Scale Features Fused Network with Multi-Level Supervised Path for Crowd Counting. *Expert Syst. Appl.* **2022**, *200*, 949–960. [CrossRef]
24. Sindagi, V.A.; Patel, V.M. Generating High-Quality Crowd Density Maps Using Contextual Pyramid CNNs. In Proceedings of the IEEE Conference on Computer Vision and Pattern Recognition, Honolulu, HI, USA, 21–26 July 2017.
25. Liang, L.J.; Zhao, H.L.; Zhou, F.B.; Zhang, Q.; Song, Z.L.; Shi, Q.X. Sc2net: Scale-Aware Crowd Counting Network with Pyramid Dilated Convolution. *Appl. Intell.* **2023**, *53*, 5146–5159. [CrossRef]
26. Shi, M.J.; Yang, Z.H.; Xu, C.; Chen, Q.J. Revisiting Perspective Information for Efficient Crowd Counting. In Proceedings of the IEEE Conference on Computer Vision and Pattern Recognition, Long Beach, CA, USA, 15–20 June 2019.
27. Liu, L.; Lu, H.; Zou, H.W.; Xiong, H.P.; Cao, Z.G.; Shen, C.H. Weighing Counts: Sequential Crowd Counting by Reinforcement Learning. *Eur. Conf. Comput. Vis.* **2020**, *16*, 164–181.
28. Song, Q.Y.; Wang, C.G.; Jiang, Z.K.; Wang, Y.B.; Tai, Y.; Wang, C.J.; Li, J.L.; Huang, F.Y.; Wu, Y. Rethinking Counting and Localization in Crowds: A Purely Point-Based Framework. In Proceedings of the IEEE International Conference on Computer Vision, Montreal, QC, Canada, 10–17 October 2021.

29. Bai, H.Y.; He, H.H.; Peng, Z.X.; Dai, T.Y.; Chan, S.H.G. Countr: An End-To-End Transformer Approach for Crowd Counting and Density Estimation. In *European Conference on Computer Vision*; Lecture Notes in Computer Science 2022; Springer Nature: Cham, Switzerland, 2022; Volume 13806, pp. 207–222.
30. Liu, C.X.; Lu, H.; Cao, Z.G.; Liu, T.L. Point-Query Quadtree for Crowd Counting, Localization, and More. In Proceedings of the IEEE International Conference on Computer Vision, Paris, France, 1–6 October 2023.
31. Savner, S.S.; Kanhangad, V. CrowdFormer: Weakly-Supervised Crowd Counting with Improved Generalizability. *J. Vis. Commun. Image Represent.* **2023**, *94*, 103853. [CrossRef]
32. Deng, M.F.; Zhao, H.L.; Gao, M. CLFormer: A Unified Transformer-Based Framework for Weakly Supervised Crowd Counting and Localization. *Vis. Comput.* **2024**, *40*, 1053–1067. [CrossRef]
33. Chen, Y.Q.; Zhao, H.L.; Gao, M.; Deng, M.F. A Weakly Supervised Hybrid Lightweight Network for Efficient Crowd Counting. *Electronics* **2024**, *13*, 723. [CrossRef]
34. Liu, J.Y.; Li, H.; Kong, W.H. Multi-Level Learning Counting via Pyramid Vision Transformer and CNN. *Eng. Appl. Artif. Intell.* **2023**, *123*, 184–196. [CrossRef]
35. Li, B.; Zhang, Y.; Zhang, C.Y.; Piao, X.L.; Yin, B.C. Hypergraph Association Weakly Supervised Crowd Counting. *ACM Trans. Multimed. Comput. Commun. Appl.* **2023**, *19*, 859–873. [CrossRef]
36. Huang, G.; Liu, Z.; Maaten, L.V.; Weinberger, K.Q. Densely Connected Convolutional Networks. In Proceedings of the IEEE Conference on Computer Vision and Pattern Recognition, Honolulu, HI, USA, 21–26 July 2017.
37. Nitish, S.; Geoffrey, H.; Alex, K.; Ilya, S.; Ruslan, S. Dropout: A Simple Way to Prevent Neural Networks from Overfitting. *J. Mach. Learn. Res.* **2014**, *15*, 1929–1958.
38. Idrees, H.; Saleemi, I.; Seibert, C.; Shah, M. Multi-Source Multi-Scale Counting in Extremely Dense Crowd Images. In Proceedings of the IEEE Conference on Computer Vision and Pattern Recognition, Portland, OR, USA, 23–28 June 2013.
39. Idrees, H.; Tayyab, M.; Athrey, K.; Zhang, D.; AlMaadeed, S.; Rajpoot, N.; Shah, M. Composition Loss for Counting, Density Map Estimation and Localization in Dense Crowds. In *Computer Vision–ECCV 2018: 15th European Conference, Munich, Germany, 8–14 September 2018, Proceedings, Part II 15*; Lecture Notes in Computer Science 2018; Springer International Publishing: Berlin/Heidelberg, Germany, 2018; Volume 11206, pp. 544–559.
40. Sindagi, V.A.; Yasarla, R.; Patel, V.M. JHU-Crowd++: Large-Scale Crowd Counting Dataset and A Benchmark Method. *IEEE Trans. Pattern Anal. Mach. Intell.* **2022**, *44*, 2594–2609. [CrossRef] [PubMed]
41. Sam, D.B.; Surya, S.; Babu, R.V. Switching Convolutional Neural Network for Crowd Counting. In Proceedings of the IEEE Conference on Computer Vision and Pattern Recognition, Honolulu, HI, USA, 21–26 July 2017.
42. Xiong, H.; Lu, H.; Liu, C.X.; Liu, L.; Cao, Z.G.; Shen, C.H. From Open Set to Closed Set: Counting Objects by Spatial Divide-and-Conquer. In Proceedings of the IEEE International Conference on Computer Vision, Seoul, Republic of Korea, 27 October–2 November 2019.
43. Zhang, S.L.; Lei, T.; Wang, Y.B.; Zhou, Q.; Xue, M.I.; Zhou, W.Q. A Crowd Counting Network Based on Multi-Scale Pyramid Transformer. *CAAI Trans. Intell. Syst.* **2024**, *19*, 67–78.
44. Gao, M.; Deng, M.F.; Zhao, H.L.; Chen, Y.J.; Chen, Y.Q. Improving MLP-Based Weakly Supervised Crowd-Counting Network via Scale Reasoning and Ranking. *Electronics* **2024**, *13*, 471. [CrossRef]
45. Sindagi, V.A.; Patel, V.M. CNN-Based Cascaded Multi-Task Learning of High-Level Prior and Density Estimation for Crowd Counting. In Proceedings of the 2017 14th IEEE International Conference on Advanced Video and Signal Based Surveillance (AVSS), Lecce, Italy, 29 August–1 September 2017; pp. 1–6.
46. Shen, Z.; Xu, Y.; Ni, B.B.; Wang, M.S.; Hu, J.G.; Yang, X.K. Crowd Counting via Adversarial Cross-Scale Consistency Pursuit. In Proceedings of the IEEE Conference on Computer Vision and Pattern Recognition, Salt Lake City, UT, USA, 18–23 June 2018.
47. Cao, X.K.; Wang, Z.P.; Zhao, Y.Y.; Su, F. Scale Aggregation Network for Accurate and Efficient Crowd Counting. In *Computer Vision–ECCV 2018: 15th European Conference, Munich, Germany, 8–14 September 2018, Proceedings, Part V 15*; Lecture Notes in Computer Science 2018; Springer International Publishing: Berlin/Heidelberg, Germany, 2018; Volume 11209, pp. 734–750.
48. Wang, Q.; Gao, J.Y.; Lin, W.; Yuan, Y. Learning from Synthetic Data for Crowd Counting in the Wild. In Proceedings of the IEEE Conference on Computer Vision and Pattern Recognition, Long Beach, CA, USA, 15–20 June 2019.
49. Ma, Z.H.; Wei, X.; Hong, X.P.; Gong, Y.H. Bayesian Loss for Crowd Count Estimation with Point Supervision. In Proceedings of the IEEE International Conference on Computer Vision, Seoul, Republic of Korea, 27 October–2 November 2019.

electronics

Article

The Role of Machine Learning in Advanced Biometric Systems

Milkias Ghilom and Shahram Latifi *

Department of Electrical & Computer Engineering, University of Nevada, Las Vegas, NV 89154, USA; ghilom@unlv.nevada.edu
* Correspondence: shahram.latifi@unlv.edu

Abstract: Today, the significance of biometrics is more pronounced than ever in accurately allowing access to valuable resources, from personal devices to highly sensitive buildings, as well as classified information. Researchers are pushing forward toward devising robust biometric systems with higher accuracy, fewer false positives and false negatives, and better performance. On the other hand, machine learning (ML) has been shown to play a key role in improving such systems. By constantly learning and adapting to users' changing biometric patterns, ML algorithms can improve accuracy and performance over time. The integration of ML algorithms with biometrics, however, introduces vulnerabilities in such systems. This article investigates the new issues of concern that come about because of the adoption of ML methods in biometric systems. Specifically, techniques to breach biometric systems, namely, data poisoning, model inversion, bias injection, and deepfakes, are discussed. Here, the methodology consisted of conducting a detailed review of the literature in which ML techniques have been adopted in biometrics. In this study, we included all works that have successfully applied ML and reported favorable results after this adoption. These articles not only reported improved numerical results but also provided sound technical justification for this improvement. There were many isolated, unsupported, and unjustified works about the major advantages of ML techniques in improving security, which were excluded from this review. Though briefly mentioned, we did not touch upon encryption/decryption aspects, and, accordingly, cybersecurity was excluded from this study. At the end, recommendations are made to build stronger and more secure systems that benefit from ML adoption while closing the door to adversarial attacks.

Keywords: bias; deepfake; deep learning; generative adversarial networks; model inversion; privacy

1. Introduction

The adoption of ML allows the field of biometrics to use different authentication methods than what is currently present. In one study, researchers used ML to classify different handwriting as an authentication method [1]. Here, the authors employed a multi-class SVM to perform the verification and identification of persons based on their handwriting using a given PIN. Although this study was conducted using a very small sample size (30 people), it showed that ML can be used to detect anomalies present in someone's handwriting in order to detect an impostor. With more training and a larger dataset, this could become a very secure method of authentication, as users tend to have different handwriting, especially when it comes to smaller details, like how specific letters are written or how the ink trails when the pen is lifted in a specific direction. In [2], template protection using DL was addressed while in [3], face and gate traits were captured by video cameras. Here, the effect of ML on the fusion process was the subject of study. In another study [4], the authors discussed the application of classical and ML methods to achieve facial recognition. They further proposed the development of a software tool for authentication. In [5], the authors checked the identification accuracy of the machine learning algorithm REPTree (a decision tree) on selected biometric datasets that had been deployed and evaluated on the data mining tool WEKA. They reported an accuracy of 95% on selected datasets. In another interesting work [6], the authors studied behavioral biometrics based on touch dynamics and phone movement. Using two publicly available datasets—BioIdent and Hand Movement Orientation and Grasp (H-MOG)—this study used seven common machine learning algorithms to evaluate performance, including Random Forest, Support Vector Machine, K-Nearest Neighbor, Naive Bayes, Logistic Regression, Multilayer Perceptron, and Long Short-Term Memory Recurrent Neural Networks, with accuracy rates reaching as high as 86%. In another paper [7], the authors studied the classification performance of biometrics using the ML methods Random Tree, the Multilayer Perceptron Neural Network (MPNN), and the C4.5 decision tree (DT) algorithms. The Random Forest classifier algorithm exhibited greater performance compared to the other techniques, obtaining a 93.5% accuracy.

In addition, deep learning (DL)-based methods represent the current state of the art for solving pattern recognition tasks. This is especially important, as in DL, the features are not hand-crafted for classification; rather, they are developed by the DL system after seeing the dataset. This means that deep learning-based biometric systems can render a lower FMR and, thus, a higher level of security [2]. Two main applications of ML in biometrics are shown below.

1.1. CAPTCHA (Completely Automated Public Turing Test to Tell Computers and Humans Apart)

Real-time CAPTCHAs are a new technology that could improve the security of biometric techniques. By requiring the user to perform some sort of action, like looking into the camera, they can verify that there is indeed a human accessing the device. Alongside that, by randomizing the requests, attackers cannot predict what to expect, therefore providing a stronger level of security. Moreover, utilizing ML to further enhance the security of CAPTCHAs can be game-changing. CAPTCHAs using ML can be trained to detect anomalies present in the patterns of users. By determining what "feels" like human input and what "feels" like bot input, the device can learn to identify differences and eventually be able to detect ML bots that act and solve CAPTCHAs somewhat similarly to humans.

1.2. Continuous Biometrics

Integrating ML with a biometric system also opens the possibility of utilizing "continuous authentication" to protect its users. Currently, most biometric systems employ a static approach, where the user is authenticated once and is logged in until they log out. This opens the door for attackers to gain access while the user is logged in. Researchers have pointed out the vulnerabilities of static authentication, where the genuine user logs into the system at the start of the session. If there is a change of user during the session, that change will remain undetectable for as long as the impostor is logged in [2].

ML can be utilized to detect subtle variations in biometrics to ensure that only authorized users are authenticated while increasing accuracy and reliability to provide a better user experience for those who use these devices regularly. "Supervised ML can be used to classify the data much more accurately".

Another study [8] that is cited in this paper analyzed the mouse movements of users as a method of continuous authentication by using data collection software that ran in the background. In this study, features such as click elapsed time, movement speed, movement acceleration, and relative position of extreme speed are utilized by a Support Vector Machine (SVM) technique to classify the behavior as belonging to the genuine user or impostor.

Despite all the advantages that come about as a result of ML adoption, there are some downsides too, which are the main focus of this paper. Attacks on data that introduce biases and backdoors may undermine the accuracy and integrity of ML models. ML models' "black box" qualities are used in model inversion attacks to extract private biometric information. Deepfakes, created utilizing deep learning algorithms, may fool speech and facial recognition systems and allow for illegal access and identity theft. The security of these systems is also threatened by adversarial attacks, like forging real samples or changing precise biometric data. Additionally, vulnerabilities are amplified by the transferability of attacks between related systems. Furthermore, biased training data may lead to misidentification and unjust outcomes by introducing prejudice and discrimination into biometric systems. To improve the security and fairness of biometric systems, this article emphasizes the necessity for strong solutions, such as using enhanced deepfake detection tools and addressing biases in training data. In addition, the user's privacy should be a main consideration while designing biometric systems. The following research questions are addressed in this paper:

Q1: We have a rich body of literature on the positive impacts of ML on biometrics. Is there a disadvantage to this adoption? And, if so, how do we address the problems?

Q2: In general, does the introduction of ML techniques make the system more vulnerable or less? If more, what are the remedies?

1.3. Inclusions and Exclusions

The consequences of using a database for training the ML module of a biometric system are included in this study. Pertinent aspects such as adversarial attacks, data poisoning, model inversion, and, more importantly, GANs (basis of deepfakes) are also included. We did not entertain the encryption/decryption of data, as this calls for a different treatment. Furthermore, a popular subset of ML, deep learning, is not the focus here, and the listed negative impacts in Section 2 apply to deep learning as a subset of ML.

The rest of this paper is organized as follows. Section 2 examines the potential negative effects of ML adoption in biometric systems, focusing on model inversion attacks and data poisoning attacks that give ML models biases and back doors and examining the adverse effects of deepfake technologies on biometric systems. The transferability of attacks between comparable systems is also covered here. Recommendations to overcome the adverse effects are presented in Section 3. Section 4 offers a futuristic view of biometrics and other concluding remarks.

2. Negative Impact of Machine Learning on Biometrics and Methodology

In this section, we elaborate on some of the negative impacts of ML on biometrics. It is emphasized that the list is not exhaustive, and there may be other disadvantages that are not mentioned here due to space limitations. Furthermore, we explain the methodology at the end of the section.

2.1. Adversarial Attacks

Biometric systems depend on ML models to effectively categorize and verify people based on their distinctive biometric features. These models are, however, open to adversarial attacks that seek to alter or disrupt the input data in such a manner that the model erroneously classifies it. In the realm of biometrics, adversarial attacks may take many different forms. Making bogus samples is one typical method. An attacker can create fake biometric data replicating authorized people's characteristics or new identities [9]. To trick the model and gain unauthorized access, the attacker injects these fake samples into the system. By showing a synthetic but seemingly realistic visage that closely matches the face of an authorized user, for instance, the attacker may try to deceive a facial recognition system. Altering accurate biometric information is a different kind of adversarial attack. An attacker may try to get around the system's authentication procedure by changing the properties of a person's biometric attributes, such as fingerprints or speech patterns [10]. This manipulation might include physical changes, like the application of synthetic fingerprints, or digital changes to the biometric information that has been recorded in a database. The intention is to trick the system into erroneously considering the changed biometric data, allowing unwanted access or facilitating identity theft.

2.2. Data Poisoning

ML algorithms use training data to find patterns and provide precise predictions. Regarding biometric systems, the training data generally comprise individual biometric samples. The performance of the biometric system may be harmed if an attacker can introduce biases or malicious models by manipulating the training data used to develop the method [11]. Attacks known as "data poisoning" include adding erroneous or malicious samples to the training data. An attacker hopes to influence the model's learning process in a way that provides inaccurate or skewed outputs. For instance, an attacker may provide many samples from a specific demographic group, causing the model to behave biasedly when authenticating group members. Backdoors may be inserted into the model as part of data poisoning attacks. Attackers could introduce specific samples or patterns that function as triggers to the training data, leading the model to react incorrectly to inputs. By using these covert backdoors, unauthorized users could get around the system's authentication procedure. The security and integrity of the training data must be guaranteed to prevent data poisoning attacks. This entails putting into practice methods like data validation, anomaly detection, and data sanitization to find and eliminate potentially poisonous samples. The training data should be monitored and audited often to detect potentially harmful biases or strange trends.

2.3. Model Inversion

An assault known as a "model inversion attack" may be used to exploit ML models, especially those employed in biometric systems. These attacks include a hostile actor querying the model to rebuild or obtain sensitive data. Regarding biometrics, the possible repercussions of model inversion attacks are especially problematic since they might endanger people's privacy by enabling attackers to reproduce the original biometric data, such as a face image or fingerprint, using the model's replies. A model learns to make predictions or categorize data by examining patterns and correlations during training. However, the underlying workings of the model often need to be more transparent and easier to access. The "black box" characteristic of ML models refers to this opacity [12].

An adversary uses a model inversion attack to try to reverse-engineer it by taking advantage of the model's "black box" characteristics. The attacker wants to retrieve private data that the model has learned during its training phase by giving it carefully constructed inputs and seeing how it responds. This extracted information may include personal information or particular traits related to the biometric data being utilized. Model inversion attacks pose a severe privacy risk for biometric systems [13]. For identification or verification, biometrics depends on distinctive physical or behavioral traits, such as fingerprints or facial features. The system's security safeguards may be circumvented if an attacker can recreate the original biometric data by querying the model, allowing illegal access or impersonation.

2.4. Deepfakes

Deepfake technology uses ML techniques, especially deep learning, to produce synthetic media that are very convincing and lifelike. This technology makes it possible to change images, films, and audio recordings, often in a manner that makes it impossible to tell the difference between the actual and fake objects. Attackers may use deepfakes to trick voice- or face-recognition-based biometric systems, enabling them to pass as someone else. Deep learning models are trained on a lot of data, including photographs or recordings of the intended subject, to produce deepfakes. By comprehending and imitating the patterns and characteristics seen in the training data, these models are trained to create very exact imitations. Deepfakes can change material in various ways, such as by swapping out faces in movies or changing speech in audio recordings.

Deepfakes constitute a severe security issue in the context of biometric systems. For instance, voice recognition systems depend on distinctive vocal traits to verify or authenticate people. Attackers, however, may use deepfakes to duplicate someone's voice with startling precision, making it difficult for the system to distinguish between the natural person and the artificial imitation. Deepfakes that effectively modify a person's look or imitate another person's facial characteristics may also deceive face recognition algorithms [14].

Unauthorized access, identity theft, or the fabrication of false identities might result from this. The creation of reliable detection techniques is necessary to stop deepfake assaults. Developing algorithms and approaches that can recognize deepfakes based on differences in the synthesized media is a current area of research for engineers and researchers. These detection methods examine numerous media features, such as visual artifacts, inconsistent facial expressions, or strange audio patterns, to distinguish between authentic and artificial information.

2.5. *Transferability of Attacks*

The situation where an attack that takes advantage of flaws in one biometric system may be used in other similar systems is known as the transferability of assaults. The context of ML-based biometric systems makes this idea especially pertinent. Suppose a hacker can effectively locate and exploit vulnerabilities in one of these systems. In that case, they may be able to utilize the same attack method to penetrate other systems that use comparable ML models or algorithms. The effect of vulnerabilities is amplified by the portability of attacks across many systems, potentially impacting various platforms. To identify and verify people based on distinctive biometric qualities like fingerprints, facial features, or speech patterns, ML-based biometric systems use algorithms and models trained on big datasets [15]. During the authentication process, these models analyze the training data to identify patterns and correlations that will help them make choices about people's identities.

These models, however, are not flawless and may be exposed to numerous kinds of assaults. For instance, an attacker may try to trick the system by delivering a biometric sample that has been altered such that it seems fundamental to the model but differs from the original biometric attribute. This can result in impersonation or illegal access. When an attack is successful against one system, it shows that the ML models or algorithms being used include more profound flaws. These deficiencies may result from shortcomings in the training set, design errors in the model, or restrictions in the overall system layout. Hackers may be able to use the same flaws in similar systems by knowing these vulnerabilities. Assaults' transferability severely hampers the security of biometric systems. Because attackers may use the same attack technique to compromise other systems with comparable properties, identifying and exploiting a vulnerability in one system can have far-reaching effects. This places the responsibility for addressing vulnerabilities in their systems and the broader consequences for other systems in the field on developers and researchers.

2.6. *Bias and Discrimination*

ML algorithms' bias and discrimination are a growing source of worry since they have the ability to reinforce and amplify preexisting societal biases and prejudices. When trained on skewed or underrepresented datasets, these algorithms may unintentionally learn and perpetuate biased behaviors, producing unjust results and harming people. Biometric systems are one area where prejudice and discrimination may have a significant impact. Biometric systems employ physiological or behavioral traits like fingerprints or facial features to identify and validate people. These algorithms may incorrectly identify or reject people based on their demographic characteristics, such as race or gender, if the training data used to construct them are biased or unrepresentative. For instance, a facial recognition system may need help in correctly identifying people with darker skin tones if it is trained on mostly light-skinned faces and lacks variety in its training data [16]. Certain demographic groups may have increased rates of false positives, which might result in misidentification and unfair repercussions. Similar to the previous example, a gender bias may develop if a system is primarily trained on data from one gender, which can result in the incorrect identification or exclusion of people from other genders.

Such prejudices and discrimination in biometric systems might have detrimental effects, primarily when these systems are utilized for crucial tasks like access control or law enforcement. Misidentifications may result in unjustified arrests or access rejections, disproportionately harming certain groups and reinforcing systemic prejudices. Hackers may use the possibility of prejudice and discrimination in biometric systems to their advantage [17]. To further their goals, adversaries may consciously influence or exploit the system's fundamental prejudices. Because a particular ethnic group is more likely to be mistakenly identified by a face recognition system than others, an attacker may try to get around one by using this prejudice.

2.7. Scalability Issues

When ML models employed in biometric systems are used in extensive applications, they encounter difficulties known as scalability concerns. The amount of computer power and processing time necessary for authentication likewise rises dramatically as the number of users and transactions rises. Security holes and chances for attackers to take advantage of flaws in the system are only two issues that might result from this. The additional processing resources needed to accommodate many users is one of the significant issues. Biometric data are analyzed and matched using ML models, which often utilize sophisticated algorithms and extensive calculations. The system must process more data as the user base grows, which might place a burden on the computing resources [18]. This may result in slower reaction times, more latency, and decreased system performance.

The duration of the authentication procedure is another problem. Biometric systems must contrast the user-provided biometric data with the reference templates in the system's database. The time it takes to complete this matching procedure might drastically grow as the number of users and transactions rises. The authentication procedure may take longer, harming the user experience and the system's effectiveness. Scalability problems may lead to security flaws. For instance, the system may need help verifying each request in a timely way when it is overloaded with many users and transactions. Attackers may take advantage of this by conducting denial-of-service attacks or barrage the system with phony requests, which would overload its capacity and perhaps circumvent security measures. Furthermore, scalability problems could allow attackers to take advantage of architectural flaws in the system. Additional components, interfaces, or integrations will likely be added when the system is scaled up to serve a broader user base. These upgrades could become entry points for attackers to enter the system and undermine its security if not adequately evaluated and guarded.

2.8. Methodology

The methodology used here consisted of conducting a detailed review of the literature in which ML techniques have been adopted in biometrics. In this study, we included all the works that have successfully applied ML and reported favorable results after this adoption. These articles not only reported improved numerical results but also provided sound technical justification for this improvement. It is well understood that integrating ML with biometrics brings forth more robustness and discrimination power (for classification) to a biometric system. Nonetheless, the vulnerabilities and biases introduced as a result of ML adoption should not be ignored, and this is the main objective of this review.

3. Recommendations to Prevent Flaws in ML-Based Biometric Systems

3.1. Strong Training Data

Robust training data are the cornerstone of every ML model that succeeds. The collection of examples used to train the model and give it the ability to predict or categorize correctly is known as the training data. To guarantee the validity and efficacy of the final model, these data must be reliable and of a high caliber. It is critical to develop trustworthy data-gathering techniques. Data training includes defining the criteria for picking data sources and guaranteeing their trustworthiness and authority [19]. Data may come from various sources, including public databases, surveys, user-generated content, and specialist data suppliers. It is critical to validate the data's validity and correctness by referring to numerous sources or using data validation procedures. Another characteristic of good training data is that they accurately portray real-world settings and include various samples. The data should consist of the necessary traits and patterns the model must learn to generate reasonable predictions. Biased or skewed training data may lead to biased or faulty models. As a result, it is critical to properly curate the training data to minimize any biases and guarantee that they are representative of the target population. It is vital to safeguard the training data from modification or compromise. Unauthorized changes to the training data might add inaccuracy or purposefully mislead the model. Implementing robust data security measures, like encryption and access limits, may assist in protecting the integrity of the training data. Regular audits and monitoring can also help detect any suspicious activities or data breaches.

3.2. *Adversarial Defensive Mechanisms*

Adversarial assaults are purposeful efforts to trick or manipulate a machine learning model by exploiting its flaws. Adversarial defensive mechanisms are tactics and procedures created to recognize and thwart such assaults, strengthening models' integrity and imperviousness to manipulation. Adversarial training is one strategy for adversarial defense. This method entails adding hostile samples to the training data. Adversarial examples are samples deliberately altered to fool the model while seeming like the original samples. By including these malicious cases during training, the model can better comprehend and manage these perturbations, strengthening its defense against adversarial assaults. Robust feature engineering is another protective strategy. Features may be constructed to strengthen the model against adversarial assaults rather than depending exclusively on raw input data. These qualities may capture higher-level semantic information that is more resilient to disturbances. For instance, models may be created for picture classification tasks emphasizing vital elements like textures or forms more than pixel values.

Adversarial defense may also be improved via ensemble approaches. The total model becomes increasingly resistant to adversarial assaults via the independent training of numerous models and the combination of their predictions. Assaults by adversaries often target certain flaws in individual models. Still, using a variety of projections from an ensemble makes it more complicated for adversaries to design successful assaults. Continuous research and development are necessary to keep one step ahead of hostile threats. Researching new defensive tactics and upgrading current ones is essential since attackers' methods constantly evolve. This entails investigating adversarial attack detection techniques, strengthening adversarial training methodologies, and encouraging research community partnerships to exchange information and ideas.

3.3. *Regular Model Updates*

The efficacy and security of biometric systems must be maintained via regular model upgrades. As technology develops, new attack routes and flaws can emerge that unscrupulous actors might exploit. It is crucial to regularly update and enhance the ML models employed in biometric systems to remain ahead of these threats. Organizations may quickly detect and fix vulnerabilities in their designs by staying up to date on the most current advancements in biometric security research and best practices [20]. Keeping up with new attack methodologies, biometric spoofing techniques, and adversarial ML developments are all part of this. Regular model upgrades make the incorporation of better algorithms and tactics to fend off these changing threats possible.

A problem called concept drift, which happens when the statistical characteristics of the data used to train the model change over time, may also be addressed using regular model updates. Aging, accidents, and environmental changes are just a few variables that might alter biometric data. The system may keep its accuracy and dependability by incorporating new data into the models and considering these changes. Regular upgrades also guarantee that the biometric system complies with changing regulatory standards [21]. Businesses must modify their biometric systems to comply with these evolving regulatory frameworks as privacy and data protection regulations continue to change. Regular updates make it possible to put privacy-enhancing strategies into effect, use secure data handling procedures, and adhere to data storage and retention policies.

3.4. Integrated Biometrics

Multi-modal biometrics is the process of authenticating a person using several biometric modalities. Multi-modal biometrics integrates two or more modalities, such as voice, face, fingerprint, iris, or behavioral attributes, for identification purposes rather than depending only on one biometric feature, such as a fingerprint or face [22,23]. There are significant benefits to using various biometric modalities. It first makes it harder for attackers to simultaneously impersonate or change several biometric traits. For instance, it can be difficult for an attacker to duplicate a person's vocal rhythm and facial features perfectly. The entire security of the authentication process is increased by this multi-modal method, which considerably increases the difficulty for attackers to trick the system. By lowering the rates of erroneous acceptance and rejection, multi-modal biometrics improve accuracy and dependability. The method may increase confidence in identifying a person by merging different biometric modalities. The system may fall back on one modality to provide proper authentication in situations when one modality needs to be more accurate due to various reasons.

Additionally, multi-modal biometrics enables enhanced resilience against individual and environmental fluctuations. For instance, the system may use other accessible modalities, such as the person's face or voice, for verification if their fingerprint is momentarily hidden by moisture or damage. However, it is crucial to consider the compromises brought about by multi-modal biometrics, such as a system's increased complexity, cost, and user experience. Multiple biometric modalities may need more hardware, processing power, and computing resources to integrate and manage [18]. User acceptability and convenience should also be considered when deploying multi-modal biometric systems since they may need different enrollment processes and longer authentication times.

4. Conclusions

Biometric systems' capabilities have unquestionably been improved by machine learning, but this technology also introduces vulnerabilities that need to be addressed. The security and fairness of biometric systems are seriously jeopardized by adversarial attacks, data poisoning attacks, model inversion attacks, deepfakes, the transferability of attacks, and biases and discrimination. Strong remedies are needed to reduce these hazards. The ability to discriminate between real information and phony information may benefit from improved deepfake detection algorithms. Several potential future paths may be investigated to achieve this goal. This is especially important as research on GANs has progressed tremendously since its inception in 2014. There is a constant need for research and improvement in deepfake detection methods. The countermeasures to identify and distinguish between real and altered biometric data must improve along with deepfake technology. This will be crucial in preserving the reliability and integrity of biometric systems. Efforts should be concentrated on enhancing training data security. Attacks on data that are intended to poison them make clear the necessity for robust data validation, anomaly detection, and data sanitization techniques. The reliability and accuracy of biometric models may be improved by routinely monitoring and reviewing training data to help avoid biases and malicious models from entering the system. Transparency and comprehensibility should be given top emphasis in ML biometric models. Enhancing these models' interpretability may provide users insights into how they make decisions, allowing them to see weaknesses and fix them. It is feasible to manage and reduce the dangers posed by model inversion assaults by understanding the basic principles of ML models. Biometric technologies may continue to develop as safe and dependable instruments for identification and authentication across a variety of areas by resolving these flaws and encouraging fairness.

Author Contributions: The background information, literature survey, and summarization of the state of the art were performed by M.G. The identification of positive and negative impacts of ML, potential promise and threats, and recommendations to researchers in the field were prepared and compiled by S.L. All authors have read and agreed to the published version of the manuscript.

Funding: This research received no external funding.

Data Availability Statement: No specific dataset was used. The pertinent information is properly cited throughout the manuscript.

Conflicts of Interest: The authors declare no conflicts of interest.

Abbreviations

ML	Machine learning
DL	Deep learning
CAPTCHA	Completely Automated Public Turing Test to Tell Computers and Humans Apart
SVM	Support Vector Machine
PIN	Personal Identification Number
FMR	False Match Rate
GAN	Generative Adversarial Network

References

1. Scheidat, T.; Leich, M.; Alexandar, M.; Vielhauer, C. Support Vector Machines for Dynamic Biometric Handwriting Classification, AIAI-2009, Workshops Proceedings. 2009. Available online: https://citeseerx.ist.psu.edu/document?repid=rep1&type=pdf&doi=90ee60f5df2d679dc851f13ca28165eb03519042 (accessed on 12 October 2023).
2. Rathgeb, C.; Kolberg, J.; Uhl, A.; Busch, C. Deep Learning in the Field of Biometric Template Protection: An Overview. *arXiv* **2023**, arXiv:2303.02715v1.
3. Kumar, A.; Jain, S.; Kumar, M. Comparative Study of Multi-Biometrics Authentication Using Machine Learning Algorithms. In Proceedings of the 2024 11th International Conference on Reliability, Infocom Technologies and Optimization (Trends and Future Directions) (ICRITO), Noida, India, 14–15 March 2024; pp. 1–5. Available online: https://ieeexplore.ieee.org/abstract/document/10522125 (accessed on 8 December 2023).
4. Saurova, K.E.; Hayitbaeva, D.K. Artificial Intelligence based Methods of Identification and Authentication by Face Image. *Acad. Res. Educ. Sci.* **2024**, *5*, 123–130. Available online: https://cyberleninka.ru/article/n/artificial-intelligence-based-methods-of-identification-and-authentication-by-face-image/viewer (accessed on 8 December 2023).
5. Shakil, S.; Arora, D.; Zaidi, T. Feature based classification of voice based biometric data through Machine learning algorithm. *Materialstoday* **2022**, *51*, 240–247. [CrossRef]
6. Pryor, L.; Mallet, J.; Dave, R.; Seliya, N.; Vanamala, M.; Boone, E. Evaluation of a User Authentication Schema Using Behavioral Biometrics and Machine Learning, Computer Science, Cryptography, Cornell University. *arXiv* **2022**, arXiv:2205.08371. Available online: https://arxiv.org/abs/2205.08371 (accessed on 19 December 2023).
7. Umasankari, N.; Muthukumar, B. Evaluation of Biometric Classification and Authentication Using Machine Learning Techniques. In Proceedings of the 2023 International Conference on Artificial Intelligence and Knowledge Discovery in Concurrent Engineering (ICECONF), Chennai, India, 5–7 January 2023. Available online: https://ieeexplore.ieee.org/abstract/document/10083610 (accessed on 19 December 2023).
8. Mahadi, M.; Mohamad, M.; Kadir, M. A Survey of Machine Learning Techniques for Behavioral-Based Biometric User Authentication. *Recent Adv. Cryptogr. Netw. Secur.* **2018**, *31*, 43–59. Available online: https://www.intechopen.com/chapters/60937 (accessed on 19 December 2023).
9. Siddiqui, N.; Dave, R.; Vanamala, M.; Seliya, N. Machine and Deep Learning Applications to Mouse Dynamics for Continuous User Authentication. *Mach. Learn. Knowl. Extr.* **2022**, *4*, 502–518. Available online: https://www.mdpi.com/2504-4990/4/2/23 (accessed on 18 January 2024). [CrossRef]
10. Rosenberg, I.; Shabtai, A.; Elovici, Y. Adversarial ML Attacks and Defense Methods in the Cyber Security Domain. *ACM Comput. Surv.* **2021**, *54*, 1–36. [CrossRef]
11. Sudar, K.M.; Deepalakshmi, P.; Ponmozhi, K.; Nagaraj, P. Analysis of Security Threats and Countermeasures for Various Biometric Techniques. In Proceedings of the 2019 IEEE International Conference on Clean Energy and Energy Efficient Electronics Circuit for Sustainable Development (INCCES), Krishnankoil, India, 18–20 December 2019; pp. 1–6. [CrossRef]
12. Li, K.; Baird, C.; Lin, D. Defend Data Poisoning Attacks on Voice Authentication. In *IEEE Transactions on Dependable and Secure Computing*; IEEE: Piscataway, NJ, USA, 2023.
13. Shafee, A.; Awaad, T.A. Privacy Attacks against Deep Learning Models and Their Countermeasures. *J. Syst. Archit.* **2020**, *114*, 101940. [CrossRef]
14. Dionysiou, A.; Vassiliades, V.; Athanasopoulos, E. Exploring Model Inversion Attacks in the Black-Box Setting. *Proc. Priv. Enhancing Technol.* **2023**, *2023*, 190–206. [CrossRef]

15. Jones, V.A. Artificial Intelligence Enabled Deepfake Technology: The Emergence of a New Threat—ProQuest. Available online: www.proquest.com2020.www.proquest.com/openview/60d6b06b94904dccf257c4ea7c297226/1?pq-origsite=gscholar&cbl=18750&diss=y (accessed on 12 January 2024).
16. Minaee, S.; Abdolrashidi, A.; Su, H.; Bennamoun, M.; Zhang, D. Biometrics Recognition Using Deep Learning: A Survey. *Artif. Intell. Rev.* **2023**, *56*, 8647–8695. [CrossRef]
17. Mittal, S.; Thakral, K.; Majumdar, P.; Vatsa, M.; Singh, R. Are Face Detection Models Biased? In Proceedings of the 2023 IEEE 17th International Conference on Automatic Face and Gesture Recognition (FG), Waikoloa Beach, HI, USA, 5–8 January 2023. [CrossRef]
18. Popescu, G. Biometric Technologies and the Automation of Identity and Space. In *Handbook on Geographies of Technology*; Edward Elgar Publishing: Cheltenham, UK, 2017. Available online: http://www.elgaronline.com/abstract/9781785361159.xml (accessed on 27 June 2023).
19. Alhomayani, F.; Mahoor, M. Deep Learning Methods for Fingerprint-Based Indoor Positioning: A Review. *J. Locat. Based Serv.* **2020**, *14*, 129–200. [CrossRef]
20. Hasan, M.K.; Ghazal, T.; Saeed, R.; Pandey, B.; Gohei, H.; Esmawi, A.; Abdel-Khalek, S.; Alkhassawneh, H. A Review on Security Threats, Vulnerabilities, and Counter Measures of 5G Enabled Internet-of-Medical-Things. *IET Commun.* **2021**, *16*, 421–432. [CrossRef]
21. Zhang, C.; Costa-Perez, X.; Patras, P. Adversarial Attacks against Deep Learning-Based Network Intrusion Detection Systems and Defense Mechanisms. *IEEE/ACM Trans. Netw.* **2022**, *30*, 1294–1311. [CrossRef]
22. Wang, J.; Pan, J.; AlQerm, I.; Liu, Y. Def-IDS: An Ensemble Defense Mechanism against Adversarial Attacks for Deep Learning-Based Network Intrusion Detection. In Proceedings of the 2021 International Conference on Computer Communications and Networks (ICCCN), Athens, Greece, 19–22 July 2021; pp. 1–9. [CrossRef]
23. Akulwar, P.; Vijapur, N. Secured Multi Modal Biometric System: A Review. In Proceedings of the 2019 Third International Conference on I-SMAC (IoT in Social, Mobile, Analytics, and Cloud) (I-SMAC), Palladam, India, 12–14 December 2019. [CrossRef]

MDPI AG
Grosspeteranlage 5
4052 Basel
Switzerland
Tel.: +41 61 683 77 34

Electronics Editorial Office
E-mail: electronics@mdpi.com
www.mdpi.com/journal/electronics

www.ingramcontent.com/pod-product-compliance
Lightning Source LLC
Chambersburg PA
CBHW061507210926
51850CB00008B/1843
* 9 7 8 3 7 2 5 8 5 9 3 1 3 *